HEWERS OF THE FORESTS

FISHERS OF THE LAKES

The History of St. Edmunds Township

Compiled by
The Township of St. Edmunds

Editor
CATHY WYONCH

Cover Design by
STAN McCLELLAN

ISBN 0-9692347-0-8

COPYRIGHT 1985 ©
Printed by Stan Brown Printers Limited
Owen Sound, Ontario

Handbound by The Old Stable
Owen Sound, Ont.

TOWNSHIP of ST. EDMUNDS

TOBERMORY - ONTARIO
NOH 2RO

This account of the history of St. Edmunds Township is the culmination of the efforts of many people to whom we are extremely grateful.

Early in 1983 Linda Smith approached the Township to express an opinion that the cultural roots of the community should be explored more fully. Council concurred with Linda and it was from her suggestion that this book evolved.

Subsequently, Council applied for and received a Summer Canada Student Employment grant from Employment and Immigration Canada to work on a history of the Township. Unfortunately, Linda Smith was unable to continue work on the project. Three students, Melony McLay (supervisor), Karen Robertson and Andrew Hodkinson were employed and work began on the book in May of 1983. These students completed a tremendous amount of work and in their four months of employment produced a book that basically resembles the one you are now reading.

Faith Ross and Wendy Mills were employed in the summer of 1984, with the assistance of an Experience '84 Program grant provided by the Ministry of Citizenship and Culture, to continue work on the project. Faith and Wendy undertook additional research and re-wrote and re-typed some sections of the book.

Since that time many hours have been spent by municipal staff and interested residents, particularly Iola Stabenow, in typing, proofreading, editing and all aspects of finalizing the book.

We hope that you enjoy reading our efforts to preserve the heritage of our municipality and any efforts or omissions are sincerely regretted.

Bradley W Davis

Council of St. Edmunds Township
1982-1985

TABLE OF CONTENTS

ACKNOWLEDGEMENTS

We wish to express our appreciation to the following people. Without their invaluable knowledge and generous assistance, this project could not have been completed.

Patrick Folkes — for his advice and suggestions, for reading the first draft of this report, and for the generous use of his historic material concerning the pioneers and marine traffic without which this book would have been incomplete.

Wiarton Echo — for the use of their photographs and newspaper articles dating back to 1879, and for assisting us in our research.

Owen Sound Sun Times — for the use of photographs and articles.

Ministry of Natural Resources — for the use of one of their inhouse reports.

Stan McClellan — for the use of his slides and information

Reverend Chung and the United Church of Canada Archives — for the use of information pertaining to the United Churches in Tobermory.

Viola Adams — for the use of her report on the United Church Women.

Nona Scott — for her information on the Anglican Church

Heather Middleton of the Board of Education Office in Chesley — for her time and trouble taken in listing the names of teachers.

Angus Ralph — for explaining school related issues.

Vida Jordan — for sharing her valuable tapes with us.

Charles Smith — for his photographs and stories.

Mrs. Shaw — for assisting us in our library research.

Rusty Raney and Clarence Spears — for their information about fishing.

Kathy MacLeod and Elaine Mills — for transportation.

Mr. and Mrs. A. J. Watson — for their stories and poems.

Mr. W. A. Spears — for helping to date photographs and identify people in them, and for his information.

Jim Rae — for his information on lumbering.

Joe George — for his information on tourism.

Pauline Knight and Barbara Dinsmore — for typing the first draft.

Cathy Wyonch, Dona LaFontaine, Brad Davis — for their assistance, information and support.

Iola Stabenow - for all her work in the final stages.

Tom Hopkins — for searching for newspaper articles and advertisements.

Stan McClellan - for the dust cover design and photograph and history of Big Tub Lighthouse.

Nelson Maher of Stan Brown Printers - for his suggestions and advice.

Cathy Wyonch - for editing and pulling it all together.

And a special thanks to all those people who welcomed us into their homes for interviews and who lent us their photographs.

INTRODUCTION

One hundred and fourteen years have passed since 1870, the year in which the Township of St. Edmunds was first opened for settlement. With the passing of each generation, valuable information concerning the early days of the township is lost. Another factor leading to the loss of information is the fact that St. Edmunds is presently undergoing a period of resettlement. People with longstanding ties to the area are leaving, and people originating outside the area are moving in. This book is therefore an attempt to gather as much information about the history of St. Edmunds Township before, for the above reasons, it is forever lost.

Within the historic boundaries of the book, the social and economic aspects of life in St. Edmunds have been examined.

The social aspects include stories about individuals illustrating their character and how they have adapted to the changes in the community over the years. Through these stories, the pleasures and hardships in the lifestyle of these people in this small, isolated community are described. Organizations within the community are discussed to illustrate how they influence the individual by shaping his/her beliefs, morals, and conduct; providing support and services; establishing law and order; educating; and providing recreation. These organizations also change through time reflecting external influences acting on the community.

The economic factors discussed illustrate that the economy of St. Edmunds has shifted throughout its history to four different resource bases: agriculture, timbering, fishing, and tourism. The people of St. Edmunds have therefore developed many different skills and have held a number of different jobs during their lifetime. This indicates that specialization in a single job is rare in this community. The overall picture of the economy of St. Edmunds shows that it is fragile due to its seasonality and susceptibility to external factors.

The text of this book consists of a blend of information from a number of different sources. Memories of the Township's residents are combined with information from newspapers, scrapbooks, diaries, letters, photographs, and other authors' research in order to give what we feel is an accurate description of the history of St. Edmunds Township.

1983: Melony McLay   1984: Faith Ross
Karen Robertson   Wendy Mills
Andrew Hodkinson

CHAPTER ONE
IN THE BEGINNING

"Four hundred million years ago, warm tropical seas flooded this area. From the sediments deposited on the sea's floor, the escarpment was elevated. A million years ago, glaciers almost a mile thick advanced and retreated four times. Left behind in the last glacier's wake were boulder-strewn areas, finger lakes pointing toward the direction of the glacier's retreat, and two perfectly carved harbours set at the top of the Bruce Peninsula" (1).

THE FIRST PEOPLE

As there has been little archaeological research carried out on the Bruce Peninsula, it is not known for certain when the first humans arrived in the area that is now known as the Township of St. Edmunds. Due to the lack of archaeological data, it is necessary to rely upon the written records of the earliest explorers to provide information about the people who once occupied this area. According to these sources, the first accounts of people coming to this area are found in the legends of the Ojibwa Indians who were also called the Chippewa. The name "Ojibwa" comes from the Algonkian language that the Ojibwa spoke, and refers to the puckered seams of the Ojibwa's moccassins (2).

In their legends, the Ojibwa describe a migration from their original territory north of the Great Lakes, southward to the area that is now known as Mackinaw, Michigan. At Mackinaw, the Ojibwa Nation decided to separate into four tribes who would occupy different areas of the upper Great Lakes (3). One tribe decided to keep the name "Ojibwa", and occupied the Lake Superior region. Another tribe took the name "Mississauga" from the area that they occupied around the mouth of the Mississagi River on the northern shore of Lake Huron. The third tribe was the Potawatomi who lived on the western shore of Lake Huron in what is now Michigan. The final tribe is the one that concerns us the most for these people chose to live around the shores of Georgian Bay, on Manitoulin Island, and on the Bruce Peninsula. These people were the Ottawa meaning "buyers and sellers", for they were renowned for their trading skills.

THE OTTAWA

As the land that the Ottawa occupied was rocky and barren for the most part, they survived by hunting, fishing, gathering edible vegetation and fruit, and trading. The Ottawa tribe was made up of a number of bands that were scattered throughout their territory. Each band had its own leader, hunting territory, and political independence from the other bands. Their religious beliefs, reflecting those of the whole Ojibwa nation, had good and evil spirits who were conjured by the shaman of the band. For relaxation, the Ottawa had many games, some of these were betting games played with bone dice. Another game that the Ottawa invented was the game of lacrosse, one still played today.

Trading was a very important part of the Ottawa's life. Prior to the arrival of the whiteman, the Ottawa would trade such things as medicinal roots and herbs, furs from the tribes to the north, tobacco from the Petun (or Tobacco Indians) who lived in the area south of the Bruce Peninsula, and corn from the Huron of southeastern Georgian Bay. By 1600, their trade routes stretched from the eastern shores of Georgian Bay westward to Michigan and along the shores of Lake Superior. They travelled these long distances by canoe, another skill for which they were renowned.

As well as making long trading trips, the Ottawa would also travel long distances during the summer months to raid the villages of their enemies. Therefore one can see that the bands of Ottawa were very mobile, probably not very large, and probably did not stay in one location for a long period of time. This makes it difficult to determine how densely the Ottawa populated the Bruce Peninsula, especially the area that is now St. Edmunds Township.

THE HURON INDIANS

Of all the Ottawa's trading partners, the Huron were the most important. The land that the Huron Nation occupied was that between southeastern Georgian Bay and Lake Simcoe. Unlike the Ottawa's territory, the Huron's land was rich and fertile; therefore, their economy was based on horticulture, not hunting and gathering as was that of the Ottawa.

The Huron were important to the Ottawa for a number of reasons. The Huron grew the corn, a highly valued trade item as it often prevented many people from starving to death in the late winter when food was scarce. The Huron were actually better traders than the Ottawa and it was the Hurons who taught the Ottawas to trade. The most important reason however, was the fact that the Huron traded directly with the French traders in Quebec, and therefore the Huron controlled the availability of the highly valued trade goods. These trade goods were such things as iron knives, axes, glass beads, copper cooking kettles, woolen blankets, and clothing. Such trade goods were given to the Indians by the European traders in return for furs. The French dominated the fur trade in the lands north of the St. Lawrence.

The Huron Nation was actually a member of the Iroquois family of tribes. In spite of this relationship, the Huron and the Iroquois were bitter enemies. This hostility was a direct result of the fur trade that had begun when the first whiteman reached the shores of Canada.

The Iroquois lived in and dominated the area south of Lakes Ontario and Erie. They traded with the English and Dutch who dominated the trade along the Atlantic coast south of the St. Lawrence River. The furs in this area were of poorer quality than those from the colder, northern area that the Huron dominated. Most importantly, the furs in the Iroquois' territory were becoming scarce due to overtrapping, and therefore the Iroquois had to find another source of furs. For this reason, they expanded into other Indian tribes' territories to gain furs.

After expanding into as much territory as they could south of Lakes Ontario and Erie, the Iroquois looked to the north and saw their Huron relatives handling a vast number of prime quality furs. The Iroquois then proposed to the Huron that the Huron join an Iroquois alliance and share their furs. The Huron of course had no intention of sharing their furs with the Iroquois as they were now the middlemen between the French and the other Indian tribes. This made them a very wealthy nation. With this refusal, the Iroquois and the Huron became enemies.

The wars between the Iroquois and the Huron began in the mid to late 1500's. Each year the Iroquois and the Huron would make raids on each other's villages and trading parties, and it soon reached the point where the Iroquois controlled the lower Great Lakes and the upper St. Lawrence. This forced the Huron to travel to Quebec by the Ottwa River, thereby avoiding the Iroquois.

SAMUEL DE CHAMPLAIN

It was during these turbulent times that Samuel de Champlain began his explorations of the land lying north and west of Quebec. His first visit took him as far west as the Huron Nation around Lake Simcoe, where he spent 1615-16. On his way to the Huron Nation, he met about three hundred Ottawa at the mouth of the French River where they had been gathering blueberries. Due to the men's hair which was styled in a high scalplock, he called them the "Cheveux Relevez". Champlain visited the Ottawa again in 1616 at one of their villages on southern Georgian Bay. Champlain did not travel as far westward as the Bruce Peninsula in his explorations.

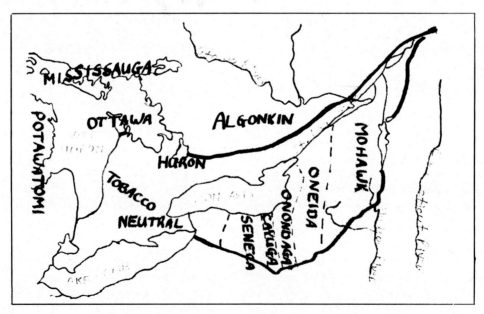

Approximate distribution of Iroquois, Ojibwa and Algonkin tribes in 1525. Except for the Ottawa, Mississauga, Potawatomi and Algonkin tribes, the tribes named on the map are of Iroquois heritage and their area of control is marked by boundaries of dark lines.

THE HURON DISPERSAL

After Champlain's visit, the hostilities between the Iroquois and the Huron increased dramatically. The Iroquois also began to make raids on the allies of the Huron. In order to defend themselves, the Ottawa joined the Potawatomi and the Lake Superior Ojibwa to form an alliance, "The Council of Three Fires" (4). The Huron had earlier formed a confederacy called the "Wendat" (5). The strength of the Iroquois increased as they were able to obtain guns from the English and Dutch. The Huron were at a technological disadvantage at this point, for the French were not trading guns in as great a quantity.

In 1648, the Iroquois took the offensive against the Huron. They raided three Huron villages late in the fall of that year, and then, rather than returning to their territory south of Lakes Ontario and Erie, they wintered in Ontario. In the spring of 1649, before the snow had left the ground, the Iroquois attacked the Huron in full force. Weakened by starvation, epidemics of European diseases, and surprise, the Huron Nation was decimated. It was during this raid that the Jesuit priests were killed along with many others. Any Huron who survived fled to take refuge with the Ojibwa tribes, the French, or even with other tribes as far away as Oklahoma (6). Other Hurons were adopted into the Iroquois tribe, a common Iroquois practice.

This decimation of Huron is known as the "Huron Dispersal of 1649".

THE FATE OF THE OTTAWA

Having conquered the Huron, the Iroquois then turned their fury against the allies of the Huron. After numerous battles, the Ottawa attempted to make peace with the Iroquois at the mouth of the Saugeen River at the base of the Bruce Peninsula in 1652, but to no avail. Soon the Ottawa were driven out of the Georgian Bay area. Many of the Ottawa did not escape the Iroquois' onslaught. In 1883, William Leslie visited Flowerpot Island and found a number of skeletons that may have been Indians. Similarly in 1967, Constable Fred Keates was called in to investigate a skeleton found by Hugh Black in a rock cleft near Dunks Bay (7).

The Iroquois who occupied the Bruce Peninsula after having vanquished the Ottawa were mainly from the Seneca tribe. They used the Peninsula as a base from which to attack Indians who tried to pass by and trade with the French at Quebec. The Iroquois continued to make raids on many other tribes, but by the late 1600's, their power began to wan due to two factors. The French were now supplying their allies with rifles as they still desperately wanted furs. The second factor concerned the social structure of the Iroquois tribes. For many years the Iroquois had been adopting the survivors of tribes that they had defeated into their own tribes. Soon a very large proportion of the Iroquois Nation was made up of these adoptees. These adoptees did not have the same impetus for battle that the Iroquois did and many historians therefore feel that the desire for war decreased a great deal and peace gradually returned.

THE FRENCH MISSIONS

During 1670-71, the Ottawa recovered Manitoulin Island from the Iroquois with the aid of the French. Earlier in 1668-69 a Jesuit, Father Allouez, claimed to have converted one band of Ottawa to Christianity. With the Ottawa's return to Manitoulin Island, the Jesuits are thought to have set up the Mission of St. Simon (also know as St. Simon and St. Jude) (8).

Conflicting claims arise about the location of this mission. It has been suggested that St. Simon was actually built prior to 1670, and that according to an old map, it was located on the Bruce Peninsula near Dyers Bay (9). To add to the confusion, J. M. Bluth, a landowner on the Big Tub in Tobermory, found rocks piled in such a way that they resembled a fireplace measuring three feet long by two and a half feet wide and three feet high (D). A historian, Fritz Knechtel, suggested that this fireplace was either the remains of St. Simon or a French fort, Fort Suppose, that according to a map drawn by the French cartographer, Lahontan, was in the area of Tobermory (11). Unfortunately, this fireplace was destroyed by hydro workers in 1958 (12). Another interesting point is that in 1873, when the Indian Agent, William Bull came to St. Edmunds, he was told by one man that there was an "ancient Stockade" made of cedar posts that were "quite plainly to be seen" located in the forests between Baptist Harbour and Tobermory (see Appendix G).

It is still not known what these remains represent. They could be anything from the remains of a French fort or mission, to the remains of a fisherman's or trapper's encampment of the 1800's.

THE OTTAWA *and* THE FRENCH FUR TRADERS

Following the "Huron Dispersal", the French were without a dependent supplier of furs, a role that the Huron had fulfilled prior to 1649. The Huron had acted as middlemen for the first half of the 1600's, trading with other tribes further to the north and west for furs in exchange for European trade goods. The Huron then delivered the furs to the French. The Ottawa were first introduced to the French in 1653, after a small party of Huron who had taken shelter with a band of Ottawa, guided the Ottawa to Quebec (13). After this, the Ottawa quickly filled the void that the Huron left in the fur trade. In 1667, the Ottawa told a French Jesuit missionary that the Ottawa Nation controlled the Ottawa River route to Quebec and that no other people could navigate it without their consent (14). The Ottawa controlled the fur trade until the French were able to penetrate the region around the Great Lakes and build forts and fur trading posts in the late 1600's and early 1700's.

One of the French explorers who explored a section of the Great Lakes was Rene Robert Cavalier, Sieur de la Salle. La Salle built a small ship, the "Griffon", at Niagara in 1679. He then sent it to Green Bay, Wisconsin, where it picked up a load of furs. The people who watched the "Griffon" sail out of Green Bay three centuries ago were the last to ever see her. Somewhere on the Great Lakes, the "Griffon" disappeared. The riddle of the "Griffon" has never been conclusively solved, although there are more than ten shipwrecks around the Great Lakes that are proclaimed to be the "Griffon". One of these was found by Orrie Vail of Tobermory in 1955. Vail's claim is discussed further in Chapter 16.

In the 1700's, the Ottawa with the aid of the Potawatomi began to take advantage of the Iroquois' diminishing strength by expanding back into regions that had been lost to the Iroquois many years before. As a result, the Bruce Peninsula was resettled by various tribes of the Ojibwa nation including the Ottawa. A relatively new tribe that arrived on the Peninsula was the Sauk (or Sauking or Saugeen). The Sauk had migrated from southeastern Michigan to this area.

THE TREATIES

By the 1800's, the number of European settlers coming into Canada had increased to the point that the Federal Government was coming under pressure to open up new parts of the country for settlement. This pressure led to the drawing up of treaties in which the Indians surrendered (or ceded) their land to the Crown represented in Canada by the Federal Government in exchange for protection and care.

In 1827, a treaty was drawn up between the "Indians of Western Canada" and the "Province of Upper Canada". This treaty surrendered part of the "Western District" which included parts of the counties of Perth, Huron, Bruce and Grey (15).

In 1836, the Treaty of Manitouwaning was drawn up by Francis Bond Head. In this treaty, a reserve for the Sauking (Saugeen) was secured on Manitoulin Island. The second section of this treaty surrendered the townships of southern Bruce County to the government. However,

at this time, all of the land north of an imaginary line drawn between the mouth of the Saugeen River at Southampton and the mouth of the Sydenham River at Owen Sound, still belonged to the Saugeen Indians. For this reason, the Peninsula was known either as the Indian Peninsula or the Saugeen Peninsula.

By 1855, hostilities had arisen between the white settlers and the Indians who lived along the imaginary line. As the number of settlers coming into the area had increased, more farm land was needed. Some settlers saw that the land north of the dividing land was fertile and so they crossed over and began to farm on the Indians' land. The disputes that ensued were settled at the Allenford Pow-wow in 1855. At the Pow-wow, a treaty was signed that surrendered most of the Peninsula except for a few reserves.

After 1855, the land surveys were continued on the Peninsula, as the Indians were confined to a reserve on Cape Croker and a hunting reserve in St. Edmunds Township. The control of the Peninsula was now in the hands of the Federal Government and the white settlers began to move in.

Throughout the 1800's and until World War I, it was quite common to see Indian encampments at Tobermory. Many of them had sailboats from which they would fish. At Tobermory the Indians would camp on North Point or on a small bay that was located where the Ferry Dock now stands. The Indians sold their catches to either the merchants or the fish companies in Tobermory.

Another spot where the Indians were often found was at Rattlesnake Harbour on Fitzwilliam Island. Rattlesnake Harbour was a busy fishing station from the 1800's until the early 1920's. After the decline in the fishing industry, the Indians were only seen infrequently around Tobermory. However, artifacts of these people have been found throughout St. Edmunds, and some are now on display in the St. Edmunds Museum.

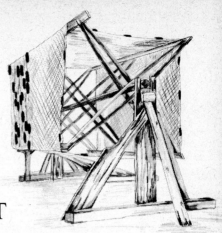

CHAPTER TWO

PRELUDES TO SETTLEMENT

NAMING THE TOWNSHIP

After the Saugeen Indians surrendered the Saugeen Peninsula as the Bruce Peninsula was then called, the Indian Department of the Federal Government took control over it. As Lord Bury was the Superintendent of Indian Affairs during that period of 1855-56, the honour of naming the newly designated townships on the Peninsula was granted to him. He chose the names of these townships from the names of his family and friends. On the northernmost township of the Peninsula he bestowed the name of St. Edmund. This name was a derivative of his family's seat, the city of Bury St. Edmund in Suffolk County, England. Accordingly, he named the proposed townplot the "Townplot of Bury", and the proposed road connecting the Townplot of Bury to the Lindsay Townline was called the "Bury Road".

The origin of the name of Bury St. Edmund is rather interesting and will be briefly examined here (1). The town now called Bury St. Edmund was founded in 638 A.D. by Seigbright, the fifth king of the Angles, who originally named it "Bury". The second half of the name comes from King Edmund the Martyr who was crowned at Bury in 855 A.D. Unfortunately King Edmund was killed by the Danes during one of their raids on that part of England. The Danes beheaded Edmund and threw his head into the forest. According to the legends connected with King Edmund, the animals of the forest respected this holy man so much, that a wolf carried the head to the place where the body was buried. From this legend comes the wolf found on the official insignia of St. Edmunds Township. King Edmund was later canonized and a shrine was built for him at Bury, therefore the name of the city was changed from simply "Bury" to "Bury St. Edmund." From this name comes the following rhyme:

"Bury St. Edmund? Certainly!
if you'll find me his head.
Who would have thought he'd be wandering about
a thousand years after he's dead?"(2).

There are many other rather violent episodes in the history of the English city of Bury St. Edmund that will not be mentioned here. Thankfully, the history of the Canadian St. Edmunds has not been so turbulent. Perhaps one of the few disputes in the Township of St. Edmunds has been the spelling of its name. Officially the name of the township is spelled "St. Edmunds", however variations found on signs and maps and in books include St. Edmund, St. Edmund's, and even St. Edmonds!

NAMES OF PLACES *and* FEATURES IN ST. EDMUNDS TOWNSHIP

The name of the townplot of St. Edmunds Township has changed several times in the last century. The first official name given to the townplot area was "Collins Harbour". It received this name during Admiral H. W. Bayfield's hydrographic survey of Lake Huron in 1820-21 (3). Lord Bury's name of the "Townplot of Bury" replaced "Collins Harbour" in 1855. However it was the name of "Tobermory" that was in common use since the 1830's that outlasted both of the above official names (4).

The name "Tobermory" comes from the Gaelic "Tober Moray" which means "well of the Virgin Mary". This name was given to the area by Scottish fishermen who noticed its resemblance to the town of Tobermory on the Isle of Mull in Scotland. It is thought that these fishermen would sail from southerly ports on the Great Lakes to fish around Tobermory as early as the 1830's (5).

The origins of other place names were noted by Norman Robertson, an early historian of Bruce County (6). He noted that Cameron Lake was named after John Cameron, a man who was well-known to both Indians and whites throughout the Peninsula. Cyprus Lake was named after the Mediterranean island of Cyprus. Andrew Lake and George Lake were named respectively after Scottish and English saints. Emmett Lake was originally supposed to be named after an Irish saint, but a young man who worked in the Wiarton office of the Indian Land Agent, B. B. Miller, persuaded Miller to name the Lake after him rather than a saint.

There are many other names whose origins have been lost with time. Other names have been conceived by the local population and some of these are listed in a later section of this book.

SURVEYING ST. EDMUNDS TOWNSHIP

The Indian Department decided that the land on the Peninsula should become available to settlers as soon as possible and therefore had the land surveyed. In 1857, J. S. Dennis, who later became the Surveyor-General of Canada, and H. C. Boulton were sent to survey the plots in St. Edmunds Township. Surveying the land was necessary so that sales could proceed in a systematic and efficient way.

In 1869, Charles Rankin received instructions to resurvey the line of the proposed Bury Road. On September 26th of that year, he and seven men landed at Dunks Bay, and proceeded to slash out the Bury Road (7). It took six weeks for them to hack their way from the Townplot of Bury to the Lindsay Townline. After finishing this work, Rankin wrote that this was "one of the most troublesome explorations and pieces of line running...that I have ever met with" (8). Rankin's overall impression of the Township of St. Edmunds was negative as is revealed in the following report:

> "Some party, it is apparent, whether Mr. Dennis the surveyor or the then authorities of the Indian Department was culpable in the matter of incurring so useless an expense as the subdivision into one hundred acre parcels of the extensive part of rock of which this township is chiefly composed" (9).

It is clear that Rankin thought that there was very little chance of agriculture being successfully practiced in St. Edmunds. The soil was thin, there were far too many rocks, and there were many areas that had been burned out, a sure sign of frequent brush fires. It would be difficult for a settler to wrest a living from such a harsh landscape. This thought had earlier been expressed by A. G. Robinson, the Chief Engineer of the Lake Huron Lighthouse Works. He wrote the following report to his superiors:

> "The next harbour is called Tober Moray...It lies at the Extreme End of the Indian Peninsula, and from its position, it is admirably situated, but as the country in its vicinity is totally unfit for agricultural purposes, I suppose it will never attain any further importance than what it is now, viz a Harbour of Refuge" (10).

In spite of the negative observations presented by Robinson and Rankin, the Indian Department decided that the Township of St. Edmunds would be opened for settlement with an economy that was to be based on agriculture.

THE BEGINNING OF SETTLEMENT IN THE TOWNSHIP OF ST. EDMUNDS

In 1869, H. Langevin, the Secretary of State announced that sales of land in St. Edmunds Township would begin in 1870. Due to a government decision, the lots in the townplot were not put up for sale at that time. It was not until 1886 that these lots were sold, and the reasons for this delay are not known.

Some of the conditions of the land sales are described here. The price of land was set at eighty cents per acre. Land could be purchased by paying one-fifth of the total price at the time of sale, and the remainder was paid in installments (11). Before the actual ownership of the land was passed to the settler, the settler had to perform certain settlement duties. These settlement duties were designed to keep speculators from buying up large tracts of land, but as they were not strictly enforced, speculators did manage to buy land in St. Edmunds Township. The settlement duties included such requirements as building a dwelling that was at least eighteen by twenty-five feet, occupying the land within six months of its purchase, clearing and fencing at least five percent of the land, and remaining on the land for at least three years (12). With the above conditions set, the land sales began.

LAND SALES IN THE TOWNSHIP OF ST. EDMUNDS

The record of land sales from 1870-1883 can be found in Appendix C of this book. This list, compiled by Patrick Folkes, consists of the first sales of land from the Crown to the first buyers (13). Although this list is extremely useful in answering a number of questions, it must not be used as a directory for the population of the area in any given year.

The first sale of land in St. Edmunds Township took place on July 11, 1870. This consisted of the sale of Lot 47, Concession 1 West of Bury Road (W. B. R.) to John Wesley Colwell. The second sale of land also took place that same day when Abraham Davis bought Lot 48 Concession 1 West of Bury Road (W. B. R.). and Lot 48 Concession 1 East of Bury Road (E. B. R.). This property is in the area of the "Tip of the Bruce" Golf Club. John Colwell never assumed ownership of his land so it was later resold to Charles Earl.

Abraham Davis and Charles Earl were the first settlers in St. Edmunds Township. It is not known precisely when they arrived in the township, as some sources say November, 1871, and others say in the early spring of 1872 (14). Both of these men were from Collingwood, where it is thought that Davis was a farmer and Earl was a fisherman (15). Until 1875, the Davis and Earl families were the only two settlers in the northern half of the township. They only had the occasional squatter such as John McKay and John Seaman of Dunks Bay as company (16).

In the southern half of the township there was greater activity underway than in the northern half. In 1870, Darius Doty a speculator, began to buy shoreline property around the Johnston Harbour area. Doty was a member of the Doty family of Goderich, a well-known name in the shipbuilding field. In 1871, A. A. Thompson, another speculator, began buying the shoreline properties of Baptist, Eagle, and Little Eagle Harbours. In 1872, Thompson bought the Johnston Harbour area from Doty. It seems that he was trying to develop a monopoly on the harbours along the Lake Huron side of the township.

In 1872, John Leathorn and James Cockwell bought land along the Crane River in the area now occupied by the Hidden Valley Lodge. This was the beginning of one of the most prosperous farming and lumbering concerns in St. Edmunds Township. Also in 1872, George Campbell, Donald McIntosh, and Adam McTavish bought lots around Cameron Lake. Unfortunately they did not fulfill their settlement duties and so they lost their land.

In 1873, William Grant joined Leathorn and Cockwell in the Crane River area, and the farming and lumbering concern grew. It was also in 1873 that the Indian land Agent who was in control of all the unsold land on the Peninsula arrived in St. Edmunds Township. William Bull had travelled from the Indian Land Office in Wiarton, to inspect the land and timber in the three northernmost townships of the Peninsula (17). His diary entries for part of his visit can be found in Appendix G. At the time of his visit, he noted that Earl was a tenant on Davis' land, and that Earl had cleared six acres but had not erected any buildings. This probably explained why Earl was squatting in an old fisherman's shanty at Dunks Bay, where John McKay, a fisherman, was also squatting. Bull explained the land in St. Edmunds Township and reported the following:

> "There is a block of land of about 4000 acres adjoining the Town plot. . . This block of land, like all the land in the Peninsula is more or less broken with rock and stone, but it is equal to the average of the lands already settled" (18).

Although Bull noted that Davis was the only other settler in this area, he said nothing about his circumstances.

In June, 1875, Jacob Belrose and his family settled on Lot 47, Concession 1 E. B. R.. Jacob's children are believed to be the first born in St. Edmunds Township. Also arriving in 1875, was John Shearer. Since Tobermory had been named after the town of Tobermory in Scotland, the Scottish government decided to send Shearer to Ontario to teach the fishermen of Tobermory how to fish using the gill net method. Shearer was surprised to learn upon his arrival, that the Indians had already taught the fishermen this method. Rather than returning to Scotland, Shearer bought Lot 49, Concession 1 E. B. R. It is thought that Shearer acted as the first teacher of St. Edmunds Township's first school for a short time in 1882. The last arrivals of 1875 were Alexander (Archie) Hay of Lot 47 and 48, Concession 3 W. B. R., and Thomas Lee of Lot 1, Concession 7 E. B. R..

In 1876, Michael Belrose purchased Lot 50, Concession 3 W. B. R. and joined his brother in the township. Michael had previously been a police constable and his experience would later be put to use in St. Edmunds. Captain Alexander Marks arrived from Southampton and settled on Lot 49, Concession 3 W. B. R. also in 1876.

Other settlers trickled into the area over the next few years. These included George and Neil Currie in 1878; Robert, John Cuff, and James H. Hopkins, William Simpson, Thomas and George Bartman, Benjamin and Alexander Butchart all arrived in 1879; Donald McDonald, the first postman, arrived in 1880; Benjamin and William Young, in 1881; and Solomon Spears in 1883.

It was estimated that by 1880 there were about fifteen families in the area below the townplot known as the Settlement (19). Unfortunately, there was little else there for them as the following description written about the settlement states:

> "There is neither store, school, church, doctor, minister nor mechanic of any kind in the Settlement. Their surplus produce of any kind is shipped in small coasting craft to Owen Sound, Collingwood, Port Elgin, etc." (20).

Without doubt, life for the earliest settlers in St. Edmunds was rough, but in the 1880's, St. Edmunds began to prosper, and the population of the area increased dramatically. Reasons for this increase included the sale of townplot lots in 1886, and the numerous lumbering companies that were coming into the area and opening mills.

SETTLING THE TOWNPLOT

In 1886, the townplot lots were put up for sale. Prior to this however, people had begun to squat on the townplot lots as they were so conveniently located. A map of the townplot in 1882 has been included in Appendix F to show the squatters who were inhabiting the area at that time. Charles Earl had moved from Dunks Bay to the north shore of the Big Tub. Alexander Green not only lived on the Little Tub, but he had also built a sawmill at the foot of the harbour. William Spears, Benjamin Young, Frank Candler, John Robinson, William Allison, and Robert Cachrane all lived around the Little Tub. Of these, the only settlers were Earl, Spears, and Young. The rest were either mill hands, timbermen, or fishermen (21).

In 1885, the Department of Marine and Fisheries bought three lots at the entrance of the Big Tub for a lighthouse. In the 1870's, previous to this, Charles Earl had taken it upon himself to hang a lantern on a tree where the lighthouse was later built. Earl's lantern guided ships into the Big Tub where they could take refuge from storms and high seas. In gratitude for this service, sailors gave Earl such goods as coal, flour, and coal oil (22). Later the government awarded Earl an annuity for his services.

With the townplot lots available, the village began to grow and for a short time it prospered.

HARDSHIPS FACING THE EARLY SETTLERS

When the early settlers arrived in St. Edmunds Township, the only building there was a fisherman's shanty at Dunks Bay. The settler therefore had to immediately begin to work to erect himself some type of shanty or shelter, and then begin to clear his land of trees and stones. Many settlers arrived in St. Edmunds without their families and sent for them only when they had a shelter built and a little bit of ground cleared. From this little bit of land, the settler had to earn enough money to pay his taxes, make his land payments, and have enough left over for the food items he needed to survive upon. As most settlers came to St. Edmunds upon ships, few had livestock. It was not until 1877, that Henry Bradley Davis and Archie Hay pooled their money to buy the first team of oxen in the Settlement. This team would have made clearing and plowing the land much easier.

Other forces operating against the settlers were the weather and fires. In 1884, brush fires and poor crops dealt the settlers a severe blow. The situation was so serious that potatoes, grain, flour, and cereal were distributed to the suffering (23). In the spring of 1885, the authorities decided to allow the settlers of St. Edmunds an extension of their land payments. In 1888, disaster struck again in the form of a drought which lasted from May until August. This drought was then followed by an early frost in September (24). The settlers' situation was again desperate so they petitioned the Superintendent of Indian Affairs in Ottawa for another extension on their land payments (25). The government officials again decided in the settlers' favour, and allowed the settlers one year to pay off land payment arrears, and two years to pay timber fees and dues (26). This petition is found in Appendix D. Fires and drought again left the settlers impoverished in 1896.

The year of 1903 was another distressful year for the people of St. Edmunds. Heavy snowfalls plagued householders throughout the early winter months of the year. During that summer, brush fires laid waste to hundreds of acres of timber. The fire began on August 21, 1903, and continued until a downpour washed out the blaze on August 24.

The greatest catastrophe that ever hit the land of St. Edmunds Township occurred in 1908. A great brush fire razed the Bruce Peninsula destroying everything in its path. The damage done to the southern section of St. Edmunds paled the damages done by fire in 1903. After the fire of 1908, the population of St. Edmunds Township plummeted to a low point, and did not rise to its former population until the 1970's. The decrease in the population reflected the exodus of the timber companies from the township. Without the extensive stands of timber to support them, many small lumbering companies that had operated were forced to close and dismiss their employees. This meant that the workers left St. Edmunds Township and travelled to other areas where lumbering was still being profitably carried out.

Not all of the settlers' difficulties came from the elements. In a small, isolated community such as the Settlement, there were bound to be personality conflicts. The following is the story of one such conflict taken from the Wiarton Echo in 1880.

THE DAVIS-EARL FEUD

It seems that Abraham Davis and Charles Earl lived peacefully together until 1877. In that year, Davis wrote a letter to the Indian Department which accused Charles Earl of illegally cutting timber on unsold lots. Davis' strongly worded letter alerted the Indian Department so they soon sent an official to St. Edmunds to investigate this charge. Strangely enough, the official found that it was not Earl who was involved in illegal activities, but the writer of the letter, Abraham Davis!

From then on, the Davis and Earl families were involved in a bitter feud which included many of the families in the Settlement who sided either with the Davis' or the Earls. John Shearer had his well ruined when someone poured coal oil into it. Of course the Earls immediately accused the Davis' and Mark Earl, Charles' son even wrote a poem about this incident. The content of this poem has mostly been lost, but its opening lines were:

"Here's to you old dirty face,
We look upon you with disgrace!"

Of course it did little to restore relationships when all the children recited this poem whenever they saw a Davis.

Things went from bad to worse, and in 1879, both Charles Earl and Abraham Davis received jail sentences. That fall, Earl received a sentence of thirty days in the Bruce County Jail at Walkerton after he hit Abraham Davis over the head with a stick. Abraham Davis immediately retaliated by attacking Earl's son, Patrick, and by doing so, he earned a three month jail sentence. Also after this incident, Patrick Earl was fined five dollars and costs for threatening to shoot Abraham Davis. Henry Bradley Davis attempted to defend his father, and hit Patrick Earl in the face, physically marring him.

All during this time, Michael Belrose had been investigating the feud. While questioning George Nelson, Abraham Davis' son-in-law, Constable Belrose found a far more serious offense...murder! George Nelson told Belrose about an incident that had happened in 1874. This incident was later called "Cape Hurd Murders" when it was reported in the Wiarton Echo of 1880.

THE CAPE HURD MURDERS

In January, 1874, Abraham Davis and George Nelson journeyed to Cape Hurd in order to find wreckage of ships that had drifted ashore. They planned to burn the wreckage in order to recover the wrought iron nails, as the nails were rare in Tobermory, and expensive to buy. This was intended to be an overnight trip as they knew that this job would probably take quite a long time. On arriving at Cape Hurd, they built a rough shelter out of boards, and then went to work. At nightfall, they returned to the shelter and proceeded to build a fire and prepare their meal. While they were doing this, three Indians approached them and began a conversation with George. All this time, Davis sat by the fire holding his double-barrelled shotgun in his hands, not saying a word. After talking for a short time, the Indians went down to their camp which was only a short distance away. After finishing his meal, Davis began to tell Nelson that the Indians had previously stolen some lumber from him, and that he had wanted to shoot them then but had been restrained by the fear that the Indians would turn on his family and kill them all. Davis kept on and insisted that tonight was the perfect night for him to take revenge. He told Nelson that he could kill the Indians, and set their bodies adrift in their sailboat. By this time, Davis had worked himself into a frenzy, he gripped his gun and said "here's the lady that's good for two of them, and we're good for the other one with the axe!". Davis continued to talk hysterically and made threats not only against the Indians but anyone else who had ever offended him. After two hours of this frenzied talk, he grabbed Nelson and asked, "Are you going to help me kill these beggars?". Nelson struggled to free himself and tried to calm Davis, but Davis threatened to kill him with the axe. Nelson pleaded with Davis to come to his senses but even as he did so, Davis fired his gun at the Indians and managed to kill two of them. The other Indian immediately tried to escape to his boat, Davis clubbed him with the butt of the gun. Davis had dropped his gun after hitting the Indian and could not find it in the dark, so he grabbed an oar from the boat, and beat the Indian to death. Davis then threw the bodies into the boat, threw in some rocks, and then pushed the boat out from the shore. He then took the axe and made a hole in the side of the boat so it would eventually sink. As the boat slowly drifted away with its macabre cargo, Davis walked to the shore, found his gun and reloaded it. Davis then turned to Nelson and demanded that he promise that he would never tell anyone about the events of that night. When Nelson made no reply, Davis pointed the gun at Nelson's head and demanded his promise. With this form of persuasion, Nelson gave his promise. After a sleepless night, the two men headed back to Davis' house.

In the spring of that year, 1874, Davis turned Nelson out of his house. Nelson fled to Southampton where he lived in fear of Davis until 1880, when he finally told Constable Michael Belrose his bizarre story.

As a result of Nelson's testimony, Abraham Davis was again arrested. It is ironic that he was just climbing into his wagon to leave Walkerton after having served his three month sentence for assault, when he was charged with three indictments, each one for having "murdered a person to the jury unknown" (27).

After a lengthy court battle, it was decided that there was not enough evidence to convict Davis, and so he was set free. A. B. Kleen, Davis' lawyer, received part of Davis' farm as payment for his services.

In 1885, Abraham Davis was appointed lighthouse keeper of the Big Tub Lighthouse, which had been built on the same spot where Davis' enemy, Charles Earl, had once hung his lantern to guide ships to safety.

On November 6, 1895, Abraham Davis disappeared. He was last seen sailing out of the Big Tub Harbour on his way to Devil Island where the two ships, the "City of Owen Sound", and the "James G. Worts" were stranded nearby. Davis' boat was later found near Howdenvale, but his body was never found, hence his headstone at Dunks Bay Cemetery marks an empty grave. Although it could never be proven, many people believed that Davis had not died accidently, but had met his death at the hands of an enemy, either Indian or white, who was seeking revenge for some past wrongdoing.

As for Charles Earl, he lived until 1888, when a mixture of old age and alcoholism finally overtook him. Before his death, he had been a bootlegger, and ran a still somewhere on the northern shore of the Big Tub. Apparently when the road was being extended around the Big Tub, the still's "secret location" was finally discovered.

After Charles Earl died, two of his sons, Patrick and Thomas, left St. Edmunds for either northern Ontario or the west. A third son, Mark, stayed in Tobermory and earned his living in various ways which included singing and reciting poetry he made up about the people and events of Tobermory. There are too many stories to be recited here about Mark Earl and his dog Prinnie, but when Mark died in Walkerton hospital in the 1930's, the feud between the Davis and Earl families finally ended.

OTHER ASPECTS OF LIFE IN ST. EDMUNDS

It must not be assumed that violent incidences were normal in the early days of St. Edmunds Township. On the whole, such incidences occurred only rarely. Early reports from St. Edmunds in the Wiarton Echo spoke of many other things that were more typical of life.

Tales of generosity and of the whole community coming together to help one another are evident in many reports. For example, in 1894, after Alexander Butchart's house, barn and stables were destroyed, the community held a lumbering bee so the family would quickly have the wood they needed to rebuild their home and farm buildings.

Tales of personal courage are often found. One such incident occurred in 1901, when Nellie Marwick dived into the water to save her drowning friend Agnes McIver, who had fallen out of a boat.

Examples of humour are found in many reports. In 1901, bets were placed on whether it was faster to travel to Tobermory from Wiarton by water or by land. Hector Currie, fearing the water, travelled over the "four thousand hills of the Bury Road", and Robert Gillies travelled aboard the steamer, the "Milton". The Wiarton Echo was pleased to announce that both parties arrived on the same day, and therefore there were no winners or losers!

Natural phenomena were also reported upon as news items. In 1904, Wesley Belrose encountered an unusually large lynx near the McArthur lumber camp, and it is reported that he "quickly showed it his heels". A bald eagle was shot by D. Huether, and in 1906, Henry Davis grew a twenty pound turnip.

Life in the Settlement and in Tobermory reflected that of many other small villages. As the population of these areas grew, one report mentioned that "our village is expanding on all sides, with houses springing up among the trees". By 1901, the population had reached 623, and by 1911, it dropped to 423. Of Tobermory, one person wrote the following:

> "We prefer to live in a small village, where people sympathize with you in your troubles, and if you haven't any troubles, they will soon hunt some up for you" (27).

As was stated earlier, the reason for Tobermory's sudden growth from the 1880's to the early 1900's, was lumbering. It is relevant therefore, that the lumbering industry in St. Edmunds Township is examined thoroughly.

Old Mark Earl and his dog Prinnie about 1920

Miss Nellie
Marwick
1903

Threshing Bee early 1900's

CHAPTER THREE

LUMBERING

The world was hungry for lumber when Bruce County was first opened for settlement. By the time that the settlers were entering St. Edmunds Township, the assault on the forests of Ontario had wiped out the vast forests of the Ottawa Valley, and had extended into the area of the Great Lakes. In St. Edmunds, primeval forests of rich and valuable timber waited for the timbermen. In the east lay the hardwoods; maple, beech, elm, oak, ash, and birch. In the west lay the conifers; spruce, cedar, tamarack, hemlock, and the pine which was considered to be the most valuable of all. For these prizes the timber barons would compete, striving to denude the land as quickly and as efficiently as possible. In 1870, the Cook Brothers came to St. Edmunds. This company was one of the largest timbering operations on the Bruce.

Trees on the lots that a settler purchased could not be cut down and sold for a profit without a special license. In 1875, the Superintendent of Indian Affairs allowed the settlers to buy a four dollar license which would allow them to cut and sell the timber from fifteen acres of their land without paying dues on that timber (1).

By 1877, pine was considered to be so valuable that an Order in Council restricted its harvest:

"All Pine Trees being or growing upon any Indian Land hereafter sold, and at the time of such sale, or previously included in any Timber License, shall be considered as reserved from such sale, and such land shall be subject to any Timber License covering the same, which may be in force at the time of such sale, or may be granted within three years of the date of such sale; and all pine trees of larger growth than twelve inches in diameter at the butt, may be cut and removed from such land under a Timber License lawfully in force; but the purchaser of the land, or those claiming under the purchaser, may cut and use such trees as may be necessary for the purpose of building, fencing, and fuel, on the land so purchased; and may also cut and dispose of (but the latter only under a Settler's License duly obtained from the local Indian Superintendent or Agent) all trees required to be removed in actually clearing the land for cultivation, fencing and fuel, as aforesaid, shall be cut beyond the limit of such actual clearing before the issue of the Patent for such land: and any Pine Trees so cut and disposed of, except for said necessary building, fencing and fuel, shall be subject to the payment of regular dues, and fifty percent added thereto for trespass fine" (2).

This order effectively squeezed out all small operators and competition that the larger lumber companies had. The Cook Brothers did not have any competition in St. Edmunds, so they moved in with large work gangs, and proceeded to remove vast tracts of lumber. As early as February, 1870, the Cook Brothers applied to the Superintendent of Indian Lands in Toronto for a license to cut timber on seventy-one square miles of land in St. Edmunds and Lindsay Townships. After their request was relayed to the Honourable Joseph Howe in Ottawa, the Cook Brothers received their answer. It was felt that their request of seventy-one square miles was excessive, and fifty square miles of timbering rights must suffice...still one tenth of the area of the Bruce Peninsula. The license was issued in 1871, and it stated that all types of timber must be cut, not just pine. This stipulation was overlooked as the Cook Brothers cut whatever they wanted to, which meant exclusively pine. In May, 1871, Simon Cook applied for and received a license to cut pine sawlogs and squared timber as well on forty-seven square miles of land in St. Edmunds and Lindsay Townships. In the end, the Cook Brothers managed to obtain cutting rights on ninety-seven square miles of land rather than the seventy-one they had originally applied for.

One might wonder how the Cook Brothers managed to obtain the cutting rights on so much land. This is probably explained by the fact that Hiram Cook, the eldest of the Cook Brothers, served as the Member of Parliament for North Simcoe from 1872 until 1878, and for East Simcoe from 1882 until 1891!

There was still a great demand for lumber in the late 1800's both on the domestic and international markets. The Cook Brothers sent the valuable white pine to markets in Toronto by schooner, and to the markets in Quebec in huge log booms. There was still a great demand locally for lumber, and sawmills were located in Tobermory, Lions Head, Wiarton, Owen Sound, and in many other smaller centres.

For settlers coming into St. Edmunds, lumbering was both a curse and a blessing. It was a curse in that it restricted lumbering on their own land, and a blessing in that it provided employment during the winter months, the season in which the trees were cut and either loaded on sledges and pulled by horse teams to the mills, or piled on the ice so they could be towed to mills in booms after the ice melted. The lumber camps also provided a market as the camp cooks would buy surplus farm produce from the settlers, therefore providing another source of income for the settlers. Another point about lumbering that should be remembered is that settlement often followed after the sawmills were built. This point is well illustrated in St. Edmunds Township by the sudden increase in the population after the sawmills were built, and by the small settlements that sprang up around the sawmills. Such small settlements were found at McVicars on the Crane River, Johnston Harbour, Casseis' Cove (Boat Harbour) on Cove Island, and of course, Tobermory.

In spite of the number of local settlers who worked in the lumber camps during the winter, far more men were needed to make up the large gangs needed to timber. Many of the extra hands who were hired were rough, transitory men who drifted from job to job. Lawlessness among the timbermen was common, and St. Edmunds is not without tales of criminal behaviour by timbermen. The following story tells of three wild timbermen who pushed the settlers of St. Edmunds too far.

LYNCH LAW IN ST. EDMUNDS

According to the local legends, this event took place during one winter lumbering season during the late 1800's. Although the residents of St. Edmunds Township were fairly used to the wild ways of the gangs of lumbermen who arrived each year, it seems that during this particular season, there were three lumbermen whose wicked ways surpassed those of the average lumberman, as they regularly terrorized the residents of the township. As the winter passed, the settlers became so used to hearing about the pranks and damage done by these three men, that these three were soon blamed for every unpleasant deed, whether or not they were responsible for it. As time and patience wore away, a desperate mood crept into the township. Finally, after months of midnight disturbances and alarm, the three lumbermen were attacked by a band of vigilantes who set into their task with the utmost ferocity. The battered bodies of the three men were thrown into the forests and abandoned. A few days later in remorse, a number of men took the bodies to the cemetery on a sand ridge overlooking Dunks Bay. There the three were interred in an unmarked grave, where they still rest among the graves of those who had murdered them.

THE CRANE RIVER SETTLEMENT

Not all of the lumber operations in St. Edmunds were carried out by such huge operators as the Cook Brothers. One particularly successful operation was found on the Crane River (3).

In 1872, James Cockwill bought three lots near the Crane River. In 1873, his son-in-law, William Grant, bought another two lots. In 1874, Cockwill bought another lot from another son-in-law, John Leathorn. It was upon this last lot, Lot 7, Concession 1, E. B. R., that the first sawmill and shingle mill in St. Edmunds Township was built in 1872, by James Cockwill and William Grant.

The Grant-Cockwill establishment successfully combined farming and lumbering, both of which are still practiced on the same property today. In the early 1870's, Grant and Cockwill were listed as farmers, by 1879, they were listed as mill owners. The number of employees of the mill and the farm grew to the point that a small settlement sprang up around the mill.

In 1880, the Grant-Cockwill holdings were sold to William and Peter McVicar. These two men continued to build up their holdings in eastern St. Edmunds, so the small settlement around the Crane River was now called "McVicar's". As this settlement was located on the Bury Road in those days, McVicar's became known as a stop on the route between Lions Head and Tobermory. The main building was a registered post office. The Hidden Valley Lodge which replaced this building is also a registered post office. In 1900, the Wiarton Echo reported that the McVicar house was the "largest and most comfortable house north of Lions Head".

In 1881, Peter McVicar built a sawmill at Johnston Harbour. Another small settlement sprang up around the sawmill. The structures built here included a sawmill, a boarding house with room for twenty men, stables, blacksmith shop, barn, school, icehouse, and a number of log cabins. A dock was built which had a depth of ten feet. At the dock, schooners for transporting lumber would tie up. In 1916, Jim Rae remembers that two schooners, the "Bert Barnes" and the "Davis", would sail between Goderich and Johnston Harbour, making the return trip in three days. He also remembers that on some evenings, the deck of the "Davis" was used for square dances, so it was not all work and no play, even in those days.

The settlement at Johnston Harbour was eventually sold to Charles Pedwell, a member of a well-known lumbering family in southern Ontario, in the early 1900's. By the 1920's this settlement was abandoned, and was finally destroyed by a forest fire in either 1928 or 1929. Today all that remains are the foundations of the mill, an icehouse, a number of stone cribs, and cut wood lying on the bottom of the harbour around where the mill once stood.

THE CHANGING SCENE

Until 1880, the only holders of timber licenses in St. Edmunds were the Cook Brothers, the Grant-Cockwill establishment, the McVicars, Abraham Davis and Charles Earl. After this date, the number of licenses increased, as will be shown in the following.

In 1881, a mill was built on the Little Tub in Tobermory by the Maitland Rixon Company even though they had not purchased the land upon which the mill stood. This mill soon became important to the settlers in the Settlement, as well as the squatters in the townplot, because it supplied employment and building supplies. In 1883, the mill was destroyed by fire, and the economy of the area was affected so badly that the residents of the area drew up a petition which asked the Minister of the Interior for land upon which the mill could be rebuilt legally (see Appendix E). The Minister replied favourably, and the mill was rebuilt that same year.

Another mill built in 1883, was the Lynburner Mill in Lindsay Township on Lots 39 and 40, Concession 13, E. B. R. Although this mill was in Lindsay Township, it was important to St. Edmunds because settlers in the southern part of the township supplied it with timber, and bought lumber for building there. This sawmill continued working until 1905.

By 1882 the timbering situation in Canada had changed. The valuable white pine had been almost completely logged out but other types of trees remained. The situation was so serious, that Sir John A. MacDonald and A. Van Koughnet, the Deputy Superintendent General of Indian affairs decided that the issuing of timber licenses had to be analyzed carefully. In 1884, Sir John A. MacDonald had reached his final decision. Timbering in its present style had to be stopped. Now timbering was only to be carried out in areas where farming was not possible. The Cook Brothers, who still maintained contact with the government through Hiram Cook, seem to have been forewarned of the likelihood of such a decision, and therefore they shrewdly sold their business and licenses to an investor group known as the British Canadian Timber and Lumbering Company before the 1884 decision. Needless to say, with reduced areas available to timber, the British Company could see no future in timbering on the Bruce Peninsula and made no efforts to apply for new licenses.

Lumbermen and townsfolk hauling logs over the snow late 1800's.

The settlers benefited from this decision, and by 1888, the 1877 Order in Council was rescinded, and the restriction on timbering pine was also lifted. With the disappearances of large companies controlling timbering in St. Edmunds, smaller groups began to engage in timbering. Even the Maitland Rixon & Company moved its sawmill from Tobermory to Owen Sound in 1889. Still lumbering survived in St. Edmunds, for in 1890-91, there were twenty to thirty shanties in operation in western St. Edmunds.

In 1892, the Southampton Lumber Company opened a sawmill at Pine Tree Harbour. Like the Lynburner Mill, this mill was in Lindsay Township, and it also obtained timber from St. Edmunds.

In 1895, a new sawmill was built on the Little Tub in Tobermory by Richard Badstone. Shortly afterwards, it was sold to Hector Currie. Two more mills followed the Badstone Mill, E. M. Meirs' in 1900, and Simpson and Culvert's in 1901. All of these mills were located on the Little Tub in Tobermory and operated at the same time. One can easily imagine the noise that the three mills produced and visualize the huge piles of timber and finished lumber that were found all around the edges of the Little Tub.

The Simpson and Culvert Mill had been bought from J. P. Newman of Wiarton and moved to Tobermory. Later Simpson and Culvert sold the mill to Hector Currie and John Neil, who in turn sold it to William Gillies. Gillies later sold the mill to Ed Erb, its last owner. The mill was eventually destroyed in the 1940's by a tornado that scattered debris from the mill as far away as Bear's Rump Island.

In 1900, the Forest Bailiff for Tobermory said that the timbering industry settled down, and the timbermen were now "walking the straight and narrow path". Tobermory was well established by this time, and the local businesses were receiving outside contracts. One such contract was received by the Meir's sawmill, and consisted of an order for 20,000 fish boxes for the Buffalo Fish Company.

Sawing logs 1910-1920

In 1906, timbering in St. Edmunds experienced a slowdown due to the lack of snow. This meant that more horses were needed to drag trees out of the forests than usual, hence the price of a horse team rocketed to the rate of four dollars a day!

In 1905, Thomas Cassels came from Cockburn Island and made a lumber camp at Cassel's Cove (Boat Harbour) on Cove Island. The Owen Sound Hunt Club, who appear to have been the owners of the island at that time, allowed Cassels to build a stable, bunkhouse, barn, frame house, and a small crib dock. The Cassel family occupied that frame house, and two other families occupied two other cabins. The frame house was of exceptional quality, and contained a kitchen designed to feed everyone in the camp. Twenty-two men and five women were employed at the camp at the height of its production. The women, Mrs. Cassels and her two daughters, Mrs. Sam Ellis, Mrs. Berry, Mrs. Young, and Mrs. Pettigrew all worked together to provide the huge meals eaten by the hungry timbermen. Supplies of livestock, produce, and even kegs of fish were supplied to the camp by the people of Tobermory.

The men were given room and board, and were paid monthly after working six days a week. The men were away to the bush by six thirty, after breakfast. Lunch consisted of bread and meat, and it was almost seven-thirty in the evening before the more distant crews arrived back at the camp for the evening meal. Sundays were strictly observed as a day of rest and strict Methodist prayer. When an organ was brought over to the island by sailboat, it too was incorporated into the Sunday worship, even though the only person who could play it was an Indian named Gabe Shegeck, whose entire repertoire consisted of a single Catholic hymn! Other forms of amusement on the island were ice-skating, hockey, or walking across the ice to Tobermory. Unfortunately, walking on the ice was risky during the early spring, and one man, George Young, fell through and was drowned before he could be rescued.

Gillies Mill

William Gillies Sawmill 1911
Left to Right: **Bob Adams, George Fitzhenry, Pete Fosher, John Black,
Donald Gillies, Robert Gillies (lower), Fred Smith, James Blake (boy),
William Gillies, John Gillies, Adam Youngston, Louis Hellyer.**

The timber taken from Cassels' Camp was mainly used for posts and railway ties. Using axes to shape the wood, and drawknives to cut around knots, the men prepared the wood for loading onto tugboats that sailed from Tobermory in the spring. The wood was dragged from the forest on flat, horse-drawn sledges, and was then stacked in piles along the shores of the harbour. The Cassels' operation on Cove Island lasted until the winter of 1909-10. After the operation finished, the Cassels' house was moved by boat to Tobermory, and the rest of the buildings were stripped and left to decay, as was the fate of most lumber camps.

By 1910, the timbering industry in St. Edmunds had definitely come to the end of its big boom. The rapid removal of trees practiced by the timbermen had practically denuded many areas of St. Edmunds. Brush fires were responsible for destroying a large part of what the timbermen had left behind. With the decline of timbering, St. Edmunds slipped into an economic lull that endured until the tourism industry took hold.

Lumbering continued on in small piecemeal operations scattered across the township. Even nearby islands such as Flowerpot, Bear's Rump, and Cove, were timbered, although most of the wood coming from the islands was of poor quality. In 1937, when Yeo Island was being timbered, the following story that was told in the Wiarton Echo occurred.

Five timbermen planned to go to Yeo Island to cut wood for posts. As Yeo Island is fifteen miles away from Tobermory, the timbermen said that they would light a big fire as a signal in the case of an emergency. With this precaution made, the woodcutters left. Later, the men of Tobermory sighted a fire flickering in the distance. Believing it to be the emergency signal, the men struggled to free the "John and Alex" from the ice, so they could rescue the woodcutters. Eighteen hours after the alarm had gone up, Captain J. W. Ramsay arrived on Yeo Island only to find all the woodcutters in good health as they declared that they had not signalled Tobermory. Together with his crew of rescuers (Warren Adams, Martin Young, Bill Spears, and Aaron Dean), Dean returned to Tobermory to find that the fire that they had sighted was a housefire on Manitoulin Island!

Later, in 1941, Barney Hopkins and Jim Rae harvested timber not from the forest, but from the bottom of the Little Tub! Using grappling tongs, they managed to pick up twenty oaks and maples.

Lumbering was the first economic boom experienced in St. Edmunds. The population grew steadily under this industry, and the population at the height of the lumbering boom in St. Edmunds Township was not met again until the 1960's. As the speculators and other timbermen removed the most valuable timber from the forests of the township, the lumbering industry will never again rise to the peaks experienced from 1870 to 1910.

Some lumbering did continue on a smaller scale. In 1950, Ashford Pedwell built a sawmill on Lake Scugog on the Johnston Harbour Road. This mill operated until 1955, when it was stripped and abandoned. W. I. Watson's sawmill still operates, as does Percy Robin's Mill on the Johnston Harbour road. Interestingly enough, the mill at the area known as McVicars still operates, an enduring symbol of the settlers' desire to harvest the forests of St. Edmunds Township.

Little Tub Harbour scene around the turn of the century depicting the lumbering industry.

CHAPTER FOUR

FISHING

The oldest record of white men coming to St. Edmunds in any numbers, is found in the story of the fishing industry. Fishing was one of the oldest lures that brought men to the area from all parts of Ontario and Michigan. Fishermen left few marks on the area, as they came only for short periods of time, and left as silently as they arrived.

METHODS OF FISHING

There are three major methods used for catching fish. The *Owen Sound Sun Times* reported in 1941, that fish were caught because of three personality faults:

"For the fish who doesn't keep his mouth shut there's the hook;
For the fish who sticks out his neck there's the gill net; and
For the fish who's too stubborn to back down the pound net stands ready" (1).

The first method, hook fishing, was the cheapest, as it used bait nets set on shoals and banks. At the first of the year, hooks were usually placed on the bottom, and then later, the lines were floated so the hooks were midway between the surface and the bottom.

The second method, the gill-net, was more costly. The gill-net comes in different mesh sizes, depending on the type of fish one wishes to catch. The gill-net is so named because it catches the fish by the gills. The nets are set in deep or shallow water, according to the habitat of the fish that one wishes to catch.

Finally, the third method is the pound net. The pound net is made in the shape of a box and is hung on poles pounded into the bottom of the lake. Another net, called a lead, is hung leading from the shore to the pound net. At this point there is an opening in the box-shaped net that fish swim through and can not escape from. This net is designed to catch fish that swim along the shoreline.

The most commonly used net in the fishing industry around Tobermory was, and still is, the gill-net. One of the drawbacks of the gill-net is that it requires a lot of upkeep as it must be dried and mended after it is used.

THE HISTORY OF THE FISHING INDUSTRY IN ST. EDMUNDS

The first method of fishing in the waters around St. Edmunds began in 1831, when Captain Alexander McGregor found large schools of fish near the Fishing Islands in Lake Huron south of St. Edmunds (2). In 1834, a Detroit fishing company signed a contract for three thousand barrels of fish per year at one dollar per barrel. This success was bound to create a stir, and soon the Canadian government became aware of the fact that large quantities of fish were being sent to the United States. The government, by an act of Parliament, in conjunction with the Sauking (Saugeen) Indian Chief Metaqul, created the commercial fishing licenses. As a result, Captain McGregor was banned from the rich fishing grounds that he had discovered, and the newly formed Niagara Fish Company took over operations there.

In 1848, the Niagara Fish Company had failed and was sold at a much reduced price to the Southampton pioneers Captain John Spence and Captain William Kennedy. By 1851, these two were leasing fishing operations to others, and finally withdrew from the business in order to join an Arctic expedition to search for Franklin Island.

By 1850, many fishermen were involved in commercial fishing around the Fishing Islands and the waters between Tobermory and Manitoulin Island. They fished these waters in fleets of sailing schooners which were of two designs. Patrick Folkes has discovered an argument

17

Early Scenes at Tobermory

It was a common sight to see Indian sailing boats from Manitoulin Island in the harbour at Tobermory. While the men were out fishing, the women remained at work in the teepees in the dock area. A typical scene is the above photo, with the Tobermory native owned sheds and fishing reels for nets in the background. 1900 or earlier.

that the sailors from Lake Huron had with the sailors of Georgian Bay concerning the design of the fishing boats (2). Apparently, the fishermen from Lake Huron believed that the design most suited to fishing was a boat with a square stern and a large wooden centreboard. The Georgian Bay fishermen felt that a sharp sterned boat with an iron centreboard was the most efficient and would bring in large quantities of fish most easily.

Arguments about types of sailboats became trivial around 1882, when the first steam tug arrived in Tobermory. After that, steam tugs rapidly replaced sailboats. As the steam tugs burned wood as fuel, another source of income was created for the residents of St. Edmunds. Many cords of wood formed the huge stacks of wood that lined the shores of the Little Tub.

Soon there were a number of steam tugs operating out of Tobermory. The first steam tug in the area was the "Clucas", owned by McKay and Clark of Goderich. When the "Clucas" first arrived in Tobermory, she was captained by John McKay. After McKay, she had a number of captains: a Young, a Chapman, Angus McKenzie, Malcolm McDonald, Alexander Craigie, and George McAuley. Another tug in Tobermory was the "Juno", owned by Malcolm McKenzie of Southampton, and later by the Booth Fish Company. The "Juno" was captained by Neil Matheson, who also owned the tug "Evelyn". Two other tugs operating in the area were the "Seabold" owned by the Booth Fish Company and captained by Duncan McInnis, and the "Queen", owned by Captain Craigie. The "Queen" hauled fish and lumber, but was not actively involved in the catching of fish.

PRESERVING FISH

Fish hauls were good, and the prices obtained on the markets, including Toronto, were consistently high. The major species of fish caught was the lake trout. Fishing took place not only in the warm months of the year, but also in the winter. In 1899, it was reported that men were icefishing and hauling their catches ashore by sleighs and toboggans.

As the fishing industry expanded, it was necessary that some means of preserving the fish had to be practiced. In Tobermory, there were two different methods of preservation, freezing and salting.

Salting fish is a very old method of preservation. The first step in this method is to fillet the fish, and then rub as much salt as possible into it. The fish were then packed into a keg with approximately one hundred pounds of fish in each keg. After each keg was packed, the lid was put on the keg. A hole in the lid was left open, and through this hole brine was poured until it covered the fish, and then the hole was corked. Kegs for the fish were made in Tobermory by Alex Young, whose cooper shop stood where the Ferry Dock Restaurant is now located. Salted fish had to be soaked for twenty-four hours before they were eaten, in order to remove the salt. Even after soaking, Mr. W. A. Spears remembers that "the fish tasted good, but it kept you running for the lake afterwards".

Keeping the fish on ice was another method of preservation. In the days before electricity and automatic ice making machines, getting ice was hard work. Ice was "harvested" in February when it was thickest. Many men were employed in harvesting ice in Tobermory. Ice was cut in blocks that were four feet long, twelve inches thick, and twenty inches wide, and were then loaded onto sleighs. In the olden days, these sleighs were horse drawn and there are stories of horse teams falling through the ice, sometimes to be rescued and other times not.

Orrie Vail displaying his catch in 1910-12.

Crews of the "Clucas", "Juno" and "Evelyn"

Bottom Row: **Norman Smith, Jim Cooper, Frank McInnis, Donald McIver, Sam Craigie, Stanley McInnis**
Second Row: **Malcolm McLeod, Murdock Murray, Andy Clendenning, Ken McIver, Dan Martin, Alex Craigie Jr., Elmer Martin**
Third Row: **Captain Neil Matheson, Art Martin, Malcolm Matheson, Dan McIver, John Murray, Roderick Smith**
Top Row: **Alex Craigie, Murray Murdock Jr., Walter Vail, Isaac Hopkins, Captain Duncan McInnis, and Danny Smith**

The ice blocks were stored in small buildings called ice houses. Sawdust was packed around the ice blocks to insulate them so they would not melt. Ice was taken as it was needed, and packed around the fish so that they would stay fresh.

One of the first commerical ice houses in Tobermory was built by Robert Gillies, near the present ferry dock, in 1903. He later sold his company to F. T. James of Toronto, and James then sold to G. W. Golden and Sons of Tobermory.

In 1905, a tug that was well-known in the Tobermory area was launched. The "David Marwick" was built by Albert Leslie, William Leslie, and George Belrose, and became the basis of their fishing business. These three men also built an icehouse and a dock as their business prospered.

In 1916, W. J. Simpson, W. W. Ransbury, and George H. Smith also built an ice house and began selling fish. Later Ransbury would leave his partners, and buy out the Booth Fish Company's ice house, dock, and fish nets.

There are many stories about fishing to be found in the newspapers of the early 1900's. Some of these tell about the size of fish, such as Orrie Vail's two lake trout that went to the Ford Exhibit in Detroit in 1910. One fish weighted thirty-seven pounds, and the other forty-eight pounds, weights unheard of today. Other stories tell about the severity of storms, such as the storm that occurred in 1913, that sent waves crashing against the Big Tub Lighthouse, almost destroying it.

Tobermory served as a drydock where boats were built and repaired. A number of steam tugs had their beginnings in Tobermory.

There are other stories about shipwrecks and loss of life that are unfortunately part of every community whose economy depends on the surrounding waters. One such tale is the loss of the "Kingfisher" in 1927.

The "David Marwick" late 1930's or early 1940's

THE LOSS OF THE "KINGFISHER"

One late autumn day in 1927, Walter Vail, and Frank, Louis, and John Desjardine were aboard the Kingfisher as she made her way through a storm toward the safety of Whisky Harbour on Fitzwilliam Island. The small boat was only three hundred yards away from the shore when a mountainous wave suddenly caught the vessel and capsized her. As the boat overturned, the engine tore loose and plummeted toward the bottom of the lake, trapping Louis beneath it. The other three men were thrown into the water, and after fighting their way to the surface, they managed to grab hold of some wreckage. It was only then that they realized that Louis was not with them. They repeatedly called out his name and scanned the crashing surf hoping that he would appear, but there was no sign of him.

After being in the water for approximately half an hour, the men were finally swept close to land. They quickly scrambled ashore and took stock of their situation. It was now dark and the storm was still raging, and to make matters worse, it had begun to snow. The men decided that they would follow the shore and hoped that they would soon find shelter. It was nearly four hours later when the men did find shelter. They were nearing the end of their strength when they finally spotted an Indian lodge. They quickly woke the Indian family who immediately supplied the men with warmth, dry clothing and food. The three men stayed with the family until they were able to return to Tobermory.

THE FISHING INDUSTRY IN THE 1930'S AND 1940'S

By the 1930's, the fishing industry had undergone a number of changes. The major change in commercial fishing was that most of the steam tugs had been replaced by gas powered tugs. This in turn caused a number of gas pumps to appear on the docks in the Little Tub. The second greatest change was that sport fishing had increased dramatically and guide fishing was now a full-time operation rather than a sideline.

Tobermory soon became well-known for its skilled guides and good fishing grounds. In 1932, there were reports of Alf Carver guiding a fishing trip that had caught fifty-one Lake Trout in one day, and several of those fish weighed more than twenty pounds. Many such stories floated down the Peninsula, and sport fishing soon meant a great deal to the economy of St. Edmunds.

One might think that with all of the water around St. Edmunds, fishermen had no worries. This was not true, however, as in 1928 the government decided to impose a limit of three miles for all commercial fishermen. This law was made in order to protect the sport fishermen. The commercial fishermen decided to protest this law as many of the shoals located near the islands were rich fishing grounds. The fishermen had now found another antagonist apart from nature...the government.

In 1936, fish catches hit a low that had never before been experienced, and the commercial fishing industry began to suffer as catches of lake trout decreased dramatically. It was not until the 1940's that the full extent of the damage to the lake trout was realized.

1927 photo of young Bill Davis in fish box with nets in background.

There were a series of boat sales in 1939. Archie Simpson bought T. A. Golden's boat, Hector Butchart bought the "Barney" from Barney Hopkins, and Martin Young bought the "Mary Ellen" from Fred Grieves. Also that year, Ivor McLeod had bought the Buckeye Fish Company from W. J. Simpson. Even more promising was the fact that three boats were being built for John Desjardine, August Whipp, and Cliff Craigie. These transactions demonstrated the confusion that was evident in the fishing industry at this time. Some people felt that the industry was indeed in trouble and so they were getting out before they lost their holdings. Others felt that there was still and would continue to be money in fishing and so they continued to invest in equipment.

The year 1939 ended in a violent storm that destroyed Tom Spear's boat after dashing it against the rocks. The "Golden Fisher" broke loose from its moorings but fortunately it was caught before it was damaged.

It was 1943 before another storm occurred that caused such damage. In that year, a seiche acting like a tidal wave lifted John Desjardine's boat out of the water and dropped it on the dock. It also flood the village down as far as Craigie's Restaurant.

The only boat sold in 1943 was the "David Marwick" which the Leslies sold to Cecil Davis.

The year 1943 was an important one to commercial fishermen as the Ontario Federation of Commercial Fishermen was formed that year. T. A. Golden, who was President of the Lake Huron, Georgian Bay Commercial Fishermen's Association, was appointed vice president of the Ontario Federation. The Deputy Minister of the Ontario Department of Games and Fisheries agreed to co-operate with the Federation but stated that sport fishing had to also be taken into account. The Federation requested that the Ministry restock the Great Lakes with lake trout, and the Deputy Minister agreed to plant eight million fingerlings, and to continue the program in the future.

By 1944, T. A. Golden was able to compile figures that demonstrated that the lake trout had decreased by eighty-three percent in Lake Huron. Georgian Bay had slightly better statistics, but the North Channel was in worse condition than either of the other two bodies of water.

A bitter battle between the Fisheries Department and the Federation headed by Golden began. The Federation claimed that the Department was not doing enough for the commercial fishermen. According to the Federation, the Department was not planting enough lake trout fingerlings and that was the reason for the scarcity of lake trout. The Department immediately accused the fishermen of overfishing and refusing to agree to a closed season in which the lake trout could naturally restock themselves. Besides man however, there were two other reasons for the decline of the lake trout that were gradually becoming known.

From the Owen Sound Sun Times 1941

Common Sight Along Peninsula

Fish nets out to dry are a common sight along the Lake Huron, Georgian Bay shores. Here a fisherman prepares for another run.

From the Owen Sound Sun Times 1941

Matchless Harbor of Tobermory

The busy fishing centre and quaint tourist village of Tobermory are glimpsed in this attractive harbor scene. In the background are the business places. The craft tied up at the dock are all gas boats operated by tourist guides. The long line of gill nets drying in the sun represent the commercial fishing for which the Peninsula is famous.

THE DECLINE OF
THE LAKE TROUT

As was mentioned above, man was in part to blame for the decline in the lake trout through overfishing and resource mismanagement. Nature too was to blame, for the sea lamprey and the Atlantic smelt also played a large part in the disappearance of the lake trout.

It was the sea lamprey that was soon identified as a major predator of the lake trout. The sea lamprey was able to move from the sea, up the St. Lawrence River and into the Great Lakes after the completion of the Welland Canal in 1932. The lamprey immediately attacked the larger species of fish found in the lakes such as the lake trout and the whitefish. Before a means of controlling the spread of the lamprey could be found, the lake trout fisheries in the Great Lakes were wiped out. In 1950, Orrie Vail, a Tobermory fisherman, sent specimens of lamprey bearing red spots to various authorities hoping that the red spots were an indication of a disease fatal to the lamprey. He and the fishing community in general were disappointed when experts told them that the red spots were not a sign of disease, but a sign of aging as the spots appeared on the lamprey after they spawned (1).

Lake Trout caught on Georgian Bay in the 1930's

View of Little Tub Harbour in late 1940's or early 1950's.

FISHING IN THE LATE 1940'S AND 1950's

By 1946, most of the boats previously involved in commercial fishing were no longer fishing. This was the year that ended many commercial fishermen's careers. The fish market prices were very high for fish that were hard to catch in any quantity such as the lake trout, and were very low for any other type of fish.

T. A. Golden was again elected as the head of the Lake Huron and Georgian Bay Fisherman's Association, but there was little to be done for the commercial fishing industry.

Barney Hopkins about 1945

Fishing decreased again and by the 1980's there were only a very few men still practicing commercial fishing out of Tobermory. Russel (Rusty) Raney is now the captain of the "Dyker Lass". Bud Edmondstone, Billy Wipp, Alf Lee and Peter Dean, owner of the "W. A. Spears", are all that remain of an industry that dates back prior to the founding days of St. Edmunds Township.

The year 1947 was marked by the burning of the thirteen year old steam tug, the "John and Alex". The boat caught fire early one winter morning, and by the time the fire was noticed, the boat's owners, W. W. Ransbury and Sons, decided that nothing could be done to save her. Audrey Coultis towed the burning boat away from the dock to prevent the fire from spreading to other boats, and the boat's hull gradually broke up near Golden's dock in the Little Tub. The origins of the fire were never explained and the loss of the boat was estimated at approximately fifteen thousand dollars.

By 1949, the Lee Brothers, the Ransburys, and the Goldens were amongst the few fishermen still fishing in Tobermory. Later that year, the Goldens sold out to the Lees.

Little changed in the community in the 1950's. In 1952, Russel Schope bought the "Dyker Lass", a familiar boat around the Little Tub even today. Fishing did not improve, and by 1954 the whitefish catches dropped by forty-five percent. Tobermory fishermen began to venture further afield in the search for fish and employment. Tragedies still occurred on fishing expeditions. One example of how tragedy affected families in the small community of Tobermory is found in the Wilson family. In 1945, Lavern Wilson lost her father, Vern Bravener, after

Tobermory fishermen in the mid-1940's.
From left to right: **J. W. Ransbury, Lloyd Ritchie, Walter Hopkins, Murray Chisholm, and Johnny Martin.**

he drowned off Cape Hurd while fishing on the "Golden Fisher". In 1955, Mrs. Wilson's husband, John Wilson, was washed off the "Ciscoe" while on a fishing trip in Lake Erie. In the same incident, another Tobermory man, Harold "Buck" Young was rescued.

The Atlantic smelt was the other natural factor affecting the lake trout population. The Atlantic smelt had been introduced purposefully to the Great Lakes by man for commercial fishing. The smelt population increased rapidly and was soon found throughout the lakes. It is felt that the smelt affected the lake trout in two different ways. Firstly, the lake trout and the smelt consumed the same food. Because of their numbers, the smelt ate most of the food and did not leave enough for the trout to thrive on, and therefore their numbers decreased because of the lack of proper food. Secondly, the lake trout ate the smelt. Some people feel that the smelt somehow affected the trout's digestive system and the fish died because of that.

It is evident that there were various reasons for the decline of the lake trout population that included both man and nature. These factors combined to cause the end of the commercial fishing industry on the large scale that it had practiced prior to the 1940's in the waters surrounding St. Edmund's Township.

Cecil Davis, Husky Young and visitor pulling nets.

Fishing vessel in the harbour, early 1900's.

The "John and Alex" 1930's

Recent photo of "Dyker Lass".

Recent photo of John Desjardine cleaning fish.

Little Tub Harbour Early Fishing Scene

Little Tub Harbour 1920's.

CHAPTER FIVE

VOYAGING TO TOBERMORY

ASPECTS OF THE MARINE HISTORY OF FATHOM FIVE PARK
THROUGH TRAFFIC: THE RISE OF SAIL & STEAM

By Patrick Folkes

The passage of ships through the waters of Lake Huron lying between Tobermory and Manitoulin Island is one of the principal features of the maritime heritage of Fathom Five Provincial Park. The origins of this traffic lie in the three decades following the end of the War of 1812 and the occasional passage of small trading boats and the stories of the armed ships of His Majesty's Provincial Marine based at Penetanguishene. From this modest beginning, navigation on Georgian Bay evolved into a dynamic and complex enterprise which saw the utilization of almost every type of wood, iron, and steel vessel afloat on the Great Lakes. Although the tugs, steam-barges, sidewheelers, and the great fleets of sail have vanished, the bulk carriers and package freighters of the nineteen 'seventies still ply the historic channels of Tobermory.

In 1848 the southern townships of Bruce County were opened for settlement. The initial wave of homesteaders came ashore along the Lake Huron coast between Clark Point and the Saugeen River. Traditionally, the first settler reached the new country on the 'Fly', sailed by Captain A. Murray MacGregor, son of Alexander MacGregor who, in about 1831, established the pioneer fishery on Main Station Island at the base of the Bruce Peninsula. The 'Fly' set a precedent and for several years the preferred route was by small two-masted schooner or "packet boat" from Goderich. The demand for the transport of passengers and supplies gave a fresh impetus to the growth of the Goderich fleet and a prosperous shipbuilding industry was soon launched. As the hamlets of Kincardine and Southampton expanded among the fresh stumps, locally owned and built craft appeared among the coasters. By 1855, there was a fleet of at least a dozen schooners, all less than sixty feet in length, in service.

Goderich was in part a jumping off point for northern Lake Huron and the availability of transport after 1848 ensured some continuity to that obscure trade. The 'Wing & Wing' was lost in 1848 at the Fishing Islands while on her way to Manitouwaning, the principal Indian settlement on Manitoulin Island. On September 11, 1850, the 'Emily', built that year at Goderich, arrived down from the island. A year later, in June of 1851, the 'Rose of Pine River', laden with "freight for Georgian Bay ports" was wrecked at the mouth of the Saugeen River. Of these early voyages into Georgian Bay and thus through the waters of Tobermory almost nothing is yet known. Many of the pioneer Goderich and Bruce County navigators were Scots and it is probable that because of these northern trips Bayfield's "Collins Harbour" came to be known as Tobermory, in memory of a similar place in their homeland. In any event the name was in common use by 1852. An early familiarity with the area is also suggested in Captain Alexander Marks, a member of the Marks family of Southampton, schooner-builders during the late 'fifties and early 'sixties, who took up land near Tobermory in 1876.

The successful development of sail between Goderich and Southampton inevitably led to the demand for steamer service. Not only did it hold the promise of a more regular coastal passage but also held the possibility of opening a route into Georgian Bay and upper Lake Huron. In May of 1853, a public meeting was held at Southampton with the object of forming the Saugeen Navigation Company which would purchase a steamboat to connect Goderich and Sault Ste. Marie. The necessary funds, however, were not forthcoming and the scheme collapsed.

In 1856 the sidewheeler 'Ploughboy' was finally placed on a regular passage between Detroit and Southampton, with occasional runs through to Owen Sound, Meaford, and Collingwood. During 1857 and '58 the 'Ploughboy' ran solely on Georgian Bay. In 1859 she sailed from Detroit to Sault Ste. Marie by way of Windsor, Kincardine, Owen Sound, Meaford, Collingwood, Little Current and Bruce Mines. Yet the through passage was not a profitable nor a practicable one and the North Channel and Georgian Bay were in fact better served by the Collingwood steamboats. The steamer passage from southern Lake Huron, through the Tobermory straits, and into Georgian Bay died in infancy. Although the 'Ploughboy' was the first steamer to operate on a scheduled track along the entire coastline of the Bruce Peninsula, it was the Peninsula itself which formed a permanent barrier to its success.

Simultaneous with the expansion of shipping on Lake Huron, the Georgian Bay marine experienced a similar though more varied growth. By 1850 the forests and farms fronting the coast of the Bay between Owen Sound and Coldwater were in full development. Goods and passengers were brought in by schooner from great distances, frequently from as far away as Toronto. It was on such a passage that the Penetang schooner 'Lilly' was lost off Tobermory in September of 1852. As early as the spring of 1848, the Cobourg schooner 'Atlantic' had cleared Toronto for Owen Sound and Nottawasaga Bay. In July she departed Georgian Bay with the first recorded cargo of lumber for Chicago. During 1852 and '53, the brig 'Sophia' was advertised as sailing from Toronto to Owen Sound and the "Hen & Chickens" (Collingwood). The 'Sophia' was a pioneer of other voyages as well. In the spring of 1849 she was fitted out for a trip to the California gold fields by way of Cape Horn, but because of an insufficient number of passengers, she was sent instead on a voyage to England.

The Georgian Bay timber trade pioneered by the 'Atlantic' gathered momentum during the eighteen fifties. Almost every sailing ship which passed outbound through the Tobermory straits was laden with wood — square timber, sawlogs, cordwood, posts, railway ties, lumber, shingles, lath, or barrel staves. Sail dominated the trade for the first twenty years, then waned as steam-barges — the famous "lumber hookers" — and later iron bulk freighters appeared. Of the vessels lost within the region of Fathom Five Park, many were entering or leaving Georgian Bay in that pursuit. They represent a wide spectrum of the fleet so engaged during the latter half of the nineteenth century. The schooners 'Cascaden' (1871) and 'China' (1883) were lost on the inbound passage. Among the outbound timber ships which were wrecked were the schooners 'Castalia' (1871) and 'Charles P. Minch' (1898), the steam-barge 'W. L. Wetmore' and tow 'James C. King' and 'Brunette' (1901). During the 'seventies and 'eighties, whole forests passed out into Lake Huron. Within sight of the headlands of Tobermory, in fair weather and foul, from April through November, an endless procession advanced over the horizon — tugs drawing great rafts of pin sawlogs from Collin's Inlet and the French River, big three-masted schooners lumber-laden from the mills at Parry Sound and Matchedash Bay, and the wallowing "lumber hookers" westward bound from a dozen different ports. These are among the strongest images lingering in shipping records and in the dwindling memories of those who yet remember the timbering boom.

The completion in 1855 of the Ontario, Simcoe and Lake Huron Railway to Collingwood, and the subsequent arrival of railroads at such points as Midland and Owen Sound, was of fundamental importance to the growth of shipping on Georgian Bay. The movement of cereals from Chicago and other ports on Lake Michigan has long been a dominant feature of Great Lakes navigation. From the late eighteen 'fifties, the Georgian Bay offered a marked short-cut, by way of railroads, to markets in the East and the grain ships were soon streaming.

VOYAGING TO TOBERMORY

In the late 1800's, the easiest way to arrive in Tobermory was by boat. Regular steamship service to Tobermory began in the 1870's. Prior to that, many ships had called in to the harbours, but usually these were unscheduled stops made only when the weather was bad and the ship needed a safe port in a storm.

The first boat that made regular stops at Tobermory was probably the "Prince Alfred". The "Prince Alfred" competed with the "Wiarton Belle" for business along the east coast of the Bruce Peninsula.

It is known that some of St. Edmunds early settlers arrived in this area by boat. It is rumoured that the first settlers, Charles Earl and Abraham Davis, arrived on the black sailing vessel, the "Nee Chee". James Simpson and some of the "Backline Hopkins" arrived aboard the "Prince Alfred". Young W. J. Simpson arrived on the "Jane Miller", a boat that plied its trade between Owen Sound and Manitoulin Island. Unfortunately, this boat went down with all hands on Colpoys Bay in 1881.

By 1882, the "Josephine Kidd" had replaced the "Jane Miller". She was owned by the Maitland and Rixon Company, a business that had lumbering and mercantile interests at Tobermory.

The "Forest City" on Bear's Rump Island 1904

STR. J. H. JONES, WRECKED 10 MILES FROM LION'S HEAD ON THE EVENING OF NOVEMBER 22ND, 1906. ALL PERISHED.

The Steamer 'J. H. Jones' in the Little Tub before 1906

Other steamers that called in at Tobermory included the "Telegram", "City of Grand Rapids" and the "J. H. Jones".

But these also had violent ends, especially the 'J. H. Jones' that had been very important to Tobermory. She was also the most important boat to the Crawford Tug Co. (valued at $12,000). She was built in Goderich in 1888 and visited Tobermory many times. In 1894, Captain McAuley, well known to residents of Tobermory, brought the steamer in. The "pork and tobacco" famine caused

by the winter was relieved by new supplies from the "J. H. Jones". In 1900, the Dominion Fish Co. (the "J. H. Jones" owners) sold the steamer to the Crawford Tug Co. The details of her sinking were unknown except that she encountered stormy seas. It was surmised that she turned on one side in the gale. The passengers and crew would remain trapped inside as the steamer slid into the water. The loss was closely felt by Tobermory for among the dead were the Fellon boys. The destruction of the family was so complete that the name would never continue in Tobermory. Also reported among the dead were Marmaduke and Orrie Vail. However, these two corrected the newspaper with a curt letter explaining that they were still alive.

As roads were improved, the boat passenger service began to die, and by the twenties it took a great drop. Out of the ashes of this first decline a new line began. In March, 1921, Captain Norman McKay organized the Owen Sound Transportation Company. The competition that the Owen Sound Transportation Company had was from the Dominion Transportation Company which was a subsiduary of the Booth Fisheries Corporation. The Dominion Company built boats that were specifically designed for the Great Lakes, that is, the boats were small and made of wood. The Owen Sound Transportation Co. had two ships, the "S. S. Manasoo" and the "S. S. Manitoulin" (formerly the Madjeska). The "Manasoo" was added to the company in 1928, and she went down that same year in Colpoys Bay. Only five men from the entire crew survived to tell how the ship's hull had been punctured and the ship had gone down almost instantly.

'The Telegram'

Steamer C. P. R. ashore on bad neighbour shore on July 3 or 4, 1914. Steamer Alberta unloading some of the freight.

The "Islet Prince" was another ship that encountered difficulties. She had come into the harbour at Tobermory in order to inspect the damage that had been done when she had sheared off one of her four propeller blades. The captain decided that rather than wasting time in dry-dock while the propeller was repaired, they would simply get some dynamite and blow off the blade that was opposite the one that had been lost, and this would restore the balance of the propeller. A crewman was ordered to attach a large charge to the blade as those on shore watched the whole procedure with an air of misgiving, and men who had boats in the harbour scurried to get their boats away from the "Prince". After a lot of discussion, debate and preparations, the charge was fired. The explosion did blow off the desired blade, but it also blew off the rest of the propeller as well as most of the stern! Windows around the harbour were blown out, and wreckage littered the shore as the concussion from the explosion rolled around the harbour. Onlookers who had taken shelter looked up just in time to see the "Islet Prince" settling to the bottom of the Little Tub as men scrambled around on its deck. Fortunately there was no one killed and no injury, save for the pride of the captain. Needless to say, the "Islet Prince" spent far longer in the dry-dock than she would have with the original damage (1).

The 'Islet Prince' about 1936

Even though the Owen Sound Company was reduced to one ship, they would have a replacement by 1931. After experimenting with a Tobermory-South Baymouth service in 1930, they obtained a franchise for the operation from the Province of Ontario in 1931. They also purchased the "Normac" (named after Captain Norman MacKay), a steel vessel that held 15 automobiles per trip. The cars had to let air out of their tires to fit all of them in. This had been done for all previous ferries and this practice would not be abandoned until the 1960's.

By 1936, the competition between the two companies had reached a head. With both competing to their utmost, they were losing money heavily. The Dominion Transport Company arranged a 'partnership' in which both companies retained ownership and expenses of their vessels and set up schedules that would not conflict.

Ferry Steamer leaving Tobermory, for Manitoulin Island, Ont.

'Caribou' at Dock late 1930's — early 1940's

In 1945, the Dominion Transportation Company acquired the total capital stock of the Owen Sound Transportation Company, but the Dominion Company chose to rename itself the Owen Sound Transportation Company. Prior to this merger, the Dominion Company owned the wooden-hulled "S. S. Manitou", and the "S. S. Caribou". The Owen Sound Company owned the steel ships, the "S. S. Manitoulin" and the M. S. "Normac".

After the merger, the "Manitou" was immediately scrapped and the "Manitoulin" took over the Owen Sound-Manitoulin Island-North Channel freight and passenger operation. The "Caribou" and the "Normac" were used on the Tobermory-South Bay Mouth ferry service.

The reason for the merger of the two companies was complicated. During the war, the government froze the freight and passenger rates and therefore the company operated at a loss. However, the Federal Government gave a $35,000.00 subsidy each year from 1943-45 to support the company. The ferries had gone from transporting 1,500 automobiles in 1931, to 7,198 in 1945. The freight and package business had fallen off due to the new highways. The ships were outdated, as they ranged from thirty to fifty-five years old. Both of the ships had room for twelve cars and fifty passengers. Most importantly, their equipment was outmoded which forced the captains to take all kinds of risks as they were forced to

rely on instinct, experience, and such dangerous practices as listening for the echo of a whistle in order to see how close the shore was in a fog and judging the proximity of the shore by the scent of the pine trees!

With the new merger, the company was able to approach the Federal Government and negotiate a subsidy contract for $65,000.00 each year. They then applied the subsidy toward the building of a new ferry, the "S. S. Norisle".

In 1947, the "Norisle" came into service at the same time that the battered, wooden-hulled "Caribou" was scrapped. In 1947, the "Norisle" and the "Normac" were both running the Tobermory to South Bay Mouth circuit.

By 1949, it became evident that the S. S. "Manitoulin" was ready to be scrapped. However, the freight route up the eastern side of the Peninsula was still demanded by many people, so either the "Manitoulin" had to be repaired or a new ship had to be built. As the "Manitoulin" was over sixty years old, it was decided that the Collingwood shipyards should be engaged to build another ferry. To help replace the "Manitoulin", the government raised their annual subsidy to $100,000.00 a year. The S. S. "Norgoma" was built to handle the "Manitoulin's" Owen Sound-Manitoulin Island-North Channel operation.

By 1963, the "Norgoma's" run was so weak, and the "Norisle's" so strong, it was decided that the "Norgoma" would be transferred to the Tobermory-South Bay Mouth run as well in 1964. By this time, the "Normac" was only used occasionally during the peak summer period to aid the "Norisle".

The statistics showed that the ferry service were indeed a growing concern. In 1947, 12,744 autos had been handled, in 1963, 18,871 were handled, and by 1969, the traffic skyrocketed to 25,822! This increase reflected the rapid growth of the tourist industry on the Peninsula.

Tobermory Ferry Dock mid-1940's.

S. S. "NORISLE"

The New Tobermory-South Bay Mouth Ferry

Now Under Construction at Collingwood Shipyards for

The Owen Sound Transportation Co., Ltd.

This entirely new and modern ship is of all-steel construction and entirely fireproof. The first commercial passenger and cargo ship to be built on the Upper Lakes since 1913. The S.S. "Norisle" will have the following dimensions and characteristics insuring the public a first-class ferry service between Tobermory and South Bay Mouth:

Length	214 ft.	Beam	36 ft.
Depth	16 ft.	Speed per hour	12-14
Carrying Capacity			50 Automobiles
Passenger Accommodation—Day			200
Passenger Accommodation—Sleeping			100

The S.S. "NORISLE" will be placed in service in the Tobermory-South Bay Mouth ferry service immediately on completion and will provide adequate and comfortable accommodation for passengers crossing from the mainland to Manitoulin Island and return.

Until the completion and delivery of the S.S. "NORISLE," the Company requests the indulgence and patience of its many passengers and friends should unavoidable delay occur at certain peak periods during the Summer operation of the ferry service.

Pending delivery of the S.S. "NORISLE," the following will be the time-table on the Tobermory-South Bay Mouth service:—

FOUR TRIPS DAILY

IN EFFECT FROM
JUNE 28 TO SEPT. 2 inclusive

Leaves Tobermory		Arrives South Bay	
	6:00 a.m.		9:00 a.m.
	10:00 a.m.		12:30 p.m.
	1:00 p.m.		4:00 p.m.
	4:00 p.m.		6:30 p.m.

Leaves South Bay		Arrives Tobermory	
	7:00 a.m.		9:30 a.m.
	9:30 a.m.		12:30 p.m.
	1:00 p.m.		3:30 p.m.
	4:30 p.m.		7:30 p.m.

TWO TRIPS DAILY

IN EFFECT FROM
JUNE 3RD TO JUNE 27TH and
SEPT. 3RD TO SEPT. 30 inclusive

Leaves Tobermory		Arrives South Bay	
	10:00 a.m.		12:30 p.m.
	4:00 p.m.		6:30 p.m.

Leaves South Bay		Arrives Tobermory	
	7:00 a.m.		9:30 a.m.
	1:00 p.m.		3:30 p.m.

ONE TRIP WEEKLY

IN EFFECT FROM
OPENING OF NAVIGATION to JUNE 2ND
and OCT. 6TH TO OCT. 28TH inclusive

Leaves Tobermory	Arrives South Bay
Sundays -- 6:00 p.m.	Sundays -- 8:30 p.m.

Leaves South Bay	Arrives Tobermory
Mondays -- 6:00 a.m.	Monday -- 8:30 a.m.

All Schedules Eastern Standard Time — Subject to Change Without Notice — No Reservations Accepted on Ferry Service

Sorry! All Cruise Trips Are Sold Out

The popular 5-Day Cruise and the Week-End Cruise are both sold out for this year and people are now being turned away. We would suggest making reservations now for the season of 1947. This is what one lady from Port Huron, Michigan, wrote us: "I hear such thrilling accounts of your cruises! How soon can you accept reservations for the 1947 season? You see, we are determined to get in on your popular cruises sooner or later."

We suggest, if you would like to cruise with us in 1947, you make your reservations now.

Schedules show the time at which boats may be expected to arrive at and depart from the ports, but their arrival and departure at the time stated is not guaranteed, nor does the company hold itself responsible for any delay or any consequence arising therefrom. We solicit the co-operation and patience of the patrons of the Ferry and assure them of a greatly improved service, much more accommodation and a faster passage when the new "Norisle" is launched and commissioned.

For Further Information, Enquire

Owen Sound Transportation Co. Ltd.

Owen Sound, Ont.   Phone 78

The "Norisle" at the Tobermory ferry dock about 1950

The "Norisle" at dock in the 1960's.

Pictorial Souvenir History of Tobermory to Manitoulin Island Ferries.

A — M.S. Normac 1932 - 1962.
B — S.S. Norisle 1946 - 1974.
C — M.S. Norgoma 1963 - 1974.
D — M.S. Chi-Cheemaun 1974 -

Aerial view of M.S. Chi-Cheemaun and ferry terminal area 1980's.

The company once again urged the Province of Ontario to improve the service. This was the moment that the company learned of the government's plan to take over the ferry operation in 1972. By 1974, a new faster, larger ferry was put into service. The name of this ship was chosen in a contest sponsored by the Ministry of Industry and Tourism. From among the two hundred names entered in the contest, the name "Chi-Cheemaun", which means big canoe in Ojibwa, was chosen. This name had been entered in the contest by a man from Cape Croker, Donald Keeshig. The ship was christened in that name on June 15, 1974, at the Collingwood Shipyards.

The following are the ship's original statistics:

Length: 365 feet five inches
Beam: 62 feet 4 inches
Draft when Loaded: 13 feet
Service Speed: 17.25 knots
Auto Capacity: 113
Passenger Capacity: 630
Maximum Vehicle Height: 17 feet

Today, with improvements, the boat has even more impressive statistics.

What of the fate of the other ships, the "Normac", "Norgoma" and the "Norisle"? The "Normac" sunk later in Toronto Harbour while serving as "Captain John's Harbour Boat Restaurant". It had been damaged earlier in a collision by a Metro Toronto Parks boat and within a month, it surprised the owners by sinking.

The "Norisle" left under tow in 1974, for Manitowaning on Manitoulin Island where it now serves as a restaurant-museum. The "Norgoma" is now a marine museum on the Sault Ste. Marie waterfront.

The "Chi-Cheemaun" is still running, as it has for ten years, serving both the passengers for transportation and Tobermory for business and tourism.

Chi-Cheemaun at dock 1983

Ferry terminal and parking area 1983

Ferry dock and loading ramp 1983

OVERLAND TRANSPORTATION ROUTES

As Tobermory and St. Edmunds became more developed, so did the roads that stretched up the Peninsula to them. It was surprising that with the township depending so heavily on water traffic for supplies, a road to Stokes Bay was open as early as 1873. However, this lumberman's road was not a winter road and could only be travelled by foot. It was on this road that Mr. George Pepper travelled to visit a Mr. Cockrell at Stokes Bay. On September 20, 1879, he left to return to his home in Tobermory. From his experiences recounted in the *Wiarton Echo* on October 10, 1879, it was clear that it was not an ideal path with which to keep in touch with the outside world:

"On the following Tuesday Mr. G. Webb arrived at Tobermory, having also come from Mr. Cockrell's and discovered that Mr. Pepper had not yet arrived home. Considerable alarm was manifested and Messrs. Young, McDonald and Earle organized a party to go in search of the missing man. Two men were despatched down the Huron shore as far as Johnstons Harbour, and another party took a boat and went up the Georgian Bay, firing a gun every few minutes. When the latter party were about nine miles east of Dunk's Bay, they discovered Mr. Pepper sitting on top of a cliff, known as Halfway Bluff. Although Mr. P. had a fine view of the magnificent scenery and abundance of fresh air, he was almost exhausted, having been travelling through the woods for three days exposed to the weather and without a morsel of food. It will probably be remembered by some of your readers that about four years ago Mr. Pepper and another gentleman were lost in the woods in the same township and found in exhausted circumstances by the tug 'Sunport Davis'. In future we think Mr. P. will be inclined to keep out of the woods as much as possible."

As early as 1881, pathmasters (old road superintendants) were appointed to look after St. Edmunds roads. In that year John Shearer, Neil Currie, Richard Hopkins, Richard (?) Belrose and Thomas Cockwill were appointed pathmasters. In 1883, H. Rixon and Company were reported to have improved the Bury Road and roads around the harbour (which Rixon claimed cost $1,600). Pathmasters continued to take care of the roads, even though some argued with their methods. An 1895 Wiarton Echo correspondent criticized the pathmasters for not building a water culvert to avoid a road pothole opposite W. J. Spears' house; the pathmasters were only filling the hole in with sand. And the roads were rough as John Shearer found out that same year:

"Mr. James (sic) Shearer lost last week a fine old horse. As Mr. Shearer is pushing and active we suppose the old beast succumbed to the bad roads. For the past month the roads have been very heavy and consequently it is very hard on horses."

By 1900, the road connecting Tobermory to Dyer's Bay followed the Bury Road to Crane River, turned east at McVicar's twisted around Shouldice Lake and finally joined Highway 6 to Dyer's Bay.

It was in 1900 that the railroad rumours started. An application in the provincial legislature was supposed to have been presented for a railroad charter. It was to span the Manitoulin Island and, via ferry, join up with the Tobermory line which would run through Lion's Head, Wiarton, Owen Sound and Meaford. Of course, nothing came of this and up until the present time the railroad has only reached as far north on the Bruce Peninsula as Wiarton. The speculation was such that the *Wiarton Echo* published this article in 1901.

"Manitoulin and North Shore Railroad"
"A railroad project of great interest to the Peninsula would make Tobermory an important village and give Wiarton a quick connection with Toronto, and an all year outlet to Algoma. A railway ferry similar to that of the Straits of MacKinac would maintain communication during the entire year between Manitoulin and Tobermory. This route would shorten the distance between Toronto and all points in new Ontario by at least 75 miles, and divert the traffic of northern Ontario to the west side of Georgian Bay and secure the same for Ontario, instead of letting it drift to Quebec."

This article shows that the early settlers wanted the best for their area even if their dreams were unrealistic for their small population could not economically support a railroad. However, in 1902, the Port Elgin Times advocated that a rail line join Tobermory and Port Elgin. In 1903, Mayor Solomon Spears declared that if the railroad building commenced in the fall, he would take steps to incorporate Tobermory as a city. As late as 1910, the Wiarton Echo was still carrying stories on the possibility of a railroad when it wrote that a number of gentlemen were seriously considering building an electric train to Tobermory.

The railroads never materialized but the roads did. The St. Edmunds Council began a push to get grants from the Provincial Government to create more and better constructed roads. However, it was not until tourism became an increasingly important economic factor that the roads were brought up to the standards that the rest of the country enjoyed.

When the Township was first settled, there were only trails. The first roads were those found around the Tobermory Harbour, and these roads were made of the sawdust from the sawmills that were located around the Harbour. For many years, the Bury Road was little better than a trail. Gradually, the trail was widened by increased usage and progressed to the state of a single lane clay track. The road's condition did not change until 1928-29, when it was finally covered in gravel. Still there were enough hills and curves in the Bury Road that it was said that it made even fishermen seasick! Accidents concerning front end collisions happened quite frequently as drivers could not see around curves. Sharp corners, steep hills and flooded out sections of the road did little to encourage tourists into the area. These conditions endured until the Provincial Government took over the responsibility for the Bury Road in 1937. After this date, improvements were made. Hills were levelled, the road was straightened and eventually a double lane hardtop road emerged. This road was renamed Highway 6 as it was incorporated into the Provincial Highway system after its completion in 1954.

Of course all of these changes in the highway took time. However small the building of the highway may seem to us now, it was another route by which the Township of St. Edmunds was linked to the outside world. One tourist was so impressed by the change in the road over the years, that in 1931 he wrote to the Wiarton Echo to praise the "ingenuity and scientific methods of the modern road builders".

Even though the roads were improved, the winter weather could still isolate the small community by freezing the shipping lanes and blocking the roads with snow. In 1941, Toronto newspapers reported that there were food shortages in Tobermory as a result of heavy snowfalls closing the roads. The Wiarton Echo correspondent denied this report as rumours by saying that "Gibbons Bakery provided plenty of bread, and the lake supplied plenty of fish". The rumours of shortages prompted road crews to open the roads in record time though. In 1942, Thomas Belrose's bus was snowed in at Wiarton. Later that year he sold the bus to Carroll Davey, but went into the business again in 1945, when he and his passengers were again stranded in Wiarton, this time for three days!

The first gasoline truck to come up the road at Tobermory is shown in the above picture. The solid tires are an interesting feature. 1919

The first car to visit the community is picture above, dating back to about 1916. The width of the road, as shown in the picture, explains why the car is well into the bush.

1964 Bus Schedule

In 1947, flocks of tourists necessitated the paving of parts of the highway. This action caused tempers to flare since people demanded other stretches of the highway be repaired. Besides making the road more accessible for summer tourists, the paving allowed earlier snow removal. This eased such problems as the seige of snow earlier in 1947, that only ended when a convoy loaded with supplies arrived on January 8th. The 12 day isolation scared many, especially Mr. and Mrs. Cecil Bartley whose child was failing due to a lack of proper formula.

In 1951, an angry article in the Echo referred to the still rough highway. They spoke of it as "one of the most hump-backed, switching, winding, and in spots, dangerous pieces of pavement in the Blue Water District". In response to such criticism, highway construction reached its peak in the 1950's. By 1953, Crane River and Willow Creek were diverted to flow under newly built bridges. Over the years, the highway has been resurfaced and is now an easily travelled route to Tobermory. Unlike one century ago, most traffic arrives in Tobermory via this overland route.

AIR TRAVEL

The last way of arriving in St. Edmunds is by airplane. Seaplanes were landing on the Tobermory Harbour in the early 1920's. The first landing on land occurred in 1945 when an intrepid pilot landed on a farmer's field after being guided there by the farmer, Gordon Gibbons.

The history of flight in St. Edmunds has been marked by fatal crashes, which continue with distressing frequency. In 1971, five members of the Leaver family were killed and a sixth member was seriously injured when the pilot of the plane attempted to land using visual flight in a heavy fog. Other planes have crashed in the waters off St. Edmunds. In 1950, a pontoon plane left Tobermory for Algoma in a heavy fog. The wreckage of the plane was found off Manitoulin Island, but its two passengers were never found. Many other planes have been forced to land at unplanned spots when the weather or equipment failure dictates that they must do so. Sometimes searches for these planes last up to two days before they are located by air searches or marine traffic.

After using a field as a landing strip for a number of years, a runway was finally built in 1967. This runway was sponsored by three London and Sarnia tourists. It was located near Highway 6 on the Warner Bay Road. The owners, the B. J. Company, cancelled their operating license in 1971 after the Leaver crash. The ownership of the airport then passed to the Tobermory Island Development Limited who had purchased it hoping that it would attract customers to their development. In 1979, they closed the airport as the Niagara Escarpment Commission was blocking their plans for land development. By July, 1979, the Township had reopened the airport and planes were again landing there. The Township, aided by the Ministry of Transportation and Communications, bought the airport for $60,000.00 in 1980. By 1981, an additional $35,000.00 had been spent to upgrade the facilities at the airport in order to attract more people into the area, and to ensure the safety of those using the airport.

The transportation routes that now exist in the Township of St. Edmunds were developed as a battle against isolation. The first lifeline that the small community had to the outside world was the marine traffic. This link, however, was broken by the long winter that meant no contact outside of the immediate community for approximately four months. This was one of the pressures that led to the establishment of an overland route to the south. Gradually, this route developed into the present highway. The addition of the airport was more a method to attract people to the area rather than a vital link in the transportation system. Although St. Edmunds never received a railroad connection, it has overcome the problem of isolation.

Seaplane in Little Tub Harbour 1919.

CHAPTER SIX

THE PROBLEM OF COMMUNICATION

St. Edmunds Township has always been separated by distance from the outside world. As a result, the community is closely knit and interrelated. It is a common joke that any person who has not been in the community for over fifty years is considered a newcomer. Well over half of the residents of the Township are able to trace their family back to the years that the Township was settled over a century ago. It was not until fairly recently that this insularity was broken by constant contact with the outside.

MAIL DELIVERY

A settler in 1894 had this to say about the problems of communication in St. Edmunds:

"It is too bad to think that Tobermory has been settled for 12 or 14 years and we are without a road and only have one mail a week. The telegraph office is closed all winter and the people of Tobermory might be all dead and the outside world would know nothing about it. It is too bad for good loyal subjects to be treated in this manner. In talking among ourselves sometimes we wish we were Indians and then the Government would look after our interests a little" (1).

It was not until 1881 that a regular post was started. This was eleven years after the first settlers had arrived. The first mail carrier was Benjamin Butchart and the first postmaster seems to have been Alexander Green, who ran a local store in Tobermory. The mail carrier travelled on foot to Stokes Bay to pick up the mail. One can understand the hardships involved in this job, but still some people complained about Butchart's services. In response, Butchart wrote the following:

"I can truthfully say that not withstanding all the storms and other difficulties which I have had to contend with in the last six months, I have only twice missed the regular trip. The great storm in January when neither man nor beast could travel was the cause of one trip being

missed, and the other was caused by floods in February, when the road was completely inundated. You have no idea what the roads are like; for miles it runs through a burned district where there are dead trees that stand with their roots clinging to the bare rocks, and after every wind the road is blockaded and I must take my axe and clear it away before I can proceed. Yet, not withstanding all the difficulties, I am ever at my post, and when the performance of my duty is neglected it is only when insurmountable difficulties arise." (2)

By 1895, the people of St. Edmunds were still demanding more frequent mail. Since an election was forthcoming, they stated:

"First and most important we must have our mail twice a week. We cannot see on what grounds the Government refuses this boon to the settlers of this township, but grants it to Stokes Bay three times per week". (3)

At this time the mail carrier was Neil Currie and by 1900, it was Thomas Bartman. Still the mail route remained slow and treacherous.

In 1913, Andrew Belrose, the community's longest serving postmaster, took up the postmaster's job. Andrew took the time to reply to children's letters to Santa Claus although the fact that the letters were written on stationary from the St. Edmunds Treasury Office might have aroused some suspicion from older children!

Tom Belrose's snowmobile used to deliver mail 1936

In the wake of World War II, the mail service to Tobermory was again under attack. It still took two days for the mail to travel from Wiarton to Tobermory. By 1946, the mail delivery changed from three times a week to daily service. Occasionally the weather interfered with the delivery of the mail, just as it does today.

In 1948, Andrew Belrose who had been assisted by his daughter, Hilda Belrose and Eunice Wheildon, completed his thirty-sixth year in the postal service. Later when he died, Hilda temporarily filled his post until Harry Davis took up the position. That winter, Thomas Belrose, the mail carrier, missed one of the ten deliveries that he had missed in nineteen years. This record was due to his trusty snowmobile.

The Post Office was located at the Belrose Inn while Mr. Belrose was Postmaster. When Harry Davis took over as Postmaster, the Post Office moved next to Peninsula Supply, and from there to the building now occupied by Fathom Five. From this location the Post Office moved to its new and present location. Now the job of post carrier has none of the hazards that it held a century ago.

POSTMASTERS		Cause of Vacancy
1881-1883	Alexander Green	resigned
1884-1885	D. M. McDougall	resigned
1887-1889	W. J. Simpson	death
1893-1903	Mrs. Maria Currie	resigned
1903-1913	Mrs. Margaret Currie	resigned
1913-1948	Andrew Belrose	death
1948	Hilda Belrose	temporary help
1948-1967	Harry Davis	promoted
1967	Mrs. Mary Davis	temporary help
1967-70	William Larry Scarr	promoted
1970-85	Mrs. Gladys Morris	retired

1983

THE TELEGRAPH *and* WIRELESS STATIONS

In 1887, another form of communication appeared when the Great Northwestern Telegraph Company extended its overland cable as far north as Tobermory. The small building that was the Telegraph Office was located where the Smith's Bait Shop now stands. The telegraph pole for the telegraph station was located on the hill where the Catholic Church now stands. The eyebolts used to hold the guidewires of the pole are still there.

One of the earliest operators was W. J. "Operator Billy" Smith. Mr. Smith began this job in 1889 at the ripe old age of sixteen years. He held this post until 1892 when he took the job of Line Supervisor of the cable north of Wiarton. The line ran from Wiarton to Lions Head, then across to Stokes Bay and up to Tobermory. One can imagine the hardships endured in this job as the Supervisor had to travel by foot along the cable in order to locate and repair any damage to the line that would cause it to cease functioning. Mr. Smith was the Line Supervisor until 1913, when the Telegraph Station was closed.

Besides working on the Telegraph, Mr. Smith also posted the expected weather conditions on the telegraph pole. It was operated with a red lantern, a large drum and a cone. A single red lantern hoisted to the top of the fifty foot pole indicated a westerly gale. If the cone was at the top, it meant an east wind. If the cone and the drum were both hoisted to the top, a heavy gale was expected.

The Telegraph Station was closed in 1913 after the Wireless Station opened. The weather signals however, were posted daily by Mr. Smith until 1951, sixty-two years after he had begun this service.

Construction on the Wireless Station began in 1911, and by 1912, this station was transmitting and receiving messages in Morse Code from the marine traffic on Lake Huron. The Tobermory Wireless Station, located on North Point, was one in a network of wireless stations built around the Great Lakes in those days of heavy marine traffic.

In 1914, after the outbreak of World War I, the Wireless Station was considered to be a very important link in communication, and was therefore considered to be at risk of sabotage from the enemy. The War Department sent Captain E. R. Clarke and a squad of fifteen men to guard the station. A huge fence was erected around the Station at this time to further ensure its safety. One resident remembers that up until 1914, Indians from Cape Croker and Manitoulin Island had used North Point for a camping area from which they would fish in their sailboats, and then sell their fish in

The interior of the Wireless Station 1914. Take note of all the equipment.
Operator is possibly A. E. Argue.

Tobermory. With the appearance of the soldiers and the construction of the wall, the Indians were scared off by all of this activity, and from then on they gradually stopped camping in Tobermory.

The War Department gradually realized that the enemy was not likely to attack the Wireless Station, and so they withdrew the experienced men who had been guarding the station and replaced them with a guard made up of local men and new, untrained recruits in late 1914. A guard was placed on the station for the duration of the war though.

An interesting story that is rumoured to have taken place at the station in 1912 concerns a message that the operator picked up. Apparently, due to the atmospheric conditions, the Tobermory Wireless Station picked up the distress call from the "Titanic" just before she went down after striking an iceberg ninety-five miles south of the Grand Banks of Newfoundland.

In 1930, W. J. Tetley was operating one of the best equipped Wireless Stations on the Great Lakes, but the Wireless Station was quickly becoming outdated. By the fall of 1933, the Wireless Station was closed. However, due to a petition from the people of St. Edmunds asking the Federal Government to keep the station open during the Depression years, the station was reopened. The station finally closed its doors forever at the end of 1939, and the buildings and the property were sold to private citizens. It is now the Trail's End Lodge.

Erecting the Wireless Pole 1911

Soldiers who guarded the Wireless Station during the First World War relaxing by ice sailing.

41

The reason for the closure of the Wireless Station was the improvement of communication services by telephones and radios. In 1930, Mr. and Mrs. Fred Smith and Mr. and Mrs. Martin Hopkins bought the first radios in Tobermory. It was these two instruments that were harbingers of the improvement of communications that meant the death of the Wireless Station.

Moving the Wireless Pole from the water to station 1911

"Operator" Billy Smith and wife Mae.

Dwelling for the Wireless Operators Early 1920's

Wireless Office (left) Wireless Operator's House Early 1920's

TELEPHONES *and* TELEVISIONS

In 1899, William Gillies started a telephone exchange in his home in Lions Head. By 1904, he had extended his line to Dyers Bay. From there he continued the line to Tobermory, so that before the First World War the people in Tobermory had telephones. The Gillies Telephone System served the people of the northern half of the Peninsula until 1934 when it was sold to Wesley Taylor.

In 1939, Taylor extended the dialing telephones to Tobermory. Since Jim Rae was the first person to subscribe he was honoured by being given the telephone number 2222.

In 1954, Taylor introduced the automatic dialing system. At this time, there were fifty-four telephones serving the five hundred and thirty residents of St. Edmunds.

In 1973, an American syndicate bought the Taylor Telephone System. In 1979, they introduced the seven digit telephone number to their service. This meant that callers could tie in to the Bell Telephone Company without going through the operator. The telephone service in St. Edmunds is now equivalent to that found in the rest of the country.

In 1953, Cecil Arscott and Fred Grieves introduced the first televisions into the area. Since then, the reception has been improved dramatically by a CTV rebroadcasting station. Today, satellite dishes are used by some residents to pick up more than the two stations that most people in the area now receive.

CHAPTER SEVEN

LOCAL GOVERNMENT

The circumstances that led St. Edmunds Township to self-government included a long series of unions with other townships. It began with all four northern townships being united in one government on June 21st, 1872. At this time, St. Edmunds had very few settlers, so their input was very limited. Albemarle was the senior township with Eastnor, Lindsay and St. Edmunds merely waiting for a chance to break off on their own. Five years later, Eastnor became the senior township of the new united townships of Lindsay, St. Edmunds and Eastnor. The break was not to be a peaceful one and arguments were quick to break out. Financial troubles, stemming from the over-assessment of the three northern townships, forced Albemarle into a four year legal battle. This was only to be solved when Eastnor, Lindsay and St. Edmunds paid Albemarle $300.

The union of Eastnor, Lindsay and St. Edmunds on June 8th, 1877 was also destined to last a short time. The Bruce County Council passed by-law 188 on June 10, 1882, freeing Lindsay and St. Edmunds. Unlike the previous partnerships, this Lindsay-St. Edmunds union was to last twenty years or twice the amount of time that both previous unions lasted put together. It was not until January 8th, 1883 that a council for the United Townships of Lindsay and St. Edmunds was put together. Even in 1882, St. Edmunds' population was small. Some people with ties to St. Edmunds were influential on the council. Most noted is Alexander McDonald who served well over half the amount of time for Reeve when Lindsay and St. Edmunds were united. Also Peter McVicar, whose family would also later have a considerable effect on the township in creating the small village of McVicar. Agitation began to grow and an effort was made to have this final union dissolved.

On June 6th, 1902, the Bruce County Council passed by-law 488. It would separate the townships and allow St. Edmunds to be self-governed by elections that winter. The by-law which marks the beginning of St. Edmunds as a separate township is as follows:

"And whereas it appears that the township of St. Edmunds being the Junior Township of said union has at least fifty but less than one hundred resident freeholders and tenants on the last revised assessment roll of said Township.

And whereas sixty eight (being at least two thirds) of the resident freeholders and tenants of the said Township of St. Edmunds have petitioned the Municipal Council of the County of Bruce to separate the said Township from the union of the Townships of Lindsay and St. Edmunds being the union to which the said Township of St. Edmunds belongs.

And whereas the Municipal Council of the County of Bruce considers the said Township of St. Edmunds to be so situated, with reference to streams or other natural obstructions that its inhabitants cannot conveniently be united with the inhabitants of an adjoining Township for municipal purposes.

And whereas it is deemed expedient to grant the prayer of the said petition.

Therefore the Municipal Council of the Corporation of the County of Bruce enacts as follows:

1. The Township of St. Edmunds in the County of Bruce is hereby separated from the union of Township of Lindsay and St. Edmunds and is hereby created a separate Municipality and a corporate body politic.

2. The first municipal election for the said Township of St. Edmunds shall be held at the Town Hall in connection with school section number one near Tobermory in the said township.

3. Alonzo H. Bryan of the said Township of St. Edmunds, farmer, is hereby named and

appointed the Returning officer who is to hold the first municipal election for said township.

Dated and passed in open Council at Port Elgin this 6th day of June A. D. 1902.

W. S. GOULD,   J. J. DONNELLY,
County Clerk,   *Warden.*

The winner of the first St. Edmunds election was Solomon Spears who became the first reeve. With his council of Henry Bradley Davis, William James Simpson, John Henry Smith and William Henry Hopkins, Solomon Spears met for the first council meeting on January 12th, 1903. In the settlement school house of S. S. No. 1 they passed their first by-law — to appoint the first clerk, James Campbell. In this meeting they also arranged for clerical and treasury supplies, appointed John Cuff Hopkins the first treasurer, and secured salaries for the council. The reeve and the councillors received identical pay; $1.50 a day and mileage for St. Edmunds meetings and $2.00 a day and mileage for Lindsay business. Settling with Lindsay would take a fair length of time and in their first meeting they promptly instructed the clerk to open talks with the Lindsay reeve.

The 1903 council of Solomon Spears that adjourned "to meet again at the Call of the Reeve" not only dispensed with the ususal posts that needed to be awarded, but also created interesting by-laws — some of which have never been repealed.

On March 1903, by-law 7 was passed prohibiting "from running at large in the Township of St. Edmunds", horses, bulls, pigs and geese that, "if found on the roads or highways are liable to be impounded". The odd part about the law is the roads and highways are big words for the trails comprising the transport routes of St. Edmunds. For even until 1911, their "road superintendants" were called "pathmasters".

On Hallowe'en Day another interesting by-law was issued by the council. It prohibited "shooting or discharging fire arms within one half mile of the village and harbour at Tobermory". They were also not allowed to discharge "firearms on the Public Roads in the Settlement". They had originally put in "within a half mile limit of" but crossed it out and inserted "on".

The council handled itself fairly well and ran into few troubles in its first year. Solomon Spears was the head of a large family. Many of the earliest settler's children married into his family, making him the grandfather of much of the village. As would be the case in the history of reeve-ship in the council, it would be the strong families of the community that usually formed the government. Solomon Spears also had previous experience in Township matters during the Lindsay — St. Edmunds union. He was a friend of Bruce County historian Norman Robertson and contributed much to the St. Edmunds section of Robertson's book.

In the following year, 1904, another leader of a prominent family rose to power. Though relatively young (age 34), William James Simpson was to hold the reeveship for almost two years. Among the original settling families, he was a man of many talents and interests. He was a settler, a fisherman, and a timberman whose varied abilities lead him to fulfill almost every office in the council and a second term as reeve in the 1920's. In his term of 1904-5, his by-laws dealt strictly with business and efficiency. There was nothing unusual in his term except his instructions to his councillors that stated in dealing with a person, they could use strong language, but they were prohibited from swearing at the person. Simpson also secured a Little Lake Bridge maintenance agreement with Bruce County that was favourable for the township.

In May, 1905, Simpson was replaced by his predecessor, Solomon Spears. Simpson probably resigned although it is not known why. During Spears' reign, many fascinating by-laws were passed.

On June 16th, 1905, a by-law was written that charged all shows and entertainments five dollars a day to operate. This money was collected by Spears and personally given to the treasurer.

On July 15, 1905, the Noxious Weed Act was passed as by-law 43. All parties having cultivated land were compelled to pull out all obnoxious weeds on their lands. As strange as this act sounds, Thomas Bartman was appointed to enforce the act, and in 1936, the post of Weed Inspector was begun and still functions today.

Liquor was a serious debating point in the days of prohibition in many townships. In by-law No. 60 that was passed in 1907, there was a paragraph prohibiting the sale of "spiritous, fermented or other manufactured liquors" in "every tavern, inn, or other place of public entertainment". This retailing of alcohol must have been a burning issue, for by March 1st Solomon Spears had reversed his stand and allowed "all persons wishing to keep a Hotel or any place they keep for accommodation of the travelling public" to sell liquor for a hefty $60. fee a year.

On May 15, 1907, the Harbour Garbage Act was passed prohibiting the throwing of "any refuse or other matter from said Vessel or Crafts" in the harbour.

William Gillies was a man of strong morals if the by-laws he passed are any sign. In 1908, he came into office. He was heavily connected with his general store in Tobermory, and had timbering interests. His two year reign was to last until the winter of 1909. His clerk was none other than Solomon Spears' son, Lytle, who had replaced A. H. Byrand (Deputy Returning Officer 1902) in the middle of 1907.

By-law No. 90 is a gem of the era, written on March 31st, 1908, it states:

"That any person or persons found guilty of any of the following offences viz Posting up any indecent placards, writings, or pictures, or the writing of any indecent words, or the making of indecent pictures or drawings on walls or fences in public places, vice, drunkenness, profane swearing, obscene, blasphemous or grossly insulting language and other immorality and indecency. The carrying on of disorderly houses and houses of ill fame, gambling houses and etc. And be it further enacted that any wares found in any house be seized and destroyed.

And be it further enacted that this by-law is to be construed so as to refrain from running at large any vagrant mendicants and persons found drunk and disorderly in the streets, highways or public places or at or near a place of public entertainment or indecent public exposures of the person and other indecent exhibitions, shall be liable to be prosecuted (sic) according to law."

If the residents of St. Edmunds ever wonder what constitutes a legal fence for the township of St. Edmunds they should consult by-law 93 on May 26, 1908:

"Wire fence: — four and one half feet high. Partly stone and Partly wire: — four and one half feet high. All bail fence: — four and one half feet high. Large fence: four and one half feet high."

In the winter of 1910, William Gillies chose not to run for another term of reeveship and W. W. Ransbury was elected the new reeve by acclamation. W. W. Ransbury is another patriarch of an important family in St. Edmunds. He heavily invested in fishing and formed W. W. Ransbury and Sons. He was familiar with council, serving the previous three years (1907 - 1909) as a councillor before choosing to run as reeve.

It was during his term that the infamous St. Edmunds dog versus council war was to begin. In the previous by-law prohibiting certain animals from running loose it should be noted that dogs were not mentioned. In By-law 131 of March 1910, it is stated that "all dogs within St. Edmunds must be securely chained in an outhouse or kept under lock and key or muzzled. Any person allowing their dog to run will be prosecuted (sic)". The fine was not to exceed $20.00 for the first offence and $200.00 for the second offence. Dog-owners were to be on the look-out.

Also in the same year, the first by-law aimed at improving the roads was written. By-law 118 was to invite any parties to suggest the ways of improving "main and leading roads of St. Edmunds with stone and gravelling of a substance at a total estimated cost of $1,000". This was a response to Provincial Grants that were available.

1910 was the year that the council's two major problems were brought to the surface. The dog problem was more complex than the by-law earlier suggested for vigilantes had for a long time taken the problem onto themselves. Strychnine was put out as early as the 1880's to kill dogs and the councils by-law 136 was probably in response to that. On September 12th, 1910, a by-law prohibited people from putting out poison for the purpose of killing any game.

By 1911, William Gillies was back in power for three years. His first by-law is a long, detailed notice explaining who is available for statute (obligatory) labour and how much they must do. A person could get out of working by paying a cash alternative.

No fast driving would be permitted, especially after dark. In the minutes of October 7, 1911 it was stated that no vehicle go faster than a walk around the village and no faster than five miles an hour in the township.

William Gillies worked on expanding the roads and securing provincial grants. His by-law 147b on October 5th, 1912, detailed the work to be done and money to be spent. Its major interest was to obtain provincial funding.

By 1914, W. W. Ransbury was in for another year term. Past reeve, Gillies announced on March 22, 1916 that he had enlisted in the army. The Echo correspondent stated he "is not altogether a spring chicken but he wants to get into it all the same." Ransbury continued expanding roads which by this time had gone beyond pathmasters. By 1911, they were called overseers, but the roads had ceased to be divided into straight divisions by 1913. In 1914, as it would be for years to come, the council adopted the task of planning and overseeing roads. Little mention was made of the previous semi-autonomous pathmasters/overseers as the council began to assign work in specific areas.

Andrew Munn came to power as reeve in 1915, and was to hold his position for six straight years until the winter of 1921. He had lost to W. W. Ransbury in 1914 by a vote of 42 to 38 just as a Vail, a Smith, and a Davis had been refused council seats. Andrew was head of the Munn family in the township and his son became an influential person — particularly in the Road Department.

World War I began and a grant of $10 was made to each accepted recruit (e. g. Clifford Hopkins and Howard Belrose). Later it fell to $7 and even $5. With roads and expanding expenditures, the St. Edmunds corporation borrowed $1,000 from the Royal Bank in August of 1915.

The dog war was also in full swing, for by-law 193 of October 9th, 1916, set forth the first dog tax. It charged $1 for the first male dog and $2 for each one after it. Female dog licenses cost $3 for the first one and $5 for each additional license. If the assessor did not receive such a fee and found dogs on a person's land, the dogs were to be destroyed by the constable. The reason was simple for such strict legislation — dogs were blamed for the death of sheep. In the final paragraph the council promised to pay for 2/3 the cost of damages done to sheep by dogs of unknown owner. This led to the appointment of sheep valuators and later livestock valuators. The council had become bound to protect the livestock within the limits of the township.

Financial problems plagued the council again and they arranged for a loan from the Royal Bank — One thousand dollars ($1,000) in 1917. Vandalism also hit that year with the single streetlight becoming an object of fun. Signs were posted on the streetlight forbidding people to interfere with it. This did not deter the council from planning the erection of new streetlights and early the next year they looked into purchasing new ones.

Always interested in the commerce of Tobermory, the Council leased land to Marmaduke Vail, Orford Vail, and David Vail to establish an ice house on December 15th, 1917.

Of course roads were still of high concern. Geoff Nightingale, a clerk in the late 1970's perused the minute books and discovered that:

"Driving down the Bury road in our cars and trucks seems a simple task these days, but we couldn't be doing it without actions of early councils. On April 30th, 1918 (James H.) Hopkins and Bartman moved that the clerk be authorized to notify each person owning property adjoining the Bury Road in the Townplot of Bury that council has decided to sell the timber on the Bury Road the width of three rods in the centre of the road allowance. Parties wishing to purchase timber in front of their property may do so by handing to the clerk a written tender stating the amount they are willing to pay. Tenders to be in by May 20th, 1918 and the timber to be cut by December 1st, 1918."

Influenza, which took such a fatal toll on soldiers in 1918, sent some councillors home sick in the latter half of that year. By 1919, the war was over and to commemorate the dead, a local Memorial Committee was formed. It was given the duty to erect a monument to the soldiers — a monument which now stands near the harbour.

The streetlights were installed by 1920 and on January 12, 1921, Mr. George Fitzhenry was appointed to light them until May 1st at $20 a month.

On March 17, 1921, the Dog Tax and Sheep Protection Act was passed. It detailed a precise set of instructions for the assessor to note so as to make sure all dogs were accounted for. Dog tags were issued, each with its own serial numbers. This tagging was done in hopes of restricting the number of dogs and their movements.

The speed limit was raised to 15 miles per hour below the harbour but "10 miles an hour around the harbour for motor cars and etc."

The winter elections yielded another leader — W. J. Simpson. This reign was to last from 1922 to 1925.

Roads were to take a new step in this administration. The problems of expanding the roads was finally placed on a road superintendent's head. John Cuff Hopkins became the first to hold the title, although his traces can be found among the earlier pathmasters and road overseers. With his appointment came mechanical equipment to repair the roads. The machine of the time was a horse-drawn grader, hand cranked and manned by two men. It cost $50 and was labelled "Sawyer and Masey

Co. Model #4". John C. also received information from the department of highways on his new job and was granted a salary of $3.25 per day to supervise all work on roads.

On April 30th, 1925, the Bruce County regained maintenance rights on Little Lake Bridge and St. Edmunds was freed of that responsibility.

Fishermen were not forgotten and in a motion by "Operator Billy" (W. J.) Smith and Frederick James Smith, it was demanded that Tobermory receive more young fish. This cry would become louder by the 1930's and break into a yell by the 1940's.

By 1926, W. J. Simpson had relinquished his chair to another former reeve, W. W. Ransbury. Simpson had defeated T. A. Golden in 1925 by a landslide vote of 85 to 37, but 1926 brought a switch that allowed neither of them to take the chair. Instead, W. W. Ransbury gained his 3rd term as reeve. A fisherman himself, he promptly applied for 10,000 Black Bass Fry for Hay Bay.

In 1926, the council also bought a stone crusher and had moved further into building roads with cheaper gravel.

In 1928, plans for a sidewalk began — to be built of cement and four feet wide. Of course, fifty per cent of the cost had to be paid by the townsfolk bordering the walkway.

The dog war had expanded as well, for by-law 360 on May 26th, 1928, banned dogs from "running at large for a period of 30 days". The fine for "neglect or refusal to comply with the provisions of this by-law" was $10.

The sheep-dog battle did not cease and council decided instead to veto claims for monies by insisting that no dog killed sheep — it was the wolves (not covered in the by-law and therefore free to act outside the law). This of course did not please Bill Cosgrove, Walter Warder, W. E. Shaw or Andrew Munn who had sheep claims at the time.

Perhaps this helped to created W. W. Ransbury's overthrow in 1929. William Simpson was elected by a slim nine vote margin. Thus Simpson took his final third term of office that would last for two years. In all he had served eight years as reeve.

During the next two years the council set up their library (by taking over "Tobermory Library" assets with by-law 387), set up a community hall fund, and borrowed heavily to support these ventures and still apportion money to road maintenance. Fishing still interested the council which responded to the Fisheries three mile limit (commercial fishing banned within this limit) with a statement harshly protesting its injunction.

The elections in the winter of 1930 brought Cecil Davis to the reeve's chair. For the past three years he had served as a councillor. His father, Henry Bradley Davis, had also served as a councillor. Henry had been the councillor to head the list of the first council in 1903. For some years Cecil Davis was the community milkman. About the beginning of the war, he sold his dairy farm, bought a comfortable home in the village and a fishing tug. He later sold his boat and carried on as a seasonal guide. Mr. Davis had five of his children in the Armed Services, a record which was notable even in Tobermory, where there was an average of one enlisted soldier for every household. His reign as reeve was to last six years.

In building the Community Hall they were reduced to extreme actions such as by-law 412. Passed on June 9th, 1931, it provided for, "a field day consisting of music, banquet in the evening" and enforced a Public Holiday in Tobermory. In fact, any daring business who tried to open their doors that day would be fined $50. The following by-law arranged a bank loan of $10,000 but was strangely always followed by brackets containing $1,000.00. On July 6th, 1932 another field day was created (allowing stores to open only until noon) with a $50 fine to all who did not comply. Further financial troubles were apparent in the February 4th, 1933, by-law 444 which allowed private bonds to be accepted as security for the treasurer and tax collector.

Later that year the townships pleaded to the federal government to keep open the Wireless Station. The fall of 1933 saw at least 50 families on relief and the council not only administering funds but also seeking ways to get around the unemployment of the Depression. They asked the government for aid to expand the roads, especially around the harbour. This "relief roadwork" was agreed to by the government who signed an agreement on December 15th, 1934, for $3,000 of relief to be used to expand roads. The council interviewed applicants who wished to work for this relief money and road foreman, J. C. Munn submitted the list of applicants. However, money was hard to get and pay was small — 22-1/2 cents per hour for men and the road foreman, J. C. Munn, got 34 cents per hour.

The cemetery board was established in 1934, as were some laws on moral conduct. By-law 979 was passed on April 12th, 1930 (p. 30! Book #2).

"No person shall make use of any profane, swearing, obscene, blasphemous, or grossly insulting language or be guilty of any other immorality or indecency within the Township. Nor shall any person or persons exhibit, sell or offer for sale or circulate or cause to be circulated any indecent or lewd book, paper, picture, plate, drawing, photograph, or any other object of that nature, or kind, or perform any indecent, immoral or lewd plays within the Township.

No person nor persons shall frequent or keep a house of ill-fame or disorderly house within the Township.

No person shall engage in, or take part in any charivari or other like disturbance within the Township.

No person or persons shall ring any bell or bells, blow any horn or horns, about or make any other unusual noise in any of the streets or public roads of the Township, which is calculated to disturb the inhabitants, provided always that nothing herein contained shall prevent the ringing of bells in connection with any lawful business, or with any church chapel, meeting house or religious service or fire bells or fire alarms".

Any person who violates any of the provisions of the above by-laws shall incur a penalty not exceeding fifty ($50) Dollars exclusive of costs and in default of payment of fine, may be sentenced to a term not exceeding six months in jail."

In 1935 a reeve had a car destroyed and since it was Cecil's term we assume it was his car. The author Warren Adams wrote:

The Wreck of the Model T
Our Reeve rode to the village
On a bright sunshiny day,
And there he parked his Model T,
But the darn thing ran away.

Down the hill it ran quite quickly,
Now I am not here to boast,
But they say she was doing 70
When the darn thing hit a post.

And the Reeve was doing 60,
As he sprinted o'er the ground,
But the Ford, it beat him to it,
And spoiled the scenery round.

A crowd then quickly gathered,
For a wreck all like to see,
And they found a cussing Reeveship,
And a ruined Model T.

W. A. Adams
(The Canadian Echo
October 10, 1935)

In the middle of his 1936 term, Cecil Davis accepted the job as clerk, a job he would keep until 1962. In his place, J. W. Ransbury (son of previous three time reeve W. W. Ransbury) served his term for six years until 1941 when he left for World War II.

By-law 520 became his effort in the dog war. It raised license fees but lightened restrictions in killing untagged dogs. His next by-law was even liberal enough to grant a speed limit of 30 miles per hour.

Before a fisherman (W. W. Ransbury and Sons), he instructed the clerk to apply for ten million trout fry, ten million whitefish, two million black bass and one million speckled trout. The fishing situation was indeed worsening.

In that year, the Bury Road was adopted as part of the provincial highway and the province asssumed responsibility for it. By 1939, the community hall was also completely paid for. It seemed that J. W. Ransbury had eradicated two of the problems that plagued councils before him.

During J. W. Ransbury's 1941 term he left to fight in the war in the R. C. A. F.

To replace Ransbury came a unique man, Weir Grieve. Grieve was one of the few men who had become reeve without having longstanding roots in the area. On January 12, 1942, Grieve was appointed reeve.

Grieve was an interesting character. He was born in Glasgow, and received a degree in law from the University of Glasgow. In World War 1, Grieve served as a captain, and then remained in Europe after the war. He then travelled to North America and toured the United States before settling in Tobermory in the mid-1920's. Besides being the Wiarton Echo correspondent for many years, he was also a councillor for three years before rising to become reeve.

Weir Grieve
Reeve 1941-47

Also in 1942, Margaret Golden became treasurer replacing Margaret Ellen Ransbury. A few interesting actions of the council of this period were: to draft a by-law to have "slot machines, pinball machines, etc. banned from the township", and to request the Federal Government to take steps to appoint a harbourmaster and to have S. C. Craigie fill the position. Work shortage problems plagued the war years, just as there had been a surplus of workers available during the Depression years. On June 22, 1944, the council stated that boys under sixteen could not be employed by the council except with parental consent since the township did not want to be liable for accidents.

When the war ended and more men returned to the township, the council started on a road expansion program. On February 5, 1947, by-law 654 was passed, and St. Edmunds finally became "wet", that is, able to sell liquor.

At the end of 1947, J. W. Ransbury returned to resume his reeveship. In this post-war era, two major problems were tackled. These were again road building and the problem of dogs running at large. A second war memorial was erected beside the earlier one during this year. Roads were again a major concern for the council in December, 1952, when J. W. Ransbury passed his final act as reeve — by-law 704 expropriated land around the harbour to the wireless station to make way for roads.

J. W. Ransbury would not return for the next term, perhaps his double-job in 1952 had tired him. For that year he was not only reeve of St. Edmunds but the Bruce County Warden. He was the first St. Edmunds man to hold that position. Nine nominations were made for the position but all were withdrawn when J. W. entered his name into the race.

Archie Simpson, son of W. J. Simpson — another previous three time reeve, took the reeve's chair in 1953. The main aims were financially stabilizing the township while expanding the roads. Still, in their first meeting they saw the way clear to grant Alex Holmes a license for his pool table. A second agreement was also signed with the Liquor Control Board on 1955. These liberal actions were only contrasted by firm action on road expansion supported by three Royal Bank loans. Their bank loans, however, were only "to meet, until the taxes are collected, the current expenditures of the Corporation for the year". In 1955, the council, though perhaps late, asked the Federal Government to increase efforts "to stamp out the lamprey eel and restore the trout fishing industry in these lakes."

In the winter of 1957, a councillor who had served the three previous years took the office of reeve. John Daniel Wyonch began an eight year term of office. The son of Charles Wyonch and Charlotte Hopkins, he came from old family lines in the community. During his long term, roads were further expanded but no further dog laws were passed. Two by-laws were directed at fox bounties but during those years the problem must have died down. During his term, building permits were created with by-law 745 on August 5, 1957.

J. D. Wyonch sailed into the sixties with no one opposing him. In 1961 he won again by acclamation but a new councillor was elected — the first female councillor — Gladys Morris (nee Davis) placed second behind also new councillor J. P. Johnstone, Jr.

The returns were as such:

J. P. Johnstone Jr.	157
Mrs. Gladys Morris	142
A. S. Ralph	123
John Hopkins	114
Bessie (Betty) Smith	105

Gladys was concerned about the cliff across from the liquor store. She feared that some day a car or person would go over it and down the steep drop. Two years of attempting to get council to put up guard rails there during meetings, met with no success. She decided the only way to ensure its construction was to run for council. In honour of her efforts the people called the landmark "Gladys' Monument". The rail did serve its purpose, for a hearse carrying her dead Aunt Hazel Hopkins (nee Young) was stopped from going over the cliff. In 1982, a car went over the cliff just past the rail. The driver claimed he would have been stopped by the rail except he swerved to miss the people sitting on it. Luckily there were no serious injuries.

In 1962, the council's road expansions led them to request more road crushers from the populace. Though no new dog by-laws were passed, Roy Hatt successfully asked the council for $510 in damages done to sheep by dogs. In 1962, Cecil Davis resigned as clerk, a position he had held for 27 years. In appreciation of his services, the council secretly placed a gold watch on his Christmas tree.

By 1964, the idea of a Centennial Park on 27 acres of land owned by Thomas Spears was discussed. On October 13th the council inspected the lot and decided to request approval from the Ontario Municipal Board.

On December 15th, 1964, a shock hit the council as a newcomer that had swept councillor polls defeated former reeve J. D. Wyonch. J. P. Johnstone Jr. received 144 votes to J. D. Wyonch's 117 votes. With this 27 vote majority he took office in 1965. He was one of the few newcomers to hold the reeveship, the other being Weir Grieve. J. P. Johnstone was born and educated in Walkerton and later spent four years overseas in World War II in the 19th Field Regiment. After association with the 60th air squadron he was discharged with the rank of sergeant major. He married Shirley Taylor the year before he moved to St. Edmunds in 1952. He had served as a school trustee before he moved into local politics.

His term of 1965 would only last the year and J. D. Wyonch returned for 1966-1967. In his two year term he established Centennial Park and made sure of large celebrations. When J. D. lost to Johnstone again in 1968 with a vote of 195 to 164, he would never return to the reeve's chair. Leaving with him in 1968 was clerk Clarence Spears, a man whose skills had allowed him to undertake various positions on council (such as last township assessor).

J. P. Johnstone Jr. recovered the reeve's chair in 1968 but had aims that were much higher as he also became the Warden of Bruce County. During the next eleven years as reeve he instituted many new by-laws in favour of the changing economic role of the township. Slowly Tobermory became more tourist oriented with tent-trailer laws, garbage disposal laws, lottery and bingo fees, parking laws and the harbour, sewer systems, taxi fees, by-laws accommodating riding academies and snowmobile facilities, and many by-laws dealing with recreation (such as 986, 989, 990). Although popular during elections as reeve, during his terms he angered rate payers on such subjects as the uni-lateral move to buy a $50,000 gravel pit. On June 8th, 1977, eighty St. Edmunds ratepayers held a meeting at St. Edmunds Community Centre in an attempt to meet with the Council. Although the council was meeting next door they failed to attend the meeting because it was not on their agenda. Somehow, despite these arguments which were compounded by such actions as hiring outside truckers to haul the gravel from the gravel pit, J. P. Johnstone was once again elected in 1978.

In the spring of his 1978 term, J. P. Johnstone died. After J. P. Johnstone's death on April 19, the council was thrown into disarray. The deputy reeve Harold Powley was eventually named reeve on May 3. He had been on council for four years, two which he served as deputy reeve.

The third outsider to ever gain the seat was a native of Toronto who had moved to St. Edmunds in 1966. Harold Powley is the owner and manager of the Tip of the Bruce Golf Course. Betty Smith moved into the place of deputy reeve, becoming the first woman ever to hold that position.

The election in 1978 brought a new reeve to the chair. Brad Davis gained the chair for a two year term, and was then elected again in 1981 for a three year term. Brad is a direct descendent of one of the first settlers and son of Cecil and Mabel Davis. This shows that the Davis family is still active in municipal life in the fourth generation.

Six Reeves
Back Row left to right: **Archie Simpson, Daniel Wyonch, J. P. Johnstone.**
Front Row left to right: **Cecil Davis, Weir Grieve, John W. Ransbury**

J. P. Johnstone Jr.
Reeve 1965, 1968-78
Warden of Bruce County

J. W. Ransbury, Reeve 1936-1941, 1948-1953, Warden of Bruce County in 1952.
Shown here with son Paul, wife Dorothy, and daughter Donna.

50

MUNICIPAL OFFICIALS

DECISION   MAKING   BODY

REEVE

DEPUTY REEVE

COUNCILLOR · COUNCILLOR · COUNCILLOR

STAFF

CLERK   ●   TREASURER   ●   ROAD SUPERINTENDENT

BUILDING INSPECTOR

Municipal Office 1983

REEVES
United Townships of
Albemarle, Eastnor, Lindsay and St. Edmunds
June 21st, 1872

1872-73	Thomas H. Lee
1874-77	Ludwick Spragge

United Townships of
Eastnor, Lindsay and St. Edmunds
June 8th, 1877

1878-80	David Scott
1881	William Hale
1882	Robert Watt

United Townships of
Lindsay and St. Edmunds
January 8th, 1883

1883	Peter McVicar
1884	J. Weatherhead
1885	James Shute
1886	J. Weatherhead
1887-1900	Alexander McDonald
1901-02	John Shute

Township of St. Edmunds

1903	Solomon Spears
1904-05	W. J. Simpson
1905-07	Solomon Spears
1908-09	William Gillies
1910	W. W. Ransbury
1911-13	William Gillies
1914	W. W. Ransbury
1915-21	Andrew Munn
1922-25	W. J. Simpson
1926-28	W. W. Ransbury
1929-30	W. J. Simpson
1931-36	Cecil Davis
1936-41	J. W. Ransbury
1941-1947	Weir Grieve
1948-52	J. W. Ransbury
1953-56	Archie Simpson
1957-64	J. D. Wyonch
1965	J. P. Johnstone Jr.
1966-67	J. D. Wyonch
1968-78	J. P. Johnstone Jr.
1978	Harold Powley
1979-	Bradley H. Davis

Clerks

1903-06	James Campbell
1906-07	A. H. Bryan
1907-09	Lytle Spears
1909	W. J. Simpson
1910-1934	Lytle Spears
1934-1936	Dr. Harold Spencely
1936-62	Cecil Davis
1963-1968	Clarence Spears
1968	Caroline Sear
1968-71	Alex Holmes
1972	Roy Hatt
1972	Victor Greygoose
1972-77	Glen Cameron
1977-80	Geoff Nightingale
1981-	Cathy Wyonch

Deputy Clerks

1968-71	Ella Holmes
1976-79	Dona La Fontaine

Deputy Reeves

1973-74	Angus Ralph
1975-76	Joe George
1977-78	Harold Powley
1978	Betty Smith
1979-	George Harpur

Treasurers

1903-07	John C. Hopkins
1908	Harvey Pettigrew
1909-10	John C. Hopkins
1910-11	Daniel A. Martin
1912-14	Solomon Spears
1915-26	Andrew Belrose
1927-42	Margaret Ellen Ransbury
1942-49	Margaret Golden
1950-72	Roy Hatt

Hereafter the office of treasurer was combined with that of clerk.

Treasurer — Tax Collector

1980-	Dona La Fontaine

Councillors

Henry Bradley Davis 1903-05, 1911
William James Simpson 1903, 1921
John Henry Smith 1903-04, 1906-07, 1919
William Henry Hopkins 1903-04, 1912-12
Edward Young 1904
William Matheson 1905
William Gillies 1905-07
Andrew Belrose 1905-13
W. W. Ransbury 1907-09, 1915-16
Thomas Bartman 1908
Neil H. Currie 1909
Andrew Munn 1909-13
Thomas M. Belrose 1910, 1918
Arthur H. Watson 1919, 1930-31
Samuel McCormick 1910, 1915-16
Andrew Wardrop 1911
George W. Golden 1912-16, 1919-21
H. F. Murphy 1914
George Butchart 1914
James Allen Watson 1914-17, 1921
Alfred K. Adams 1917, 1919-20
James H. Hopkins 1917-21
John McCartney 1920
John C. Hopkins 1921-23, 1925-26
W. R. Hopkins 1922
W. J. Smith 1922-26, 1933-44
John Clifford Dean 1922-23
Thomas Spears 1923-24
Thomas Andrew Hopkins 1924
Thomas Albert Golden 1924, 1930-34, 1935-36
Frederick James Smith 1925-29
John A. Martin 1925-27, 1929
J. C. Munn 1927-29
Cecil Davis 1928-30
W. J. Tetley 1928-30, 1931-33
A. R. Craigie 1931-32

J. W. Ransbury 1931-36
G. B. Hopkins 1933-35
Ira Wellington Vail 1935
Gordon Hopkins 1936-40
Albert Leslie 1937-42
George Harold Smith 1937-38
Weir Grieve 1939-41
James Watson 1941-44
Orrie Vail 1942
Lloyd Ritchie 1942-50
Stewart Peacock 1943-46, 1955-56, 1965
Scott Watson 1945-50
Arthur James Watson 1945-46
William A. Spears 1947
Howard Chisolm 1947-48
Melvin J. Martin 1948-49, 1952-53
Carl Hopkins 1949-51, 1953
Angus Ralph 1950, 1958-65, 1968-74
M. McArthur 1951
Cecil Watson 1951
Harry C. Davis 1952-54
J. H. Rouse 1952-61, 1966-67
Archie Simpson 1952
William Ivan Watson 1954-61
James Daniel Wyonch 1954-56
Gladys Morris 1957-64
Lorne Lyons 1957-61
J. P. Johnstone 1962-64
John James Hopkins 1962
Lynn Watson 1963-64, 1966-73, 1979-
Borden Hopkins 1965 67
Murray Ransbury 1966-72
Thomas J. Adams 1968-72, 1976
Joe George 1973-76
Larry Bell 1973-76
Nelson Watson 1974-76
Harold Powley 1975-78
Betty Smith 1975-78, 1981-82
Pete Dean 1977-78
Lloyd Adams 1978-80
Dr. George Harpur 1979-
Ron Peacock 1979-80
Winston Hollis 1981-
Tom Hopkins 1982

Assessors

1903	Harry Pettigrew
1904	Daniel Smith
1905	Daniel A. Martin
1906	Daniel Smith
1907	Daniel A. Martin
1908	Harry Pettigrew
1909	Daniel A. Martin
1910	Harry Pettigrew
1911	R. A. Hopkins
1912	Harry Pettigrew
1913	W. W. Ransbury
1914	William Henry Smith
1915	Arthur Henry Watson
1916	W. J. Simpson
1917-19	Arthur Henry Watson
1920-24	John A. Martin
1925	Howard A. Belrose
1926-27	William Davis
1928-30	Thomas Andrew Hopkins
1931	James Allen Watson
1932-35	Thomas Andrew Hopkins
1936	Arthur Henry Watson
1937	W. J. Simpson
1938-41	Archibald Simpson
1942	Thomas Andrew Hopkins
1943-51	Archibald Simpson
1952-56	Lloyd Adams
1957-64	Clarence Spears

Hereafter the duties of the assessor were no longer done in the township.

Auditors

Daniel A. Martin 1903-08
William John Smith 1903, 1905, 1908-11, 1913-15, 1917-18, 1930
William Gillies 1904
C. Miers 1904
Lytle Spears 1905
Neil Currie 1907
Harry Pettigrew 1909-10, 1912
James Allen Watson 1911
W. W. Ransbury 1912-13
Thomas Albert Golden 1914-16, 1920-23, 1926-29, 1937-42
W. J. Simpson 1916, 1918-20
R. F. Mercer 1917
Arthur Strappe 1919
John Ward 1921
Thomas Spears 1922
William Alexander Young 1923-35
Hugh C. Wilson 1924-25
A. A. Leslie 1931-36
Carlton Young 1936-38
Oscar Smith 1939-46
Roy Hatt 1943-46

Hereafter the auditing is done by professional accountants beginning with James Van Overbeck, Owen Sound, Ontario, in 1947.

Fence Viewers

Robert Hopkins 1903-04
Samuel McCormick 1903-04, 1918-20
Andrew Belrose 1903-04
George Bartman 1905-07, 1921
Archibald Currie 1905-08, 1910-11
George Butchart 1905-07, 1916-19
Arthur Henry Watson 1908, 1911, 1921
James Hopkins 1908
Fred Belrose 1909
George W. Golden 1909
Thomas Bartman 1909
James Allen Watson 1910-11, 1922-31
James Henry Hopkins 1910-15
Robert Allen Hopkins 1914, 1935-50
Thomas M. Belrose 1914-17
W. H. Hopkins 1914
Edwin Belrose 1915
Edward James Hopkins 1916-20
Thomas Spears 1920
William Leonard 1921
T. H. E. Munn 1922-34
Percy Adams 1922-34
William Davis 1932-34
Alfred King Adams 1935-39
John Masterson 1935-47, 1948
Clarence Spears 1940-54, 1956-68
Star Munn 1947
Earl Lambkin 1949-74
Scott Watson 1951-54
Archie Watson 1955-76
J. P. Johnstone Jr. 1969-75
J. C. Munn 1975-
Dave Wyonch 1976-
Sheldon Belrose 1977-

Pound Keepers

Thomas Bartman 1903-08
Hanson Lindburg 1903-04
Thomas Bruin 1903
Harry Pettigrew 1904-08
Arthur Watson 1905
Robert Hildrick 1905
Phillip Forbes 1906
Michael Belrose 1906-08
Archie Currie 1909
Arthur Henry Watson 1909
James Hopkins 1909
Fred Belrose 1910-13, 1915
George W. Golden 1910-13
George Bartman 1910-16, 1920-21
William Lynch 1911, 1914
Henry Bradley Davis 1913, 1915, 1917-18, 1920-23
Andrew Munn 1914
Harry Murphy 1914
Neil Matheson 1915-15
James Henry Hopkins 1916
James Bartley 1916-18, 1920
Robert Allen Hopkins 1917-18, 1920
George Butchart 1918-19
Andrew Belrose 1918, 1920
Sam McCormick 1919
Edward J. Hopkins 1919
Howard Leslie 1919
W. E. Shaw 1921
Marmaduke W. Vail 1922-23
Percy Adams 1931-33
James Allen Watson 1931-33
John Whitmore Hopkins 1934-40
William Davis 1934-40
Star Munn 1941-53
Charles Wyonch 1941-63
Archie Watson 1950
Aaron Dean 1952-71
Dave Wyonch 1964-

Pathfinders — Road Superintendants — Road Foreman
Pathfinders — Road Overseers

Harry Pettigrew 1903-04, 1906, 1911-?
George H. Smith 1903-04, 1906
Archie Currie 1903, 1909-10
George Bartman 1903-04
William Matheson 1903
Archibald McDonald 1903-05
John G. Hopkins 1905
Thomas Adams 1903-04
Thomas McBride 1903-04
Andrew Wardrop 1903-06, 1908-10
Edwin Belrose 1904-07, 1911
Marshall Locker 1904-05
James Henry Hopkins 1904, 1912
W. W. Ransbury 1905, 1908-09
John Henry Smith 1905, 1911
James Campbell 1905-06
Phillip Adams 1905
Lytle Spears 1905-06, 1911
William Lynch 1905-06
James Hopkins 1906-07
Arthur Henry Watson 1906-07, 1911
Richard Badstone 1907
Julius Koch 1907
William Matheson 1907
John C. Hopkins 1907
George Graham 1907
Hector Currie 1908
Sam McCormick 1908
George Bartman 1908-10
William Henry Hopkins 1908-10
George Butchart 1908, 1911

Robert Allen Hopkins 1908-10, 1912
Edward Hopkins 1909
James Allen Watson 1909-10
Peter Fochie 1910
Henry Bradley Davis 1910

Hereafter they are called Road Overseers — 1911

James Lynch 1911
Thomas Belrose 1912
Thomas Robbins 1912

During this period, men were directly given road orders by the council who gained provincial aid at this time. Some Road Overseers mentioned are

Thomas Belrose 1914
George Butchart 1914

Road Commissioners

R. A. Hopkins 1920
Percy Adams 1920
William Leonard 1920

Road Superintendants

John C. Hopkins 1924-28
Fred Myles 1929-?
William Weir 1947-49
William Weir 1949-71
J. C. Munn 1971-72
Carl Adams 1972-73
J. C. Munn 1973-74
Merrit Munn 1974-76
Wesly Rydall 1976-77
R. G. Nightingale 1977-78
Rex Liverance 1978

Road Foreman

A. H. Watson 1929
J. C. Munn 1928-70
Merrit Munn 1973

The jobs of road supervising often were either done by both superintendant and foreman or done separately without one or the other being appointed. Today we have no road foreman.

Tax Collectors

1903-04	Harry Pettigrew
1905	Robert Allen Hopkins
1906	Lytle Spears
1907-08	Marmaduke Vail
1909	Solomon Spears
1910	Robert Allen Hopkins
1911-12	James Allen Watson
1913-14	Robert Allen Hopkins
1915	William Gillies
1916	Arthur Henry Watson
1917	Robert Allen Hopkins
1918	James Allen Watson
1919	Lytle Spears
1920	John A. Martin
1921-23	Cecil Davis
1924	James Allen Watson
1925-26	Cecil Davis
1927-33	William Davis
1934-35	Alfred K. Adams
1936-38	Garfield Hopkins
1939-40	Thomas J. Spears
1941	Cecil Davis

1942	Scott Watson
1943-49	Clarence Spears
1950-60	Roy Hatt
1961-68	Clarence Spears
1968-71	Alex Holmes

Hereafter the job of tax collector merged with that of the treasurer.

Sheep Valuators

1916	James Henry Hopkins
1917-28	Thomas Belrose
1929-36	Charles Pedwell
1929-71	Percy Adams
1937-43	William Shaw
1944-52	A. E. Pedwell
1953-56	Clifford Woods
1957-65	Cyril Eagles
1966-71	Dave Wyonch

Livestock Valuator

1975-77	Glen Cameron
1978	J. P. Johnstone
1978	Harold Powley
1979-	Dave Wyonch

Weed Inspectors

1936	James Allen Watson
1937-40	William Davis
1941-42	Robert Allen Hopkins
1943-44	Scott Watson
1945-64	Borden Hopkins
1965-74	J. C. Munn

Hereafter the County Weed Inspector was used.

Deputy Returning Officers

A. H. Bryan 1902
James Campbell 1903-04
Thomas McBride 1903-04
Michael Belrose 1905
Robert Hilditch 1905-06
W. J. Simpson 1906
Robert Allen Hopkins 1906-09, 1911-12, 1920
William Lynch 1907-12
William Leslie 1907
Daniel Smith 1908
John C. Hopkins 1909
John H. Smith 1910, 1913-17, 1920
James Allen Watson 1910, 1918
Nathaniel Ransbury 1911
William H. Smith 1912
Thomas Belrose 1913-17, 1919, 1921
Lindsay Myles 1913
Matthew Green 1914
William Parker 1915, 1917-21
Charles Pedwell 1916, 1936
George Hamilton Smith 1918, 1921, 1948
Fred J. Smith 1919
Howard Belrose 1922-23
Lytle Spears 1922-23
Alexander Young Jr. 1922-26
Thomas Andrew Hopkins 1923, 1925, 1927, 1932, 1942, 1949
J. C. Munn 1924
Martin Hopkins 1924, 1928, 1938, 1940, 1944-45, 1947, 1951- 59
William Davis 1925
William Cosgrove 1926-28
Percy Adams 1929-30, 1933-34, 1936-38, 1945
Martin Young 1929-30, 1937
J. A. Martin 1931-32
James Allen Hopkins 1931

Arthur Henry Watson 1933
Harry Pettigrew 1934
T. H. E. Munn 1935
Isaac Hopkins 1935
Borden Hopkins 1939-40
Howard Leslie 1939
Clarence Spears 1942, 1947-48, 1951-62
Scott Watson 1943-44
Mrs. Sam Craigie 1943
Orlon Dean 1946
W. A. Spears 1946
Clifford Woods 1949-50, 1956
John Currie 1950
Llody Smith 1955-60
Carl S. Hopkins 1961
Clifford Allen Hopkins 1962
Mrs. Margaret McArthur 1963-64, 1966-68
John Hopkins 1963
Lloyd Ritchie 1964
Mrs. Lena Cosgrove 1965
Mrs. E. Davey 1965
Mrs. Helen Edmonstone 1966
Mrs. Clara Reitz 1967-68, 1970
Earl Lambkin 1970

Hereafter mention of Deputy Returning Officers in the by-laws is omitted.

Reeve Salary

1903-05	$1.50 per day and mileage in St. Edmunds
	$2.00 per day and mileage in Lindsay
1906-24	$2.00 per day and no mileage
1925-44	$2.00 per meeting
1945-47	$5.00 per meeting
1948-54	$6.00 per meeting
1955-63	$250.00 per year
1964-65	$300.00 per year
1966	$400.00 per year
1967-70	$600.00 per year
1971-73	$700.00 per year
1974-75	$1000.00 per year
1976	$1500.00 per year
1977	$2000.00 per year
1978	$2100.00 per year
1979-80	$2565.00 per year
1981	$3000.00 per year
1982	$3360.00 per year
1983	$3528.00 per year

Councillor Salary

1903-05	$1.50 per day and mileage in St. Edmunds
	$2.00 per day and mileage in Lindsay
1906-24	$2.00 per day and no mileage
1925-44	$2.00 per meeting
1945-47	$3.00 per meeting
1948-58	$4.00 per meeting
1959-65	$75.00 per year
1966	$125.00 per year
1967-70	$175.00 per year
1971-73	$300.00 per year
1974-75	$500.00 per year
1976	$750.00 per year
1977	$1000.00 per year
1978	$1100.00 per year
1979-80	$1515.00 per year
1981	$1800.00 per year
1982	$2016.00 per year
1983	$2117.00 per year

Deputy Reeve Salary

1973	$500.00 per year
1974-75	$750.00 per year
1976	$1000.00 per year

1977	$1200.00 per year
1978	$1300.00 per year
1979-80	$1725.00 per year
1981	$2200.00 per year
1982	$2464.00 per year
1983	$2587.00 per year

Clerk Salary

1903-04	$45.00 per year
	$10.00 for delivering ballots to Wiarton
1905	$45.00 per year
1906-07	$50.00 per year
1908	$55.00 per year
1909	$45.00 per year
1910-16	$65.00 per year
1917-19	$80.00 per year
1920	$120.00 per year
1921	$110.00 per year
1922	$75.00 per year
1923-28	$90.00 per year
1929-33	$100.00 per year

Hereafter the clerk was also paid for road bookkeeping as well.

1934-39	$225.00 per year
1940-42	$250.00 per year
1943-46	$275.00 per year
1947-49	$325.00 per year
1950-51	$375.00 per year
1952-55	$300.00 per year
1956-57	$350.00 per year
1958-62	$400.00 per year
1963	$650.00 per year
1964	$700.00 per year
1965	$750.00 per year
1966-68	$1050.00 per year
1969	$1400.00 per year
1970	$1450.00 per year
1971	$1900.00 per year

Hereafter the clerk assumed the duties and pay of Treasurer and Tax Collector.

1972	$5000.00 per year
1973	$6400.00 per year
1974	$8500.00 per year
1975	$10500.00 per year
1976	$12500.00 per year
1977-78	$13500.00 per year

Hereafter road bookkeeping was no longer part of the clerk's duties.

| 1979 | $14000.00 per year |

Hereafter the positions of treasurer and tax collector became separate again.

1980	$14000.00 per year
1981	$11000.00 per year
1982	$14000.00 per year
1983	$14750.00 per year

Assessor Salary

1903	$25.00
1904-05	$40.00
1906	$45.00
1907	$44.00
1908	$35.00
1909	$30.00
1910-12	$40.00
1913	$60.00
1914	$45.00
1915	$60.00
1916	$45.00
1917-18	$60.00
1919	$70.00
1920-21	$75.00
1922-24	$50.00
1925	$45.00
1926	$50.00
1927-28	$55.00
1929	$75.00
1930	$100.00
1931-36	$75.00
1937-42	$100.00
1943-46	$125.00
1947-49	$175.00
1950	$200.00
1951-57	$300.00
1958-62	$350.00
1963-64	$400.00

Hereafter assessing no longer done by township.

Treasurer Salary

1903-05	$35.00
1906-20	$40.00
1921	$60.00
1922	$40.00
1923-28	$50.00
1929-30	$100.00
1931	$150.00
1932-37	$100.00
1938-49	$150.00
1950-62	$300.00
1963	$350.00
1964-65	$400.00
1966	$700.00
1967-68	$800.00
1969	$900.00
1970	1000.00
1971-	$1100.00

The treasurer's duties were adopted by the clerk from 1972-79 until the duties were split and a treasurer-tax collector position was created again.

1980	$11000.00
1981	$14000.00
1982	$15600.00
1983	$16380.00

Tax Collector Salary

pay not mentioned for 1903 — 1905

1906	$60.00
1907	$50.00
1908-12	$55.00
1913	$65.00
1914-15	$60.00
1916-17	$75.00
1918-20	$70.00
1921-22	$50.00
1923	$70.00
1924-28	$50.00
1929-30	$60.00
1931-34	$50.00
1935-37	$75.00
1938	$85.00
1939-49	$75.00
1950-51	$125.00
1952-56	$175.00
1957	$225.00
1958	$275.00
1959	$325.00
1960-63	$300.00
1964	$350.00
1965-66	$450.00
1967-68	$700.00
1969-70	$750.00
1971	$800.00

Hereafter job through clerk-treasurer and later treasurer tax collector.

Deputy Clerk Salary

1976	$3.50 per hour
1977	$3.75 per hour
1978	$4.00 per hour
1979	$4.50 per hour

Hereafter the Deputy Clerk assumed the role of treasurer-tax collector.

Auditor Salary

1903-28	$5.00
1929-42	$15.00
1943-44	$17.00
1945-46	$25.00

First professional charge 1947 $115.00

CHAPTER EIGHT

TOURISM THROUGH TIME

Originally a lumbering and commercial fishing port, Tobermory today is the centre of a thriving tourist trade and the mecca of scuba diving enthusiasts for the whole of Central Canada and the northern American states.

Many long time residents have watched Tobermory's economic base change from a small commercial fishery to the intensive tourist industry that it knows today. When the lake trout fell off drastically because of the increase in the smelt population and the appearance of the lamprey eel, the residents of Tobermory were forced to adapt to the change. Tourism began to flourish and the fishermen started taking tours by boats to the Islands around Tobermory. According to the late Lloyd Smith, the tours would include going ashore and cooking for the visitors, "Trout and potatoes, and tea as black as ink".

Many of the fishing tugs have now been converted into crafts to take divers out to the sites of the more than fifty wrecks that lie in these crystal clear waters — the federal government has recently charted most of them as part of Fathom Five, Canada's first and only underwater park. Today these wrecks invite exploration for learning and enjoyment, and are a part of Tobermory's most important industry — tourism.

MERCHANTS AND BUSINESSES

The first store in Tobermory, according to the late Captain William J. Simpson, was established in 1881 by Maitland-Rixon and Company. They bought ties, posts and cord wood, for which there was a brisk demand. A line of steamboats running from Collingwood to Chicago called at the harbour regularly for wood. There were four boats on the run, the "Northern Queen", the "Lake Erie", the "Canada" and the "Columbia". All used wood and each took forty cords of it on every call. The company's store was a large log building on the property later owned by Albert Leslie Jr. It was like a lumber camp van and besides being used as a store, served as a boarding house and as sleeping quarters. In the fall enough supplies had to be brought in by boat to last until a fresh supply could be brought in the spring. Captain Simpson recalled that sometimes food became very scarce. In March, 1882, when the supply of flour was used up, nearly every settler had a supply of Indian corn to fall back on. John Shearer, an old Scotsman, was the local miller. He had a large coffee mill and for grinding the meal took part as toll. The result was that he had meal and some to spare. One year for six weeks, Captain Simpson remembered, he and his father and sister lived on Johnny cake, cornmeal mush, and maple syrup. The last mentioned was plentiful in those days.

It is believed that Alexander Green was the first man to run the store belonging to the Maitland-Rixon Company. Mr. Green, who was connected with James Maitland and Henry Rixon, constructed a saw-mill at the head of Little Tub on lots 87 and 88, Bury Road, probably during the fall and winter of 1881/82. Green lived on Lot 3, Carlton Street, and also had a dwelling on Lot 14, Head Street, occupied in 1882 by the late William Lytle Spears. On January 1, 1884, Alexander Green was bought out by Rixon and apparently left the store and the township.

Another Tobermory resident around at this time was William John Smith. He came in 1889, when he was barely sixteen years old, to act as an agent and operator for the Great North Western Telegraph Company of Canada. At that time, Mr. Smith recalled, there were only four houses and the present United Church building on the south eastern bank of the harbour and only four or five shanties on the other side. In 1889, William Hill was running Tobermory's first store that had been earlier operated by Alex Green. Mr. Smith remembered it being the only store in the district. Besides being patronized by the few families at the harbour, the store served the settlers in what is now known as the Settlement.

Six years later, in February 1895, *The Wiarton Echo* wrote about a Mr. Spence who had a good stock-in-trade of general merchandise near the harbour in Tobermory:

"Mr. Spence is doing a rushing business here this winter. Great processions of teams laden with shanty supplies leave Tobermory every day. The great secret of his success is the cash down plan. Everyone having timber to sell can rely on getting his pay with as much certainty, as one having an account at the Bank of Montreal."

Later in the same year there seemed to be some controversy over the price of merchandise in the store owned by Mr. Spence. The Tobermory correspondent wrote,

"There is some talk of the price of store goods being too high and rumors are afloat that another store will be started. Some people do not know when they are well off. They are a good deal like the Ancient Egyptians dissatisfied with old-time slavery. No better man to the settlers ever was in business at Tobermory than Mr. Spence. He has always given a fair price for timber and farm produce and has sold his store goods at very reasonable prices. More than that he always pays promptly and to the last farthing what is coming to any man. He has relieved the needy settler times without number and instead of misrepresenting him they should at least be fair. No better thing ever happened to Tobermory than Mr. Spence setting up business and relieving the settler from the power of the men that compel all those whom they owe to travel eighty miles before they can get their money."

The merchandise of Mr. Spence does seem quite reasonable when compared to the prices of today. The following is a market price from Tobermory in 1895:

Oats per bushel . . . . 50cts to 60
Potatoes per bushel . . . . 50cts to 60
Hay per ton . . . . $15 to $17
Butter per lb . . . . 20cts to 25
Eggs per doz . . . . 20cts to 25
Pork per lb . . . . 12cts to 14

Baise Munn believes that his father, Andrew Munn, came to Tobermory in 1896 as an employee of the Maitland-Rixon Company. The following year he ran the store in Tobermory that was owned by these Owen Sound lumbermen.

On August 30, 1900, Thomas Pettigrew was in Tobermory finishing and putting in shelves and counters in what would soon be a large general store owned by the Gillies Brothers.

As early as 1901, tourists were enjoying Tobermory. Even in those early days, the Tobermory correspondent for the Wiarton Echo predicted that "this is the place for a summer resort". Growth of the small village was apparent as the Echo later states that "the village is expanding on all sides, houses are springing up among the trees". Mr. John Spears was building a new butcher and cooper shop. Shortly after its construction, the butcher shop was sold to Robert Gillies. The same business was later sold to Thomas Bruin, who boasted of "small profits and quick returns".

By 1903, Tom Bruin's son, Leonard, had opened a new store in the old Ludwig's home (now owned by Jim Rae). Leonard worked with his brother, Fred, in this business venture. Later in 1903, *The Wiarton Echo* reported that:

"Robert Gillies, one of our enterprising merchants, paid a visit to Owen Sound last week, but there appears to be no truth to the rumour that Bob went over to bring a supply of household goods back."

The report is indicative of the role that the merchant played in the small, isolated community.

There are other tales told by merchants, and this one following is said to have taken in the Gillies General Store. According to the story, Granny Adams went into the Gillies Store one day, carrying a roll of freshly made butter. Once inside, she asked Mr. Gillies if he would trade a roll of his butter for her roll. As his curiosity was aroused at this unusual request, Mr. Gillies asked her why she should want to do this. "Well", she explained, "while I was making my butter, a mouse somehow managed to fall into by bowl of cream and when it drowned, I picked it out". "Now, knowing this, I can't eat my own butter but someone else who didn't know about it, well...it wouldn't hurt them". Mr. Gillies thought the situation over and finally, with a twinkle in his eye, he agreed to trade her. He took Mrs. Adams' roll of butter into the back and marking it so that it looked different, he came out to the front and gave her back her own roll of butter.

When she returned to the store a few days later, the store owner asked her how the butter was. "Fine", she remarked, "whoever made that butter sure knew how to make butter!" Laughing, the merchant told Mrs. Adams what he had done. She just smiled and coolly said "Well there, that just goes to show, what you don't know won't hurt you!"

Another event concerning Gillie's store, took place on Hallowe'en night, 1901. The Lion's Head correspondent wrote to the Echo:

"Mr. S. C. Cooper spent the latter part of the week at Tobermory. He and Mr. Bridge spent Hallowe'en there. In the morning Mr. Bridge found his rig on top of a resident's house and Mr. Cooper, his on top of Gillies Bros. Store. Some of the boys helped get them down and let them go on their way rejoicing."

Gillies Bros. store was later sold to a family by the name of Leslie and was operated for a number of years as "Leslie's Store". By 1941, the same building was owned and operated by Bunstons and advertised "good home-cooked meals served at all hours". Mrs. Bunston was the former Vera Vail, sister of the late O. C. Vail and originally from the village.

In 1944, Mrs. Carroll Davey leased the former Leslie store. She redecorated it and carried on a restaurant business there. In 1961, the Liquor Control Board of Ontario opened a beer and liquor store on the property once owned by the Gillies family. The Board obtained a ten year lease on the property, then owned by Lloyd Adams. Mr. Adams removed what was left of the old building on his lot, and then erected a new building that was thirty-two by seventy-two feet in size for the use of the Board.

In 1904, Fred Bruin left Tobermory and went to Lions Head to help his brother in his butcher business.

Matheson Tourist Home, early 1920's.

"Evelyn". The Matheson family had moved to Tobermory in 1894, and purchased a home from Tom Bartman before buying the Matheson House. After Captain Matheson's death, Mrs. Matheson operated the boarding house for many years.

Marion McLeod and Fodie Matheson, the daughters of the Mathesons, remembers many things about working at the boarding house. She remembers that the boarding house was well-known for its fish dinners, so a twelve quart basket of lake trout was prepared each day for the evening meal. The boarding house was quite different from the motels of today as the water had to be carried to the guests' rooms, and coal oil lamps provided light. Naturally, the boarding house was the busiest in the summer, as guests would arrive on the steamers that came to Tobermory for fish and lumber.

THE MATHESON HOUSE — THE GEORGE'N

The Matheson House was built and operated as a boarding house by J. H. Smith at the turn of the century. By 1905, there was a hot time in Tobermory over the licensing of a hotel. Julius Koch, who purchased the Matheson House (now the George'n) from J. H. Smith, was seeking a license. Mr. Crittenden, the Methodist minister, was vigorously opposing it. The minister was reported as arguing that "the village has all that it can handle without a hotel". The application for the license was eventually refused by the License Commissioners due to the strong opposition against it. Meetings held in 1906 and 1907 at the Pacific Hotel in Wiarton again saw the Commissioners refuse Koch a license.

The business was then purchased by Captain Neil Matheson, who was described as "a fine type of Scotsman". Captain Matheson also commanded various fishing tugs during his life, such as the "Juno" and the

The George'n 1983.

Mrs. McLeod eventually sold the business to Mr. and Mrs. Carroll Davey who renamed it the "Davey Hotel". Mrs. Davey rented rooms and had a restaurant as well. In 1971, the Daveys sold the business to its present owners, Mr. and Mrs. Joe George, The George'n is now rented out to divers and dive clubs that are recommended to the Georges by clubs that they know well. The Georges give the divers a place to stay and three meals a day. Never in its history though, has the building ever received a license to serve liquor although it was thought to have been built for that purpose.

THE GOLDEN'S STORE — PENINSULA SUPPLY

After years of sailing on the Great Lakes, George W. Golden decided to open a store in Tobermory. The store was such a success that Golden operated it for thirty-seven years before he sold it in 1945, three years before his death.

It seems that the Golden Store was originally built by Harry Pettigrew, who had intended it to be a hotel. When Pettigrew learned that he could not get a liquor license, he decided to turn the building into a general store. Unfortunately, in 1906, the Pettigrews were forced out of business when the steamer, the "J. H. Jones" sank, carrying all of Pettigrew's winter merchandise to the bottom of Georgian Bay.

As well as establishing the store, Golden and his sons established the "Golden Fish and Transport Company" providing transportation overland between Tobermory and Wiarton.

In 1945, Mrs. Carroll Davey became the successor of G. W. Golden, and the store was appropriately renamed "Davey's Store". The store also had a number of rooms upstairs that were rented out, as well as a number of cabins that were later sold to Stewart and Grace Peacock to become part of Peacock Villa.

William Ross and his sister, Dorothy McCoy, bought the store in 1947. They renamed it "Peninsula Supply Co." and have been operating successfully for thirty-seven years.

Peninsula Supply 1983.

MARTIN'S BLACKSMITH

Around 1917, a Mr. Martin built a blacksmith shop where the Hi-Way Market now stands. Little is known about how long he operated for, but many residents remember him for his handiwork.

JIM RAE'S BARBERSHOP

Jim Rae came to Tobermory as a barber in 1922. Sixty-two years later, he is still the only barber in the village, and he is still cutting hair. His one room barber shop with its one hundred year old chair and bottles of hair cream closely resemble scenes that Norman Rockwell has painted. Mr. Rae's shop was originally located on the shore of the Little Tub at the corner across from the Cenotaph. He later had it moved alongside his house which is beside the library.

The barber shop used to be closed all day as Jim was a guide during the day, and then would cut hair until eleven o'clock at night. The days when Jim charged a dime for a shave and a quarter for a hair cut are past, but he still has the best price on the Peninsula.

THE RED ROOM RESTAURANT — G&S DIVE SHOP

This shop opened as a restaurant by Mrs. William Henry Hopkins — popularly known as Aunt Ruth.

In 1939, Grace and Stew Peacock opened the Red Room Restaurant, so named for its red and ivory interior. After seven years of hard work, the Peacocks sold their restaurant in 1946 to Mr. and Mrs. Howard (Pid) Chisholm. Thereafter, the business was known as Pid's Restaurant. The next owner was Mrs. Carroll Davey, who also ran a restaurant there. Mrs. Davey eventually sold the building to its present owners who now run the G & S Dive Shop on the premises.

Golden's General Store, late '1920's.

PEACOCK VILLA

Peacock Villa began with fifteen cabins purchased from the Goldens by Stew and Grace Peacock. Later the Peacocks added four new units which they would rent for the princely sum of $2.50 per night. Running the Villa meant long work hours that began in the early morning and ended often in the middle of the night as late guests arrived. After years of hearing people ask if the Peacock Villa was located on the water, they built the Mariner Motel in 1957 and operated both the motel and the Villa. After Stew's death, Grace sold the Mariner and in 1979 turned the Villa over to her daughter Penny.

THE MARINER MOTEL

In 1957, Bert Munn was hired to build the Mariner Motel for Grace and Stew Peacock, but both of the Peacocks could be found sawing and hammering alongside Bert. Originally five units were built, but over the years twelve more were added. In the early years of operation, Grace and Stew called it the "Mariner Motel and Botel", the word "botel" came from boat owners who would dock in the Little Tub and stay in the Peacocks' establishment.

The Mariner was sold to Roger Salen in 1967. Since then, the Salens have made a large number of changes. Now in addition to the motel, the Salen family also owns the Chart Shop, a number of tour boats, and dockside gas pumps.

Peacocks Restaurant 1939.
Bert Morris and Stew Peacock.

Peacocks Restaurant and Golden's Store 1939.

Mariner Motel 1957.

G & S Dive Shop.

Mariner Motel 1983.

THE BIG TUB LODGE

The Big Tub Lodge holds the distinction of being the only lodge located on the Big Tub. It was built in 1946 by Mr. Lyons. After operating it for a number of years, he sold it to Mr. Townsend. Mr. Townsend in turn sold it to Mr. Mannen. Mr. Mannen built the dive shop on the property which attracted even more divers to this already popular spot. Roy Blais, the present owner, bought the lodge from Mr. Mannen in 1979. Since then, Mr. Blais has made a number of changes to the property such as adding motel units, tearing down old cottages, and making a campground. Now the motel boasts sixteen units and a dining room. It is interesting to note that because of its rustic appearance, the dining room has been used as a set in several movies.

The property that the lodge is built on has a long and interesting past. It has been used for over a century by ships and boats seeking refuge from storms on the Great Lakes. The Big Tub itself lies in an east-west direction and is 1440 feet long and about 35-40 feet deep. It is ideal for docking as the water is about 35 feet deep off the steep, natural rock walls. Huge steel rings have been pounded into the rock by people tying up there in the past. Another sign of past users of this port are the names and dates of boats that have docked there. A huge coal pile once covered part of the area that is now the campground. Divers often bring up lumps of coal from the bottom of the Big Tub off the campground. One of the docks located off the Big Tub Lodge is made of British Columbia fir, and has been floating since 1920. Needless to say, there is quite a lot to attract people to the Big Tub Lodge.

In 1946, the "Norisle" docked at Big Tub, close to the Lodge, as the new dock at Little Tub was not yet completed. The Norisle used coal for fuel, hence the coal pile.

TENES STORE — WHISPERING PINES

Tene and Bill Willaughan had a small business of cottage and boat rentals in 1957 at Dorcas Bay. It was a long way to a store, so Tene started keeping a few items for retail sale. Before long, she was operating a small General Store.

They sold the cottages and moved to Highway 6, close to the entrance to Cyprus Lake Park, around 1970. In 1978, the Whispering Pines Store was sold to the present owners, the McKays.

DAVIS GENERAL INSURANCE

Around 1944, Cecil (Ted) Davis started an insurance business. Cecil operated the insurance business for many years until his son Brad took over in 1960. It was operated for a couple of years out of Tobermory and Lions Head, then Brad moved the business to Lions Head where he and Doug McLay formed the partnership "Davis & McLay" in 1969.

The insurance business was sold to an employee, Eric McLay, in 1975 and is still operated in Ferndale under the "Davis & McLay" name.

LITTLE TUB BOUTIQUE

The Little Tub Boutique was started by Ethel Haythorne in 1979 as a gift shop located next door to Circle Arts. The next year the shop moved to a house at the corner of Highway 6 and the road to the Ferry Dock and a ladies' sports wear section was added. The shop then moved to its present location at the Ferry View Motel in 1983.

HILLTOP FOOD MARKET

The Hilltop Food Market was opened in June of 1973 and is located just south of the village next door to Ransbury's Hardware. It is owned and operated by Karen and Lynn Watson. The Hilltop Food Market also has a small one-bay garage and gas pumps which have been leased out since 1984.

RANSBURYS HARDWARE

Murray & Kay Ransbury started a small hardware store in the basement of their home on Highway 6 just south of Tobermory in November, 1965. They joined the Pro Hardware organization in 1966. In 1973, they built the present store adjacent to their home, and added on an addition in 1978 which is used as a warehouse and work area.

BELROSE INN AND GENERAL STORE

In 1920, Andrew Belrose opened a general store and inn on the Little Tub in Tobermory. Under Mr. Belrose's management, these businesses grew to be ranked among the best in the area.

Andrew Belrose was the son of Jacob Belrose who came to St. Edmunds in 1875. In 1898, Andrew married Mamie Spears and took up farming. In 1912, he was appointed postmaster, a position he held for over thirty-five years.

In 1930, Andrew modified his building by raising the roof and installing a dining room. This renovation increased the number of rooms that he had available and the dining room was an added attraction for the inn. Later Andrew installed a service elevator in the building, the first elevator built on the Peninsula. Another innovation that Andrew introduced to Tobermory was a wind-driven generator that supplied enough electricity for the Inn, the store, and the village library. Rather than the technological changes, many older residents remember the homemade ice cream that was available at the Belrose Store for five cents per cone.

After serving the public for over thirty years, the Belrose Store was closed in 1951 after the death of Russel Belrose, Andrew's son. Miss Hilda Belrose then took over the operation of the Belrose Inn until her death in 1981. The Belrose Inn is now privately owned, and the General Store building now has three businesses in it.

Building that would eventually become Belrose Inn 1920's.

Belrose Inn 1940's.

In front of Belrose Store, late 1930's or early 1940's.
Left to Right: **Andrew Belrose, Russel Belrose, Tom Belrose (owner of snowmobile), Britain Belrose and Dell Smith.**

Belrose Inn and Store 1930's.

Belrose Store 1940's.

Today, 1983, the Belrose Inn is privately owned and the store building has three businesses in it.

RITCHIE'S RESTAURANT — DIVERS DEN

Prior to owning a restaurant of their own, Laura and Lloyd Ritchie worked in a restaurant owned by W. W. Ransbury, Laura's father. In 1940, the restaurant was destroyed by a fire that started in the home of "Butcher Bill Smith" and then swept on to consume his adjoining butcher shop and Ransbury's restaurant before it could be controlled. After the fire, Mr. Ransbury offered to give the land that the restaurant had stood on to Lloyd and Laura if they would build a new restaurant on the same spot. The Ritchies took him up on his offer, and soon "Ritchie's Restaurant" was standing in the centre of town.

While Laura operated the restaurant, Lloyd operated a cabin cruiser, the "Neewash II". The boat slept eight people, and tourists and fishermen would hire it for cruises that lasted up to a week long.

In 1945, Jim Austin bought "Ritchie's Restaurant" and remodelled the premises into a grocery store. Shortly afterwards, Chess and Eunice Wheildon bought the business and continued to operate the grocery store. The property changed hands again in 1947, when Don McIver bought it and opened a new restaurant. The next owner was Tom Adams who opened a bake shop. After him, Albert Smith opened the "Smith Family Bakery" there. The building then passed into the hands of the owners of the "Divers Den", the business that presently occupies the premises.

GOLDEN'S SERVICE STATION
LIGHTHOUSE GARAGE AND TAKE-OUT

Charlie Golden built and Bert Morris operated the garage until 1956, when Lloyd Ritchie managed to sell the "Neewash II" one night at midnight, and bought the garage the next morning. Lloyd greased cars and repaired tires until 1972, when he sold the business to Hughie McConnel. McConnel sold the business to Jim and Bess Kritikos in 1976, who presently own the business.

Divers Dens 1983, formerly Ritchie's Restaurant.

GIBBONS BUTCHER SHOP

Gordon Gibbons opened a butcher shop when he first arrived in Tobermory in 1935. His shop was located in the building adjoining W. J. Smith's home. In 1938, Clayton (Cap) Young took over the business which was destroyed in the same fire that burned W. W. Ransbury's restaurant in 1940.

GIBBONS BAKERY —
PEACOCK'S GROCERY STORE

In 1940, Gordon and Elizabeth Gibbons had opened a bakery. This business eventually closed and the building was torn down by Ivor McLeod in 1960. Ivor had bought the grocery business that belonged to Bud Hopkins, and moved it into the centre of the village after he built a new building. In 1961, McLeod sold his business to J. C. Wiseman of Owen Sound. The store was then bought by William Haythorne, who eventually sold it to its present owner, Ron Peacock. Ron Peacock expanded the business by building a new laundromat alongside the store.

THE VILLAGE INN — BEE HAVEN

By 1947, Gordon and Lizzie Gibbon had opened the "Village Inn", after reconstructing a house previously owned by Jim Austin. The Gibbons ran the business for five years before selling it to the Brenners. Chess and Eunice Wheildon took over the inn and renamed it "Wheildon's Guest Home". Mr. & Mrs. Neil Brodhegen purchased the inn from the Wheildons and renamed it the "Bee Haven". The Bee Haven is presently owned by the Sandersons who do not operate it as a business at the present time.

In 1961, Gordon and Lizzie opened a restaurant on the highway south of the Hi-Way Market. They called it the "Highway Village Inn", taking the name from the former Village Inn. The Gibbons ran a successful restaurant for many years, and upon retirement, they sold the building to Fred Symes, its present owner. The building is still standing.

Lighthouse Gas Station and Take-Out 1983.

RESTAURANTS OPENING IN THE LATE 1940's

There were a number of small restaurants that opened in the late 1940's. In 1946, J. J. Tony Davis opened the "Propellow Restaurant". It was situated on the upper floor of what had been Cecil Davis' net shed. J. A. Craigie opened the Craigie Restaurant by the docks of the Little Tub, and Stew Peacock and Mrs. Charles Golden were also running food services.

Mrs. Golden sold her business, the "Hill-Top Restaurant", to Mr. and Mrs. Zarnke, Don Fry and Pearl Hopkins in 1946. In 1947, Mr. and Mrs. Cecil Davis opened the "White Spot" restaurant. This restaurant had previously been the Leslie's net shed before it was converted. The Davis's then sold the restaurant to Mr. and Mrs. Fred Green and Bruce Young. The building was eventually taken down.

HOLIDAY HAIR STYLE

This business was started in the summers of 1957, 1958 and 1959 by Tilly Vaughan in the home of Mr. and Mrs. Whit. Hopkins.

In 1960, she opened at her present location, the "Leslie" house, next door to the Blue Bay Motel.

She is open year round and now has fifth generation families as her customers.

THE FERRY-VIEW MOTEL

Scarcely a summer passes without the sounds of construction coming from this prosperous motel beside the ferry dock. The motel was built by W. Ransbury and John in 1952. They owned it until 1968, when Don and Joyce Weir bought it from them. In 1976, the Weirs sold it to its present owners, Missinaibi Holdings Ltd., managed by Albert and Gloria Smith.

When the motel first opened, it had eight units. Today, the motel has twenty-eight. Before the motel was built, the property was part of the Ransbury Brothers fishing establishment. Their docks, ice house, packing plant, net shed, and drying reels all stood on the shore of the Little Tub. A little further inland stood three small houses.

ERB'S MILL AND LAUNDRY

Mr. and Mrs. Ed Erb constructed a sawmill in 1945 on the site where Tom Spears had had a mill. It was destroyed by a tornado on May 2nd, 1956. The mill was never rebuilt.

Mr. Erb lost his right hand in an accident at the mill. In 1952 his wife started a laundry business which she closed in 1977 after her husband's death. Mr. Erb continued to work as a builder and do electrical work after the loss of his hand as well as help with the laundry business.

GUIDE BOAT BUSINESS

In the 1920's, 1930's, and early 1940's, there was a number of men involved in commercial trolling. These early men were:

Warren Adams	Andy Hopkins
Whit Hopkins	Herb Hopkins
Edwin Butchard	Alex (Candy) Young
Harley (Buck) Young	Ivor MacLeod
Del Smith	Fred Smith

Day Guides in the late 1930's, 1940's, and 1950's were:

Lloyd Smith	Sam Craigie
Lawrence (Oat) MacLeod	Alf Carver
Russel Belrose	Art Martin (Sr.)
Cecil (Ted) Davis	

Guide boats which took parties to the north shore of Georgian Bay for a period of 2 days to 2 weeks from 1939 to 1965 were as follows:

James Rae	Barney Hopkins
Carl Hopkins	Bill Ransbury
John Ransbury	Archie Simpson
John Desjardine	Lloyd Ritchie
George (Cy) Simpson	Stew Peacock

The fishing and commercial guide business was very prominent in the early days, but gradually came to a total stop by 1965.

The Ferryview Motel, late 1950's.

The "Neewash" 1950's.

BAYVIEW RESTAURANT — TOBERMORY GARAGE RESTAURANT

After returning home from the Second World War, Dan Wyonch built himself a large garage to work out of. Dan, in 1946, was the one licensed mechanic in town. The garage was located on Highway 6 as you enter the village of Tobermory.

In 1964, Dan and Eva Wyonch bought a house on the ferry dock where the Norisle docked, right next to the coal pile. This house belonged to Doris (Dodie) Lee, and had at one time been her father's (Jeff Weir) net shed. The Wyonches did some remodelling and opened the Bayview Restaurant running it until the land was expropriated in 1974 to make room for the new ferry dock and terminal.

At this time, Eva decided she needed a larger restaurant and Dan lost his garage. Work was started remodelling what once had been Dan's garage. Eva and Dan opened the Garage Restaurant on July 9th, 1974, operated it for 2 years, and sold to their daughter and son-in-law, Goldie and Clayton Meilhausen, the present owners and operators.

HIDDEN VALLEY LODGE

The 1800 acres of property was purchased in 1952 by J. P. Johnstone from the Pedwell Family. It was originally purchased as a beef cattle farm and lumber operation; however, it quickly became a tourist business as well. It became known by photographers, naturalists and artists such as Robert Bateman. At first, guests stayed in the main Lodge, but as business grew, motel units were built in 1963 and 1967.

Many interesting guests have stayed at Hidden Valley through the years, including Lord and Lady Hunt, and the Duke of Edinburgh Gold Award Winners from 14 Commonwealth countries in 1967.

The business is still operated by the family of the late J. P. Johnstone.

GINGHAM GATE BOUTIQUE

This small boutique of 20' by 10' is located next to the Circle Arts in the home of Mrs. Edith Hilliard. Mrs. Hilliard started this business in 1975. She sells only hand made crafts which are made by herself, her two daughters, and friends of the family.

Doris Lee's home formerly Jeff Wiers net shed.

Bayview Restaurant.

Tobermory Garage late 1940's.

Garage Restaurant 1980's.

TOBERMORY DAIRY

Gordon Hopkins had started a small milk delivery service which he sold to Cecil (Ted) Davis in 1933. Cecil purchased the farm across from the Munn farm and increased the size of the dairy and delivery service. The milk was delivered by a horse-drawn wagon in the summer and a sleigh in the winter.

In 1942, Cecil sold the dairy to Roy Hatt. Mr. Hatt put in a pasteurization plant and continued to improve the dairy. In 1964, Mr. Hatt sold the dairy to Bill Willaughan. Mr. Willaughan operated it for a very short time, then he sold the dairy to Wiarton Dairy.

CRAFTSMAN JEWELLERS

Our first visit to Tobermory in 1967 was for a diving holiday. We continued until 1969, when as a family we worked on Subluminos, "Canada's first underwater habitant".

In the spring of 1972 we first opened Craftsman Jewellers in the building which is adjacent to Circle Arts.

A move was made in 1979 across from the Divers Den. Then in 1980, we moved to our present location next to Peninsula Supply. Craftsman Jewellers is owned and operated by Betty and Keith Evans.

CRAIGIE'S RESTAURANT AND COTTAGES

Albert and Samuel Craigie started a gas service business at the head of the harbour for both cars and boats. Sam sold out to "Abbie", and he built a restaurant with a small dance floor. This became the 'in' place for the young people in the late forties and early fifties.

Abbie added cottages at the back of his home on Highway 6 and they were later moved to a waterfront location next to the Tobermory Lodge. This business is now a restaurant and cottages and been there for 52 years. Today it is run by Abbie's daughter, Shirley.

Abbie Craigies Restaurant.

LANDS' END PARK

Lands' End Park is located at Hay Bay on the water, with a sandy beach and good fishing. It is owned by three brothers: John, Norman, and Robert Stevens, and their wives.

The campground was started in 1973 and opened in August, 1975. They now have 126 campsites, some fully serviced, others partially serviced, along with boats, canoes, and paddle boats.

UNCLE CLAUDES CAMPING AND TRAILER PARK

Claude and Cecilia Russ purchased 50 acres of land 2 miles south of Tobermory, close to Hi-Way Market, in 1981.

In the spring of 1982, work began remodelling existing buildings and landscaping the grounds. They excavated two small lakes and the camp also has access to the Tobermory Bog which is visited by many naturalists.

They now have 100 campsites and the Tobermory Family Festival is an annual event held at the campground.

VAIL, BUNSTON, MARTINS AND LAVOIE CABINS

In the late thirties, forties, and early fifties, there were a number of overnight cabins belonging to the above families, along the shore and road where the ferry now docks.

Mrs. Bunston served meals in her home, and Mrs. O. C. Vail served fish dinners only to the yacht people and a few cottagers.

These cabins are all gone except for a few at Bettie Smiths (daughter of the Art Martin family), and a couple at La Voies.

WATSON'S LUMBERING AND BUILDING SUPPLY LTD.

Owned and operated by Ivan (Pop) Watson. Pop left Tobermory as a young man and returned in 1944 and started a building business.

In the early days, he built a saw mill, did logging for his mill, and built cottages, motels, homes, etc. Along with his construction business, he had a hardware and building supply store.

Pop built his own pleasure craft and retired in 1976 to enjoy it.

There is an antique shop in the old hardware store on Highway 6, owned and operated by his wife, Willow. His son Lynn is still building and son Doug has a haulage business in sand and gravel. Pop passed away in 1980.

RALPH BROS.

It was in January 1946, that two young men in their early thirties decided to leave the Niagara area and start a business at Tobermory. They were Ernie Ralph with his wife Eileen and children David and Linda, and Angus Ralph with his wife Jean and daughter Judy. A partnership was formed known as Ralph Bros. and they purchased property at Warner Bay on the Lake Huron shore from Bert and Charlie Golden. Their plans were to build rental cottages on the sand beach, but first a road had to be built from Bobs' harbour to the Bay. The work was hard and the days were long. Six cottages were built the first year and although they were without electricity and indoor plumbing, the tourists enjoyed the good fishing and clean air. The following year, several more cottages were built. Much of the lumber used in the construction of the cottages was from their bush and processed at their sawmill.

The demand for more and better accommodation became apparent and soon another 1500 acres were acquired from the Golden family and the shoreline around Warner Bay. Eagle Harbour on to Dorcas Bay was developed in registered sub-divisions. The men sold lots and built summer and some winterized homes for the next 17 years when the partnership ended.

RUBY'S TAKE-OUT —
FERRY DOCK TAKE OUT —
FERRY DOCK RESTAURANT

Ruby Ransbury opened a take-out food service in the front sections of Ransbury's Fish House in 1971. Ruby sold this business to Tom McAfee in 1974, who then added a boat with tours to Flowerpot Island.

After Mr. McAfee's death in 1979, Brad Davis bought the business, which also included a new glass-bottom boat, the "Seaview III". In 1984, Brad rebuilt the business with a cafeteria style restaurant which has seating for 135, an indoor-outdoor bar, and a gift shop. The business is now known as the Ferry Dock Restaurant.

PATHWAY CRAFTS

In 1981, Loyais Golden opened a craft shop at her summer home. This house had belonged to her in-laws, Elsie and Charlie Golden, and is located close to the docking area at Little Tub Harbour.

She now has 32 people doing crafts for her, many of them local. She encourages local people to put their crafts in her shop.

CEDAR VISTA MOTEL

The Cedar Vista is located a short distance south of Tobermory on Highway 6. At the present, the motel consists of eight units and is owned by Lynn Buck. The motel was built in 1956 by Art Dalmer, who operated it for a number of years. Other owners and operators in the past included Kathleen and Winston Hollis, and the Davis-McLay partnership. The house attached to the motel is actually a log cabin from the days that Tobermory was just being settled. The sign outside the motel is the same one that Art Dalmer put up when he first opened the motel.

CEDAR GROVE COTTAGES

The Cedar Grove Cottages were built in 1960 at Cameron Lake by Tom Taylor. He had 4 rental cottages and a residence. In 1973, Bev and Betty Butler purchased the property and they improved on the residence and the grounds.

In 1979, the Butlers sold the property to Gary Goodyear. The Butlers later built Cameron Lake Store. Mr. Goodyear, the present owner, added to the residence, built another cottage, and up-graded the property.

Cedar Grove is on the northwest shore of Cameron Lake and is the only commercial business on this beautiful inland lake.

NEPTUNE PARK

Mr. and Mrs. Ray Jenkins bought a piece of land in 1952 from Howard Bowman at Bob's Harbour. They erected a dwelling and 5 rental cottages and called it Jenkins' Cottages & Boat Rental. In 1970, Vern and Grace Leonard purchased the business and renamed it "Leonards' Camp Ground". Vern insulated and redid the 5 cottages, and then he sold it to Robert Woolner in 1974.

Mr. Woolner sold Neptune Park to Richard and Pauline Sowa in 1977, when they added an addition to the residence and opened a small store. The Sowas are the present owners and operators.

BUD'S MEAT MARKET — VERNAS DRY GOODS

Bud's Meat Market, which now houses the Fathom Five Park office, was built in the late thirties, but was not opened until the spring of 1946 when Bud returned from serving in the Second World War.

After the Belrose Store closed, it became impossible to handle the business in the small store, so he moved to Belrose Store in the spring of 1952. There, Bud operated a General Store and his wife Verna started Vernas Dry Goods in one end of the store.

Bud sold the General Store business to Ivor MacLeod and Verna had Bert Munn build her a new store in 1959, at its present location, across the harbour from the old store.

Verna, with the help of her daughter Susan in the summer, still operates Vernas Dry Goods.

THE TRAIL'S END LODGE

The Trail's End Lodge is another historic building in Tobermory. Once this building housed the Wireless Station, an important link in the Great Lakes communication network. The name of the lodge comes from the fact that it is located at the end of a road.

The appearance of this historic building has not changed much over the years. It was originally built to house the families of the two Wireless operators, and so it consisted of two identical houses and the Wireless Office under one roof. The Wireless Station was sold to W. W. Ransbury, after it was no longer in use.

In 1945, Hillis and Geo Froats read a for sale ad in the Toronto paper, placed by Mr. Ransbury. They drove to Tobermory from their home in Ottawa and liked what they saw, so they bought the Station from Mr. Ransbury.

In May, 1946, the Froats moved to Tobermory and were soon taking in guests. There were ten bedrooms, but they never refused any one, as many people had to spend the night in cars while waiting their turn on the ferry to Manitoulin Island.

The Froats were held up for a year in receiving hydro, but they added an addition on the east end of the Wireless building, put in 2 wood cook stoves, and started serving meals in the station building.

The Froats family owned and operated the Trail's End Lodge for 28 years, but had to sell because of poor health.

Today the interior has been renovated so it contains nine rooms that are rented out to divers by the present owner, Arthur Amos.

Trail's End Lodge, late 1940's.

HARMONY ACRES

The riding stables were built in 1974 by Earl Craig and a snack bar added the following year with the help of Marina Wyonch to be known as the C & M Ranch. In 1979, it was sold to Laurie Adams and Simon Iemants, thus changing the name. The snack bar was in operation with open air musical coffee houses until 1981.

There is now a cozy 15 site campground nestled under maple hardwoods; a stable housing approximately 20 horses and ponies; and a whole menagerie of both domestic and exotic animals running around the place.

There are a variety of horse trips offered catering to all styles of riders (and non-riders). One can ride into the more remote areas of St. Edmunds to the rocky shores of Georgian Bay, through cedar swamps, under beautiful hardwoods, and past the "majestic" weathered tree stumps left standing triumphantly from the fires of the late 1800's, just as our forefathers had once done!

THE HI-WAY MARKET

Originally built in 1948 by Percy Watson, the Hi-Way Market was constructed of cord wood walls. In one small building were living quarters, an office, a grocery store with a fresh meatstand, and a garage with a BA gas station. There was a nice lawn and apple orchard on the north side.

In 1959, Cleve and Jean Adams and their family bought the store. Local farmers would bring in cream and eggs to trade for other staples. Expansion began in the mid 60's: the BA Gas Co. became Gulf Oil, the living quarters became a small laundromat and office, the store expanded out into the garage and a new garage was built next to the orchard.

As tourism increased, the Market expanded again, adding on a storage area. Then in the 70's, the laundromat became a Variety store; a new laundromat was built along with a larger Service Station. Long storage buildings were built around the back as the Market began producing its own ice, became an outlet for Canada Lafarge Cement, and a Brewers Warehouse Bottle Returns.

Now in the 80's, the orchard is gone and the cord wood walls covered, but a modern Supermarket complex still offers Grade A fresh meats and groceries in the same friendly atmosphere that began back in 1948.

THE TIP OF THE BRUCE GOLF COURSE

The Tip Of The Bruce Golf Course stands on the land that was once owned by St. Edmunds' earliest farmer, Abraham Davis. In 1962, Edward Born purchased the one hundred acre farm from the Davis family. Born built a 250-yard driving range and a nine hole golf course on the property before he sold the property to its present owners, Mr. and Mrs. Harold Powley. The Powleys have since installed an outdoor roller rink and a mini-golf course.

Tip-O-the-Bruce Golf Course on land formerly owned by Abraham Davis and his son Henry.

For a THRILL PACKED HOLIDAY
or a Quiet, Restful, Family Vacation

COME TO

TOBERMORY

**Tobermory Beckons You To The Very Tip Of The Bruce Peninsula—
Nearly Surrounded By The Beautiful Waters Of Georgian Bay And Lake Huron**

COME AND ENJOY

FISHING
LAKE TROUT
SMALL MOUTHED
BLACK BASS
GREAT NORTHERN
PIKE
And Pan Fish
CABIN CRUISERS
with Experienced Guides

BOTANICAL
and
Geological
Wonders
Rare Plants
and Birds
Flower Pots
on Islands
etc.

ACCOMMODATION
CABINS
CAMPS
COTTAGES
GUEST HOMES
INNS
MOTELS

Business Services
S.S. Norisle — Ferry Service
to Manitoulin Island
MODERN STORES
To Supply All Your Requirements
Pasteurized Milk - Fresh
Fruits and Vegetables
Fishing Fleets Return to Our
Harbor Daily
REAL ESTATE FOR SALE
Fine Building Lots on Sandy Beach

WRITE SECRETARY, TOBERMORY TOURIST ASSOCIATION
For Descriptive Folder and List of Guides, Camps and Business Places With Rates.

Example of the type of advertising promotion put forth by Tobermory Tourist Association in 1953.

Tobermory 1948.

72

Mariner Motel advertisement 1960's.

Hill-Top Restaurant 1942.

Village Inn 1961.

THE RANSBURY LODGE —
ROCKCLIFFE LODGE — CROW'S NEST

W. W. Ransbury was the first owner of the Ransbury Lodge. As well as owning the lodge on the Little Tub, he owned the Shell station and a restaurant nearby the lodge, and cabins that were located at the Gap, close to where the Anglican Church now stands. Besides these businesses, he also owned the "John and Alex", a fishing boat.

Alex Holmes bought the lodge and the Shell station from Mr. Ransbury in 1946. Mr. Holmes renamed the lodge the "Rockcliffe Lodge".

The lodge then took on the air of a men's club, and women rarely ventured through its doors. On winter's evenings, local men would meet to play pool and gossip. The local correspondent for the Wiarton Echo could often be observed in the lodge picking up any interesting story that he could find. Most of the local women did not condemn the hall's existence, but one used to refer to it as a "den of iniquity". In 1959, the lodge was destroyed by a fire that was caused by faulty wiring.

Today the Crow's Nest stands in front of where the lodge once stood. The Crow's Nest caters to the tourists with a gift shop and coffee shop.

Ransbury Lodge, mid-1940's.

Crowsnest 1983.

CIRCLE ARTS

The Circle Arts was opened by Allan Smutylo in 1969. In 1970, Allan Smutylo and his wife moved to Tobermory and took up full time residence. From 1970-1980, Smutylo produced a series of oil paintings, water colours, and prints of a number of St. Edmunds' residents and landscapes. Each of these works portrayed the spirit and character of the people and the harsh beauty of the land and water around St. Edmunds. In his work, Smutylo produced a pictoral record and therefore contributed to the history of St. Edmunds Township.

In 1980, Ben Goedhart bought the Circle Arts from Smutylo. Thirty different artists have work for sale at the Circle Arts as the Circle Arts lives up to the objective that it began with fifteen years ago. That objective is to increase the awareness of Canadian art to the public.

THE HAPPY HEARTS PARK

Happy Hearts is located on the Cape Hurd road. Peter and Sue Paquette purchased 25 acres of land from T. A. and Amelia Golden, and started construction of a mobile home park in 1972. The mobile home site was opened in 1973 with 15 sites.

In 1974 and 1975, more work was completed and presently the park has 15 sites for mobile homes and 65 sites for tents and trailers. The park also boasts a modern recreation hall and an inground swimming pool. Happy Hearts was sold to Wilson and Gayle Campbell in 1983.

In 1980, a unique entertainment was built at the Happy Hearts Park. This was Ontario's third water slide. Many campers and summer residents find the water slide an exciting ride as they speed down a 216-foot flume consisting of tunnels, dips, bends, and finally end up in a pool at the bottom of the flume.

Gillie's Store — Leslie Store — Bunston's Store — Liquor Store and Blue Bay Motel, 1900 - 1983.

Gillies Store.

Blue Bay Motel 1983.

Liquor Store 1983.

THE BLUE BAY MOTEL

The Blue Bay is the most recently built motel in Tobermory. It was built in 1971 by its present owners, Lloyd and Vi Adams. The motel stands on the hill overlooking the bustling Little Tub, in the same place the Leslie General Store once stood many years ago. The motel has fifteen units, and its owners are justifiably proud of the view of the harbour.

HARRIET'S LUNCH —
FERRY DOCK RESTAURANT

Harriet's Lunch was built in 1949 by Mr. and Mrs. Fred Grieves. Behind Harriet's Lunch stood the house in which Harriet had formerly operated the Little Tub Lodge. In the same house, Harriet's mother, Mrs. Isaac Hopkins, had operated a home bakery. In 1962, the Grieves sold Harriet's Lunch and Gift Shop to Mel and Della Cramm. In 1964, the Cramms sold out to Tom McAffee. Mr. McAffee operated the business until 1974, when the government bought the property and tore down the buildings to make room for the new ferry dock.

Mrs. Isaac Hopkins at door of her Home Bakery 1930's.

Little Tub Lodge 1940's.

Harriet's Lunch showing roof of Little Tub Lodge behind, 1950's.

THE HIGHWAY MOTEL

In 1953, Mr. and Mrs. A. J. Watson began to haul logs out of the bush and started construction on a four unit motel on the highway, south of the village. The Highway Motel was opened in 1954. Following a successful summer, the Watsons increased the size of the motel by adding on four more units. In 1957, following the loss of their home and office in a fire, A. J. built a new house and added on two more motel units and a new office. All of the units were finished in knotty pine which Mr. Watson hauled, sawed, and planed himself.

In 1963, the motel was sold to Doug Turner and Ruby Williamson. During the thirteen years that they owned it, more units were added onto it.

In 1976, Mr. and Mrs. DuBois purchased the business. At the present time, the motel has thirty-seven rooms, a licensed dining room, and a lovely, now heated pool.

Highway Motel 1960's.

Coach House Inn 1983.

77

Site of Tobermory Lodge, late 1940's.

Motel units, Tobermory Lodge 1983.

THE TOBERMORY LODGE

Dorothy and Cecil Arscott and Ralph Dan came to Tobermory in 1949, looking to buy land on which to build a motel. After scouting around the area, they chose the property where the Tobermory Lodge now stands. Mrs. Arscott remembers the long hours that she and her husband put into clearing the land. Mrs. Arscott had a hand in the building of the motel as well. By 1950, the cottages and motel units were ready, so the Arscotts opened the Tobermory Lodge and Motel Resort.

During the time that the Arscotts operated the lodge, they received one of the few Duncan Hines Gold Star Awards for their food and accommodations. By 1955, their business was doing so well that the Arscotts built two new motel units and a new kitchen.

In 1971, the Arscotts sold the Tobermory Lodge to Brad Davis and Doug McLay. Under the new ownership, the lodge underwent extensive reconstruction and today the lodge offers thirty-nine motel units, nine chalet units, and five cottages. A heated swimming pool, tennis courts, and a licensed dining room make the lodge a popular spot. The Lodge is now owned by Brad and Virginia Davis.

Chalets, Tobermory Lodge 1983.

Reception desk of original lodge, early 1950's.

Pool area Tobermory Lodge 1983.

THE GRANDVIEW MOTEL

In 1954, Mr. and Mrs. A. Hudson began to build the Grand View Motel on what had formerly been the Leather property. When the motel opened, there were eight units. By 1955, the Hudsons had begun the construction of four more units. The new motel proved to be popular, and the Hudsons received an award for the second best landscaped motel in Ontario.

In 1967, the Grandview was sold to its present owners, Mr. and Mrs. Jack Sanderson. Over the years, the Sandersons have added a few more units and have remodelled the dining room which does indeed have a grand view.

Grandview Motel 1983.

BANKING FACILITIES

In 1972, for the first time in the history of St. Edmunds Township, banking facilities were available for the convenience of the residents and tourists.

The opening of a branch of the Royal Bank in Tobermory was the result of planning between the Township Council and Len Tokey, the manager of the Royal Bank in Lions Head. At first the bank operated two mornings a week in the Township Council's Office. Reeve J. P. Johnstone expressed pleasure in securing such a service for Tobermory.

About ten years later, Tobermory received more permanent service when Royal Place was built by Lloyd Adams. Royal Place houses the Royal Bank and the new office of the O.P.P. The bank held its Grand Opening as part of the Big Canoe Day Festivities.

FATHOM FIVE PROVINCIAL PARK

The great influx of divers into the waters around St. Edmunds prompted the Provincial Government to establish Canada's first underwater park. The Fathom Five Park manages the waters within a five mile radius of Tobermory. The attraction of this park lies in the fact that there are approximately twenty-six shipwrecks lying on the bottom of the lake within its boundaries. Underwater geological features are another of its attractions, but the park was established to protect the wrecks from vandalism and theft.

Attached to the underwater park is the Fathom Five Information Centre. This building on the Little Tub has knowledgeable personnel on hand to answer questions and a number of exhibits set up dealing with the wrecks as well as the flora and fauna found in St. Edmunds. Under Stan McClellan, the Fathom Five Park has flourished. A registry has been set up in the park office so that the numbers of divers in the park can be monitored. This facility is used for safety and statistical purposes. For the safety of both the divers and the wrecks, the park waters are patrolled by the Ministry of Natural Resources and the O.P.P.

The popularity of the Fathom Five Park is evident any day during the summer both in the number of divers out diving and in the number of visitors in the Fathom Five Park office.

THE BRUCE TRAIL

The Bruce Trail has attracted many people to the area over the years. This four hundred and thirty mile long footpath has terminal points in Tobermory and Queenston Heights. As the trail runs along the Niagara Escarpment, there are many opportunities for hikers to view spectacular scenery and many different species of flora and fauna.

More than two hundred and fifty people have hiked the trail in its entirety and countless others have wandered along sections of it. Many people, however, remark on the beauty of the section that runs through St. Edmunds. The following is a brief history of the cairn.

THE BRUCE TRAIL CAIRN

The Bruce Trail Cairn marks the beginning of the 430 mile Bruce Trail from Tobermory to Niagara. Unveiled on June 10, 1967 by Rene Brunelle, who cut the ribbon to open the Bruce Trail. The cairn was designed by Ruth Arnsberger of Wiarton and built by Ivan Lemeke of Barrow Bay. The arrow in the symbol at the top was donated by Ebel Quarries of Wiarton.

Cairn marking the north end of the Bruce Trail.

On August 8, 1967, there was a ceremony to mark the beginning of the Duke of Edinburgh Gold Award Winners' hike from Tobermory to Owen Sound. There were 27 participants from 14 Commonwealth Countries taking part. Lord Hunt unveiled the plaque on the Cairn listing the names and countries of the participants. Lord Hunt of Lanvair Waterdine, Scotland, was the Director of the Duke of Edinburgh's Award in the United Kingdom from its beginning in 1956 until he retired on December 31, 1966. He also directed the successful British Expedition of Mount Everest in 1953. This was Sir Edmund Hilary's famous climb of Mount Everest.

Lord and Lady Hunt hiked for the first 3 days with the group leaving at Cabots Head. Also taking part in the hike were 3 local people, J. C. Munn, Tom Adams, and J. P. Johnstone. Baise and Tom hiked with the group for the first 2 days through the Peninsula section. J. P. Johnstone was the area co-ordinator of the hike and hiked with the group for the entire trip. He was also a Director of the Bruce Trail Association.

TOURIST ASSOCIATIONS

By the 1920's, Tobermory had quite a collection of businesses ranging from eating places to guide boats to tourist accommodations and yacht facilities. The foundation for tourism in St. Edmunds had indeed been laid.

In 1931, *The Wiarton Echo* described the progress that had been made in Tobermory:

"Today the Little Tub is Tobermory with its docks, piers, fish huts, warehouses, gas tanks, wharfs, its modern general stores, and its up-to-date dwelling houses it does one good to go back in memory to the early days and count up the things that were pledged to our generation by the courage, fidelity, vigour, and vision of the early settlers".

Fifty years later, Tobermory again has a new look that would astound the author of this newspaper article.

In 1930, ferry service linking the Peninsula and Manitoulin Island gave a boost. Although the first ferry, the "Kagawong", could only carry eight cars, tourists did endure the poor roads and the sometimes long waits to make use of the facility. By this time, people realized that the flow of tourists into the area depended on the roads leading into the area. In 1937, the "Bruce Tourist Association" had been formed, and they called upon the provincial government to assume the upkeep of the Allenford-Tobermory road. Also during that year, MLA John Sinclair predicted a great future for tourism on the Peninsula calling it a "mecca for tourists". He also supported the request for a paved road leading to Tobermory.

By the mid-1940's, tourists were coming to Tobermory in large numbers by land and by water. By the mid-1950's, the Tobermory Tourist Association had been formed and had made an order for 10,000 folders to advertise the attractions and businesses in Tobermory.

In 1956, the Bruce Tourist Association was able to show that the tourist industry in that county was worth ten million dollars annually. The Association also pointed out that the money made from the tourist industry in the summer months was the money that people of the area spent during the winter months. This point showed that the effect of tourism on the local economy lasted for the entire year, and was not just seasonal. Also, they indicated that the taxes from summer residents benefited the people who lived in the area for the entire year a great deal.

In 1977, the Tobermory Chamber of Commerce became a recognized member of the Ontario Chamber of Commerce. Since then, the Chamber has worked hard to obtain the best for the tourist industry as well as the community.

THE HANDICRAFT PROGRAM

In the early 1950's, the revenue from lumbering and commercial fishing had fallen off a great extent, so like so many other small communities, Tobermory was looking for alternative ways to provide employment and income for its inhabitants. To aid in the economic development, it was decided that a handicraft program would begin in the village.

It was decided that the finished goods could be sold at a store located at the ferry dock. Between the ferry passengers, the yachters and the tourists who visited Tobermory, a market for the goods was available without having to go to outside markets. The small store was built by Ivan Watson.

The instructors came from the Ontario Department of Education and offered courses in weaving, metal-working, and leather-working. Many people, adults and children, were interested in joining these classes.

The program lasted for only a while as it did not produce the financial goals that had been hoped for. The small store was taken down and now stands on the highway being used for an unrelated purpose. However, the program was not a failure since the skills were learned and practiced by the villagers. Sometimes, items made by skills learned in these classes are found at craft and bake sales held in the village today.

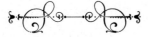

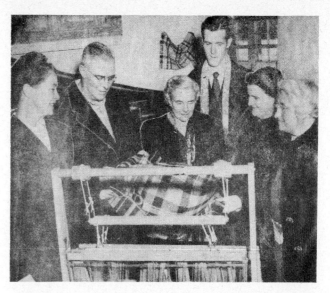

Tobermory, long a popular tourist centre, is preparing to enter that big industry in another way...that of making handicraft products to sell to the tourist trade. In 1951 the department of crafts of the Ontario Department of Education sent a staff to give instruction. On the left is Mrs. D. E. Arscott, in charge of the project, while looking over a product of such work, *left to right:* C. Davis, Clerk of the Township, Mrs. J. W. Ransbury, Mrs. Gordon Gibbons, while behind is Principal H. Hessel of the Tobermory School and Mrs. John Noble, teacher at the Settlement School.

Recovered from the wreck of the schooner Charles P. Minch, wrecked at Tecumseh Cove, Cove Island, October 27, 1898. The schooner was built in Vermilion, Ohio in 1867. The rig was a 3 masted schooner, with a length of 1547 feet.

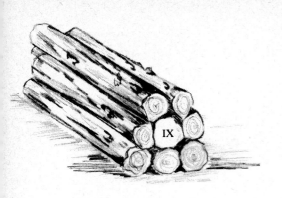

CHAPTER NINE

LAW ENFORCEMENT *and* RESCUE AGENCIES

THE TOBERMORY POLICE

Policemen were non-existent in St. Edmunds in the late 1800's and a great deal of money had to be spent if justice was to be wrought. Criminals' punishments were often handled by the settlers, a dubious form of justice. In 1895, the Tobermory correspondent of *The Wiarton Echo* wrote the following article:

"We agree with the Hanover Post in regard to the appointment of a Police Magistrate at Wiarton with the power to deal with the roughs and toughs of the Peninsula. The present arrangement is too costly and too cumbersome both to the parties aggrieved, and to the county. Many a poor man is compelled to submit to tyranny, injustice, and lawlessness on account of the enormous amount of money required to obtain justice. It is astonishing to see how some notorious scoundrels are permitted to harass and annoy peaceful and law-abiding citizens, and enjoy complete immunity from the penalties of the law. It is the boast of these rascals that they can do as they please and defy the law. We are glad that the Hanover Post has called attention to this matter. We hope that the Government will see that this state of affairs does not continue".

In 1907, A. B. Bryan was appointed Police Magistrate for St. Edmunds and other nearby townships. The Orange Hall in Tobermory was designated to be used as the Police Court when it was in session. The council passed a motion ordering the payment of fifty cents each time the building was used as a court.

In 1917, Marmaduke Vail was appointed the first Municipal Constable. His job was to enforce the Temperance Act. Constable Vail remained at this post for many years, and by 1920 he was earning ten dollars a year for his services.

As time went on, Constable Vail's duties multiplied. To assist him at his job, Mr. Spears built him two dummies or mannequins in 1926. One of these dummies was stationed at the corner near Golden's store, and the other was erected near Leslie's store. These dummies served two purposes: they reminded automobile drivers to keep to the right of the dummies as they went around the corners, and they reminded drivers to slow down in the village. To ensure the safety of school children, "go slow ahead" signs were erected on either side of the school building.

In 1928, A. H. (Dell) Smith took over as constable. In 1928, he received ten dollars as payment, and by 1935, he was receiving twenty-five dollars a year.

Occasionally, a police constable was called up from Lions Head or Wiarton to assist in certain areas. These included cases of theft, traffic accidents, and the illegal cutting of timber along township roads.

In the 1940's, Constable Smith's duties increased. He now collected dog taxes, patrolled dances to keep order, and performed the office of truant officer and sanitary inspector for the Township. His wage was now fifty dollars a year.

In 1942, Constable Smith died. It was difficult to get a policeman for the village as so many men had gone to fight in the war. Starling Munn offered his services for two years, but could not offer them for full time as he had a farm to attend to. Bert Morris was the next Constable. During his term, the duties of Community Hall Caretaker and Public Toilet Custodian were added to the job description. For these duties, he received a salary of five hundred dollars a year. The next constable was Gordon Gibbons. The duties of caretaker for the Community Hall and public toilets was removed from the Constable's duties, and he was paid two hundred dollars a year, but he received a new uniform and two pairs of trousers free of charge from the Council.

The last constable was Lyle Smith. After numerous requests that the Ontario Provincial Police take over the St. Edmunds area, the Lions Head Detachment of the O.P.P. finally took over in 1968.

In 1973, a three man detachment of the O.P.P. was stationed in Tobermory from May until October. A police station was built on Highway 6 by Lloyd Adams. These three men were Gary Woodroffe, John McIntosh, and John Phillips. For the rest of the winter, the Lions Head Detachment kept an eye on the Township.

By 1981, the police staff consisted of one corporal, six constables and a clerk. Also added to the O.P.P. facilities was the "H. H. Graham", a thirty-three foot cruiser. The boat is used to patrol the water for violators of the Criminal Code or the Canadian Shipping Act, assist boats in distress, and search for accident victims.

St. Edmunds Township has come a long way from no law enforcement to the eight member police staff that is present today during the summer months. In the winter months, after all the tourists have fled south, the generally quiet village is watched over by the Lions Head O.P.P.

THE TOBERMORY FIREFIGHTERS

Fire has always been a menace to Tobermory residents and continues to be to this day. There is, however, a great difference now in the equipment, the know-how and the number of men available.

Houses were always in danger in the past as most were made of wood. The open flames, used widely for cooking and lighting, also presented a hazard. The only means of preventing extensive damage to a whole area was through the use of a bucket brigade. Men would make a line between the nearest water supply and the place on fire, and run buckets of water to the front of the line to be splashed on the building. This was a slow method of fire fighting and it was of little help in saving the burning building, but it did serve the purpose of preventing the fire from spreading to other buildings.

Fish sheds and lumber mills were not immune to the effects of fire. In 1939, Oscar Smith's net shed burned down, but the building beside it was saved because of the bucket brigade. This brigade was again helpful when Mrs. W. J. Spears' house caught on fire. The local men had been attending a funeral and, just as it was ending, the news came that Mrs. Spears' home was on fire. The men hurriedly left the funeral, all in their best suits, to help put out the fire.

As Geoff Nightingale wrote:

"One of the most significant municipal developments (in the 1940's) was the creation of a fire department for St. Edmunds, the result of a petition by rate-payers. At the meeting of February 5, 1940, Council decreed that in response to a petition by 56 tax-payers, a suitable motor and pump with 1000 feet of hose be procured for reducing the fire hazard in the municipality, that a responsible committee be appointed to assure its operation and that a by-law be drafted fixing 75% of the cost on S. S. #2, and the balance on the remainder of the municipality".

To this end a Johnstone Thremble fire engine and 1000 feet of hose was bought in 1940. The first fire department was set up that year and consisted of Chief: Howard (Pid) Chisholm and his brigade of men; W. O. Smith, Charles Golden Sr., W. W. Ransbury, John Currie, and Thomas Knight (who had led the petition for the brigade). This was the village brigade and another brigade made up of Scott Watson, Gordon Hopkins, and E. J. Hopkins was to fight fire in the Settlement area.

The following article from *The Wiarton Echo* tells of a near catastrophic fire in 1940 which called for help from the whole community:

"The village of Tobermory received a rude awakening at 5 o'clock Saturday morning, when fire broke out at the home of Mr. Bill Smith and swept through the adjoining butcher shop and residence of W. W. Ransbury before it could be checked. Only the prompt response and hard work of almost the entire population prevented a major catastrophe, as the home of Mrs. Alex Young Jr., and Ransbury's lodge and gas station were all within 25 feet of the burning buildings".

The fire engine came in use for various other purposes so that in 1942, council passed a by-law requiring anyone who used the engine and hose for purposes other than fire, to pay the fire chief for drying the hose, and expenses for gasoline and oil. Apparently the pump could throw out the water in a strong stream "like nobody's business" and was kept handy near the harbour from which it got its water. When used in the Settlement area, a good well was needed nearby. A small building to store the fire equipment in was constructed in 1942 between two sheds on the timber crib-work portion of the Public Wharf.

Alex Holmes became the chief of the brigade in 1950. he was paid $100 to $150 per year to fight fires but as Geoff Nightingale wrote, "(his) pipe was considered by many to be the Township's biggest fire hazard". Mr. Holmes had a volunteer brigade of five or six men who had no protective clothing and had to carry four or five gallon water packs on their backs. Besides the water packs, there was a hand pump and a hose on a reel with which to fight fire.

One incident that Mr. Holmes remembers occured when the firefighters' outboard engine failed to start. The water could not get to the fire and consequently the house burned to the ground. Cottagers from Cameron Lake saw what had happened and said that it was a shame that the department did not have decent fire equipment. One of them knew of a good deal on a truck in a Ford plant in Detroit. Council agreed that a fire truck was needed so in May of 1954, Reeve Dan Wyonch and Alex Holmes went to Detroit to get it. In their excitement over the new truck, they drove it all the way home from Detroit forgetting that licence plates were needed to drive it legally. The fire truck got to Tobermory safely and it was only then that the two men realized that they could have been stopped and charged.

After acquiring the new truck, council passed a by-law stating that no equipment was to be loaned from the fire truck. A fire hall was badly needed to house the truck so canvassers were appointed to raise money for this purpose. The fire hall was started in June of 1954 and was completed early in 1955.

It was fortunate that this new equipment had been procured when it was, as a forest fire broke out in June of 1955. Fifteen local men turned out to fight the fire, some working for as long as 13 hours and receiving renumeration at 70 cents per hour. Apparently outside help was also needed as, in the minutes, the council later voted to thank the Department of Lands and Forests for their assistance in the recent fire. Also in the minutes, Alex Holmes was authorized to engage men as replacements at any time during a fire.

In 1958, J. D. Wyonch was appointed fire chief and, during his term, a bad ground fire started half a mile behind Roy Hatt's dairy farm. Outside assistance was again called in and the fire was fought all night, finally subsiding in the early morning.

Lorance McFarlane took over as fire chief in 1961 and during his first year the fire department tried to prepare local residents for emergencies by showing them films on artificial respiration and teaching them first aid.

The early sixties saw many fires which created a lot of damage. Causes of fires were attributed to: carelessly tossed cigarette butts, lightning, faulty wiring, lighting matches near a gas tank, sparks from an acetylene torch, an overheated stove, and spontaneous combustion. Damage was done to homes, cottages, a car, a bulldozer, storage sheds, barns, and about one and a half acres of land on Bear's Rump Island. In September of 1968, there must have been quite a fire as 28 men were paid for firefighting as recorded in the minutes.

In 1965, the fire truck received repairs and an engine replacement. Later that month, Lorance McFarlane turned in his fire chief badge and the council decided to hold a special meeting to discuss this new problem. It was decided that the firemen should receive more pay and that the fire chief was to have more responsibility and more training. During this meeting, Mr. McFarlane was reinstated as fire chief and from then on was responsible to the Township for all equipment and men. Mr. McFarlane resigned from his position in 1968 and William Haythorne became the new fire chief. At that time, Mr. Haythorne received a salary of $200 a year and the firemen were given $4 for each fire practice that they attended.

In mid-1974, the fire hazard in the area was extreme. Wet weather had not been experienced for quite some time and the ground fuel was at the driest level it had reached in the past four or five years. St. Edmunds was fortunate that during this time, only three small forest fires needed extinguishing. Started by unattended campfires and a "controlled" brush burning, the fires were sighted by aircraft and put out immediately so that only 10 square feet of land was burned each time.

By 1977, the need was felt for new fire equipment and a new fire truck. To this end, the Tobermory Firefighters put on a fire fighting display and dance to raise money. Additional money was raised through candle sales, raffles, the sale of fire extinguishers and smoke detectors, and through public donations and memberships. By February, 1978, a cheque for $1054.50 was presented to the council to purchase new gear for the department. Ten complete outfits of hats, coats, gloves, and boots were bought with this money and the Rotary Club later donated a valuable breathing apparatus called a MSA Air Mask

The department in 1978 consisted of fire chief Joe Dean, deputy chief Don Johnstone, two captains and 14 firefighters. With only one fire truck and several firefighters working out-of-town and not always able to come in emergencies, firefighting was no easy task. To back the firemen, an Association of 28 individuals and organizations had been formed early in 1977 and was instrumental in making the Township's firefighting capability more effective over the next few years.

In December of 1978, the fire department received a new $50,000 fire truck. This Ford C-904-840 pumper was purchased from C. E. Hickey and Sons Limited of Hamilton. The Ontario Municipal Improvement Corporation loaned the money to the council to be paid back over a ten year period at an interest rate of 11%. The old fire truck, a home-made effort built on an old mail truck chassis, was converted into a water tank truck. A 60 foot high tower was installed beside the Township Office to connect St. Edmunds with the Bruce County Mutual Aid Fire Radio System which would relay help to any area during a major fire.

In 1981, a public meeting was held to review the reorganization of the department, to discuss future plans, and to appoint officers. It was decided that a lot of fire equipment needed replacing, so various fund raising projects were planned by the Association and the firefighters' wives. Dances were held and a gas barbecue and fishing rod were raffled off. By June, the council approved the purchase of a five ton truck, a 1200 gallon water tank to be fitted on the truck, and a pump for the tanker. The old tanker truck and a rack and hoist were resold to help pay for the new equipment. By September of 1981, a new 50 by 60 foot steel fire hall had been constructed on Nicholas Street at a cost of $50,538.

Today the volunteer fire department has the men and the equipment to fight fires effectively. Practices are held frequently and many men have received their licenses enabling them to drive the fire truck and the Township's newest vehicle — an ambulance.

THE COASTGUARD

In 1978, a Coastguard post was established at Tobermory. The Coastguard operates from this post from May until November when most boating occurs. The eight men at this post are divided into two crews consisting of a coxswain and three crew men. While one crew at a time is on a fourteen day duty tour, the men reside in a mobile home. The men are on duty from 8 a.m. until 4 p.m. and then are on standby in case of emergency.

The Coastguard has defined their duties into three levels. Their primary duty is search and rescue procedures. In complicated cases of search and rescue, the Coastguard works closely with the Rescue Coordination Centre in Trenton who coordinate all men and equipment used in such operations for all of Ontario. Their secondary level of duties consists of promoting boating safety to the public. The third level of duties is the maintenance of navigation aids such as lights and buoys. All of these duties as well as the usual equipment maintenance serve to keep the crew on duty very busy.

The Coastguard vessel by Tobermory is the "Coastguard Cutter #108" which was built in 1973. This boat is self-righting a property that makes it invaluable for use in storms and high seas. The "108" is equipped with various types of radios, radar, radio direction finder, and emergency medical equipment as well as a life boat, survival suits and life jackets.

All of the "108"'s equipment comes in handy as the Coastguard handles fifty to sixty calls each year. Most of these calls are not from people in life threatening situations, but about two life or death situations occur each season. Such calls usually come from boats in distress or scuba divers.

Considering the number of people involved in water related activities, it is fortunate that Tobermory has a Coastguard post or the number of casualities from accidents might be much higher.

Township of St. Edmunds Fire Department

Official Opening of the new fire hall— June, 1982.

CHAPTER TEN

TOBERMORY MEDICAL HISTORY

Back before professional doctors or trained nurses were frequent visitors of the Tobermory community, the village truly had to "take care of its own". Martha Watson recounted the story of Little Jimmy (James) Hopkins who broke his leg while working out on the ice. Fortunately someone came by and happened to notice him and took him home before he froze to death. As Mrs. Watson explained, in those days, "people worked alone in dangerous places".

Accidents occurred wherever men worked, often during lumbering, fishing or hunting activities. One fatal accident occurred to Burt Roe when he was out felling trees. A limb struck him on the head and knocked him to the ground, but he managed to get back up and continue working until quitting time. He became very sick when he returned to camp and died at ten o'clock that night.

Children at play or sport had the odd accident as was the case of Eddie Lynch who shot himself through the eye. The 11 year old boy had been shooting sparrows with a .22 rifle near his home at McVicars, when it ceased to fire. In examining it, the gun went off sending a shell into the lad's left eye. He was found unconscious sometime later and was taken to the Owen Sound hospital where an attempt to save the sight of his other eye was made.

People of all ages had to be wary of the harsh winter weather. Maggie Currie was one to learn the sting of

winter as she incurred frozen feet while out skating, and had to be confined to the house for several days.

Back in the late 1800's, the nearest doctors lived and practiced in Wiarton. Because of the lack of good transportation and the harsh winters, a doctor was seldom available when emergency called. This also meant that women giving birth were attended by only a midwife. Most children were born at home with the assistance of Mrs. Edith Masterson, Mrs. James H. Hopkins, Mrs. Phillip Adams or another, usually older, married woman. Mrs. Elspeth Martin was the midwife attending the birth of Henry Dean, Roxie Belrose, Wilbert Hopkins and several other children in 1907. For the assistance of these women, many mothers were very thankful as there was little in the way of prenatal care or education. Sometimes the midwife had the aid of other people as in the case of the delivery of Percy Adams' first child. Percy himself worked alongside his mother to help deliver his child and he recalls that it was quite an experience.

Louis, Martha Watson's oldest child, was born in a woodsman's log shanty on one cold winter night. The rest of her 16 children were born safely in a little frame house with only a neighbour to help. Other families were not so lucky but the women in attendance did their best. Mrs. Mabel Davis remembers when her sister, Mattie Young, was born prematurely. She was wrapped in a blanket, put in a long matchbox and kept warm on an oven door. Often the midwives would continue daily care of the mother and baby until the mother was able to take over herself.

Tobermory had its own particular health problems because of its isolation from other communities and its rather small population. Some such problem was the occasional incidence of diabetes mellitus, a result of inter-marriage. Another was alcoholism which often grew worse during the winter when the air was cold and the roads blocked, leaving families and individuals seriously isolated. Apart from these particular problems, the village suffered from many of the same diseases and illnesses that other places had to contend with.

Many diseases that are almost non-existent or of much less severity today were things to be greatly feared in the early 1900's. With little in the way of vaccinations, antibiotics, or other medicines, some of these diseases resulted in permanent disability or death.

Diptheria was serious in the early 1900's and was responsible for the deaths of Henry Dean and Cleveland Adams among others. In 1905, George Armstrong, a citizen of Lion's Head, provided medicine during the diptheria out-break and was paid $11.50 for it by the council.

Pneumonia was a great danger in the early years and a few adults as well as children died of it. Percy Adams remembers getting rheumatic fever when he was nine years old. He recalls a Mr. Cameron telling his mother that she would be taking Percy to Dunks Bay (the cemetery) in the spring. To disprove this prophesy, Percy survived and is still living today at the age of 89, out-living Mr. Cameron by a long shot.

In 1907, a smallpox outbreak occurred in Tober-mory. Julius Koch was appointed Sanitary Inspector for the duration of the outbreak. It must have been quite a serious problem as the council soon appointed John Brinkman to help him. Dr. Thompson provided the vac-cine for $26 and three months later the scare was over. Typhoid fever struck the Craigie home in 1909 and killed five of that family.

A measle epidemic threatened in 1914 when it broke out in the Leonards' home. Fortunately, the Leonards were wise enough to stay at home, thereby preventing a serious epidemic. Four years later the flu was going around and Percy Adams and his wife got it. Percy stayed in bed and had hot cloths put under his bedclothes so that he "just sweated it out".

Heart failure of some form or another seemed to be the most prevalent cause of death according to the available death certificates. Stillborn babies were fairly common also. Anemia claimed several people and the odd drowning or hunting accident occurred. One young boy was run over by a wagon but survived this ordeal when nursed by R. J. Martin. Another boy who was hit by a car 22 years later was not so lucky. When helping to build an addition on the Harbour Church in 1921, James H. Hopkins backed into a saw and was killed instantly.

Advertisements for patent medicines in the *"The Wiarton Echo"* during the early 1900's claimed to be able to cure everything from bronchitis to worms. There probably was not a large readership of the newspaper in Tobermory back then, but even among those who did see the ads, home remedies were likely far more popular and attainable.

In fact, home remedies were credited for many recoveries. Grace Peacock recalls that when she was very young, she was accidentally scalded. To reduce the pain, a salve containing cattails and lard was put on her skin. Coal oil was used for many ailments including the croup. Children suffering from this hoarse cough were given a spoonful of brown sugar with a bit of coal oil. Percy Adams recalls that poultices of coal oil were used to cure one of the Currie girls when she was sick. When the Butchart family contracted tuberculosis, one of the girls was saved by putting her on porter (alcohol). Unfor-tunately, she was the only member of the family to sur-vive. The house was boarded up for a long time after her family died, as it had been under quarantine when the family was sick.

By the turn of the century, doctors were starting to make calls in Tobermory. Dr. R. M. Fisher and Dr. Sloan, both good physicians and surgeons, were prac-ticing at Wiarton and would make the occasional visit to Tobermory or come up when an emergency arose. Unfortunately, travel was very slow and often times it was more practical to bring the sick to the doctor. Patrick Folkes' story of Mrs. Watson shows this to be true although the point about her driving the car could well be questioned as it is said that she did not know how to drive. The story runs as such:

"On one occasion, some fifty years ago, the young son of Mrs. Arthur Watson gashed his leg while using an axe. With no men of the family at home, she placed the boy in a wagon and started down the Peninsula in search of a doc-tor. At that time the Bury Road was a narrow, graveled lane which followed the route of the present highway as far as Crane River, then twisted east to the hamlet of McVicar, wandered south through the woods back of Shouldice Lake on to the present Dyer Bay road and south from there at Brinkmans Corners. Mrs. Watson lashed the team over the muddy ruts and rocky crests until she wore them out near Miller Lake. Ob-taining a car from a nearby farm, she pushed on towards Lion's Head, arriving there late in the afternoon. Unfortunately, the local doctor was a man much given to the drink, and, finding him "in his cups", Mrs. Watson immediately set out again, this time for Wiarton. She reached there late at night and had great difficulty in rousing the doctor. By now the boy was in great distress and the doctor, feeling that he did not have the means to treat him, urged her to continue to the hospital in Owen Sound. At this point Mrs. Watson was penniless, out of gasoline, and only after much haggling did she prevail upon the doctor to take them to Owen Sound. With her son safely in the hospital, Mrs. Watson back-tracked to the Peninsula, returned the car to its owner at Miller Lake, and continued on to Tober-mory with the wagon and team. The entire journey lasted three days and during that time Mrs. Watson took not a moment's sleep nor moment's rest''

Dr. Sloan, one of the first doctors to serve Tober-mory, was a relatively young man when he started his practice in 1898. He was one of the first doctors in the area to diagnose and operate on people with appendicitis. It was fortunate that he had this skill as appendicitis was a common ailment then, and previously, had often led to death. Operations were performed on a kitchen table and sometimes by coal oil lamp during night time emergencies.

Doctors that followed Dr. Sloan and Dr. Fisher in serving the Tobermory community included: Dr. Thompson, Dr. Charles Wigle, Dr. Roy Hacking, and Dr. Forge.

One of the earliest by-laws of the St. Edmunds Council was to appoint a Board of Health. This by-law of March 21, 1903, appointed: Solomon Spears — ex-officio, Jas. Campbell — secretary, William Young — for a term of three years, Harry Pettigrew — for a term of one year, William J. Smith — sanitary inspector, and Dr. Sloan — medical health officer as members of the first Board of Health to enforce the Public Health Act. From 1903 on, a Board of Health was appointed each year.

In April of 1903, Solomon Spears, reeve of St. Edmunds, wrote the County Board to say that the council was in favour of the erection of a hospital in Walkerton and that they were willing to bear their share of the $6,000 which the County proposed to raise towards it. It was announced that the minister would take up a collection in church for the hospital. Besides bearing their share of the costs for the Walkerton Hospital, the council gave $5 to aid the Children's Hospital in Toronto in 1906. Both of these donations were impressive accomplishments in those days as Tobermory was such a small community.

The council of 1920 was in favour of a memorial hospital being built in Wiarton and stated that it would consider giving a grant in aid of this project. Thus, a short time later, Tobermory was served by the Wiarton hospital. Also, in 1924, the Red Cross Outpost Hospital was built in Lion's Head to serve the four northern municipalities of Lion's Head, Eastnor, Lindsay and St. Edmunds. Despite these additions, Tobermory remained relatively isolated from medical services.

In the 1920's, doctors came up and held offices in Tobermory for one day each week and dentists practiced their trade in an office in the Matheson house. For several summers, the Haigmier brothers administered to the Tobermory residents. These two doctors came from the Kitchener-Waterloo area and had a cottage and a yacht in Tobermory. Grace Peacock recalls that they did quite a bit of surgery in their day, including two gall bladder

operations done on Mrs. James H. Hopkins and Mrs. Phillip Adams. Grace also remembers that she and two of her brothers had their tonsils and adenoids taken out on the kitchen table at home.

In 1922 diptheria struck again, killing three people. These were the last Tobermory people to die of this dreaded disease.

Dr. Bell moved his practice to Lion's Head in 1923 and would travel the long trip to Tobermory by horse and sleigh to care for the sick in the village. Many of his trips were made to deliver babies and, in his truly humour-ous way, he called these occasions "birthday parties". Mid-wives were still of great assistance and sometimes would have the whole task completed themselves before Dr. Bell arrived. Mrs. Arthur S. Martin, a former war nurse, Mrs. Evelyn Young, Mrs. Smith and Mrs. J. C. Hopkins were some of these notable women. Dr. Bell's term ended when he decided to join the Canadian Armed Forces in 1939.

In the late 1920's, the women of the community became very active in the health field. A nurse from Lion's Head came to give a talk about home nursing and sponge and bed baths to them. In 1927, the Federated Women's Institute of Ontario offered to subsidize the maintenance of a doctor in Tobermory, so the local women responded by setting up a search for one. In August of 1928, Dr. Fraser came to Tobermory. One of his first actions was to make sure that everyone was innoculated against diptheria. Dr. Fraser was to receive $1,000 in compensation by the Ontario Association of Women's Institute and was supposed to have signed a two year contract. His term, however, must have ended in less than a year as the ladies were again searching for a doctor in January of 1929.

A Dr. Anderson came up to fill this position in late January. It is said that he came up in a "cloud of snow" and a bowler hat and left hurriedly the next day, once again "in a cloud of snow". Apparently the doctor did not feel that the government subsidy of $4,000 over a two year period was enough, and so he left.

In August of that year, Tobermory was delighted to welcome Dr. Eva R. Fisher into their midst. She stayed in W. J. Simpson's home and had an office there. Later she moved down the highway. A Tobermory correspondent to *The Wiarton Echo* worte:

"The doctor and her husband arrived here Friday afternoon. Many busy preparations were made to ensure their comfort, and it is good to again see the house open upon the hill, shedding its light and healing rays abroad. A big welcome is extended to her and a deep sense of satisfaction and security is felt in having her in our midst. We do appreciate the work of the Grey, Bruce and other Institutes that are pushing forth their enterprises in order to raise sufficient funds to keep a doctor here. Already she has been called upon, and a good start has been made in her winter's work of mercy and healing ministries."

In May of 1930, some bad news was heard from the Women's Institute in Toronto. It was reported that all further support for maintaining a doctor at Tobermory was to be cancelled. Funds at the Institute were exhausted, and the Tobermory people were again going to be without a doctor.

Dr. Fisher left for a short time that year until it was arranged to pay her $300 per month. The residents helped raise the money with the Township also contributing to enable Dr. Fisher to continue her valuable work. In 1932, Dr. Fisher attended the births of Keith Austin and Bessie Currie among others. Later that year she left Tobermory as the village again could not pay her.

In December of 1932, the Township Council presented a by-law which provided for the maintenance of a doctor through the rates of the township. *The Wiarton Echo* correspondent wrote:

> "The burden of providing a doctor has been resting very heavily on the local women folk who through the local W.'s I. have struggled worthily but hopelessly with a task which was far too big a load to carry. Long ago it should have been taken from their shoulders and given over to a central council of men — for it is a man sized job — for proper oversight. If this had been done many serious mistakes might have been avoided. At last the best thing and the needed thing is being done and there should be no hesitancy in supporting the measure".

The council decided to present a by-law to the voters at the next election, asking permission to raise $500 annually through taxes, for the support of a doctor during the winter months. In 1933, the by-law was passed and Dr. Harold Spenceley was appointed medical health officer of the Board of Health. He took up residence in Tobermory, opened his practice, and soon became an active community member taking the positions of clerk and road bookkeeper in 1934. While here, he also married Oriel Vail, a local girl. Dr. Spenceley ended his term in 1936 and the village again became dependent on the occasional visits of Dr. Bell.

At a meeting of the Lion's Head Branch of the Red Cross Society in October of 1937, it was decided that a nurse should be sent to Tobermory to stay from December 15 to April 15. The reeve of St. Edmunds, Mr. Ransbury, was at the meeting and he volunteered to secure a boarding place for the nurse in the village. In making this offer, the reeve had secured his name, unintentionally, on the Red Cross Executive.

In January of 1938, Mrs. Kenny was engaged as a nurse. That same month she organized classes in home nursing for the local women. The lessons were held in the library and included topics on disease prevention, mild ailments, communicable diseases, artificial respiration, dietetics, and infant feeding. During her time in Tobermory, Nurse Kenny stayed with Don McIvor and his wife. She was a widow and very dedicated to her work.

Everyone talked with fondness of Nurse Kenny and eventually it got around to Charles Wyonch. He had never seen her before, but the day he got a look at her he was quite impressed. A neighbour asked him how his health was just after he had met Nurse Kenny and his reply was, "Oh, I'm going to be sick a lot more".

Because of the winter weather and the distance between herself and her country patients, Nurse Kenny used many forms of transportation. The postmaster and other community members, Barney Hopkins in particular, would drive her in a "June Bug" in milder weather and she herself drove a horse and cutter at times. In very rough weather she had a team of huskies and someone made her a pair of "ice creepers" for walking on icy roads and fields. These creepers were actually perforated tin cans strapped to her shoes.

Besides visiting sick patients, Nurse Kenny inspected the school children's health. In late February of 1938, an epidemic of whooping cough prevailed and many children were very sick. Aleta Marie Smith, a two month old child, was the first to die of the cough on April 1. Both Gladys Davis and Little Alice Austin had their tonsils out in that same month. In mid-April, Nurse Kenny's term ended and she was given a farewell party in the Belrose sun room. Diplomas were presented to the women completing the home nursing course and fond farewells were said.

Nurse Ruth McDonald was the winter nurse for 1939. She was a younger nurse but quite a capable one. She had a lot to handle that year. She gave a talk on tuberculosis and attended many sick people. 1939 seemed to be the year of appendicitis attacks. Cecil Davis fell prey to it in January and was taken to Wiarton for an operation from which he recovered well. That same winter, a blizzard struck blocking roads and preventing communication. The only person the storm did not stop, was Alex (Scotty) McDonald who took a baby to the Lion's Head hospital in the morning and had to make a second trip in the afternoon when Melvin Martin had a bad appendicitis attack.

Accidents also seemed numerous that year. Tom Knight broke his arm when he caught it in the rope of a piledriver, the Reverend McKnight broke his rib when he fell on the ice scraper with which he was cleaning off the skating rink, and a hunting accident left John Fisher wounded.

During the war years, the Tobermory community kept busy assisting the Red Cross in their war effort. Women would gather at Ritchie's Restaurant to quilt and knit. Bales of clothing were collected to be sent to the designated war areas and even the reeves and councillors contributed by doing canvass work. To help subsidize the cost of the Red Cross work done in their area, 102 local people contributed $104 by direct subscription in 1940. This left the amount of $621.98 to be paid by the Division who felt that the cost was well worth it as the nurse's services were much appreciated.

Never identified by name, Ontario Red Cross outpost hospital nurses in 30 centres are called "ladies bountiful"

Big problem in winter is transportation. Dog teams and covered horse-drawn cutters are used for ice - bound highways

Tobermory farmers gave this "June Bug" to their nurse. Driver is the postie

Nurse lets her little patient see the flashlight with which she will examine her throat

Eight people live in this tiny cabin on Bruce peninsula, 40 miles from the nearest hospital. Outpost nurses made 16,365 visits in 1937

NURSES on Red Cross outpost hospital duty remain strictly anonymous at their own request. No publicity-seekers they failed unanimously to provide "color" stories from the frontiers to be used in Red Cross appeals, upon which the organization depends for financing. "Nothing," they reported as one, "ever happens here. . . ." Last year 30 branches spent $300,000

No doctor aided the nurse at Lion's Head the day these babies were born

In emergencies, nurse hitches up her light cutter, does her own driving

Perforated tin cans strapped over shoes are used by nurses as "ice creepers"

In 1940-41, a nurse served the community from November to April, making 725 home visits and seven visits to schools, during which she made 172 physical inspection of students. Seven or eight cases of pneumonia occurred during this time and a flu epidemic struck in January. The nurse was fortunate to have a continuous telephone connection to Wiarton and Owen Sound where she could obtain advice from doctors.

Early in 1942, the four northern municipalities entered into an agreement to initiate a community doctors service for the area. Under this agreement Dr. Carr-Harris held office hours in Tobermory during the first few months of 1942. Bettie Smith tells this story of Dr. Carr-Harris:

"Dr. Carr-Harris came to Lion's Head with a 1939 Ford which was noted for its horsepower and he was noted for putting it to the test. He travelled at consistently high speeds on his run to Tobermory and sometimes took Gordon White who was a member of the committee of reeves who had completed the contract with the doctor. His car was not the kind of guided missile to meet in the narrow, snowplowed Peninsula roads. As the doctor rounded the old Monument Corners and went full out for Burley's Corner one day, the rear end of the car slid around and struck the frozen snow-plowed bank. There was a great clatter and the doctor said, "I think we better stop and see if we have done any damage".

When the doctor and Gordon went behind the car, there was a collection of basins, pitchers, bedpans, and a baby bath scattered on the slippery roadbed. Gordon was at a loss to know where they came from and the doctor pondered the matter for awhile and said "I wonder if they came out of the trunk?", which at the moment was tight shut! Gordon tried the handle and found the trunk empty. It was concluded that the car had hit the frozen bank hard enough to spring the body, the lid flew up, the trunk had discharged its cargo and when the lid fell down again, it locked"!

During Dr. Carr-Harris' time, Mrs. C. Horvath was also serving the community as Red Cross Nurse. She taught a war emergencies course and at the end of her term, 12 ladies were presented with certificates for it. In early April, Nurse Horvath was forced to give up her post because of poor health.

Dr. Carr-Harris' service was terminated a few months after his arrival. In March 1942, the residents of the Township gathered to hear an explanation of the Red Cross Community Doctor's Service which was to provide Tobermory with a doctor. The plan gave people the choice of paying all regular doctor's fees or subscribing to a co-operative plan with an annual fee to cover doctor's services. This co-operative plan was to cost $4 per adult and $2 per child annually. Through this plan, Dr. Donelly was dispatched to Lion's Head and his services were extended to Tobermory. Dr. Donelly terminated his services to the community in August of that year, but Nurse Horvath returned in October to carry on the Red Cross services for another winter. Early in 1943, the Red Cross society posted Dr. Frost to Lion's Head. He held office at Tobermory in the Belrose sun room on Wednesdays.

In February of 1943, a snowstorm blocked the road to Tobermory for two weeks, preventing supplies from being transported to the village. Nurse Horvath was almost out of sulfa drugs with which to treat influenza patients when Dr. Frost arrived with supplies. During the storm, the nurse had been caring for some seriously ill patients and had walked two miles in a blizzard to attend a young boy with appendicitis. On his arrival, the doctor just checked them all and pronounced the boy with appendicitis "out of danger" before returning to Lion's Head.

Dr. Frost's services were short-lived, and an elderly bachelor, Dr. Connor of Flesherton, provided some service to Tobermory for the rest of 1943. After Dr. Frost's brief sojourn, there was no resident doctor closer than Wiarton until the end of the Second World War.

In 1943, blood donor clinics were being held in Wiarton and in March of 1944, 31 blood donors from Tobermory attended the clinic. Gordon Gibbons arranged the trip down and five local people received buttons for giving their third donation.

After the war, Dr. John Kelly took up residence in Lion's Head and held office hours during the week in Tobermory. If someone was sick when the doctor was in Lion's Head, and he had to come up to attend them, the municipality covered the extra travel charge.

Two registered nurses and English war brides, Mrs. William LaVoie and Mrs. Patrick Seely, became residents of Tobermory in 1945. They stayed for many years, treating emergencies and assisting the doctors who came up on call. During the winter of 1947, a series of snowstorms kept medical supplies and food from coming in for almost two weeks. Nurse LaVoie found herself and Mrs. Mabel Davis attending the birth of Mrs. Carl Hopkin's daughter. Early that April, a plane carrying doctor W. A. Wilford of Wiarton broke through the storm, landing on the ice at Big Tub Harbour. He brought supplies for the nurses and attended several people suffering from the stomach flu.

In 1946, the Red Cross Society expressed their regret in being unable to send a nurse to Tobermory for that winter. This was not such a hardship for the locals as they still had their two resident nurses. Nurse Seeley had two children while living in Tobermory. When her husband died, she married a local, Bill Adams, and later moved out west. Nurse LaVoie resided in Tobermory well into the fifties. She delivered Mrs. Levi Wyonch's son in 1952. This was quite an event, considering that most children were being born in a hospital by that time.

Public health nurses became familiar sights in Tobermory in the late forties. Nurse Shouldice came from Lion's Head to educate the Tobermory residents in health matters. In 1948, Mary McLaughlin, another nurse, came and gave lectures on growth and nutrition, personal hygiene, and care of preschoolers. These lectures were held in the public library and twelve girls from the home economics class attended the last one.

In the spring of 1951, Doctors Mervyn and Norma Hopkinson came to the Peninsula. They held office in Tobermory for two days per week in the home of Mr. and Mrs. Chester Wheildon. The "Hoppys", as they were often referred to, also came up in the middle of the night or during harsh weather to attend to emergency victims.

This man and wife team served the Peninsula longer than any doctor before them had and, wherever they went, they were gladly greeted. Both were dedicated to their work and were well-known in their field. Norma was one of two women coroners in Ontario. Her husband, also a coroner, was a medical director of a pharmaceutical company and an award winner in obstetrics, gynecology, and psychiatry. In 1971 he received a scholarship, the money of which he used to study hormones and diseases due to hormone imbalances. The Hopkinson's served the area for twenty-five years until October, 1976, when Mervyn was killed in a house fire. This tragedy shocked the people of the area. His wife, Norma, has continued her services alone for many years.

**Dr. Mervyn Hopkinson and
his wife Dr. Norma Hopkinson.**

In 1948, the St. Edmunds council gave a grant to the Bruce Peninsula and District Memorial Hospital being built in Wiarton. By 1952, the hospital came under local management and representatives from each of the district townships were chosen to make up the hospital board. Cecil Davis was elected that first year, and re-elected in 1953. The council gave another donation of $125 to the hospital in 1956 and indicated that more might be raised by canvassing the area.

The late forties to the early sixties saw a great deal of effort put into preventing diseases by innoculating and vaccinating everyone. Beginning in the late forties, medical personnel strove to entirely eradicate the dreaded disease, tuberculosis. The Department of Health was responsible for the steps made in this direction as they sent officials to hold free chest x-ray clinics throughout the Peninsula. Local ladies assisted in the registrations and canvassing for these clinics and a mobile x-ray unit was brought in.

In 1961, Gordon Stockley of the Tuberculosis Branch, Toronto, said that only 52% of the population on the Peninsula had been tested at the last clinic. A further clinic was set up in June in the Community Hall in Tobermory and a total of 442 people attended it. This time, the usual chest x-rays were not given. Instead, a skin test consisting of only a needle or a scratch was given. Mrs. S. Craigie was the official in charge of the clinic.

Early in the fifties, school children were being immunized to protect them from whooping cough, diptheria, lock-jaw, and smallpox, diseases that had killed many children earlier in the century. Polio clinics were held in the Legion Hall in 1962. The sabin (oral) vaccine was administered to 285 people in mid-June, and in September another clinic was held. These vaccinations are very much taken for granted today, but the diseases they prevent were an unfortunate part of life and death in the past.

Indirectly related to human health, an anti-rabies clinic was held in 1958 when 85 dogs and 45 cats were vaccinated. This was considered to be a most successful clinic as 85 to 90 per cent of the dog and cat population had been treated. This, however, did not stop the wild animals from contracting rabies and endangering other livestock and humans.

In 1967, a rabid fox created havoc at Lottie Wyonch's farm. On entering the barn one morning, Mrs. Wyonch stepped on the rabid fox and was just lucky that it did not attack her. She clubbed it over the head but later discovered that it had already killed one baby lamb and had badly mauled another. Because of the fox, several barn cats had to be destroyed and Mrs. Wyonch's herd of over 40 sheep had to be quarantined for several weeks.

Medical and emergency equipment was acquired and improved on throughout the years and first aid knowledge was further acquired by many Tobermory residents.

In 1958, Captain Breen of the Owen Sound Fire Department visited Tobermory and gave a show and demonstration on the latest method of artificial respiration. He also showed the local people how to use the resuscitator which had recently been presented to the village by the Canadian Legion.

In 1962, Mr. Claude Pound was taken ill at his Big Tub cabin. The response of the Tobermory community to his call for help was rapid and, after recovering from his illness, he and his family sent the people of Tobermory a letter of thanks and presented them with a much needed stretcher. That stretcher was well used two years later when a car went into a bad tailspin sending two people to the hospital. Their note of thanks to the community read as follows:

June, 1964.
Tobermory News (Rotary)

"A special thank you from "Ye Royal Printer"

We have often said a word of thanks for our readers; this time we are saying a word of thanks on our own behalf. We wish to say thank you to all the kind friends who rallied to our assistance when we went into a bad tailspin and had to be hospitalized. We had to be taken to hospital on many occasions, but we wish to state right here and now that Tobermory does not have to take a backseat to any community, be it large or small, when it comes to making a sick person comfortable and administering to their needs. A special bouquet to Mrs. Poore, who showed excellent judgement both with her service and advice, when she insisted and convinced us that we needed medical care and got right on the phone and obtained it for us. Stew Peacock and Harry Davis had a whale of a time engineering and manoeuvering the stretcher into the hospital. We are at present designing one shaped like a pretzel twist, which will hook around corners and short turns. Thank you one and all for your assistance.

Benny''

Mrs. Poore, RN, who had assisted in the above emergency, was one of the 21 local residents who had taken and passed, a St. John's Ambulance first aid course two months before. The course had consisted of 14 hours of instructions and an examination held in the Community Hall.

In September of 1964, a hunter safety training course for Lion's Head and Tobermory district was held in the Lion's Head Legion Hall. J. P. Johnstone was chairman and people over the age of 14 applied for the training. The next month, an Alcoholics Anonymous group was formed in Tobermory.

In the early 1900's, dentists were almost unheard of in Tobermory. One news article stated that a Dr. Skinner visited the little village to "fix teeth" in 1901, but for the most part, care of the mouth and teeth was haphazard. In 1925, Dr. Campbell set up a dentist practice in Wiarton, but Tobermory residents had to travel down to him. Most people only visited the dentist when they were in great pain and, by this time, it usually meant the extraction of one or more teeth. Preventative dental care was limited at best.

Sometime in the sixties, a Dr. Crane set up a practice in Wiarton and later Dr. Loucks followed suit. Dr. Loucks continues his practice to this day.

In 1969, Dr. and Mrs. Hoffman came to Tobermory to visit friends. The dentist and his wife liked the place so much that they bought their own property and house at Warner Bay intending to retire. In seeing the need for a dentist in the community, and disliking to stop work altogether, Dr. Hoffman decided to put off retirement for awhile. He opened a dentist office in his house and took appointments in the morning. He would also take emergency cases at any time.

Dr. Hoffman soon discovered that a lot of people had no teeth or only a few, so that his major job was restoring or replacing what they had once had. One woman who came to him said, "I have so much to be thankful for. I only have two teeth but at least they meet". Dr. Hoffman did denture work and would remove troublesome wisdom teeth, but he did not do orthodontal work or serious surgery. He could treat patients at the Wiarton Memorial Hospital as he was on staff there, but most of the patients he would send to Owen Sound. The doctor tried to keep his fees low as very few people had dental insurance.

Most of the patients he treated were adults, although he did believe in preventative medicine. If the mother of a child was calm, and a good patient, Dr. Hoffman would let the child into his room to sit on the patients' chair so that he or she would grow accustomed to the dentist and equipment. Dr. Hoffman would refer most children to a dentist in Wiarton as he felt that a child should be exposed to the same dentist as often as possible and he expected to be retiring soon anyway. The dentist did, however, continue his Tobermory practice for ten years, after which he retired, and passed away in 1983.

After 62 years of practicing dentistry, he donated his original dentist equipment, which he bought a while after graduating, to the St. Edmunds Museum where it is today. There is no dentist in Tobermory now, but two brothers have a part time office in Lion's Head.

Three cases of hepatitis occurred in Tobermory in 1970. The victims were not in serious danger, but because this was a contagious disease (inflammation of the liver), Dr. Norma Hopkinson ordered innoculations given to all employees in lunchrooms and restaurants.

The Massasauga Rattlesnake, although not very common, was an issue in the 1970's. People in Ontario who are bitten by one of these snakes usually all survive due to prompt first aid and an antivenom serum treatment. In 1972, the Ontario Hospital Association advertised the fact that many hospitals provided the free antivenom serum to snake bite sufferers and promoted first aid knowledge in the case of snake bites. Rattlesnakes are almost unheard of today and there has been only one snake bite case in this area in the past nine years.

As Tobermory tourism escalated in the seventies, more divers chose to explore the shipwrecks and caves prevalent in the area. Several tragic diving accidents led people to consider the need for a decompression chamber in Tobermory. In 1970, an inexperienced diver surfaced too rapidly and died from air entering his blood stream causing the blood to foam. The next year, an expert diver and scientist died of the same cause as he had apparently been unable to get air from his tank and was forced to surface quickly.

In July of 1972, two divers were rushed to the decompression chamber in Toronto after suffering from the bends, again due to surfacing incorrectly. A woman died of the same cause in 1972, and when two men in that party, Danny Beamer and John Locmelius went down to find her, they too got the bends and were rushed to Toronto for treatment. Doctors and divers in the area began to feel that a decompression chamber should be on standby at Tobermory at all times especially when diving clubs numbering more than 100 members would converge on Tobermory for a weekend of diving.

In 1973, Mrs. E. M. Cameron informed the Ministry of Health of the lack of medical facilities and a doctor in Tobermory. The Ministry declared the area "medically under-serviced" and this began the search for a permanent doctor.

In May of 1974, Dr. George Harpur offered his services to the area. He had been practicing in Huntsville and had previously been doing research into decompression. Besides being a doctor, he is a diving instructor, an anesthetist, a coroner, and a private pilot. He moved into his temporary quarters in July and by August he was working from a cottage on the lakeshore where he had constructed two examining rooms.

The Township Council donated the land on which a medical building was to be built, and on August 27, 1974, a non-profit charitable charter was issued to the Corporation of the Tobermory Health Clinic. The committee that was to plan and oversee the development of the health clinic consisted of Rev. Peter Scott, Lloyd Adams, Dr. R. Hoffman, Ernie Ralph, and Vida Jordan. An agreement was made between the clinic's Board of Governors and the St. Edmunds Council that stated that when the clinic was complete and fully paid for, it would be turned over to the municipality.

Dr. Hoffman was the treasurer of the committee and he was in charge of raising the $30,000.00 that was needed. Many fundraising events were held and all of these contributed toward the final goal. Dr. Hoffman later said "that the people of Tobermory deserve a lot of credit for the building and furnishing of the clinic".

In 1974, the Health Clinic Committee learned that their application to the Local Initiatives Program had been accepted, and they were to receive $19,728.00 for the construction of the clinic. More money was still needed so Vida Jordan and Rev. Scott drove to Toronto to request help from the United Church. The Church agreed to lend the clinic board $30,000.00 at a low rate of interest thus taking the burden off individual shoulders and boosting the community's enthusiasm for the project. Money started to come in from individuals and businesses. By the time that the clinic was erected, over $50,000.00 had been collected.

By October 13, 1974, the clinic foundation had been laid. Many men gave their time and skill to erect the building. Plumbing, wiring and carpentry were done free of charge by local people. Peter Scott spent a great deal of time constructing the front stonework. In November, $25,000 of fire insurance was placed on the clinic, and by January, 1975, it was decided that the rent of the building should be $250 per month. As the facility was almost complete, Dr. Harpur moved in.

Donations continued to come in and by January 23, 1975, $17,500 had been donated by residents and well-wishers of the area and equipment such as an x-ray, an electrocardiograph, and a tonometer had been bought. The clinic was opened in March and in April a letter was sent to the Ministry of Natural Resources asking for reimbursement of $4,500 for the housing of the decompression chamber which was built in the form of a garage connected to the clinic.

In May of 1975, the corporate lawyers were ready to negotiate the transfer of the Health Clinic from the Board of Directors to the Township Council, but the transfer did not go through that year.

By July of 1975, $3,665.56 worth of medical equipment had been bought from Dr. Harpur and a pulmonary function analyser and a blood analyser (which enables on the spot blood testing) was acquired. Dr. Harpur sought another doctor to help him in the clinic so Dr. Silins arrived October 2, 1975. New officers were chosen for the Board of Directors that month, and the stonework on the face of the building was almost finished.

When completed, the clinic consisted of a frame structure faced with beige steel siding and covered with natural stone at the front. It contained a waiting room, a small laboratory, an x-ray room, an emergency treatment room, an examining room, a business office and a doctor's office.

By late October, the first phase of the medical clinic was near completion and phase two, the development of a decompression chamber, accessories and completion of the garage to house the chamber, was underway. The Ministry of Natural Resources agreed to fund the purchase of the chamber and equipment.

The hyperbaric chamber was delivered to Tobermory from Florida in December. Funded by the Department of Natural Resources with the support of the Department of Health, it was, and still is, used to treat divers suffering from air embolism and the bends. Air embolism occurs when air enters a diver's circulatory system from a burst lung. The bends, which are more painful than fatal, occurs when a diver comes up too quickly, not allowing nitrogen which has been absorbed into the blood to diffuse out. The nitrogen bubbles get into the blood stream causing obstruction of the blood flow.

Before the arrival of the chamber, Dr. Harpur had acquired a total of 1,800 hours of diving time, some of this time being spent trying to get the bends for research purposes. His experience aided him in his medical work and helped him to suggest better methods of diver training and rescue. To this end, the hyperbaric chamber is also used for training, educational and experimental programs as well as medical emergencies.

Besides the new chamber, the doctors' cars were equipped with citizen band radios which linked them to the clinic and the local Ontario Provincial Police branch. Donations from several diving clubs were used to finance a communication system with local dive boats.

Dr. Silins was one of the first people, besides Dr. Harpur, to be trained in the operation of the chamber.
In 1977, the issue was raised that Dr. Harpur might be away during a diving emergency, it was suggested that any doctor could operate the chamber by putting a phone path through to the Toronto chamber for instruction.

In the midst of these rapid changes, a flu epidemic broke out in 1975, keeping the doctors very busy. Lily Martin wrote this poem about the epidemic:

THE FLU BUG

"I wonder what happened to our healthy little town,
We once were quite a hardy bunch took a lot to get us
down.
Dr. Harpur's a very busy man, he's always on the jump,
One fellow get Pneumonia and another gets the the
mumps.
And if that isn't quite enough to knock them off their
feet,
They get the European flu so he can neither eat nor sleep.
But wait till spring comes rolling round
and the sun comes peaking through.
We'll perk right up, give ourselves a shake and be as
good as new".

Besides the flu, the measles and the chicken pox were nuisances in the winter of 1977, and in 1978 an outbreak of mumps occurred.

On May 22, 1976, an information meeting and the official opening of the Tobermory Health Clinic and Decompression Facilities was held. The information meeting included a welcome by Reeve J. P. Johnstone and a talk on the beginning of the clinic by Lloyd Adams. Dr. Hoffman talked of the financial structure, stating that there were no outstanding debts and that the clinic had a solid bank account. Dr. Harpur described the function of the clinic and Reeve Johnstone indicated that future plans included the possibility of having dentist and optometrist offices set up in the clinic and to have these practitioners come up once a week. Expansion plans also included an addition containing a small emergency operating room and additional lab space.

The ribbon was cut by Mrs. E. M. Cameron, Mr. Andy Harjula and Mr. A. B. MacFarlane after the dedication. Tours of the clinic were held until nine p.m. that evening. The clinic staff in attendance included: Dr. G. Harpur, Dr. G. Silins, Miss Dawn Andrews, R.N., Mrs. Bill Haythorne and Miss Shirley Kipp. Mr. Andy Harjula, Parks Co-ordinator for the Ministry of Natural Resources, said that Tobermory now had the "most modern immediate medical service of any recreational area in Ontario".

In March of 1977, Dr. Silins wife gave birth to a baby boy in the clinic. Also in that month, 29 people attended a two day course in St. John's Ambulance Standard First Aid.

By March, the hyperbaric chamber was completely operational and the emergency cost of operating the chamber was quoted as $40 per hour. To ensure that the chamber was not a liability to the ratepayers of the village, Dr. Harpur carried one and a half million dollars of insurance on himself as the operator of the chamber.

In September, an eye doctor was coming up once a month and Dr. Silins' wife was doing some consulting on hearing problems. In December of 1978, optical equipment amounting to $2,908.47 was purchased from a Dr. Pym and a television game was purchased earlier for use in the hyperbaric chamber to demonstrate the effects of narcosis.

Dr. Harpur joined the health clinic committee in 1978 and in March, Larry Bell and Lloyd Thompson were authorized to sign the documents which would complete the winding down of the Corporation of the Tobermory Health Clinic.

In February, 1979, Dr. Silins and his wife left Tobermory and Dr. Harpur once again sought another doctor. Dr. Ian Jacques joined him early in July, making him the third doctor in the Northern Peninsula. Besides Dr. Harpur of the Tobermory Clinic, Dr. Norma Hopkinson was providing service at the Lion's Head Hospital.

With Dr. Jacques' arrival, a plan to improve medical services to the North Bruce Peninsula was put to work. It included 24-hour on-call coverage available in both Tobermory and Lion's Head. To achieve this, a radio communication system between facilities and physicians was planned and a part time office was staffed in Lion's Head.

Diving accidents and deaths continued to occur every year in Tobermory, despite the use of the chamber in training and saving divers. Even so, Dr. Harpur said in 1980 that Tobermory was one of the safest places in Ontario to dive. Over 2000 divers registered with Fathom Five Provincial Park that year. In doing so, they were reminded of safety procedures and advised of risks. A diver would receive the best possible emergency treatment in the event of an accident because of the decompression chamber, the only one in Southern Ontario outside of Toronto. Local men, mostly volunteer firemen, were trained by Dr. Harpur to operate the chamber and a physician would go into the tank with the victim to administer oxygen therapy.

Other accidents occurring in the summer of 1980 included the death of a lone swimmer who overbreathed and blacked out in the water, and the case of three sailors who died of hypothermia when their boat overturned in a squall.

During the 50th anniversary year of the Lion's Head Branch of the Red Cross, $470 was raised in the Tobermory area for the society and $50 was given to it by the Tobermory clinic staff. A book on the History of the Red Cross in Lion's Head was published which contained an interesting section on service to Tobermory written by Bettie Smith. Mrs. Smith had previously been captain of a canvassing team for the Red Cross.

Also in 1980, the Tobermory community excelled itself by donating $958.38 to the Arthritis Society. Much credit for this collection was due to Gordon Gibbons who looked after the boxes, and to the ladies who canvassed the area.

In March of 1980, the clinic driveway was paved, and a sign and plaque was donated to the clinic in memory of J. P. Johnstone by the Johnstone family.

Dr. Jacques announced that he was leaving in October, and thus Dr. Harpur went recruiting again. He was successful in attracting a resident in the Family Practice Program from McMaster Medical Centre — Dr. Suke. Unfortunately, Dr. Suke would not be finished training until the following July, nine months away. The underserviced program of the Ministry of Health, recognizing the importance of the service to the Peninsula, provided interim help in the person of Dr. Laurie White. Dr. White came for the nine months, but eventually spent a full year plus three months the following summer and various weeks in between as a replacement while Dr. Suke or Dr. Harpur were on holidays.

Dr. White, Dr. Harpur and Mrs. Dawn Harpur (nurse).

In June, 1981, both Dr. Suke and Dr. Harpur took their examinations and successfully qualified as specialists in Family Medicine. Throughout the years from 1975 onward, Tobermory had seen a succession of student doctors as Dr. Harpur was now a clinical lecturer with the Department of Family Medicine at the University of Western Ontario. It was hoped that this association, while providing excellent opportunities for the students, would also encourage some to consider returning to the Peninsula or some similar area. This approach has proven successful with the arrival of Dr. J. Gibson in June of 1983. Dr. Gibson spent two months training in Tobermory as a student which led to his subsequent return.

In 1979, a Task Force was established by the District Health Council to review health care services on the Bruce Peninsula. Besides being instrumental in obtaining funds to attract a physician to the area and helping develop the radio communication network for Lion's Head and Tobermory, this task force made twelve recommendations, one of which was to suggest the integration of both institutional and community health services.

In May of 1980, the proposal came out suggesting that the Bruce Peninsula and District Memorial Hospital, the Lion's Head Red Cross Hospital, and the Tobermory Medical Clinic be united. The advantage to the Tobermory clinic was that if the clinic was included within a single hospital corporation, it would then receive government funding, which it was not receiving at its present status. This idea was a welcomed one to most of the village people, but as Dr. Harpur said at the time, "We're not prepared to give up anything we've got now in Tobermory; there are certain things that have to be allowed to stay locally available". Under the plan suggested, all equipment donated to the clinic would stay there and separate sets of books would be maintained. The clinic committee would be retained, the committee and the municipality would have representatives on the board of the hospital corporation, and the institution would have one joint medical staff.

In January of 1981, Norm Stevens was authorized to sign the second draft of the Memorandum of Declaration of Intent between the Bruce Peninsula District Hospital, the Ministry of Health, and the Municipality of St. Edmunds. In December, a ceremony was planned to mark the amalgamation and a meeting was called to form an auxiliary to look after the needs of the Tobermory Health Clinic.

In March of 1982, the Tobermory Health Clinic Auxiliary was established with officers: Peter Dean: president, Shirley Johnstone: vice president, Cathy Wyonch: secretary, Holly Smith: treasurer and Jan Gleeson: auxiliary delegate to the Hospital Board. During the first meeting, ways to raise money for medical equipment were discussed, as was the possibility of the operation of an ambulance service to be run by the volunteer Fire Department. In the summer of 1983, this later goal was achieved as an ambulance was delivered by the Medical and Health Emergency Services and housed in the Fire Hall.

Dr. Ralph Suke.

Early in 1983, Dr. Harpur and Dr. Suke started administering hyperbaric oxygen treatments to victims of Multiple Sclerosis (M.S.). The treatment involves breathing pure oxygen under twice the normal atmospheric pressure. Although unproven and controversial, it had apparently relieved the symptoms of M.S. in a number of people in the United States and other countries. This series of treatments is a preliminary to a University of Western Ontario, double-blind study, which, it is hoped, will prove or disprove the value of these treatments.

There has been a great number of changes in medical care from the time of home remedies and three day trips to the doctor to the excellent services of today. Tobermory contains full medical facilities, three doctors, an effective emergency communication system, and now, an ambulance that has already seen a good deal of use. Tobermory can boast that its medical emergency service is better than those in the larger cities, in that a general practitioner arrives at the scene of an emergency within minutes to give professional help on the spot. This results in less permanent damage and more lives saved. With seniors' apartments planned for a few years ahead and Parks Canada discussing further park expansion, ongoing planning is being done to develop medical services to even a greater extent to fulfill the future needs of the community.

The Toronto Star 1975.

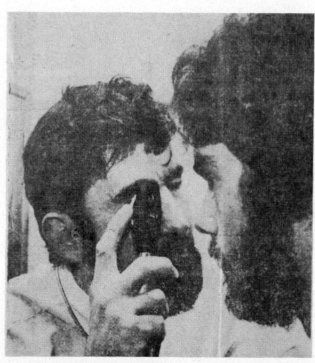

GEORGE HARPUR, Tobermory's first resident doctor in 30 years, checks out Doug Williamson at the clinic. The province subsidizes Harpur's work.

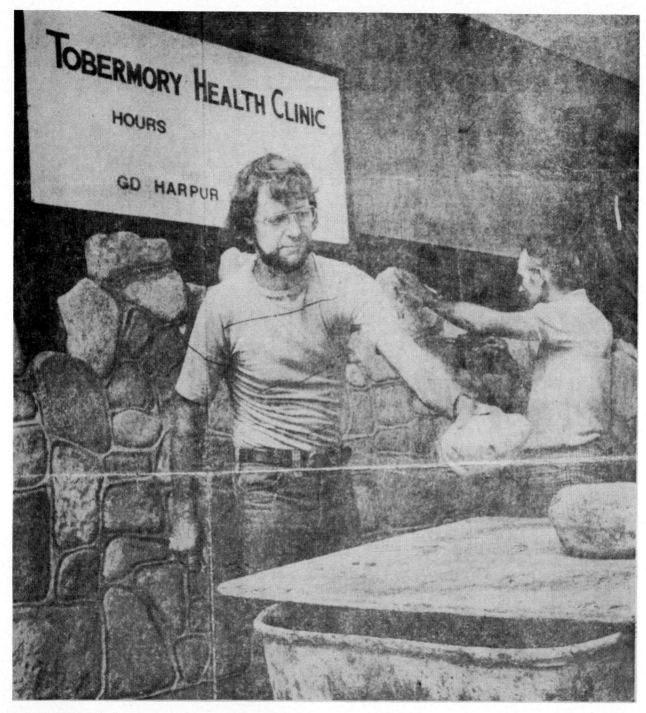

HAULING STONES from a nearby beach, Peter Scott, a United Church minister, is almost finished building the walls of Tobermory's health clinic. Helping him is Lloyd Adams, a motel owner. Residents have raised $44,000 and given months of free labor to the building project.

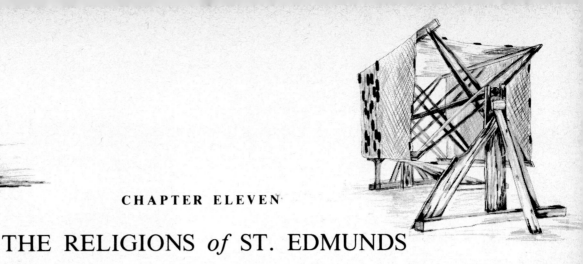

CHAPTER ELEVEN

THE RELIGIONS *of* ST. EDMUNDS

METHODIST — PRESBYTERIAN — UNITED CHURCHES

The first church service held in Tobermory was unique in that it was held on a boat tied to the shore. The Chicago 'gospel ship', the "Glad Tidings", arrived in Tobermory in 1882 with Captain Bundy at the wheel. The text of the first sermon preached came from Isaiah 55, verse 7. "Let the wicked forsake his way and the unrighteous man his thoughts, and let him return unto the Lord, and he will have mercy upon him, and to our God, for he will abundantly pardon". From newspaper articles, Patrick Folkes recounts that Captain Bundy was famous for his missionary work among seamen and remote ports on the upper Lakes. He preached in Tobermory in the newly built schoolhouse in 1883 and left some testaments and Sunday school literature (1).

In 1881, the Lion's Head Mission resolved to attach Tobermory to the Mission but nothing was done for another year or two. In 1883, the ninth General Assembly of the Presbyterian Church announced that: "The Presbytery has also opened a new station — Tobermory, at the extreme north end of the Peninsula, which promises rapid advancement". A Presbyterian student, possibly a Mr. Peter McLean, conducted the first services at the Tub, but the first regular, stationed minister was the Reverend James Walker of the Methodist Church. Ordained in 1863, he was appointed to Tobermory in 1884 and held services in the newly built Settlement schoolhouse.

In his report in 1884 to the Guelph Conference, the Reverend Walker wrote:

"This mission embraces five appointments, and is thirty miles in extent. There is great difficulty in travelling, as the country is new and very rough, and especially in winter, when the snow falls to a great depth, and all the travelling has to be done on foot. From Dyer Bay to Tobermory is between eighteen and nineteen miles, and in that instance there is but one house. But notwithstanding all the hardships we have had to undergo during the year, the Lord has been with us and blessed the work of our hands. A number of souls have been saved, and are now happy in a Saviour's love. We now report 41 members and two Sabbath schools". James Walker

In 1884, the foundation of the first Methodist church was laid and the General Assembly announced that "Tobermory closed during the winter of 1884-85, and could not open in the spring of 1885. It has not been permanently closed".

Apparently, the Reverend Walker did manage to arrive again in early April, 1885, and had quite a successful two weeks according to the following report *The Christian Guardian:*

Wed. April 15, 1885
Tobermory — Reverend James Walker, Missionary

"We have just closed a revival meeting at our St. Edmunds appointment of two weeks duration and during that time we have had wonderful manifestation of God's power in the conversion of sinners. Thirty two persons presented themselves as seekers of salvation, and most of them professed to have found the saviour. The whole neighborhood was stirred on the subject or religion. A number gave their names and more will do so. To God be all the Glory".

Later in 1885, the Reverend Philip Sparling arrived to serve the Tobermory community and in November he wrote the *"Christian Guardian"*:
"We are in the midst of a very gracious revival just now at the Settlement appointment, three miles from the Harbour. For fifteen nights the congregation seemed unmoved. At the end of

three weeks a gracious shower descended. Thirteen came forward, nine out of that number have given clear testimony to the power of saving grace. Those who came forward range from the ages of eighteen to fifty-five. We are now on the fourth week and the work increases in interest. To God be all the glory".

A report written a short while later read:

"A few days ago I sent you a few brief items from this mission. Since that time I have closed a four weeks' meeting, and, everything considered, I think a very successful one, as the number came forward at the altar represents the number of families living in the neighbourhood where the meeting was held, namely, eighteen, out of that number, eleven were converted.

Thirteen have united with the Church. Some of these are very promising young people. Having to leave immediately at the close of the meeting for the other end of the mission, I could not then fully ascertain how many would join, as there were several others seeking, who I think, will unite with us. Quite a number of those who were converted I baptized the evening I took them into the church. Altogether, I have baptized that same week eighteen persons, ranging in age from two years to fifty-five.

Since conference I have taken twenty-six into the church. In many respects this is a very interesting mission. The want of good roads makes it hard to travel as it has to be done on foot, and rivers and lakes have to be waded in spring and fall. The people are very kind and considerate and do what they can for the comfort of their minister".

During the Reverend Sparling's service, a new church was built at the Tobermory harbour. With help from Maitland, Rixon and Company, the village people and visiting fishermen concentrating all their efforts toward completing the construction of the church. As the building was almost finished, the funds were running very low. As a result, Reverend Sparling was so intent on a church being built that he made out a paper and had people sign it, pledging money for its construction. His enthusiasm was evident when he himself put the first $10.00 down. It was Captain Simpson, his father James Simpson, James H. and John C. Hopkins, William Spears, and Jacob and Michael Belrose who helped in the building of the church. They used saws and axes to cut the timber and oxen and teams to haul it out.

When complete, the little church contained seats made of wide rough boards and tiny windows which let in a dim light. Coal oil lamps were used to brighten the place. The floor and outside walls were made of wooden boards and the inside walls were plastered. A box stove was placed at the back of the church to provide heat for the building. It appears that only the bare necessities were provided as there was no bell or steeple. Membership in the late 1880's included about 28 people.

The Tobermory Harbour United Church, 1924.

1965

1983

The Reverend Dainard finished his term in 1890. The following reports were written about the Tobermory mission for the Guelph Conference during this time.

1886-87 "Tobermory is only 3 years old as a mission, and is yet in crude form. It is about 40 miles from north to south, and in width takes in the whole Peninsula. The missionary has to make all his journeys on foot. Notwithstanding many difficulties the mission has advanced and the outlook is hopeful".

1887-88 "Limited territory and limited opportunities characterize this mission. Good work has been done, however. A large number of conversions have taken place, Sunday-schools have been established, prayer-meetings and class-meetings built up, and church property improved".

The Reverend Tyler served the Tobermory community in 1891. There is no doubt that he worked hard because his mission contained several preaching points. He would hold an early morning service in Cape Chin, walk to Dyers Bay for a short service at noon and then walk or hitch a ride part way to the Tobermory Settlement church. There he held a service at 3 p.m. and, in the evening, he held a night service at the Harbour church.

Reports on the Tobermory mission in early 1890 indicated that small improvements were being made despite the difficult conditions.

1892-93 "Tobermory has prospered somewhat during the year, but here also the people are divided and many of them very poor. The prospect is that this will be missionary ground for years to come."

1893-94 "Tobermory remains about as last year as to membership, but congregations are said to be increasing, and some improvements on church property are being made."

The improvement came in the form of a parsonage which was purchased for $154 in 1893. Two years later the church spent $95 on repairs.

1894-95 "Tobermory reports church improvements. Revival services were successful. Two Sunday schools are well attended. The migratory character of the people makes it difficult to keep our congregations."

As if to prove that congregations were indeed hard to keep, 1895-96 saw a decrease in membership of 11 people bringing it down to only 13 supporters of the church. A second possible cause of the decrease may have been the doings of the Reverend Harnwell of 1894-95.

In 1894, a visiting minister took the steamer "Jones" to Tobermory and reported the following in *The Wiarton Echo*.

"On Sabbath I opened our nice little church and was greeted by good congregations. The pastor, Reverend H. J. Harnwell and his wife are very popular. On Monday evening was held the good old-fashioned tea-meeting. I was informed that whiskey is not an article of commerce at the Tub, that no hotel was needed there, nor do the people want one."

The tea meeting referred to in the paper, was held by the congregation to raise money with which to pay the "popular" ministers salary. Shortly after this effort, Mrs. Harnwell became quite sick and eventually had to be taken to Kincardine where she chose to remain for quite some time. Mr. Harnwell returned alone from Kincardine and announced that he would soon hold revival meetings. The choir was reorganized and Miss Glazier became the organist. Now all that was needed was a new choir director. *The Wiarton Echo* printed the following article in response:

Tobermory Settlement United Church 1930's.

1983

"We congratulate Mr. Harnwell on his election to the position of leader of the choir. Some adverse criticism is heard, but we think in the abscence of any local talent, it is at least excusable".

It seemed that near the end of the year the congregation's patience was wearing thin and Mr. Harnwell was quickly falling out of favour. The Tobermory "Echo" correspondent reflected the feelings of the local people when he wrote:

"The question the people here are asking is, "Has Rev. Mr. Harnwell resigned the pastorate of the church here?" It is now nearly four weeks since the Rev. gentleman left here. For the last three or four months he has condescended to pay us a flying visit once every two or three weeks, but now he intends to make it four. The people here have patiently borne with this kind of thing since July last, but patience like everything else has its limits. Mr. Harnwell finds time to preach in different parts of the Peninsula while his own charge for which he has been paid to serve, is left to its own resources. It is most unfair and dishonest for the Rev. gentleman to treat the people of Tobermory in this manner".

In 1897 when W. J. Smith proposed to Helena May Belrose, the couple had to journey to Hepworth to be married. They must have been surprised to find the familar Mr. Harnwell preaching there. It took the couple three days to reach home as the snow in the valleys was up to the telephone poles.

Services did, however, go on without Mr. Harnwell. Mr. D. F. McKenzie and a Reverend Coll took the odd service with the latter also preaching and serving ice cream at an ice cream social held in aid of the Sunday school. A children's social was held in 1895 but a storm left attendance low. It was an interesting program, however, as Mr. Glazier of Wiarton spoke on "Loyalty", the children did readings and recitations, the choir sang, and several adults made speeches.

Amidst the everyday life of the church, the Methodists and Presbyterians were vying for the churches on the Peninsula. This meant that in Tobermory, one year there would be a Presbyterian minister and the next, a Methodist one. In 1892, a committee was appointed from each church to define denominational boundaries on the Peninsula. In 1895, a report to the Presbyterian church read:

"In one of the fields, Indian Peninsula, the Methodist Church has been corresponding with our Presbytery, with a view to exchanging various stations in that district. It is likely this will be accomplished, but whilst making the field more workable, it will not lessen expense for the present at least".

The next year it was reported that:

"The arrangement entered into with the Methodist Church to divide the field has been faithfully carried out on both sides to the advantage of both".

This arrangement led the Presbytery to give the two Tobermory churches to the Methodists in 1896, in exchange for a Methodist church further down the Peninsula.

Further notes written in the Guelph Conference report show slow but steady improvements being made.

1896-97 "Tobermory's constant removals have made returns small, yet a rising generation appreciate the gospel teaching. A few have been added to our Church and others are seeking Jesus".

1897-98 "The Epworth league has been a centre of good influence. The Sunday School has been reorganized. Our special services resulted in reclaiming some backsliders, and a decision for Christ upon the part of many young people and Sunday school children. Missionary money is in advance".

1898-99 "The work has progressed; this can be seen in increased givings, deeper tone of piety, and the increased usefulness of an increasing membership. Missionary, E. L. and S. S. work is heartily sustained owing to more knowledge of these departments."

1899-1900 "God has bccn with us and has manifested His presence by forwarding the work in point of finances, the fitting up of church property and the spiritual advancement of the people".

John Worral came to preach in 1900 and in 1901 he reported a year of success. Both the parsonage and the churches were "beautified" and the financial situation had improved. The next year, under the leadership of Richard Facey, the membership increased by 19 bringing the number of church supporters up to 44, a record to date. Mr. Facey reported that, "A spirit of unity promises better prospects for the future". The Reverend Facey made a name for himself that year as it was reported that "the Pastor, trying to 'run logs', fell into the 'drink' ". Apparently the only thing hurt was his pride.

By 1903, membership had jumped to 61 people and missionary George King reported that improvements were made to the Settlement church and that it was expected that repairs to the church at the harbour would also be made.

In 1903, the indenture for the one-acre lot that the Settlement church stood on was written up and signed by pastor George King and trustees John C. Hopkins, James H. Hopkins, and Thomas Bartman. This deed transferred the land from former trustees to a new board of trustees for the price of $1.

Missionary Arthur Cooper reported in 1904 that:

"The spiritual life of the churches has improved. Financially we have had an exceptional year despite the long, hard winter. Our Settlement people have reshingled their Church, spending about $25. The Harbour church has had a complete renovation. New seats have been put in and the seating capacity greatly increased. Larger lamps have replaced the old ones and a new pulpit has been given to the church. Another encouraging feature of the report is the way in which the people have contributed to the connexional funds. The missionary givings are fifty per cent ahead of last year, which was the largest in the history of the mission".

In 1904-05, things did not go as well as was hoped. Some success was had at special services held in the winter but much of the time the roads were blocked with snow so the missionary, George Cassmore, could not get through. To add to his problems, there was a sickness in his family and so he was eventually forced to make another long and uncomfortable journey south.

By the summer of 1905, Tobermory had a new minister, Mr. Robert Crittenden. His daughter, Bertha, married Walter Vail of Tobermory.

By the end of 1906, church work was moving along well. The annual report stated that the parsonage had been repaired and the debt on the Harbour Church had been paid off. Ministerial and missionary givings were up, and special services had inspired many people.

The Methodist churches were busy in 1909 as they held many socials and tea meetings. In July, a "Magic Lantern Show" was put on in the Settlement Church for all of the young people. Valuation of the two churches was done for insurance purposes that year. The total seating capacity of both churches was two hundred, and the total property value amounted to $1,940.00. Later that year, delegates from the two Methodist churches and the Settlement Baptist Church attended a Sunday school conference in London. It was reported that a good time was had by all, and the delegates later spoke about Sunday Schools to residents gathered in the Orange Hall.

In the year 1914, the Reverend James Hyde served the community for one full term. He was followed by Robert Mercer who, with his wife, arrived in Tobermory by boat to serve the community in 1915. This was the first year that the Dyer's Bay Church was added to the Tobermory minister's duties. Mr. Mercer therefore had to leave Tobermory by horse and buggy or cutter on Saturday afternoon, stay overnight at a parishioner's home in Dyer's Bay, hold a service there on Sunday morning, and then drive north for a 2:30 p.m. service at the Settlement Church, and ended the day with a 7 p.m. service at the Harbour Church. A son was born to the Mercers while they were in Tobermory and the growing family was gladly welcomed back each summer after they finished their term in Tobermory in 1918.

**Reverend James Hyde
1914 - 1915.**

The Rev. John Ward arrived in Tobermory in 1920, after being wounded in the war. Rev. Ward was remembered for his stirring sermons and it was during his term here that a Sunday School room was added to the Harbour Church.

In 1923, lightning struck the Settlement Church destroying the chimney, breaking many of the pipes, and also making a hole in the floor.

The church attended the needs of the younger generation moreso than it had done before the 1920's. It was in 1924 that Rev. Wilson encouraged the ladies of the church to form a Sunday School group to provide teachers for the small children. With the help of Bertha Vail, this group lasted until 1934.

**Reverend John Ward, daughter-in-law Florence Ward
and Seth Ward 1920 - 1921.**

Reverend H. C. Wilson and Laurel Wilson 1924 - 1927.

In 1925, a record number of children attended Sunday School in order to celebrate Mothers' Day. Sunday School picnics were also very popular in the 1920's.

The year 1925 was an important year for the Presbyterian, Methodist, and some other churches as they joined together to form the United Church of Canada. This union meant that Tobermory Methodist Churches became United.

Rev. Albert Millen preached in Tobermory from 1927-1933. While here, he and his wife became involved in the community. Rev. Millen was instrumental in sparking interest in the production of several plays that were presented at the Community Hall. Mrs. Millen organized a Ladies Aid Group in 1927, and in 1932 it was turned into a more permanent group, the Women's Association. This group is still active today under the name of the United Church Women (U.C.W.).

The Sunday School program continued well into the 1930's. Many of the young ladies of the church took turns teaching the children the lessons, reading them bible stories, and leading discussions.

Beginning July 1, 1933, the Reverend Arthur G. Hewitt was stationed at Tobermory by the Settlement committee of Hamilton Conference of the United Church. He recollects:

"It was a Charge of two appointments — Harbour and Settlement, Tobermory itself was divided into two sections known as Big Tub, where deep water facility made adequate accommodation for Big Vesself, and Little Tub forming the village harbour. During the one year ministry, the manse was a relatively small, cold building on the west side of Little Tub, between the water and the road. I remember sitting beside the Quebec heater, which was stacked full of coal and the living-room was none too warm. My

Sunday records indicate that I was called home to Kitchener in March-April 1934. There was still lots of snow and I travelled with the Mailman behind a team of horses in a Cutter via the forty hills to Lion's Head".

According to the "Wiarton Echo", in 1935 there was a Tobermory United church club. In February they held a meeting at which Dr. Harold Spencely gave an address on "Vaccines, Serums, and Anti-toxins". His speech was followed by Ray Hepburn's talk on "Preparation Needed to Enter Teaching".

In 1937, the old parsonage, garage and furnishings were sold to raise money for a new building. That year a new manse was erected and, in February, the Women's Association led by Mrs. T. A. Golden, held an "At Home" as an official opening. Many visitors attended this event bringing useful gifts and cash presents. Much admiration was given to the living room which had been completely furnished by the Women's Association.

A Young Men's Discussion Group was formed in 1938. They met in the Sunday school and in March they held a stag social in the Orange Hall. In April the Harbour church celebrated "Stovepipe Sunday". This special service celebrated the redecoration of the church that had been done and the first steps taken in installing new stovepipes.

Reverend and Pearl Mercer 1915.

In January of 1939, the Young People's Union met to elect an executive. That year, lively discussions were held on such topics as: dictatorship versus democracy, work done by Dr. Dow in China, citizenship, and Christian culture.

In February, while cleaning off the harbour skating rink, an unfortunate accident occurred to Reverend McKnight. The ice scraper which he was using caught on a rough patch of ice throwing the minister onto the handle and breaking one of his ribs. He recovered well but left for the Scotland, Ontario United Church that June. In his place came the Reverend Arthur Jones who married soon after his induction at St. Edmunds.

Sometime around 1939-40, the Reverend Purdy from Lion's Head took an interest in the Settlement church and, as a result, had the interior of it altered. Two classrooms were put on the platform and a new railing was placed around it.

The large families of those years meant a large number of children and young people to attend Sunday School and a variety of church functions. A softball game between the two United churches, for young and old alike, made a nice ending to a supper held in the Community Hall by the Settlement church board in June. A junior choir was established in the Harbour church in 1941 under the direction of Weir Grieve, and the minister's wife, Mrs. J. N. Clarry, began a Canadian Girls in Training (C.G.I.T.) group for the young ladies. This group worked on quilts and in October, held a Hallowe'en Fete with costumes and lunch. The next year a Valentine's Day concert was held to help pay for their uniforms and later in the month the girls presented a Chinese play.

1941 was a year of celebration for the church as the last mortgage payment was made on the parsonage. Built at a cost of $3,000, it had been paid for in just over four years. The Women's Association were thanked for their part in the undertaking and a supper and concert was held. The Settlement church had to be moved back to its present location when the highway was widened. Just after the move, life was made easier when the church was wired and hydro was installed in 1941.

A mission study group was formed that year in the Harbour church and in December, both churches held Christmas concerts. In October of 1942, it was decided to hold the quarterly communion services jointly for the two United church congregations. The purpose of this was to strengthen attendance at communion.

In 1943, C. M. McKenzie took over the Tobermory charge. Unfortunately, he took ill after serving for three months and had to give up his work. From the winter of 1943 to June of 1944, there was no minister to serve the people. In March, a long article was written to "The United Church Observer". This article complained of the fact that the Tobermory charge had been without a minister for six months, even though there was a fine new parsonage and the minister received the same wage as other ministers in Ontario did. As a result of this letter, a minister, Rev. A. B. Arrol, arrived at Tobermory the

Reverend Alfred and Alice Fry 1957 - 1961.

next month. Many of the people remember this man as he was an unusual character when compared to the prior ministers that the small village had experienced. Apparently, this minister smoked, and even occasionally swore!

Sunday School was still going strong throughout the 1940's. The attendance in 1944 was up to sixty-three children. For the teen-agers, Rev. Arrol reorganized the Young People's Society. This group held many discussions on topics relevant to their age group that dealt not only with their lives, but with current events and the outside world. Social events also enlivened this club.

In 1952, Rev. Mercer was welcomed back to Tobermory. After two years of preaching in Tobermory, the Mercers retired to Beamsville. In 1965, Tobermory residents held a special reception in honour of the Mercers' Fiftieth Wedding Anniversary. Nine years later, Robert Mercer passed away.

In 1953, a new electric organ was purchased for the church. The money was raised by a canvass of the village, and the organ was bought by the U.C.W.

Rev. Alfred Fry and his wife came to Tobermory in 1957. Under the direction of Mrs. Fry, an Explorer group was formed for the girls. This group performed various social services and had a number of events that involved the community. This club continued well into the 1960's, holding parties, playing games, and participating in church activities.

The late 1950's was also a time of improvements for the church buildings. In 1957, six new stained glass windows with rounded tops were installed in the Settlement church to replace the old ones. Also that year, Mrs. L. H. McIvor, daughter of Mr. and Mrs. Martin Hopkins, painted and donated a picture of Christ to the Harbour church. A new Christian Education building was begun at the back of the Harbour church in 1959 and by 1960 both it and a new addition to the Settlement church was completed. Besides serving as a Sunday school room, the additions were fully equipped with a kitchen and, in the case of the Settlement church, a new washroom accommodation. The next year, 50 stacking chairs were donated to the Harbour church and the Women's Association decided to bear the cost of a new well being drilled there. This well was not supplying water to the church until April 1962.

In the summer of 1960, a five-day Bible Club was held for the church children. Run by the Child Evangelism Fellowship, Toronto, the program consisted of Bible stories, quizzes, flash cards, choruses and scripture memorization. The next year, 70 children registered for a two week Vacation Bible school.

Besides responding to the needs of the children in the 1960's, the church promoted the family by celebrating Mothers' Day with great enthusiasm and taking the Sunday school children into the congregation for a special service on "Christian Family Day". The C.G.I.T. was active in the early 1960's and a "Hi C" club was organized in 1964.

For the senior boys of the Harbour Sunday school, a Pro-Alis club was formed. This club held a father and son banquet in the Community Hall in 1962 with 125 men and boys in attendance.

In June of 1962, the official board of the Tobermory church decided to protest having the local beer and liquor store open all year round. Later in the year, the Young People's Union discussed the pressures of social drinking.

Improvements were made to the Settlement church that year in the form of new aluminum doors, a new floor, and an additional coat of paint on the ceiling. An investigation was made into the cost of the propane heating.

One special event in 1962 was the meeting of the Bruce Presbytery of the United Church in the Tobermory Harbour Church. The meeting was held and a fish dinner was served by the U.C.W. in the Settlement's new education wing.

The idea of combined services for the two United congregations and Sunday Schools was tried several times in 1963 and 1964 with some success.

The year 1963 saw 81 active members supporting the church, and eight burials, three baptisms and one marriage performed by the minister. In 1964, the U.C.W.

contributed money to go towards the purchase of a new parsonage furnace and the electrical lighting in the Harbour Church was changed from a two-wire to a three-wire system. The Board of Stewards found themselves selling locally compiled cookbooks in order to make money in 1965 and an oil furnace was installed in the Harbour Church. Three years later, new stained glass windows were put in the Harbour Church.

In 1971, the appearance of both churches changed slightly as the Harbour Church was panelled, and the Settlement Church received a bell tower and the Carillon Memorial Bells. Cora Wyonch, who had organized this effort, was very happy to hear them ring.

Another first for the Tobermory United Church was the ordination of the Reverend George Trigger. The ceremony was conducted at the Harbour Church in November of 1971. Over 200 people assembled to witness the ceremony as the Reverend Jewett Parr, president of the Hamilton Conference, conducted the ordination. After the service, a smorgasbord dinner was served at the Community Centre.

The fiftieth anniversary of the United Church of Canada was held on June 8, 1975. Both churches celebrated this event with special services and a fanfare of trumpets.

At the Annual General Congregational meeting of the Tobermory United Church in 1977, a committee was set up to look at alternatives to the present, two separate churches system. The alternatives suggested were: retain the present system, continue use of both churches combining the congregations and boards, close one church and use the other, build a new church to amalgamate both congregations, or build a new "Interdenominational Community Centre". The end result of this project, when the votes were all counted, was that things were to remain the same. The *Wiarton Echo,* March 31, 1977, indicated that the general feeling after the meeting was:

"You go to your church and I'll go to mine,
But let's walk together;
Our Father has built them side by side,
So let's walk along together..."

That April the Settlement church celebrated "Mildred Hatt Night" as their organist of the past 20 years retired. July saw the annual chicken barbeque held. Sponsored by the United Church and held in Centennial Park, this event remains.

In 1981, the Reverend Ken Welch preached the sermon following the induction of the minister, Reverend Peter Chung. The churches today have a combined congregation of approximately 60 people each week during the summer. Visitors and cottagers are welcome to attend and many do so. There are three women's groups: the Harbour U.C.W., the Settlement U.C.W., and a young ladies group. There is a Sunday School at the Settlement Church and a Bible Study group meets every week. Each church has an organist, but as yet there is only an active choir in the Harbour Church. Brownies meet at the church and the Orange Hall, which sits right beside the Harbour Church, can be used free of charge by the church.

The church was one of the earliest institutions to be established in the Tobermory community. The church buildings were built by the residents themselves but a great amount of help was obtained from the church conferences outside the community in the form of support money and the appointment of a missionary to the area. Through its policies and the variety of groups that sprang from the congregation, the church dealt with the social and economic issues of the times. In ensuring the longevity of the church, much time and effort was put into providing the children with religious instruction and other social activities that upheld the moral of the churchgoers. The Tobermory United Church today is much as it has always been with the exception that it is less dependent on the outside world to sustain it. Although it is still an "aid receiving" charge, Reverend Steve Lawson, the present minister in 1985, says the United Church is very near being a self-supporting charge.

FIRST MINISTERS OF THE METHODIST AND PRESBYTERIAN CHURCHES 1884-1925

James (Robert) Walker	1884
Philip Sparling	1885-86
W.B. Dainard	1886-88, 1889-90
Thomas Wiley	1890-91
R. J. Tyler	1891-92
George E. Money	1892-93
Judson Truax	1893-94
H. J. Harnwell	1894-95
John Wesley Kitching	1895-96
Charles A. Cavers	1896-97
Richard Railton	1897-98
Charles G. Cole	1898-1900
John W. Worrall	1900-01
Richard A. Facey	1901-02
George A. King	1902-03
Arthur N. Cooper	1903-04
George S. Cassmore	1904-05
Robert Crittenden	1905-08
E. Milton Carter	1908-12
Walter C. Almack	1912-13
David Dyson	1913-14
James S. Hyde	1914-15
Robert French Mercer	1915-18
Oliver (Arthur) Strapp	1918-19
Stewart Felker	1919-20
John Ward	1920-21
Alex MacGowan	1921-22
William D. Masson	1922-25

MINISTERS OF THE TOBERMORY UNITED CHURCHES 1925-1983

Hugh Wilson	1925-27
Albert E. Millen	1927-33
Art G. Hewitt	1933-34
Charles F. Tilbury	1934-35
Raymond J. McKnight	1935-39
Arthur Welburn Jones	1939-41
John N. Clarry	1941-43
C. M. McKenzie	1943
Vacant Jan. to June	1944
E. B. Arrol	1944-47
C. N. Padden	1947-49

Harold Bollingbrook	1949-50
Tom Kennard	1950-51
E. Sykes	1951-52
Robert French Mercer	1952-54
John Sutherland	1954-57
Alfred Fry	1957-61
Ken Welch	1961-63
Jan Rhynsburger	1963-65
George Trigger	1965-72
Peter Scott	1972-75
Joan MacIntosh	1975-77
John Wood	1977-81
Peter Chung	1981-83
Geraldine Bould	1983-84
Stephen Lawson	1984-

THE UNITED CHURCH WOMEN

The following extraction from the Harbour U.C.W. charter minutes was written by Vi Adams and describes the formation and activities of the United Church Women. Some additions and deletions have been made.

When we think of the ladies working in the church now as U.C.W. we are inclined to feel that this is the way it has always been. However, many of the older ladies know that this is not so, and in reviewing the minutes of the past 50 years of service to the Church, it was very interesting to compare the activities and involvement of early days to our present.

In 1932, a group of Tobermory ladies met at the home of Mrs. Millen (the minister's wife) with the thought of organizing a women's association to help in Church work. Mrs. Millen was the President, Mrs. A. Belrose vice president, Mrs. L. Ritchie secretary, Mrs. M. McLeod treasurer and Mrs. A. Leslie organist. Thirteen other members made up the membership roll.

The ladies' fund raising activities were quite similar to those of today: quilting, bazaars, suppers, concerts and crokinole parties. They appeared to work very hard for money raised. They had coin bags that would be turned in when they held 100 pennies, but the minutes tell of them having to borrow from these to buy quilt material. Admission to a concert was .25 cents and .10 cents for children. Later, they spoke of raising it to .15 cents for anyone over 12 years. During one concert, $38 was raised, so, needless to say, it was a packed house. A social evening or concert was always held after a supper so everyone really got his money's worth.

Mr. George Miles loaned the ladies $5 to buy material for a fish pond at their first bazaar. Money and a letter was sent to Robert Simpson Co. Asking them to send assorted items for the bazaar from which they eventually cleared $11.25. At this time they relied heavily on their coin bags for funds and the minutes tell of them deciding to take .50 cents from each one to buy wallpaper and window blinds for the parsonage which was in much need of attention. In August, 1932, Mr. Simpson was asked to go to Owen Sound and do the best he could with the money in the treasury to purchase a 48" bed and sagless mattress, and a light coloured piece of floor linoleum for the parsonage. Twenty-two dollars and fifty cents was given to Mr. Simpson that very night.

In September, 1933, a church banquet was planned. Marge and Madeline Smith and Mrs. O. Smith canvassed the Settlement area for vegetables, butter and milk. Salads, pies, cakes and jellies were collected in town along with dishes and silverware. Admission was .35 cents and .15 cents, however, two boys received their supper free because they had carried water for the banquet.

When the books were audited in 1933, they showed receipts of $176.31. Expenses amounted to $171.87 and a balance of $4.44 was left. The money raising bazaars mostly consisted of selling lunch, candy and material. In 1934, they decided to make up the remnant material into aprons, dresser covers, and pillow slips.

More choir gowns were needed, but there was no money to buy such things, so Mr. Weir Grieve donated $10 to the ladies for material which they made into gowns themselves. $1.90 was paid for two broadcloth gowns from Symons in Wiarton and material was ordered for $1 more. In this same year the ladies supported a motion to help in any possible way with the building of a new manse. The secretary was instructed to offer $8 for two days painting on the manse and to give the job to Archie Simpson and Walter Hopkins if they would do it at $2 a day.

Mention is made of a shower held for the manse with people donating useful equipment, utensils and money to go towards furnishing the kitchen.

In 1935 they were talking of wiring the church and helped to raise money the following year for this purpose.

In March, 1936, the 21 W.A. Members from the Harbour decided to meet in the Settlement Church and to ask the Settlement ladies to meet with them. Carl Hopkins drove the ladies out with his team of horses.

In February, 1937, an open house was held at the new manse with a committee showing visitors through and serving tea. One hundred dollars was set aside that day to help pay the manse debt. Quilters were very busy during that year and many quilting bees were held. Large quilts were sold for $10 to $12 and small ones for $8. Tickets were available and quilts were displayed in Golden's store.

In 1945, the W.A. had help in raising money as a slide show depicting scenes of Tobermory and a moving film of the local people was shown by two Port Huron men. Proceeds went to the W.A. In 1948, motion pictures including comedies and westerns were shown to benefit the W.A.

Weir Grieve loaned the ladies money in the early 1940's to pay for the building of a garage at the manse and frequent mention was made of paying him back $25 at a time until the debt was finally paid in 1944.

Although fish suppers were mentioned, it was really fowl suppers that seemed to be the most common with the ladies. The women gathered the day before to pluck the chickens, keeping the feathers for pillows. Try to envision the work in preparing for a supper in those days.

All the canvassing for food done on foot, very few had phones, and very few women drove cars even if there was one at home. Water had to be carried, wood stoves to be tended, and dishes to be brought.

In December, 1937, the ladies agreed to pay $100 towards the big loan at the manse and to try and raise $100 towards the home mission loan — it was indeed a most generous donation with many hours of labour involved.

Plays were popular money making projects produced locally and sometimes travelling to Clavering and Wiarton for half the profit. Social times and crokinole parties were held in the church while the library was usually the place for teas and small bazaars.

Several very faithful members throughout the years have kept the U.C.W. going. Margaret Golden has been an active member, going into her 50th year and president continuously for 19 of those years, and members such as Ethel Craigie — 39 years, Mary Davis — 35 years, and Kay Lyons — 29 years, have contributed greatly to the group.

In the war years most of the enlisted men were remembered with a handkerchief in a Christmas card. Another year, $2 was put in their cards and they were always remembered in prayers. Quilts were donated to the Red Cross and bales of clothing and home knitting sent west to help the farming families in the prairies who were suffering from the poverty that the dust bowl had wrought.

The Blue Cross Hospital plan was quite new at this time and was sponsored by the W.A. Mrs. Seely, an English nurse well remembered here, collected from the local subscribers. Later, other members, especially Mrs. O. Vail, took turns collecting the monthly dues.

On October 19, 1944, the minutes refer to a pot luck supper held to celebrate the 60th anniversary of the Harbour Church. At this dinner Mrs. Golden indicated that Martha Watson had been the first bride to be married in the Church. This announcement was followed by the story of Arthur Watson's wedding shirt. Apparently, a neighbour, feeling that Arthur should have a new shirt for his wedding, gave David Marwick some money and asked him to buy one in the city. Sure enough when David came back on his tug, he handed a very suitable shirt over to a grateful Arthur Watson.

U.C.W. Membership varied through the years with the most active period being from 1954 through the 1960's. With 32 ladies on the membership roll, 25 were attending on a regular basis. Even with this number, the meetings were held in the members' homes.

It was interesting to note the names on the membership roll. Most of the ladies of the village were on it at one time or another, but the names of Simpson, Belrose, Smith, Bartman, Golden, Leslie, McLeod, and Rae were consistently faithful.

One of the first customs created by the ladies was to place flowers in the church during the summer months. This custom is still carried out today. Much thought was given towards building a new church and, starting in 1945, the W.A. Group put $100 from time to time into a special building fund to remain untouched. This was finally used when the large extension of Sunday School rooms and kitchen were added. Most of the money raised by the W.A. was immediately turned over to the church treasurer as their funds were very low and a large grant had been received.

In the late 1940's, it became a custom to canvass the village for jams, jellies, fruit and pickles for the bazaars. Each member was expected to make up .25 cents worth of candy. Flower and sugar bags were bleached and made into lovely lunch cloths and pillow slips.

In the fall of 1950, the W.A. took on the responsibility of preparing for the mobile chest clinic. Much time was spent delivering and collecting information cards from each family in the community. By 1950, the W.A. was almost broke. Left with $2.91 in the treasury, the women had purchased a carpet runner for the aisle, curtains, plus quite a few other small items for the manse. As a result, they had no money left to donate to the Santa Claus fund, the Women's Missionary Society (W.M.S.), or the church building fund that year.

Insurance on the parsonage was paid by the ladies. $1,000 was carried on the contents and $1,500 on buildings. In 1953, $100 was donated to an organ fund and thoughts were turned to new pews. Nothing was done at this time as the floor needed attention first.

As well as helping to support the churches, the W.A. donated their money and efforts to: the Red Cross Society, the Muscular Dystrophy Fund, the Save the Children Fund, the Tobermory Santa Claus Day Fund, the Young People's Union and many other charities and good causes.

In 1961, the United Church suggested that the W.A. Groups should merge with W.M.S., so the Tobermory minister, Alfred Fry, held a meeting with the W.A. to explain the merger. In December of that year, it was decided that the two W.A.'s would operate as separate units but a central unit made up of women from both churches would meet at least six times per year. This new arrangement lasted until late in 1964 when the women requested that the president of the Presbyterial U.C.W. send a representative to Tobermory to advise them on how to dissolve the combined unit so that each group could operate as a distinct unit again.

A special concert was sponsored by the Harbour U.C.W. in 1962. Held in the Community Hall, the program consisted of Scottish songs and choruses, highland dancing, kilts, skits, and musical instrument selections all in honour of the anniversary of Robert Burn's birth.

In 1961, a well was drilled for the church using U.C.W. funds and, three years later, a woodshed was erected behind the church hall. The women purchased a new washing machine for the manse in 1965, and further small improvements were made on the building.

In May of 1981, the Bruce Presbytery ladies met at the Tobermory Harbour church. These 70 ladies attended a workshop on citizenship, leadership, and stewardship. Well attended by local women, this program included lunch at the Tobermory Lodge and teaching and learning through skits and dramas.

The U.C.W. had its beginnings in 1932 and ever since then it has been going on strong. Both the Harbour and Settlement groups still meet today and recently a group of younger women has been formed. As for the groups of the past, the ladies worked very hard and had many enjoyable times while being of great service to the churches and the community.

THE BAPTISTS

The first Baptist church meetings were held wherever it was convenient and conducted by students, just out of college, for the summer.

In 1898, the Baptists reported a busy summer and the following *Wiarton Echo* article expressed the Village's appreciation of their summer Baptist student.

"Our Baptist friends are having a farewell social in honour of Mr. Cross, the Baptist student, who has been laboring faithfully among us since spring. He will soon return to college, but he will not soon be forgotten in this part of the country where he has made many friends who will always be pleased to hear of his labor and success".

The Davis family, some of the original settlers of the area, were Baptists and therefore did what they could to support their church. Martha Watson recounts that one day Henry (Harry) Davis got into a bit of an argument with some local people about religion. He proudly told them, "I was born a Baptist, lived a Baptist and will die a Baptist". A woman nearby was overheard to say, "And you'll go to hell and burn up one too". Mr. Davis also believed in the baptism ritual in which one was totally immersed in water to purify the soul. A neighbour who had other ideas made it clear that he did not believe in all this. He explained that if you took a black pig, shoved it in the lake and pulled it out, it would still be a black pig — and the same applied to a bad man.

Baptist Church Ice Cream Social 1909.

The following informative excerpts were taken from the Tobermory section of the 1903 *Wiarton Echo* newspaper.

"The Baptist farewell social takes place on the church lawn on Friday, Sept. 11th, 03. A very pleasant time is expected. Mrs. Priest will sing, and favor us with some high-grade elocution. Some of her music pupils will take part. An interesting program is being prepared by our music teacher, and all are invited to enjoy the evening with us. Refreshments will be served.

The town has been favored with a visit from our semi-resident Mr. Neal Curry. The good man has evidently taken a dislike to Bachelor's Hall and has animated the solitude of the old homestead with the presence of his amiable better half assisted by Master Percy and his sister, Miss Sadie. The Baptist pastor and his wife enjoyed a hearty repast there which more than for the 'lunch' they failed to get during a former bachelor visit of our esteemed friend the Forest Bailiff''.

"The Rev. Mr. Priest will be leaving for Toronto on Sept. 16th, and we are glad to say that he will return next spring and remain the following winter. There will be a Baptist Church here in course of erection next spring''.

The newspaper article indicates that the erection of a Baptist Church was planned for the spring of 1904, however, an article written in 1901 suggests that there was a Baptist Church already standing. It was reported that Mr. Russell of the Latter Day Saints was preaching in the Baptist Church at that time. What kind of a church they had in 1901 is not known but it was certain that a Mr. Hayden was the Baptist preacher for the community that year.

The location of the Baptist Church was on the lot south of where the Health Centre now stands.

Tobermory Baptist Church 1920's.

THE CHURCH OF JESUS CHRIST OF LATTER-DAY SAINTS (THE MORMONS)

The Mormons were active in Tobermory from 1900 to the 1940's. Under the Tobermory section of *The Wiarton Echo*, the following article was printed.

1901 August — A Mormon preacher began a meeting on a log pile. After all his useless talk some of his followers became slightly angered over the spirited reception which we gave him.

A short while after the preacher came again but it was reported that he left after finding his work of no use. Near the end of August it was reported that:

"Mr. Russell, A Latter Day Saint, is preaching in the Baptist Church here. He continues his tirades in the Baptist Church against the various denominations and the authorized Bible".

The Presbyterian church watched the Mormons and reported in 1901 that:

"Mormonism has made determined efforts to proselytize the whole of the Peninsula, but so far has signally failed to get any members of adherents of the Presbyterian church".

As Martha Watson recalled, "people from the Latter Day Saints would come up to preach but there weren't many people up here who were that way inclined". This was not true of everyone, however, since in Tobermory the Mormons had the support of Benson Belrose and some of the Belrose family. Ben Belrose became a pastor and while living in Owen Sound, he would come up the Peninsula to preach for his brother Thomas's family. He also officiated at family funerals.

In 1914, *The Wiarton Echo* acknowledged the arrival of more visiting Mormons. Three followers of the Pastor Russell, who had preached in the Tub earlier, gave lectures and a slide show dealing with the history of the world since creation. They told the people that Armageddon would begin in 1915. The newspaper correspondent wrote: "the people of Tobermory are grateful for the warning".

A Sunday school made up mostly of Belrose children was quite active in the 1930's and early 1940's. William Rydall was superintendant of the Sunday school. On Christmas and Easter, special services were held and treats and toys given to the children.

As many of the Belrose family moved away or died off, the Mormons became greatly reduced in number. Since then, there has been no news of the Mormons and little is left to tell of their past.

ST. THOMAS CATHOLIC CHURCH

There were very few people of the Roman Catholic faith in Tobermory in the early days. Those wishing to attend mass had the choice of going to a church much further down the Peninsula or waiting for the priest to come to them. He would pay an occasional visit holding a service in one of the members' homes.

John Desjardine, a member of one of the two Catholic families in Tobermory at the time, remembers the hardships of worshipping in the days of no church. He tells of one crisp, Sunday morning excursion in the dead of winter. John and his family and the visiting priest struck out in a snowstorm for the wireless station where their service was to be held. These adventurous church-goer's expended much energy in breaking a trail but when their destination was reached and the service performed, all felt that it had been well worth the effort.

In the early 1930's, Father Labelle, a Jesuit Priest at Cape Croker decided to sponsor the building of a chapel at Tobermory. This was mainly for the convenience of the Roman Catholic summer tourists but it also was attended by the Desjardines. A little later the Weirs, the Woods and other local families joined. By 1936, the church was completed. Built by John Desjardine and Father Labelle, the St. Thomas Catholic Church stands in a convenient spot on top of a hill on Highway 6. Mrs. Scott remembers that during the building of the church she would often see Father Labelle up on the roof shingling it. As the people of the village passed by, they would look up and wave to the men who were hard at work there.

Father Labelle was the first clergyman to preach in the little church. Since then, there have been many other priests. One priest who was well liked and quite a familiar face to the parishioners was Father Dwyer, an energetic, enthusiastic man.

Many summer vacationers began to make their way to the little church. In 1939, the "S.S. Georgina" docked in the Big Tub for a short while in order to allow passengers to attend mass.

During the winters, services were still held in parishioners' homes as there was no heating in the church. Mass was celebrated each Sunday at 8 a.m., and then in 1958 a second mass at 8:30 a.m. was held. In the 1970's, when the Anglican Church was well established, they generously donated some communion cloths and pews to the Catholic Church.

John Desjardine, who was instrumental in the building of the church, has acted as its caretaker for many years. His family is one of the few Catholic families in an area that was settled by strict Scottish Methodists and Presbyterians.

St. Thomas Catholic Church 1940's.

1983.

ST. EDMUNDS ANGLICAN CHURCH

Before 1959, Tobermory was part of the Anglican Mission reaching out from Lion's Head. There were no Anglican services in Tobermory, so residents of that denomination had to travel to the Christ Church, Lion's Head, to attend services.

In 1958, the Bishop of Huron sent the Reverend James Horne, then rector at Lion's Head, to scout the St. Edmunds area to determine whether there was a need for an Anglican Church. From his report, the Bishop of Huron realized the need for a church and sent the Reverend Thomas Scott to St. Edmunds to establish one.

On Mr. Scott's arrival, he was given a residence at the back of Caroll Davey's vacant restaurant and the dining room was converted into a church for a short time. Before the Reverend T. A. Scott arrived, Mrs. Nona Scott, a resident of Tobermory, remembers trying to get the linens made on time for his arrival. After putting the large linen bolt in her car and coming back to Tobermory, she spent 11 days and nights making the linen cloths, completing them just on time for his arrival.

Services were held that summer in the converted restaurant. A bell was given to the church that summer but there was no church building and no steeple to put it in. A solution arose quickly, however, as Alex Holmes decided to put it outside the restaurant in its cradle and kick it, thus making it ring to call the members to the church.

That summer proved to be an interesting one for Mr. Scott and his family, for they had a house in which a tree grew in the middle of one of the bedrooms and extended out through the ceiling to the outside. As the winter came closer, the restaurant became inadequate as a church, as there was no heating. Meetings and services were then held at the Orange Hall, and sometimes in people's homes. The Scotts lived in Lion's Head for the winter and travelled to Tobermory for services.

The church that the Anglicans desired so much was completed in 1960. It had been designed by E. R. Kennedy and E. O. Erb. Mr. Erb was also instrumental in the construction of the building. Fred Lines was the chairman of the building committee, which also consisted of Mrs. J. D. Scott and Mrs. H. Arbuckle. The building's exterior was made of stained wood and large glass windows. The inside of the building was panelled and acoustic tiles were put up on the ceiling. Many of the furnishings were generously donated by the local people as well as several interested parties from outside the area.

A unique reredos (screen behind the altar) was donated to the church by Mr. H. Hamilton in memory of his father, Rev. T. J. Hamilton, who had also been the first teacher of the Village school in 1901.

The church in Purple Valley closed around 1959, so the Anglican Church in Tobermory inherited the organ and several other items from it.

The first service was held in the church in June, 1960, and a Chancel Guild was soon organized. Its tasks was to prepare for all the services and to keep the church clean. The members made all of the linens and hangings themselves.

The parish officers for the new church were: Deacon in Charge: Rev. Thomas Scott, Wardens: Mr. Stevens and Mr. Alex Holmes, Treasurer: Mrs. Carroll Davey, Secretary: Miss Dorothy McCoy, and Deacon in Residence: Rev. Wilfred Wright.

On July 17, 1960, the Service of Dedication of "The Church of St. Edmund" was held at 3 p.m. The church was filled to capacity that day and a public address system was fixed up to enable the overflow of people in the church grounds to hear the service. Clergymen attended from London, Paisley, Southampton and Owen Sound.

The Reverend W. Wright opened the service assisted by the choir and H. Oswel, organist and choirmaster from the Christ Church, Lion's Head. The Right Reverend G. N. Luxton, D. D. LL. D., Lord Bishop of Huron, dedicated the new church and told the story of St. Edmund the Martyr, after whom the church was named. The Archdeacon Carmen Queen presented a proclamation of the dedication to the church to be placed as its first document in the Archives of the Parish. Following the service, the Bishop's Reception and Tea was held at Mr. And Mrs. D. H. Stevens' summer residence.

Finally there was a church to serve the Anglican residents year round and the summer visitors of that denomination as well. Services were held at 11 a.m. and 7 p.m. each Sunday and the congregation consisted of about 12 resident families and a number of summer cottagers and visitors. In the winter, services were held about every two weeks.

The first year at the church there was no choir but there was a Sunday school program run for 23 or 24 children. Unfortunately, the Sunday school was discontinued when the Reverend T. A. Scott left late in 1964. In June of 1961, Christopher Derbyson was baptized by Mr. Scott, making him the first child to be baptized in the new church. Mr. Scott took the service that whole year round, although the customary practice was to have a deacon-in-residence hired for the summer months as was done the previous year.

An anniversary service was conducted on July 17, 1962, and many of the people who had attended the dedication service were back for the church's second anniversary. The new parish hall and the chaplain's residence was dedicated a year later. This new church cottage meant that the church could offer a summer residence to a clergyman and his family, free of charge in return for the leadership of two services each Sunday. Since that time, a clergyman has lived in the cottage and given services each summer from mid-June to mid-September.

In July of 1963, the Anglican Women's Association was organized with Mrs. E. H. Ralph as president. Throughout the next few years, the church women held bazaars, bake sales, and rummage sales; made quilts and participated in cleaning bees and various other activities.

In 1964 or 65, the Women's Association became the Anglican Church Women (A.C.W.) and joined with the Chancel Guild. This group still meets and is responsible for the orderly running of the church and for raising funds.

The Reverend D. L. Parker replaced the Reverend Thomas Scott as rector in 1965. That year the grounds around the church were landscaped and the Chancel Guild made new altar linens.

On June 12, 1971, the consecration of the church was held. This ritual celebrated the fact that in less than 12 years, the church was debt-free. This was quite an incredible feat considering the tiny membership. The Reverend Cuthbert Thomas was rector at the time and it was quite a ceremony to witness. After the Bishop had knocked thrice on the church doors, the wardens threw them open and welcomed him in. The Bishop then proceeded to go through the church asking a blessing on everything in it.

During the next 12 years, things proceeded smoothly with the Chancel Guild and the A.C.W. supporting the church. In 1984, the church will be celebrating its 25th anniversary. As Mrs. J. D. Scott says, "and that's only the first step"!

RECTORS OF THE CHURCH OF ST. EDMUND

Thomas A. Scott 1959-64, 1971-76
Douglas Llewellyn Parker 1964-68
Cuthbert W. Thomas 1968-71
Harry Brydon 1971-76
J. W. Seagram 1978-1984

St. Edmunds Anglican Church 1960's.

1983.

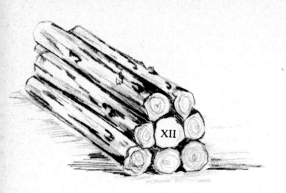

CHAPTER TWELVE

EDUCATION *in* ST. EDMUNDS

S. S. #1 SETTLEMENT SCHOOL

In 1875, the government of Scotland sent John Shearer from Glasgow, Scotland to Tobermory, Canada to teach the local fisherman the gill-net method of fishing. On his arrival, Mr. Shearer found that the Tobermory natives had already learned this craft from the Indians. As an alternative profession, Mr. Shearer chose to fulfill the educational needs of the community by teaching school. This was before the first log schoolhouse was built.

The first school meeting in St. Edmunds was held on April 28, 1880, to plan the building of a school. Michael Belrose, Jacob Belrose and Donald McDonald were appointed the first trustees and John Shearer became the first secretary-treasurer for the school board.

In 1882, a log school house was built on the corner of lot No. 46, Conc. 1, E. B. R. This twenty-four by eighteen foot building was made from squared logs which were plastered on the inside. It was built through contract with Donald McDonald and his son Alexander for $135. Many of the local settlers made the furnishings by hand. When complete, the school contained two rows of desks separated by a centre aisle, with places for four or five pupils at each desk. A blackboard was made of planed boards painted black.

Patrick Folkes indicates that Alexander Hay became the first teacher of the new log schoolhouse, but a school history written by a former teacher mentions only a Miss Ella Coglan teaching in 1882. Perhaps Alexander Hay taught for only a short period during that year and was replaced by Miss Coglan.

TEACHERS OF S. S. #1 —
LOG SCHOOLHOUSE 1882-1898

Mr. Alexander Hay ? (1882)	Miss Greenlees (1891- 1892)
Miss Ella Coglan (1882-1884)	Miss Trout (1892-1893)

Miss Astrope (1884-1885)	Miss Vance (1893-1895)
Miss McIvor (1885-1886)	Miss Glazier (1895)
Miss Kitty Couch (1886-1888)	Miss Watts (1895-1896)
Miss Greig (1888-1889)	Miss Ellis (1896)
Mr. Hawkins (1889)	Miss Fie (1897)
Miss Williams (1890-1891)	Miss Atton (1897)

By 1898, there were thirty-nine students attending classes in the little log schoolhouse. The building was soon considered inadequate because of its overcrowded conditions, and a new brick schoolhouse was built to replace it. The first board of trustees for the new school consisted of Robert Hopkins, Phillip Adams, and Andrew Belrose. Solomon Spears was the secretary-treasurer, and the first teacher was Ada Hay.

TEACHERS OF S. S. #1 —
BRICK SCHOOLHOUSE 1898-1965

Miss Leila Hay (1898-1900)	Miss Richards (1927-28)
Mr. W. G. McElhanvey (1901)	Miss Brown (1928)
Miss Halliday (1902-03)	Mr. Ray Hepburn (1929-30)
Miss Clark (1904-06)	Miss Switzer (1930-31)
Miss R. Crittenden (1907)	Mr. Roy Hatt (1931-42)
Miss McIvor (1907)	Mrs. Laura Piper (1942)
Miss Ashcroft (1907-08)	Mrs. R. Ackerman (1942-45)
Miss Burt (1908-1909)	Mr. Philip Fraser (1945-1946)
Mr. H. Carter (1909-1910)	Mrs. Alvenia Noble (1946-1952)
Mr. Cunningham (1910-1911)	Mr. M. Clark (1952-1953)
Mr. A. Richardson (1911)	Mrs. Alvenia Noble (1953-1958)
Miss Margaret Bartman (1911-1920)	Mr. William Muzzy (1958)
Miss McGillvary (1920-1921)	Mr. J. Mellor (1958-1959)
Mr. J. J. McKenna (1921-1922)	Mrs. Poore (1959-1960)
Miss C. Campbell (1922-1923)	Mr. G. Grant (1960-1962)
Miss M. Harries (1923-1924)	Miss Yvonne Bain (1962-1963)
Miss Abercrombie (1926-1927)	Mr. Loren Newman (1963-1964)
	Mr. Hieuvain (1963-1965)

Being in a central position of the Settlement community, the school hall was also used for purposes other than education. The first meeting of the first Township Council was held in the school on January 12, 1903, and the Council continued to meet there for years after that. In 1903, the Council paid the school board .50 cents per meeting, which came to a total of $5.50 for that year.

Leila Hay 1899.

Education in the early 1900's was pretty well restricted to the basics: reading, writing, arithmetic and a combination of history and geography. During recess the children were encouraged to play ball or join some form of activity, although most of them needed no en-couragement. In 1909, the Settlement boys sent off for a new football and later that year they had a match with some Toronto boys.

Borden Hopkins remembers that a favourite activity in his school days was to run upstairs to the upper storey window, stand on a stool, grab on to the flag pole and slide down it. This was usually done while the teacher was having her lunch and often 10 to 15 boys would go down, one behind the other.

In those days there was no kindergarten as school age was 8 to 14 years. Some children went to Lion's Head to try their grade 8 exams and, if successful, they might continue to grade 10 in the Village school. Soon after finishing school at the age of 12, 13 or 14, most boys would be out working and the girls would be preparing for marriage.

Enforcing school attendance was not an easy job back then and a lot of school days were missed. Often children would stay at home to help with farm or house chores when needed. Snow storms and the occasional sickness took their toll on school attendance and there were always children who just chose to take the occasional day off. In 1922, Marmaduke Vail was appointed school attendance officer for both school sections. For this service he was paid an annual salary of $25.

Class of 1901

S.S. No. 1, 1906.

In the early 1900's, the number of pupils enrolled each year generally fluctuated between 16 and 31. In 1922, the school began accepting students from the ages of 8 to 16 years instead of limiting it to 14 years. The age range was extended further to include children 5 to 18 years old in 1923, but, oddly enough, that year saw an enrollment of only 12 children. The next year enrollment more than doubled and started a steady increase of pupils into the 1930's.

In 1928, Miss Brown was hired at a salary of $87.50 per month to teach 44 pupils from grades one through eight. In October she received a raise of .02 cents per month. The pressure of this situation apparently took its toll on her as she was replaced in December by Ray Hepburn after suffering a nervous breakdown. The board must have wanted Mr. Hepburn to stay as he received a salary of $900.00 that year. The caretaker at that time, Mrs. J. C. Dean, received only $8.50 per month, even though several new duties were added to her job.

The boards of the two schools were busy in the 1930's as the depression years had begun. The boundaries for the two school sections were changed in 1930 to equalize the assessments. A row of lots had been loaned to S. S. #2 by S. S.#1 and, as the term expired, they were given back to S. S. #1. As money grew scarce, the board tried to keep expenses down while trying to accommodate an increasing number of students and trying to improve the school building and grounds.

Roy Hatt began teaching at S. S. #1 in 1931. He taught close to 40 children for the Depression-hit salary of $808.50 in 1933. Improvements were made when a government grant of $539.35 was received by S. S. #1. A frame woodshed was built by contract with Mr. T. Spears and cement steps and an iron railing were put in to replace the old plank platform. Barney Hopkins and T. Spears strengthened the floor of the hall above the school by adding new posts and a long beam.

Upkeep of the school was always a major concern. In 1926, the total expenditure for repainting and repairing the school ran as high as $203.75-1/2. One gallon of paint cost $5.25 and the painters were paid .30 cents an hour. For $40 a school bell was also bought.

In the early years, regular maintenance was provided by people hired for each particular task such as lighting fires or scrubbing and cleaning. Agnes Belrose was one of these individuals as she swept the school for a pay of $1.50 a month in 1927. In 1928 tenders were posted up calling for a caretaker for the school. The duties were to include lighting the fires, ringing the bell at a quarter to nine and sweeping and scrubbing the building.

A committee of two was organized in 1928 to select books from the T. Eaton company, Toronto at a cost of $9.15, while another order from the Educational Publications Company cost $1.10.

Of particular importance to the health and, indirectly, the education of the children was the health nurse. As far back as the early twenties, a nurse would come to the school once or twice a year to check the children's teeth and eyesight. Borden Hopkins was one of those to benefit from this program as a nurse discovered his short-sightedness and he received glasses when he was about 11 years old, thereby ending his days of having to sit at the front of the classroom.

1920

Class of 1928

In the spring of 1937, the first school garden was made. In the fall of that year, part of the platform in front of the school was removed, allowing another row of seats to be put in to accommodate the 40 students attending classes. Septic tanks for inside toilets were installed in the porch in 1938.

In 1939, Roy Hatt established the first class in manual training in the Township. A workbench and a cupboard for tools were built in the hall above the school and manual equipment was purchased.

During Mr. Hatt's term, the Women's Association held tea and crokinole meetings in the school. They were to pay .50 cents per meeting and supply their own wood for the fire, or they could scrub the hall once a month for a refund of their money.

In 1941, Mr. Hatt's salary was $950 and he taught 32 children. This was his last year at the Settlement school as he moved to the Village school the next year.

The I.O.D.E. Owen Sound (a women's group) "adopted" the school in 1942 and supplied it with Christmas presents, paint and patches for craft work and home economics. Music was taught in 1942 by Mr. Harold Bruin.

School enrollment during the 1940's remained relatively stable, usually between 31 and 36 pupils. Teachers' salaries increased each year starting at $950 in 1941 and jumping to $2,000 by 1948. Mrs. Alvenia Noble, who taught at the school for 11 years, received $1,294 in 1946 and just seven years later she received a salary of $2,400 plus $400 car allowance.

A. J. Watson was appointed truant officer for S. S. #1 for the year 1943. In 1944, the greatest number of school days lost was due to children helping at home. The second greatest cause of absence was due to what was termed "parental neglect", and last of all there was the occasional illness.

1945 was the year that the school first acquired an electric lighting system. Art classes were introduced and art supplies were bought. Also that year, Miss Ada Hay, the first teacher of the brick schoolhouse, died at the age of 89.

The Settlement school accommodated students from grades 1 to 8 only and pupils wishing to attend grades 9 and 10 were sent to the Village school. In 1945, however, the Village school was overcrowded and thus the Settlement students wishing to continue school were refused.

In September of 1947, the first school "open house" was held. Parents, friends and the pupils themselves attended and inspected the students workbooks, notebooks and crafts. The pupils put on a program and a talk on education was given by the minister. A bazaar and fish pond brought in $25 which was given to the Board to aid in the purchase of a piano for the school.

The fiftieth anniversary of the brick school was held on November 12, 1948. Present pupils, former pupils, teachers and community members attended. Mr. Clarence Spears was chairman of the program which included songs, reminiscences of former students and community members, several selections by the Adams Orchestra and a skit put on by the ladies. After the program, lunch was

Settlement School, S.S. No. 1, St. Edmunds, June 1, 1939.

Front Row: **Bert Munn, Norman Leonard, Raymond Adams, Gerald Belrose, Howard Hopkins, David Hyde, Bruce Hopkins.**
Second Row: **Lloyd Adams, Herbie Belrose, Tom Adams, Glen Adams, Melvin McArthur, Ray Hopkins, Levi Wyonch, Brant Watson.**
Third Row: **Gladys Hopkins, Doreen Lambkin, Margaret McArthur, Dora Wyonch, Dorothy Watson, Donna Belrose, Christena Watson, Loraine McArthur, Marjorie Bartley.**
Top Row: **Flora Watson, Sheila McArthur, Gladys McArthur, Myrtle Wyonch, Roy Hatt (Teacher), Grace Watson, Marie Bartley, Winona Munn, Cora Wyonch.**

served in the hall upstairs and R. A. Hopkins, the oldest man present, lit the fifty candles on the birthday cake made by Mrs. John Masterson. Mrs. Issac Hopkins, one of the first pupils of the school, blew all 50 candles out in two breaths. The visitors book was signed by all the guests, using gold ink.

Five hundred dollars was borrowed from the Royal Bank on demand note in 1950 providing the funds for the building of an inside stairway. This stairway, built in the cloak room by Mr. Earl Lamkin, provided an easier exit in case of fire and made the upstairs room more accessible and easier to supervise.

J. F. Wismer, sanitary inspector for North Bruce, drew attention to the overcrowded condition of the school in April of 1951. In September of that year there was an enrollment of 39 pupils, the same number as the year before. There was only one classroom in use as the hall above was not used regularly.

In 1952, the Board of Education wanted the Tobermory school boards to join together to create one board.

This started some dissension among the ratepayers of S. S. #1. S. S. #3 would not lose anything from this venture as they did not own a school and would pay nothing to join. S. S. #2 would lose nothing because, although they had to contribute their school, it had been given to them in the first place. S. S. #1 did lose, because they had to hand over the school and the property, plus the mill rate (the amount of money put towards schools and other services based on a person's property assessment) was increased. Besides all this, as the school tax went up, the grants that the government gave, went down.

Overcrowding was still a problem in 1953, so the board had an addition built to the school. An electric light was also installed above the entrance door.

In 1954, an Easter Tea and Bazaar was held in the school and the $70 raised went to finance an educational trip to Toronto for the pupils. Two years later, a tea and bazaar was held to provide funds for a trip to Niagara Falls.

Through the early fifties overcrowding had been a problem, but by 1959 only 21 students enrolled at the Settlement school. Enrollment remained low until 1962 when the pupils from S.S. #3, who had formerly attended the Village school, were transferred to the Settlement school, bringing enrollment up to 36 students. Cleveland Adams was given the bus contract for transporting the S. S. #3 pupils. In preparation for the new students, the school's interior was painted and ten new desks and seats were added during the summer of 1962. As the school board required a new teacher for the 1962 school year, a newspaper advertisement was submitted to various papers. It is interesting to note that the board stipulated that the teacher had to be a protestant. Two years later when the search for a teacher was again underway, this stipulation was not stated.

In 1963, the rest of the school's interior was painted and a new oil furnace was installed. It was also during that year that a measles outbreak ripped through the school sending thirty-one of the thirty-five students home.

Early in 1965, it was announced that the school S. S. #1 was to be closed. At school board meetings, various discussions were held to determine what was to be done with the schoolhouse. It was suggested that the school should be turned into a museum, but this suggestion was met with ridicule as many felt that the community didn't have enough exhibits to fill it. A petition was passed around the community and was then passed on to the school board. After further discussion, it was decided that the building should be returned to the people who had been educated in it by turning it into a museum. As a museum, it would still be used for education by teaching people about St. Edmunds' past. It was felt that this was a much more fitting purpose for the building than turning it over to the Bruce County Board of Education.

In 1965, the sixty-nine year old building was officially closed and students were sent to the Village school.

In 1967, Canada's Centennial Year, the Settlement School was opened as a museum and is now devoted to preserving artifacts that help to tell the story of the pioneers in St. Edmunds Township.

S. S. #2 THE VILLAGE SCHOOL

Children living near the harbour had a fair walk if they wished to attend the school in the late 1800's. To remedy this situation, the Reverend Cole taught school from 1898 to 1900 to children aged 6 to 20 years in the Harbour Methodist Church.

As more and more settlers moved into the harbour area of St. Edmunds, a need was felt for a local school. In 1900, a one room school was built just a short distance from the Little Tub Harbour. The building of the school was all done by the residents of the area free of charge, and, as the "Wiarton Echo" states, by June of 1900, "the new schoolhouse at the Tub (was) ready for the lath and plaster". By late July it must have been near completion because the Liberal Association held a meeting in the building and the next month, a concert was held there with a profit of $15 reported.

The Harbour school opened its doors to the village children in 1901 and C. J. Hamilton became its first teacher at a salary of $300 a year. Some of the early teachers included: Stacey Gander, Vina Shanch, Hank Carter, Mr. McCartney (a magistrate who had lost his arm in the war), E. R. Copeland, Miss A. Neely, Mr. Anderson, and Miss Ada McKenzie.

During Mr. Hamilton's term as a teacher, he was invited to sail with Mr. Jon Vaughan to Flowerpot. Unfortunately, they were shipwrecked on Plucky Island and it was over twenty four hours before they were rescued by a passing tugboat.

The number of children enrolled each year during the early 1900's ranged between twenty-five and forty-seven. As there was no required starting age, some children started school when they were five years old, and others did not start until they were seven or eight.

Outdoor activities and the odd prank added much to the children's schooldays. One prank that the boys thought was great fun was soaping the windows of the school — that was until they were caught in the act and made to clean all of the school's windows! In 1909, it was reported that the girls were allowed to join in the baseball games played in the field behind the schoolhouse.

By 1922, the school began accepting children who were eight to sixteen years old. This ruling increased the number of students to fifty-three that year. Marmaduke Vail was appointed as the school's attendance officer, a post he held until the late 1940's. The age range was changed again in 1923, and now included all those who were five to eighteen years old. This new age range increased the enrollment to sixty-three and consequently a new wing was added to the school as the "senior room". By 1925, three teachers were needed to teach the sixty-six students, these were Bert Wiggins (principal), Gladys Van Horne, and Ada McKenzie.

Vina Schaunch and some of her school students 1910.

119

S.S. No. 2, St. Edmunds, 1911.

Left to right, First Row: David Vail, Oscar Smith, George Simpson, Willard Currie, Teacher Miss A. Neely, Marion Matheson, Minerva Golden, Kate Smith, Beatrice McLeod, Margaret McLeod, Louisa Butchart, Tena Simpson, Bella Craigie.
Second Row: Reta Smith, Cora Butchart, Mabel Young, Kathleen Smith, Maretta Belrose, Irene Craigie, Laura Ransbury, Elizabeth McLeod, Mae Smith, Mildred McLeod, Alice Hodge.
Third Row: Bertha Belrose, Viney Martin, Vera Vail, Bessie Glendillion, Helen Glendillion, Marguerite Harkness, Pearl Craigie, J. B. Craigie, Lauchlan McIver, George Smith, Reg Craigie, Johnnie Ransbury, Harold Young, Don McIver, Albert Leslie.
Fourth Row: Wellington Vail, Ivor McLeod, Neil McIver, Wallace Simpson, Kyle Murphy, Marguerite Simpson, Ruby Smith, Pearl Smith, Elena McLeod, Helen Murphy, Katherine Leslie, Elizabeth Smith, Dorothy Smith, Bill Ransbury, Martin Young.

Bert Wiggins (principal) 1925.

Education past Grade Eight was not of great importance to the early settlers as most children had to work with their parents and learn their skills and trades. The end of formal education usually came around twelve to fourteen years of age. Children who had been working before and after school at farm chores, fishing, or shopkeeping, took these tasks up full time. For the very few students who wanted to further their education, the nearest highschool was in Wiarton, and the only transportation was the once-a-week passenger steamer or the stage that carried the mail to towns on the southern Peninsula.

In September of 1930, Ray Hepburn came to teach at the Village school after having spent one year at the Settlement school. Besides being principal of the three room school, he taught grades 6 to 10 and industrial arts for a salary of $900 a year. In 1933, the government required that all teachers recently graduating return to teacher's college for one more year's training. Mr. Hepburn thus returned to college and Ward Agnew replaced him for that year. Mr. Hepburn returned in 1934

Junior Room 1927

and continued his work until 1943, supplementing his income by acting as purser on the ferry. He remembers that there were often long line ups for the ferry and sometimes tourists would try to bribe him for a place near the head of the line. He never took the bribes, not even the $20 that he was once offered, and that was a lot of money in those days. At other times, Mr. Hepburn would become a commercial fisherman to pull in an extra bit of money. Besides taking extra jobs, he joined the hockey group that played on the harbour ice, and in the summer he pitched ball for the local softball team, often travelling with them down the Peninsula for a game. Days were packed full of activity, and, as Mr. Hepburn says, "We used to get up at 4 a.m. to lift the nets and in the evenings pitched ball in the Park Head-Hepworth area". Other teams were not too fond of Mr. Hepburn because he had a tendency to strike their batters out. This same ability lead him to be named "Beautiful Curve Heppy" by his own team-members.

Back then there were separate school boards for both of the schools. The board for the Village school was made up of three or four local men including the school principal. James Rae, the local barber, happened to be on the board, so often meetings were held in his little barber shop.

Most of the students were very capable. Mr. Hepburn remembers that "there was a healthy type of rivalry in those days among families". This rivalry was sometimes extended between schools as the village children called the Settlement students "Country Hay Seeds", and the settlement population returned the retort by calling the village kids "Harbour Fish Guts".

The schoolday started at a quarter to nine when the principal rang the bell and it ended at exactly 4 o'clock. In the early 1930's, subjects included the basic skills of reading, writing and mathematics. The children sat in their grade sections and while Mr. Hepburn taught one grade, the others did assignments at their desks. Recess was a fun part of the day when the children could play softball at their ball diamond. Religion was taught in the school, sometimes by the principal and sometimes by the minister. An exciting event for most of the children was the annual Christmas concert. Plays, recitals and singing were performed by the children for their parents and other community members.

Each year, a school inspector would make a visit to the school and write up a report about what he saw. It was customary for the inspector to get up and teach a lesson as a good example for the teacher. On one occasion the inspector made an error while teaching math and Mr. Hepburn quietly whispered the correct answer in his ear. Needless to say, Mr. Hepburn was not entirely impressed by the example set for him. One inspector, a Mr. Wilson, was amazed at Mr. Hepburn's well-structured class organization and asked for a copy of his schedule to use as an example elsewhere. One of the teachers, Isabel Smith, remembers Mr. Wilson as a pleasant fatherly type, unlike most of the inspectors. She remembers a Mr. Smith who was a "horrible smiley man". He would sit at the back of the room assessing everything with a constant grin. There were times, she recalled, when she would have liked to have thrown a book at him.

Mr. Smith was not the only inspector to lend a tense atmosphere to the school. Mr. John McCool was another such man who visited every school on the Peninsula, on his bike! He had a reputation as being a rather cross fellow — even the children were afraid of him. Margaret Hepburn recalls that she was late for school once and as she climbed over the fence on her way there, she heard Mr. McCool yelling from the school yard. She turned around right there and then and ran all the way home. When she returned in the afternoon, Mr. McCool, who had watched her run away, took her aside and scolded her for not coming to school. Mrs. Hepburn can still remember shaking in her boots. In 1932, Mr. McCool retired after 26 years of being an inspector.

Isabel Bain came to teach in the village in 1933. She was fresh out of college and remembers that the road up the Peninsula was hilly and rough, but when she got to Tobermory, she found it quite a pleasant place and not at all like what she had been told to expect. The Toronto school board had forewarned her that she would have to travel by dog sled and that it was a rather primitive village, but she felt quite at home almost immediately. She took up residence at Mrs. Vail's boarding house and says today that she couldn't have found a better place to live. It was quite a shock to the community, but especially to Miss Bain, when the place burned down and Mrs. Vail died in the fire.

During her first year here, she taught kindergarten and the primary grades in a sun room at the back of Andrew Belrose's store. Later the class was moved to the Orange Hall for several years until a new addition was built on to the school and her students moved there.

Kindergarten activities included: counting, the alphabet song, nursery rhymes, stories, games, crafts, a bit of reading and nature walks. When Isabel married Lloyd Smith in the early 1940's, he would come in to the classroom to play the guitar and sing songs for the little ones. The Children in grades 1 to 3 were taught reading, math, science and social studies (a new subject including bits of local history and geography).

In 1944, Isabel Smith took six years off to raise her son. When she returned to teaching she was given 21 beginners. This large class consisted of grades 1 to 3 only as kindergarten had been discontinued in the late thirties.

Mrs. Smith remembers that two-day teachers' conventions were held annually in a big city such as Toronto, Hamilton or Owen Sound. These were interesting meetings as formal and informal discussions were held concerning curriculum, discipline and other relevant issues. Outings were often made to different schools to observe.

By the late 1930's, music was being taught in the schools. Mr. Thorne was one of the first music teachers who would visit the school occasionally. In May of 1939, Tobermory's first school childrens' Music Festival was held. School children from Dyers Bay, Brinkman's

Junior Room, Tobermory, June 11, 1939.

Junior Room 1939.

Left to Right, Front Row: **Ronald Butchard, Lorance McFarlane, Lynn Golden, Dennis Hepburn, Jack Carver and George Wipp.**
Second Row: **Charles Smith, Willard Currie, Claude McFarlane, Bruce Adams, Kenneth Austin, Ronald Barber, and Keith Austin.**
Third Row: **Loyais Wyonch, Donna Ransbury, Carol Hepburn, Betty Rumley, Amelia DesJardine, June Smith, Glenda Hopkins and Bessie Currie.**
Top Row: **Jane Vail, Ruth Hopkins, Jeanne Craigie, Shirley Smith, Teacher Mrs. Lloyd Smith (Bain), Selena Smith, Betty Young, Joyce Adams, and Dona Chisholm.**

Corners and the two Tobermory schools gathered in the Community Hall for choruses, duets and solos. Music teachers that came after Mr. Thorne included Harold Bruin, Mrs. Jean Smith and Mr. Smart.

Also in 1939, the school ratepayers met and the Reverend McKnight led a discussion on Bible teaching in the schools. By 1941, his successor, the Reverend J. N. Clarry, was giving 15 minutes of religious instruction once a week in each school room.

The children of the Harbour school, with encouragement from their principal, contributed much to the war effort. In 1941, they raised $7.56 for the Navy League of Canada, and in 1942, school principal Ray Hepburn reported that:

> "from the beginning of the war to June, 1942, the children of the Harbour school in their War effort have invested in War Saving Stamps, Certificates and Victory Bonds to the amount of $426.63 and have donated $24.25 in cash to the British War Victims' Fund and the Navy League and $3.25 to the Red Cross."

By 1943, Mrs. Isabel Smith was teaching home economics and practical shop as well as the primary grades. When she left in 1945, an ad was placed in the Wiarton Echo asking for a "Protestant teacher for Junior room in a three-room school. Kindergarten, primary and home economics certificate prefered." That year, in June, the school inspector reported that progress had been made in music, manual training, home economics, art and religious instruction. In October, more equipment was purchased for manual training and home economics.

The 1940's saw more children furthering their education, some even going to the Lion's Head Continuation School which now accommodated students of grades 11 and 12.

In September of 1945, there was an overcrowding in the Harbour school, so the Settlement students wishing to attend grades 9 and 10 at the Harbour were unable to do so. Over 100 pupils attended the school but the overcrowded condition was somewhat relieved by the laxity in pupils' attendance. This was considered a problem rather than a help and the principal suggested that a new truant officer was needed — preferably one who lived in the village and could be contacted during, or immediately after, school hours.

In November, Education Week was celebrated. At the end of the week, parents, teachers and pupils gathered at the Village school. The Reverend Arrol spoke on "The

Relation of Religion to Education" and he advised parents to make sacrifices for their children's education.

Because overcrowding was still a problem in 1946, the trustees passed a motion stating that only pupils who were 5 years old or who would be 5 by the end of the year could enrol in September. In February of that year, the board changed the heating system in the school by replacing the wood burning stove with coal-burning ones.

Miss De LaPort visited the school in June to examine the children's eyesight, hearing, speech and physical health. Reports were sent to parents and a general report to the school board. Cleanliness was sometimes a problem in the school and Albert Smith remembers that the teacher would check under shirt collars to make sure that the children bathed occasionally.

Albert Smith, a Tobermory schoolboy in the 1940's and chairman of the Bruce County Board of Education in 1978-79, says that attendance during the winter was not too much of a problem as the school was often the warmest place in the community. The trick was to sit in the middle of the room as it was too hot by the stove and too cold in the corners. During warmer weather, children would miss school at seeding time and the village boys might miss some school to help their fathers with the fish nets.

The whole community operated by the school bell especially when it came time for lunch. As soon as the bell rang, people would put aside their work and break for lunch. It is said that a man, building the Wheildons' home, was nailing the floor down and had just started hammering a nail in when the school bell rang. Wasting no time, he pulled the nail out, laid it on the ground and hurried off to lunch. The biggest problem with the school bell was that the rope would would often come off the pulley. It was a great honour to the senior boys to be given the task of putting it back on.

The boys were full of pranks in those days. Albert Smith remembers one that would sometimes backfire. Some of the boys got to school a bit early in the mornings and would proceed to stuff burlap sacks down the chimney so that when the fire was lit, the schoolroom filled with smoke. Sometimes school would be cancelled because of this, but the teacher soon caught on and made the students sit in the cold, smoke-filled room until someone would admit to doing it and go up on the roof to take the sacks out of the chimney.

Disciplining the children was a challenge to many a teacher. Mabel Davis tells of a couple of incidents that occurred when Brad Davis was a child. Mabel says that Brad was pretty smart in school and he would get his work finished quickly and then proceed to tease and rile the other children. The teacher wrote a note home to Mrs. Davis explaining the problem. Mrs. Davis simply wrote back in reply "Don't you have a strap?" The next teacher solved the problem by keeping him in after school.

When the primary grades were taught in the Orange Hall, Mrs. Davis used to sweep the floor there after

school. One night she came in and found the teacher tied to a chair. She untied the poor woman and soon discovered that her youngest son had had something to do with it!

July, 1947, found the outside trimmings of the school painted and a cupboard built to hold art supplies. More home economics and manual training supplies were bought and in September, alterations were made to the main school building to enable home economics training to be carried out there. Previously, these classes had been held in the Orange Hall.

Thirty Tobermory schoolchildren had the time of their young lives in 1947, when their teacher, Mrs. Wright, took them to Toronto one weekend in October. They visited the Eaton's Young Street and College Street stores, Casa Loma, the Royal Ontario Museum, saw the motion picture "Fantasia", and heard the Don Cossacks at Massey Hall.

The board decided to buy an electric sewing machine for the school in 1947, and later the Home Economic class gave a tea at the school for their mothers and the Board members' wives. Samples of the girls' weaving, knitting and sewing were proudly displayed.

In November of 1947, the school board granted a holiday on the occasion of Princess Elizabeth's wedding day.

In 1948, the board of S. S. #2 considered the possibility of building a combined new school to serve all Tobermory children. After receiving a letter from the Department of Education outlining the procedures to be followed, the board reconsidered and decided instead to erect an addition to the old schoolhouse in 1949. To this end, Council authorized the borrowing of $20,000, and when the addition to the school was completed in the early fifties, the primary grades were moved into the main school building.

Dentists visited the school to check the pupils' teeth and in October of 1952, the schools drinking water was tested. It was found to be good and the authorities proclaimed that it contained "just the right amount of flourine for the prevention of tooth decay".

In June of 1957, St. Edmunds Council requested that Bruce County Council form a high school area comprising of St. Edmunds, Lindsay, Lion's Head and Eastnor.

The village school discontinued grades 9 and 10 for the school year 1958-59 and in 1959 the Bruce Peninsula and District High School in Lion's Head was built. By 1960, about 35 St. Edmunds pupils were attending the high school and the next year it rose to 40.

The 1960's saw a number of changes occur in the population of the school and some small improvements made to the school building. The school lobbies were repainted in 1960, and in 1962 the floor, walls, inside pipes and outside trimmings of the school were repainted. The S. S. #3 pupils, those living south of the 35th sideroad,

S.S. No. 2 1927

S.S. No. 2 1950's

S.S. No. 2 1983

had, for many years, attended the Harbour school. In 1962, they were transferred to the Settlement school, decreasing the Harbour school enrollment by at least ten.

Mabel Davis, long time caretaker, resigned from her position in 1964 and a salary of $600 a year was offered to anyone interested in the post.

A Township School Board was formed in 1964 and by 1965 it was announced that the Board would close two of the Township schools and transport the students to S. S. #2. The two schools were to be boarded and padlocked until it was decided what would be done with them. The contract to operate a school bus was awarded to A. J. Watson who was to bring the children to S. S. #2 from as far away as 29 miles.

That September, S. S. #2 saw an enrollment of 101 pupils, an increase of 33 from the previous year. Mr. Poore resigned because of ill health and Roy Hatt took over as principal and teacher of grades 6, 7 and 8.

During the previous summer, the school had been made ready for this sudden influx of students. New fire exit doors had been installed and new drinking fountains had been put in as well as general repairs made to the building. In October, plans were made to renovate the girls' lavatory facilities and the board announced that they were well-satisfied with the punctuality of the bus service. The bus driver's income had just recently been increased by $48 per month due to the extra mileage going into Cameron Lake and Dorcas Bay.

The Bruce Peninsula School was formed in 1967 and the school at St. Edmunds came under the jurisdiction of the County Board. The next year only grades one to 5 were taught as children attending further grades were bused to Lion's Head.

On Mrs. L. Smith's retirement in 1967, she was given a surprise party in the Community Centre, and later the board presented her with a chair and honoured her at a banquet. Many people were sorry to see her retire as the community was very fond of her.

Early in 1969, the Bruce County Board of Education recommended that a half-day Kindergarten class be established at the St. Edmunds Public School. Therefore, in September of that year, the Kindergarten program began, and Grades One to Six were also taught there. Students in higher grades were bused to Lion's Head where a greater number of educational facilities were available.

It was also in 1969 that the reeve, J. P. Johnstone, and a number of other reeves from the Peninsula wrote to the Minister of Education, William Davis, and complained about the high levels of education taxes that landowners in this area were forced to pay. These men felt that the schools in this area did not have the facilities of the schools in the southern portion of Bruce County, but

sixty-four percent of the landowners' taxes was spent on education — far more than what was paid by landowners in other areas. The reeves suggested that the matter of taxes be closely examined and the rates readjusted to reflect the incomes of the people who lived in the northern Peninsula area.

St. Edmunds was again angered by the Bruce County Board of Education in 1973 when the Board demanded a payment of $74,000.00 from St. Edmunds. This sum represented an increase of 31.6 percent from the previous year whereas the rest of the county only had a 3 percent increase. In the end, it was decided that the township would pay $60,000.00 rather than the $74,000.00 requested.

In 1978, Roy Hatt retired after thirty-eight years of teaching. A surprise party was held for this well-loved man and the school children put on a program entitled "A Tribute to Mr. Hatt". Three months later, the community mourned Mr. Hatt's death. Mr. Hatt had held various posts in the community as well as being a teacher. In 1947, he had been elected vice president of the North Grey and North Bruce Teachers' Institute, and in 1948 he became the president of that organization.

Throughout the 1970's and 1980's, the school children were involved in a number of money raising events. Some of the funds from these events went into bus trips and some were sent to charities. Funds were even raised for the Terry Fox Marathon of Hope.

Renovations were to be made on the school in 1979, but an informal agreement between the Bruce Board of Education and St. Edmunds to put off these renovations as plans for a new school were in the works. These plans for a new school still exist, but the building of the school has been pushed further into the future.

Photos from 1980 school reunion.

Former School Teachers, Gladys Wright, Ray Hepburn, Isabel Smith

Percy Adams and oldest surviving school teacher, Mrs. Beatty.

Front Row, Left to Right: **Donna (Ransbury) Taylor, Carol (Hepburn) Bolton, Dona (Chisholm) LaFontaine, Amelia (Desjardine) Golden, Betty (Rumley) Farrow.**
Back Row: **Joyce (Adams) Ryan, Jane (Vail) Howell, Ron Barber, Ruth (Hopkins) Lambert, Shirley (Smith) Hopkins, Isabel Smith, Oriel (Murray) Munroe, Loyais (Wyonch) Golden.**

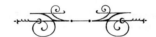

Front Row, Left to Right: **Ron Barber, Lorraine (Ransbury) Costello, T. A. Golden, Peter Golden.**
Back Row: **Muriel (Hopkins) Scott, Joan (Spears) McGrath, Viola (Watson) Adams, Hilda (Hopkins) Jorgensen, Iona (Currie) Wilson, Mrs. Wright, Jacqueline (Smith) Hopkins.**

Sitting: **Laura (Ransbury) Ritchie.**
Left to Right: **Albert Leslie, Ruby (Smith) Leslie, Dorothy (Smith) Ransbury, Pearl (Smith) Chisholm, Gordon Hopkins, Daisy (Dean) Hopkins.**

Front Row, Left to Right: **Orma (Spears) Brown, Jacqueline (Smith) Hopkins, Lorraine (Ransbury) Costello, Margorie (McFarlane) Bartley, Minerva (Hopkins) Lees, Jean (McFarlane) Hewitt, Shirley (Carver) Longe.**
Second Row: **Britain Belrose, Arthur Martin, Kay (Hopkins) Lyons, Bettie (Martin) Smith, Everitt Young, Everitt Smith.**
Back Row: **Tom Hopkins, Denelda (McFarlane) Smith, Jim Rumley, John Hopkins, John Adams, Ray Hepburn, Ernie Adams, Jim Adams, Archie Currie, Jack Barber.**

Front Row, Left to Right: **Marie (Hyde), Myrtle (Wyonch) Craigie, Donna (Belrose) Wood, Lynda (Belrose) Greig, Lloyd Adams, Lorraine (McArthur) Hoey, Ruth (Spears) Howitt, Betty (Hatt) Adams.**
Back Row: **Bud Davis, Flora (Watson), Eva (Watson) Carson, Marie (Hopkins) Price, Violet (Watson), R. M. ''Jiggs'' McArthur, Gerald Belrose, Herbie Belrose, Gladys (Hopkins) Wright, Viola (Watson) Adams.**

Class of 1910

Back Row, Left to Right: Jean Young, Maggie (Matheson) Leslie, Reta (Leslie) Menary, Francis (Cassell) Roger, Mattie (Young) Hopkins, Clara "Ted" (Young) Tetley, Tina (Smith) Lauton, Maggie Culbert, Willard Currie, John MacLeod, Gordon McLeod, Danny Butchard, George Simpson, Tina Simpson, ?.
Second Row: Irene ?., May Smith, Marion (Matheson) McLeod, Albert Leslie, Edgar Culbert, Don McIver, Harold Young, J. B. Craigie, Wallace Simpson, Laochlin McIver, Marguerite Hartness, Lizzie (MacLeod) Rae, Laura (Ransbury) Ritchie, Reta Smith.
Front Row: Kate Smith, Louisa Butchard, Beatrice McLeod, Norman McIver, Alice Hodge, Maretta Belrose McFarlane, Mabel Young Davis.
Teacher: Vina Schaunch

S.S. No. 2, 1939.

Back Row, Left to Right: Gwen Chisholm, Margaret Smith, Jacqueline Smith, Lorraine Ransbury, Mrs. Iona Craigie, Dorothy Butchart, Irene Desjardine, Betty Gibbons, Muriel Hopkins.
Third Row: Ronnie Wyonch, Peter Golden, Jessie Barber, Hilda Hopkins, Viola Watson, Margaret Ritchie, _____ Hepburn, John Spears, _____ Hepburn.
Second Row: David Vail, Jack Barber, Harvey Golden, Glen Craigie, Arnold Spears, Dick Gibbons, Bruce Young, T. A. Golden.
First Row: Bill Currie, Raymond Butchart, Freddie Young, _____ Hepburn, Gerald Adams, Ralph Davis, Albert Smith.

Class of 1900.

Back Row, Left to Right: **Jean (Young) Beatty, ?, Maggie (Matheson) Leslie, Rosie Hodge, Bella Belrose, ?, ?, Mina Hunter, Flora Matheson, Ross Butchart, ?, ?, ?, ?, ?. Teacher: Mr. Hamilton.**

Class of 1885.

Back Row, Left to Right: **Mary Hodge, ?, Tena Smith, Alex Craigie?, Howard Leslie, Elmer Martin, Ann Matheson, Tena Parker, Martha Spears, Bill Marwick, Josephine Marwick, Alex Craigie?, Ross Butchart, ?, Pearl Smith, Rosa Hodge, Ethel Martin.**
Second Row: **Kate Smith, Etta Culbert, Maggie Culbert, ?, ?, Maggie Matheson, ?, ?, Victor Vail, Willard Currie, Gordon McLeod.**
Third Row: **Johnny McLeod, Lang Butchart. Teacher: Miss McGee.**

130

S.S. No. 1, Late 1890's.

Back Row, Left to Right: **Margaret (Bartman) Ransbury, Mary (Belrose) Spears, Mina Hunter, ?, Winnifred (Hopkins) Wellaugham, Lena (Davis) Cosgrove, Elsie (Dean) Hopkins, George Young or Alf Adams, ?, ?, ?, ?, ?.**
Second Row: **?, Cecil Davis.**
Third Row: **Elsie (Hopkins) Golden, ?, ?, Whitmore Hopkins, Bill Davis, Deborah Belrose, ?, ?, Hattie (Adams) Butchart, ?, Edith (Hodge) Sadler, ?, Garnet Bartman, ?. Teacher: ?**

Old School Photos

CHAPTER THIRTEEN

COMMUNITY ORGANIZATIONS *and* ACTIVITIES

People who have never been to Tobermory and even those who have visited briefly often ask the same questions of the residents here, "but what's there to do around here? How can you live here year round?" Well, the questions might be valid ones if it were not for the pioneer background of the local people. In the past, when money was scarce, transportation limited, and winters cold and harsh, loneliness and boredom could have become rampant. This was seldom the case however, for, as many an elderly resident will tell you, you had to make your own fun then — and that is exactly what they did.

FAIR WEATHER SPORTS

Children of the past were not so catered to with plastic Fisher Price toys and safety-designed playgrounds as they are today. Toys were often homemade and included such things as stilts, sling shots, whistles, sleighs, and dolls. The harbour, the bushes, the fields and the ponds were the playgrounds of the local children. Chores often had to be done on the fishing boats, the farms or at home, leaving less time for play.

In the very early 1900's, picnics, football and baseball games, and canoeing were quite popular. In 1901, it was reported that the town boys were playing a game called "pig in the hole" which was very amusing to watch. On one occasion in 1909, Bert Currie took several young ladies out on his gasoline launch — a pleasant excursion.

Baseball was all the rage in 1909 and it is still one of the most popular summer sports today. The early thirties saw the formation of Leagues all over the Peninsula.

Swimming was enjoyed by many of the younger set as the harbour made the perfect swimming pool. It was surprising, however, to note that many of the adults, fishermen included, did not know how to swim. Swimming lessons in the past were often taught by a parent or older sibling, whereas by August, 1968, children were taking swimming lessons from the Red Cross. Since the sixties, lessons have been taught every summer, ensuring greater safety for the Tobermory children who live in an area almost completely surrounded by water.

Soccer Team, early 1900's.

Besides the usual sports activities, some rather original pastimes were developed. The following article from *The Wiarton Echo* describes one of these:

"1939 — A new nocturnal pastime has caught the fancy of our younger set this week. Each night sees an expedition tramping the mile and a quarter to Hay Bay where the smelt run is on. Lights flashed into the shallow water attract the fish, which are then scooped out with the bare hands. One party returned with 150 lbs. of the tiny fish."

Hunting as a sport has been around for many years but probably the most active hunting years were the sixties. Fitzwilliam Island was a popular place to hunt and often several tugs and guide boats would be fully occupied carrying hunters to and from the Island. The following hunting news articles were printed in *The Wiarton Echo* in the early sixties:

"Many boats left here on the weekend for Fitzwilliam Island with deer hunting parties. They included four fish tugs, the Anzac, the Northside, the Lark and the Dyker Lass and John Desjardine's and Stew Peacock's guide boats.

Due to the closing of the United States markets, the commercial fishermen are doing little fishing at present and are taking the opportunity to do some hunting."

"Many hunters have arrived in the township for the local deer hunting week and accommodation is well booked. Early on Monday morning Jack Thompson of London bagged a 120 pound doe.

Mr. And Mrs. Stewart Peacock, Mr. And Mrs. Martin Hopkins, Archie Simpson, J. D. Currie and W. R. LaVoi, returned from Fitzwilliam Island last week. They were the last of the hunters to get back on the close of the North Shore open season. Their bag was six deer. The ladies of the party took part in the hunt, but it is reported that they were unsuccessful in hitting anything. Perhaps, if they had been armed with a rolling pin in place of a gun, the deer might have found them more deadly. The party was stormstayed for several days at Rattlesnake Harbour. They ran out of butter and bread but, nevertheless, fed well on venison and biscuits."

Hunters' dances and suppers were held in the Community Hall and were quite often well-attended. Several Tobermory residents belonged to the Bruce Peninsula Sportsmen's Club, and in 1964 Lloyd Smith presented a slide show of the scenery, flowers, and birds of the Bruce to the club.

Lacrosse Team, late 1900's.

Standing, Left to Right: **T. Hamilton, two unknown Baptist students, Frank Ransbury.**
Second Row: **Charlie Harkness, unknown mill worker, Dell Smith, William Parker, William Ransbury.**
Sitting: **Unknown mill worker, T. Hyatt, mill worker, Bill Dobson, mill worker, Hugh Dobson.**

Softball Team 1932.

Standing, Left to Right: **Buck Young, Gar Hopkins, Hugh Simpson, Woodland Vail, Wally McIvor, Husky Young, Cy Simpson, Bill Smith, John Ransbury.**
Seated: **Walter Hopkins, _____ Smith, Ray Hepburn, Bill Ransbury, Bud Hopkins.**

WINTER SPORTS

For the settlers of Tobermory the winter often hit hard, piling one foot of snow on top of another and freezing the inner harbour so that the ice could vary from eight to thirty inches thick. Those who would venture outdoors enjoyed a variety of winter sports.

Skating was very popular with the young people as early as 1909. The harbour provided a wide expanse of ice for the village children to skate on, while the Settlement children found a field or pond on which to test their skates. By early April the ice became dangerously thin in some areas, usually putting an end to the skating season.

Racing down the snowy slopes on handmade toboggans was great fun for the young children. This was not generally dangerous, however, in 1914, Will Ransbury had an unfortunate accident. It was printed in the "Wiarton Echo" that, while tobogganing, Will had run into Mr. Murphy's fence and was struck from behind by a second sleigh. He suffered a couple of rather severe wounds on his head as a result.

In 1916, quite a number of young people went out on a snowshoeing party and were later entertained at Miss Golden's home in the evening. Sleigh-riding parties were more infrequent activities but occasionally a horse was hitched up and the local youngsters and adults were taken for rides.

Curling was never a major activity of the Tobermory residents, however, it did make a brief appearence in the late twenties. In 1929, Tobermory was reported as having a curling rink. The club had leased a lot on "Bachelor's Row" and the ice was in good condition. Several groups were reportedly "in full swing". In March of 1931, the "Wiarton Echo" wrote that "the Scotsmen here had their first curling on Saturday and enjoyed a fine condition of ice".

Hockey was played in the very early 1900's with crudely made sticks and pucks and nets made with whatever could be found. In 1910, one of the first hockey teams was organized and a shanty with a stove in it was put up at the rink. The club was made up of: Mr. Ransbury, president; K. McLeod, vice president; C. Harkness, secretary-treasurer; H. Pettigrew, manager; G. Smith, referee; team — Jack Murray, William Parker, Howard Leslie, John Leslie, Roderick Smith, Mack Smith, and Murdock Murray.

One of the most enthusiastic hockey teams was organized in 1939. The officers were elected in the tiny barber shop.

For those people who preferred to stay indoors for the winter, badminton was the game to play. Regular badminton games were held in the early forties and each September the executive of the club would meet to organize the games. Open nights were held occasionally

Fitzwilliam Island Hunting Trip, late 1930's.
Left to Right: **Alex Craigie, Kenneth McLeod, Herb Hopkins, Charles Golden, T. A. Golden, Barney Hopkins, Frank Desjardine.**
Sitting: **Oscar Smith, Jack Currie.**

Tobermory Hockey Team, winners of Ray Walker Trophy 1957.
Standing, Left to Right: **Sheldon Ribbel, Dale Edmonstone, Carl Hopkins, Tom Adams, George Adams, Blaine Chisholm, Lyle Smith, Moe Elder, Lloyd Adams, Brad Davis, Glen Gratis, Alex Holmes.**
Seated: **Alvin Dean, Romain Wilson, Benny Palmer, Gary McLeod, Jack Ransbury, Tom Hopkins, Ivan Reid.**

to encourage new members and, as of October, 1942, the age limit was lowered to 14 years and over. A playing fee of 15¢ was charged per night and those still in school payed only 10¢.

In February, 1945, the local badminton club was reorganized. It had been forced to suspend its operations in 1943 because of the inability to secure supplies of birds which again became available in 1945. In 1947, consideration was given to forming separate junior and senior sections playing on different nights.

In April of 1949, Claude McFarlane, Ted Young, Dick Gibbons, Lawrence McFarlane and John Wilson represented Tobermory at the Georgian Bay District Badminton Championships.

Badminton resumed in the Community Hall in 1969. Public school children played Thursday afternoons and high school students and adults played in the evenings from 7 pm to 11 pm. During the seventies and early eighties, the badminton club has remained active, providing a recreational outlet for people of all ages.

SHOWS *and* ENTERTAINMENT

Early in 1905, a by-law was passed allowing people to charge a fee for shows and entertainment. This was a useful by-law to have because, at that time, musical concerts and dances were becoming quite popular. The more

musically talented residents would combine their skills and instruments to put on a show or a dance for the town. Percy Adams, Tom Adams, and John Masterson were notable players of the violin and Jimmy Rae played the accordion. Pearl Adams, Percy's wife, was the organist of the United and Baptists churches and could play the piano as well. In later years, Lloyd Smith became known for his guitar playing and often he could be found strumming and singing for the yachters on their boats. Even today, several Tobermory natives have made names and careers for themselves in the music business.

Dances were first held in the Orange Hall but when the Community Hall was built, the dances and most social events were moved there. The school children learned how to dance from Mrs. Pearl Adams and Mrs. Murphy. Lessons were held at Mrs. Adams' home and the children were put through their drills.

Some type of social event went on every Friday in the Community Hall. Euchre, card parties and dances were often accompanied by lunches prepared by the women. As Isabel Smith says, ''there was a close family-feeling back then''. Social events were also held by the two young people's groups, the ''Unmarrieds'' and the ''Newly Marrieds''. Dances were held for almost every occasion and the Councillors' Dance was an annual affair. By the early seventies, a square dance club was formed. This group still gathers today complete with caller, music and colourful skirts and shirts.

Special events such as wiener roasts and parties were held frequently. In 1908, Mr. and Mrs. Foster held a turkey shoot and later a supper and dance in their home. The midnight supper included raw and cooked oysters and little cakes. The garden was decorated with Chinese lanterns and flowers. Wiener and corn roasts were especially popular with the young people. Ann (Long) Kelly, a girl who spent several summers working in Tobermory, recalls:

> We'd boil the corn at the restaurant after hours (which meant sometime after midnight) and then go like there was no tomorrow swinging that pot between two of us heading for "Big Tub" and the solitude of our corn roast. It was always the sort of thing you had to be a part of to appreciate, but we figured it was the greatest thing out since coal-oil lamps.

Nowadays, fish dinners and chicken barbecues are attended annually by hundreds of people.

Movies were very popular when they were available. Some would be held at the back of a woodshed with the audience sitting on wooden benches or chopped logs. In 1954, a series of movies was held during the summer in the Community Hall. Movies began at 8 or 9 pm and included westerns, love stories, and Abbott and Costello films. Colour cartoons and a serial were often shown before the main feature.

Christmas time always brought about special events, often including school and Sunday school concerts and sometimes a visit to the village by Santa Claus. In 1978, almost all of St. Edmunds Township participated in a Santa Claus parade. Businesses and local groups made up floats and many of the local children were delighted to ride some of them. In 1979, the parade was held again and enjoyed by everyone. It is now an annual event held in December.

Although barbecues and dances still go on today, much of the entertainment now is of a different nature from that of the past. The "Modern Family Games Room" is frequented by many of the local young people who play the pinball and video games with an endless supply of quarters. Several underwater movies and nature films are available for viewing at the Crows Nest Theatre, and the radio and one television channel available are not to be overlooked.

THE PLAYS

It appears that in the past the Tobermory people had quite a talent and fondness for acting. It is said that the Reverend Millen was responsible for initiating the plays in the very late twenties. Through the Reverend and Mr. Weir Grieve, the local residents became almost obsessed with rehearsing, presenting, and watching plays. Besides the minister and the librarian, many respected community members shucked off their true identities for an evening to become villains, heroes, fools, and dramatic characters for the rest of the community to laugh at or cry over.

The Community Hall, which had just been erected in 1931, had been built with the plays in mind. The stage, framed by lovely curtains and a valance trimmed with gold, was admired by everyone. Five changes of sceneries were available to suit the needs of the plays and the hall, which was fairly large, barely accommodates all the people at times. By 1932, the people felt that it was fortunate that the hall had been built when it was, as the depression would have put a halt to it if it had been started any later.

A lot of effort was put into settings, props and costumes. Music was provided by a pianist or a local orchestra group. Besides the actors, the plays required directors and stage hands too. In 1931, Cy Simpson was complimented, after a play, on his fine electrical work. Apparently he had obtained some rather fine effects with his coloured gelatine slides.

Most of the earliest plays were directed by the Reverend Millen, but by 1932, two separate groups had been formed; the "Tobermory Dramatic Society" and the "Settlement Players". These two groups would take turns presenting and would usually donate the proceeds to the church or other good causes. Door receipts sometimes amounted to over $60, which was quite a bit of money in those days. There was a friendly rivalry between the two groups back then as each one tried to outdo the other.

Weir Grieve directed one of the groups and several residents today well remember the rehearsals held in his home, "the Hermitage". Grace Peacock recalls that the rehearsals were always a lot of fun and that sometimes, after an evening's work, someone would sit down at the player piano and play some tunes for the others to sing to.

The plays themselves were often mystery thrillers, comedies, dramas, or operettas. Many had morals to them exposing the folly of drinking too much or indulging in other bad habits.

In March of 1932, the "Lion's Head Players" put on the play "Eyes of Love" in Tobermory. For this play, many of the locals lent their best furniture out to provide atmosphere. The Lion's Head group gave half of the proceeds to the Tobermory Church and kept half to be given to the Lion's Head Women's Institute. A short while later, an interesting article in the "Wiarton Echo" told of a pig disappearing off the Tobermory stage during one of the Lion's Head productions. It was later reported that the owner, W. T. Clarke of Lion's Head, got the pig back after advertising in the "Wiarton Echo".

The Tobermory groups also travelled to other communities to present plays. Shallow Lake and Lion's Head were visited frequently, even in the early spring when roads were bad. In November of 1932, Tobermory had its first presentation by the Wiarton Dramatic Society.

In April of 1932, a noteworthy play, "The Keynote", was presented in Tobermory. Local homes were ransacked to provide setting furniture and props, and the ladies rented elaborate Empire period gowns from

Toronto. Elgin Edmonstone played the violin backstage and stage electrician, Albert Leslie, handled the spotlight. In the "Wiarton Echo", this play was quoted as being "the most expensive production ever attempted here running into the neighbourhood of $25. Receipts amounted to $48". The plays were held throughout most of the thirties, but the people eventually lost their enthusiasm for them, and by the late forties nothing more was heard about them.

THE TOBERMORY WOMEN *and the* WOMEN'S INSTITUTE

Women's groups have been active in Tobermory since the early 1900's, serving their community, the war effort, and various charities.

Women all over Canada were discussing the possibility of getting "the vote" in the 1890's and the Tobermory women were no exception. On February 22, 1894, the "Wiarton Echo" printed an article submitted by one of its Tobermory readers. The article stated that there was a "heated controversy" over whether women should be allowed to vote, but that the majority of the people were in favour of granting the franchise to women. Some supporters of the women's cause said that if women were in the political arena; whiskey traffic would cease, the Sabbath would be better observed, there would be less profane language, laws would be well-administered, and the honour of women would be held "more sacred".

In April of 1905, a by-law was passed stating "that the Reeve, Clerk and Treasurer be authorized to sign the petition to entitle women to vote at Municipal Elections who held property in their own name". This was still a far cry from what we have today, but it was a step in the right direction.

The Women's Institute (W.I.) was formed in 1914 just after the outbreak of war and the women set to work knitting socks for the soldiers. During the first year in operation the ladies put together a small library and Miss. E. Hopkins became librarian. By 1916, the local women donated 147 pairs of socks and many other hospital supplies to the Red Cross to be shipped overseas. A pair of socks was sent to each of the nine Tobermory volunteers training in Wiarton.

In 1916, the W.I. held the annual picnic on the 12th of July and served refreshments at a stand for the purpose of obtaining money for the Red Cross. A game called "French Toy" was played and everyone enjoyed themselves. The proceeds from the refreshments stand amounted to $40.

By 1917, the group had over 30 members and Mrs. Walsh became president. A friendship quilt was made and completed in 1918. This special quilt contained squares on which each soldier's name and regimental number was embroidered. Donated to the St. Edmunds museum, this quilt can be seen there today.

The "Skylark Girls" were a younger version of the Women's Institute, organized in 1931 by Mrs. Russell Belrose. Although this club did not last a long time, many activities were undertaken during its existence. In September, Miss Dora Pettigrew gave an interesting paper on Florence Nightingale to the club and the next month, the club's first social evening was held.

Both the Skylarks and the Women's Institute were involved in Hallowe'en fund raising events in 1931 which were aptly described in *The Wiarton Echo*.

"A bazaar need never be bizarre. We have had many so-called events of this kind, but never one before that caught up such originality of scheme and such novelty of interest as did that of the "Skylark Girls," which was held last Wednesday evening. This had not been a hurried event, but the climax to a number of happy evenings in which dreams became plans and Hallowe'en captured as suitable background providing hobgoblins and pumpkins, black cats and witches as a decorative scheme for walls and lights. A program of sideshows gave two mystery tents and an excellent fish pond as added attractions to the hand-embroidered goods and choice souvenirs that were tastily displayed, together with a counter of pies, cookies, candy and cakes that looked very tempting indeed. The local library building had generously been loaned to these young people, and looked entrancing in its orange and black semi-weird atmosphere. Laughter was to be heard everywhere, interspersed with pleasant remarks about the display of dainty gifts. The whole was something different and thus deserved special mention. This successful undertaking, under the capable leadership of Mrs. Russell Belrose, calls for congratulations from all interested in our young folk. The proceeds were divided into an equal third for each of the societies. The church, Women's Institutes and the Skylarks. The best that can be said is keep on with the good work and golden deeds.

The W.I. Planned and executed a successful event in an Hallowe'en euchre and dance, to which were added sales of dainty gifts and embroidery, with many useful articles for the housewife and the bride-to-be. Always an item of interest is the draw for the quilt. One went to Mrs. O. C. Vail and Fred Smith. Lunch was served at the close. An interesting fish pond was provided for both the children and the adults. Friday night will be remembered as a very enjoyable evening, and one that ably augmented the doctor's fund."

In 1932, the ladies of the church got together and formed the Womens Association, later becoming known as United Church Women (U.C.W.). This, however, did not put an end to the Women's Institute as they continued to hold euchre parties, bazaars, and fund raising events.

There must have been some people in the village walking around in less clothes than was seen fit at the time, for the following letter was written to the council by the W.I. In 1934:

July 25th/34
"Reeve and Councillors"
Tobermory, Ontario

Dear Sirs:

I have been requested by the Institute to ask you to co-operate with us in striving to set our Young Folk a good example by passing a by-law to prohibit the wearing of indecent apparel in our village. We have their interests at heart.

Won't you please help us?

Very Truly Yours
For Home and Country,
Mrs. Clifford Woods
Secretary of Tobermory W.I."

In the late thirties, the women were often meeting in the public library. Hallowe'en dances were held annually and many interesting discussions were had. In 1935, dental work in the schools was discussed and Mrs. W. J. Smith was appointed as Institute representative on the Cemetery Board.

The ladies were still knitting socks in 1941, but this time they were donated to the Salvation Army. A Christmas box of 2000 cigarettes was sent to a Canadian hospital in England and later, in October, a euchre and dance night was held with the proceeds going to replenish the school medicine chest. Some of the meetings were held in the school that year. Instead of having to pay the school board for each meeting, the ladies took the option of cleaning the hall and furnishing their own wood.

Money belts for soldiers and quilts, sweaters, socks and scarves were made and donated to the Red Cross by the W.I. in 1942. Money was raised for the Red Cross through socials and card and crokinole parties so that by April of 1942, $179.99 was the group's balance on hand for Red Cross work.

Through both wars, the women of Tobermory had worked hard so that by the end of World War II, they had knitted, quilted, played cards and raised money for over 30 years. The W.I. was eventually disbanded, but the United Church Women continued, carrying out valuable services during the later years.

BOYS' *and* GIRLS' CLUBS

A Boys Scout group was formed in the thirties and, a short time later, a Cub group for younger boys was also begun. Thomas Golden, T. A. Scott, Weir Grieve, other community members, and several of the local ministers led these groups throughout the years. A great many boys joined the Scouts, completing the challenges, learning new skills and having a lot of fun. By 1943, 14 Cubs were meeting at the school on Tuesdays and 15 Scouts on Wednesdays.

The Scout group continued on for many years, meeting sometimes at the school, and in 1963, in the Community Hall. In 1967, the Rotary Club sponsored the Cubs, and Lloyd and Tom Adams became the leaders. Camping was a favourite activity of the group. In 1971, Tom Hopkins and Frank LaFontaine took the group camping and fishing at Willow Creek. In 1970, the scouts held a Walk-a-thon.

In 1948, the Reverend C. N. Paddon took charge of a newly formed boys' club. Sixteen boys attended the first meeting to hear T. A. Golden speak on his recent trip to Nassau. In December of 1948, the club decided to name itself "The Pathfinders". At that same meeting, the boys listened to Weir Greive speak on "Good Citizenship". In March, 1949, Lloyd Smith talked about his experiences while in the Air Force and a vote of thanks was given to the school board for allowing the group the use of the school for meetings.

First mention of a girl's group was made in May of 1945. It was reported that the Girl's Club had held a successful dance in the Community Hall and that the proceeds had been applied to stage improvements.

In February, 1948, the teenage girls of the village formed a club called the "Willing Workers". Dorothy McCoy became the president and teas and socials were held to benefit the church and other organizations. The next month, Mrs. Ross formed a group called the 'Little Helpers". This group of 10 to 13 year old girls met to sew and play games. In October of 1948, the Willing Workers spent a day at Wasaga Beach, seeing the sights and enjoying a picnic lunch. They visited the cottage of Eddy Allen of "Happy Gang fame", but finding him not at home, they procured his mother's autograph instead.

A Brownie Pack was in full swing by 1979. That year, 10 of the young girls were taken to Owen Sound to a fair. The Brownies and their mothers had baked cakes and candies and several came home with prizes for their efforts. There is still a small Brownie pack meeting in the church today and they enjoy the games, tasks and outings that are held each year.

THE ONTARIO FEDERATION OF AGRICULTURE THE FARM FORUM

Early in the 1940's, the Federation of Agriculture started holding annual picnics on the Peninsula. In July of 1942, the "Wiarton Echo" reported that a farmers' picnic held in Lindsay was attended by five carloads of Tobermorians. That year, 12 local farmers joined the Federation.

In October of 1943, the first Farm Forum of the Township met at the home of Percy Adams. This group, initiated by the Federation of Agriculture, listened to the Forum broadcasts on the radio and met to discuss topics pertaining to country living. Subjects covered included: marketing, health, labour shortages, farm finance, crime, schooling and much more. Most discussions were ended by an opinion count or a consensus. Some of the conclusions obtained over the years were that:

- likely 15% of St. Edmunds farmers would not be farming by 1949 on account of old age.
- future farmers would make a better living than those at present (mid 1940's)
- rural communities can be attractive.
- establishing rural high schools and introducing new subjects into the curriculum is not desirable.
- an agricultural college should be established.
- a co-operative should be formed in Wiarton.
- the decision of whether or not relief should be sent to enemy countries after a war should be left to the UNRRA.
- more adult education on nutrition was needed.
- co-operatives should be patronized to reduce the cost of goods to the consumers.
- the government should pass a law enforcing the use of darker bread by Canadians to allow shipment of more flour overseas.

Attendance at these meetings ranged from 16 to over 40 people and activities were held after each discussion. Bingo, euchre, crokinole, and '500' were played, and apple contests, bean contests, and pin the tail on the donkey were enjoyed. Music and dances were held along with the occasional social or chicken banquet. A box social was held one evening with the proceeds going to the Bruce Peninsula and District Hospital Fund.

The annual picnic for the Federation of Agriculture for the three Northern Townships was held at Star Munn's farm at the Settlement in 1948. Over 1000 people attended to hear speakers, songs, instrumental selections, and to hold races, contests and a softball game. In the evening, a comedy play was presented in the Community Hall and dancing followed. In 1952, the picnic was again held at the Munn farm.

The Farm Forum group at Tobermory eventually disappeared as more farm families turned to tourism and other occupations. As farm issues became of less interest to the community in general, the support system for farmers was no longer of much use.

THE FEDERATION OF ONTARIO NATURALISTS (FON)

In mid-July of 1947, Mr. J. B. Runnings, vice president of the Federation of Ontario Naturalists (F.O.N.), travelled from Toronto to "Singing Sands", Dorcas Bay area, to camp with his son. While there, he became very excited about the beauty of the area and the numerous varieties of wildlife and plants. He sighted some rare bald eagles and a very rare 'grasshopper sparrow' while treking

through the grounds. After two weeks of camping, Mr. Runnings took a group of 25 Tobermory residents and visitors on a hike around the Settlement grounds and pointed out many of the attractions and the variety of wildlife in the area. As a result of his enthusiasm, it was decided to form a naturalist club in Tobermory, and by March, 1948, the new club had been formed. The Reverend Paddon became the Honourary president, Roy Hatt became the president, and 16 members enrolled. That August, Mr. Runnings returned to Tobermory to give a guided field tour to residents and visitors.

One Tobermory resident who was deeply involved in the Federation was Mr. Lloyd Smith. He would often take people from the Federation or from the Bruce Trail Association out on his boat, 'The Penguin', for guided tours. Besides giving tours, he made up a slide show on the wildlife and scenery of Tobermory. This show he presented to the F.O.N., the Bruce Trail Club and the Arts Council. Mr. Smith was a talented artist as well and a collection of his work was put on display in the Circle Arts shop several years ago.

The Dorcas Bay area had been a favourite spot for the naturalists for many years, and, in 1963, the Federation bought 200 acres of land in this area. The purchase was made possible through the efforts of a special group, the Natural Areas Fund Committee. They published a well-written pamphlet about conservation and distributed it to 25,000 F.O.N. Members and their friends. As of February, 1963, $20,000 had been donated from over 1000 persons in Ontario and a part of Dorcas Bay soon became a nature reserve.

THE TOBERMORY ROTARY CLUB

The Tobermory Rotary Club was established in April of 1956 with help from the Wiarton Rotary Club and the Lion's Head Rotary Club. The first anniversary of the club was celebrated in the Community Hall. About 120 rotarians and guests showed up for the banquet and Mr. Ralph W. Harris of Toronto spoke on "A buyer's view of fire and casualty insurance". Several instrumental selections by local people completed the evening.

The Rotary Club was quite active in the 1960's. Guest speakers talked about: agricultural improvements introduced in Burma by the United Nations, Russian-style hockey and Canadian minor hockey, the Canadian Power Squadron, how the Rotary works in the British Isles and other countries, mental health, and many other interesting subjects.

Sometimes "ladies' nights" were held and the Rotary members' wives would attend the lectures. At some of these meetings, dinner would be served or a musical program would follow the talk. New officers were elected each May and each Rotary birthday was celebrated with a cake or a guest speaker.

The club was also interested in supporting boys' groups and activities. In 1962, two boys were sent by the Rotary Club to Camp Kitchigama to learn about leadership and government and to participate in recreational activities. The next year, the club decided to sponsor a

Boy Scout Troop. In October, a Tobermory Sea Scout Troop was given the proceeds from a Rotary sponsored stage show and dance at the Community Hall. In 1964, four boys and their leader stayed overnight at the Rotary camp in Tobermory and then hiked the Bruce Trail from Tobermory to Lion's Head. In 1971, the club donated $100 to the Rotary, Ottawa to assist in a student exchange from Northern Canada. As a result of their generosity, the Tobermory club received an award for their contribution to the International student exchange.

In May of 1972, the club sponsored a three hour cruise out of Tobermory on the S. S. Norisle. Tickets cost $4 per person and over 200 people from all parts of the Peninsula went on this excursion. Proceeds went to the Crippled Children Fund of Canada.

In February of 1979, the Tobermory club and other area Rotary Clubs sponsored a Snow-a-rama and raised approximately $36,000 for crippled children. To aid community projects, the Tobermory club sponsored a dance in the Community Centre that same year.

The 25th Anniversary of the founding Rotary club was held at the Tobermory Lodge in May of 1981. The three remaining charter members, Gordon Gibbons, Alex Holmes, and George (Cy) Simpson were given commemorative plaques. Dinner was followed by dancing and the evening ended with a complimentary lunch served by the Lodge at midnight.

THE ORANGE LODGE

The Orange Order, a fraternal society, was organized in Tobermory and the rest of the Peninsula at an early date. In 1895, the "Wiarton Echo' announced that patrons intended to build a large hall to be used as a meeting place. However, it was not until 1904 that the Orange Hall was erected. The "Wiarton Echo" wrote in 1904: "The Orange Hall at Tobermory was raised on Saturday (April) the 16th. They are going to rush the work to have it finished by the middle of May. John Parker Sr. is the builder".

One of the biggest events of the year for the Orangemen and most of the Tobermory community was the July 12th celebrations. On this date, the victory of the Battle of Boyne was celebrated with parades and a picnic. It mattered very little what race, age, or religion a person was because everyone came to enjoy themselves. The Indians, who were often devout Roman Catholics, would dock their boats near the ferry dock and join the activities for the day. The Orangemen and a small band marched to the Community Hall with children and women following behind. At the back of the hall, a great picnic was held with lemonade, popcorn, freshly made ice cream, watermelon, and a little candy stand. Sometimes the picnics were held at Dorcas Bay or Cameron Lake. In these instances, Alf Adams would go in with a team of horses and cut the grass with a haycutter so that the children could run races. Orange ribbons, red flags and balloons decorated the area, and often

Orange Hall 1983.

ball games were had with local teams or against a team from Cape Croker. Bill Spears remembers one such game that ended in a brawl.

Once the Orange Hall was up, the council began to meet there at a cost of 50¢ per meeting. A dance for young people was held in the hall in 1909 and it was said to have lasted well into the morning. Concerts were another popular pastime and money-raiser. One concert in 1914 held in aid of the patriotic fund included bagpipes, songs, speeches, and instrumental music selections. That month, $100 was given to the general fund to assist the British Emprire.

By 1929, people realized that the Orange Hall was too small for the crowds that attended such gatherings, so the Lodge sold the Township a piece of land on which to build a new Community Hall. After the new hall was built, most dances and concerts were held there — even the council met in the new hall.

Despite its decline in use, the Orange Hall was renovated in 1931 and social evenings for Orange Lodge members and friends were held. The Lodge remained quite active and interested members formed a group which put on plays. In 1939, the group presented the play, "The Attorney for the Defense" in the Community Hall. That summer, Orange Lodge officials conducted the service at the Harbour United Church and Percy Spears gave an address on Orangeism.

In 1923, the ladies formed an auxiliary group for the Orange Lodge called "The Ladies Orange Benevolent Association" (L.O.B.A.). This group carried out 'good works' and held many crokinole and card parties. Money raised was given to the Church or other charities and, in the forties, money was often sent to a district fund which provided clothes for war victims. A masquerade dance was held in the Community Hall in 1942 and the $32 raised was contributed to the War effort.

The ladies held a box social in 1949 for Valentines Day. In preparation for this type of social, each women would pack two of her best-prepared lunches in a box and decorate it with ribbons and paper. These boxes would then be auctioned off to the highest bidder and everyone would sit down for lunch. At some box socials, the lady who had prepared the meal would be expected to eat lunch with the man who had bought her box. Under these circumstances, many husbands and boy-friends were discreetly pointed to the box which they were to buy if they wished to avoid their lady's wrath.

The social and other events brought in a fair amount of money to to Organe Lodge which was often donated to such charities as the Children's Aid Society and the True Blue Home for Children in Richmond Hill.

July 12th celebrations continued into the forties and fifties with some variation in program. A quiet celebration was held in 1943 as the commercial fishing boats took a day off and everyone relaxed until the evening when a dance was held. Ten years later, a huge celebration marked the day and a special feature of the program was a football match between two teams of village ladies.

In 1962, the ladies received permission to put up a new ceiling in the Orange Hall. When completed, this ceiling, entirely paid for by the ladies, was considerably lower than the original roof had been. The next year a series of card parties were held in the hall and five men of the Orange Lodge received the blue degree. Plans were made in 1965 to move an oil tank to the Orange Hall and the stove was shifted around and new sanitation equipment purchased.

Since the sixties, some Orangemen have died and others have moved away. There are still a number living in Tobermory, but the Orange Lodge is not active anymore. The Orange Hall still stands and bingo is held there once a week, however, the days of Tobermory's grand 12th of July celebrations are gone.

DUNKS BAY CEMETERY

In 1908, Henry Bradley Davis gave the Corporation of St. Edmunds township the deed for four acres of land at Dunks Bay to be used for a cemetery.

On March 12, 1935, a general meeting was held with representatives from every organization present and a cemetery board was formed with Reverend Charles Tullbury for a one year term and Percy Adams and Mrs. Albert Leslie for a two year term. Today, there are five members on the board, two of them are granddaughters of Henry Davis.

THE LIBRARY

A temporary library was started in 1894, and in 1895 Mrs. Christina Simpson became the first librarian. She was paid 25¢ a week. Books were bought with money collected from the residents and were shelved in a section of the Methodist Sunday School. A Public Library

Association was formed in 1921, and the Sunday School room was still used for housing the collection. W. J. Simpson became head of the Association.

In 1929, two summer visitors, Henry E. Bodman, then the owner of Cove Island, and Halrow N. Davock, both from Detroit, chose a site and built a log cabin on it. The two men then presented the cabin to Tobermory as a public library. The cabin was twenty-four by thirty-six feet and was built of rocks and logs. The ceiling was made of British Columbia fir, two inches thick, tongued and grooved, and supported by old-fashioned cross beams. The donors also furnished the library with tables, chairs and shelves. A large stone fireplace dominated one wall and was used to heat the building.

Mr. Weir Grieve became the first librarian of the new, free public library. He continued to hold this position for twelve years. He also became the Chairman of the Public Library Board. In 1940, he began a scrapbook of newspaper clippings related to Tobermory and St. Edmunds. He faithfully compiled these scrapbooks for many years, as have librarians that followed him. Now these books represent a valuable research tool for anyone interested in the history of St. Edmunds.

In 1929, the assets and the property of the Library Association were taken over by the Township, and a Public Library was established according to the Public Libraries Act. The property and its assets were valued at $1230 at that time.

In 1935, an article appeared in the Wiarton Echo telling its readers that the generous patron of the library, Henry Bodman, had gone broke in the Depression, but later managed to recover his wealth.

In 1941, Mrs. S. C. Craigie was named as the librarian. She held the position for twenty-five years. Later, in 1942, the Library Board met to decide on books to buy, and also to buy a phonograph so that the school children could have a music instruction period as well as a library period.

In 1949, the library was updated by the adoption of the Dewey Decimal System. The librarian, Mrs. Craigie, passed her Librarian Class E Certificate, so the library now qualified for a one hundred dollar annual provincial grant.

Library early 1930's.

In 1961, the library underwent extensive renovations. Additional lights, a new oil tank, and piping fixtures were installed, and more books were bought. Later that year, Archie Simpson presented the library with pictures of Mr. Bodman and Mr. Davock. In 1963, the people of Tobermory were saddened by news that Mr. Bodman had died.

The library roof was reshingled and a new stove was added to the library in 1964. In 1965, St. Edmunds Township joined other Bruce County municipalities in requesting the establishment of a county public library system. Also that year, an assistant, Elizabeth Erb, was hired to help the librarian.

After twenty-five years, Mrs. Craigie retired in 1967. A generous donation of a book shelf and book was made to the library by Mr. And Mrs. Lloyd Adams in that year.

In 1983, a major addition was made to the library. As well as more room, the library acquired washrooms, new lighting, ventilation, and heating. Today the library is a well used facility in the community that delights summer residents as well as the year round residents of the area.

THE COMMUNITY HALL

During the early 1900's, the Orange Hall was used as the place for social gatherings and special events. By the late 1920's, the Hall was considered too small for the growing community, so, in 1929, a petition requesting the building of a Community Hall was circulated among the Tobermory residents and presented to council. A by-law was passed that year, authorizing the building of a Community Hall. Money was borrowed from the Royal Bank in 1930 for this purpose and a field day was held to help increase funds. That year, $1008 was paid to the Orange Lodge for Block "A" where the new hall was to be built.

Construction got underway and in April, 1930, the Reeve was authorized to hire men to lift stone for the foundation of the Community Hall at $3 per day. A. H. Watson was appointed foreman for the building of the foundation and Tom Spears became the overseer of the project. In the late seventies, the Township called on consulting engineers to survey the building and they remarked that the foundation was one of the most 'sound' they had seen on the Peninsula, and it was doubtful that it could ever fail.

The hall building was completed in November, and on December 15, rates were set for the use of the hall. Dances and general concerts were $5 per evening and council meetings were $2. On January 12, 1931, the newly elected council met for the first time in the Community Hall. That night, a motion was passed that the hall "be free for the councillors' dance to be held that same evening."

George (Cy) Simpson became the first caretaker of the hall. His responsibilities included: the "lighting plant", scrubbing the hall four times a year, and attending all meetings, reporting disorders to the local police officer.

Community Hall 1930's.

The following *Wiarton Echo* article outlines some of the work done on the hall in 1931:

"1931 — Feb. — Our Community Hall continues its program of improvements. Ladies Orange Lodge donated $60, and arrangements have been made for a valance of green velour trimmed with gold braid and a beautiful pair of velour curtains for the stage. A roller curtain is in use at present. Plans are being made for a new exterior back drop, tree wings and border, also a complete interior box set. The council are planning the official opening early in the spring. Two very fine deer heads have been placed at extreme left and right of the proscenium opening. The stage is 36 x 14 ft.

In June, 1931, the official opening of the hall was celebrated. The enthusiastic crowd joined the free sailing trips around the islands, attended the sports program, received free admission to the grounds, enjoyed a banquet, heard a list of speakers and the Kincardine Pipe Band, had a softball match, watched the operetta "Babette", clicked heels at the old times dance festival, and watched a motor car caravan.

In November, 1939, a dance and card party was held in the hall. During this public meeting and social, the debentures were burned as the hall had been completely paid for in less than 10 years.

The hall was used for a great variety of events including dances, elections, meetings, concerts, wedding receptions, plays, dinners, and lectures.

To celebrate the advent of hydro in 1942, a dance was held in the hall and bright lights shone over the happy crowd. That same year, the Women's Institute put on a dance to aid their war efforts, but the hydro failed them and all lights went at 10:40 p.m. This, however, did not spoil the fun as the orchestra played by ear and the dancers continued, avoiding collision through the aid of the moonlight coming in the windows.

Community Hall 1983.

In January of 1942, T. A. Golden, president of the Community Hall Board announced that order was to be enforced in the hall and that a severe penalty would be dealt to anyone smoking or whistling shrilly in the hall.

Dances continued to be held and in 1946, the hall was rented for $8 per night to show movies in. Local musicians would often rent the hall for $5 and put on a concert. Everyone came and sometimes the men would throw handfuls of coins out for the children. Yacht people would often attend the concerts and dances in the forties.

Upkeep of the hall was a concern in 1952, and the roof was reshingled as it was leaking. The caretaker was authorized to pay small, miscellaneous accounts incurred between Board meetings, and the piano was repaired and tuned for $60.

The hall roof was again repaired in 1958. That year, an all-girl orchestra, "The Bell-Aires" from Detroit, held a dance in the hall, proceeds to go towards the cost of a new resuscitator for the local fire department.

To keep the order, a constable was required to attend all dances at the hall in uniform, in 1959. In 1962, the caretaker took over the job of attending all functions at the hall. His salary was half of the hall rentals, with a minimum of $150 a year. The sign over the front door was repainted, screens were put on all the windows, and six broken windows were replaced that spring. In June, the outside trimmings were repainted and the roof was repaired for a third time. Believe it or not, in September the roof was leaking again and was once more repaired.

In 1969, the Recreation, Parks and Community Centre Board met and decided to get an estimate on the cost to repair the basement wall of the hall. Fifty new stacking chairs, twelve stacking tables, and seven pairs of window drapes were also ordered. Entrance doors and coat racks were installed. The Board began sponsoring a teenage dance every two weeks with two couples attending each week as chaperones.

Today the hall is still in use. Bingo, dances, and various other special events are held there every year. During the summer of 1983, it even served as a day care centre for very young children.

THE PENINSULA AND TOWNSHIP OF ST. EDMUNDS MUSEUM

The St. Edmunds Township Museum was officially opened in May, 1967, Canada's Centennial year. The building that houses the collection of artifacts was the former St. Edmunds Settlement School built in 1898. The opening included a speech given by William Forsyth of Owen Sound, and a ribbon-cutting ceremony. Mrs. Arthur Watson, the oldest resident of the village at that time, and John Martin, one of the first pupils of the school in 1898, cut the ribbon and then Rev. George Trigger dedicated the museum. A message from Tobermory, Scotland was read, and later the reeve and the clerk welcomed people to the museum as they set about their first tour of the museum.

At its opening, the museum consisted of one building which contained a tiny room at the back that was furnished and decorated as a pioneer bedroom. Some people loaned articles to the museum and others donated them. The main floor of the museum was devoted to articles used around the home such as quilts, irons, basins, spinning wheels, dolls, and old photographs. There are also Indian artifacts on display that people discovered when they were clearing land or farming.

The upper floor was dedicated to the marine history of the area with maps and relics from shipwrecks.

In 1969, the rudder and propeller from the steamer "City of Grand Rapids" was arranged on a concrete slab outside the main building.

St. Edmunds Museum 1980's.

As an added attraction to the museum, an old log house, built by Jacob Belrose in 1875, was donated by William Willaughan of Dorcas Bay. The house was torn down, moved to the museum site and rebuilt there. Authentic furniture and appliances from the same time were donated to furnish it. In May of 1971, the old log house was officially opened. Tom Spears, the first white boy born in Tobermory, and Martha Watson cut the ribbon at the ceremony. For the rest of that summer, demonstrations in weaving and spinning were held once a week in the old home.

In November, the museum board met with Mr. and Mrs. Stan McClellan and Mr. Patrick Folkes of the Ontario Underwater Council to discuss renovations on part of the museum. These three people offered their labour to the museum free of charge. They and the Underwater Council were given much credit later for the attractive marine display with its maps, descriptions and pieces of old boats on the second floor.

In 1977, the museum received a quilt which had been bought from the Tobermory Women's Institute in 1918. This white friendship quilt with red cross patterns consisted of squares with each local soldier's name and regimental number embroidered on them.

By 1978, school classes were touring the museum from Eastnor, Wiarton and Owen Sound. A grade five and six class from Mindemoya, Manitoulin Island came for the tour and the following *Wiarton Echo* article was written in description of the museum at the time of their visit:

"The Marine display, upstairs with the pictures of the lighthouses and the big map showing the location of sunken ships — dates — why they sank, etc. was a big attraction. The girls all liked the doll room and the old name quilt of 1918. The boys liked the old gramaphones and farm implements and they all were just a tiny bit scared of the rattle snake preserved in alcohol. The photos of our forefathers were gazed on with some carefully hidden smiles. The history of Tobermory — compiled by two grade 8 girls in 1967 was read with interest and one or two students displayed their talent for playing the old organ.

In the log cabin, the refrigerator and the old ice saw and wood stove with the sad irons. The upstairs with its beds and commodes and water jugs and old fashioned shoes and a bridegroom's night shirt were all causes of a lot of question.

Then the little parlor downstairs with the spinning wheel, love seat and organ were the proper setting for a story or two which the Assistant Curator loves to tell."

As of November, 2,685 people had visited the museum in 1980, raising door receipts of $2,258. Interior painting, cleaning and re-arranging was also done that year.

Today, two or three hours could easily be spent looking at the many interesting articles in the museum. Many of the local residents' roots can be traced through the photos, land deeds and registers there. As Geoff Nightingale so aptly wrote in 1980:

"A good museum is much more that a stuffy repository for older people's cast-offs. The Peninsula and St. Edmunds Museum in Tobermory is like a well-written history book: it "houses a million memories of the pioneer and maritime past, of the people, the events and things that helped shape today and tomorrow"".

THE WARS *and* THE LEGION

Both World Wars brought the people of Tobermory together to contribute to the war effort and to help support each other. Several groups formed during the war years, one of which, the Legion, is still in existence today.

When the war broke out in 1914, Tobermory saw its first soldiers as Captain E. R. Clark arrived with 15 men to protect the small Tobermory wireless station, which at that time was one of the few on the Great Lakes. That October, the community decided to canvass the area for oats and eventually collected 150 bushels to be sent to the war effort.

In 1915, a public meeting was held in the interests of recruiting with Lieutenant Harold Hay of Wiarton as speaker. By 1916, training sessions were being held in Tobermory. In May of 1916, the soldiers were taken to Walkerton and accommodated there until June first when the whole battalion went to camp at London. Little more was written about the casualties and the dead. Casualties in 1918 consisted of Robert Hazen (who was wounded in the leg) and Privates Samuel Craigie and James Belrose.

Throughout the First World War, the Women's Institute kept busy knitting socks and sweaters and making medical supplies for the Red Cross. Cigarettes were often sent overseas to the local boys and various fund raising projects were undertaken to further aid the Red Cross.

By 1918 the war was over, leaving six Tobermory men dead. Norman and Stewart Campbell, John McLeod, Fred J. Millwood, Angus Smith and Harry Willaughan were killed in action. In 1919, a local memorial committee was formed to erect a monument to honour these men and the other soldiers who fought in the war. This monument is located in the middle of the village by the Little Tub.

Memorial Day Services are held at the cenotaph every year complete with the parade, prayers, speeches and observance of the minute of silence and Last Post so typical of services throughout Canada.

In 1932, a reunion banquet was held for ex-servicemen, their wives and friends, and afterwards, a dance was held for the general public. Later that week, the Veterans held a feast for eighty-eight children.

Cenotaph 1920's.

Iona and Gladys Davis — Navy

The Tobermory Branch of the Canadian Legion was formed in 1938. In August, the mayor of Wiarton presented Tobermory's newly-formed branch of the Legion, Branch #290, with its charter and installed its officers. The first president was A. S. Martin, the vice presidents were T. A. Golden and Martin Hopkins, and the secretary was Weir Grieve.

When the Second World War began, many Tobermory men enlisted. By January of 1942, a request was sent to the Ontario Command of the Legion, asking that the Tobermory branch be allowed to remain dormant for the rest of the war. The problem lay in finding enough officers to take the available positions as most men had joined the services and no remaining member wished to be the secretary. After receiving a letter from the provincial secretary asking them to reconsider their proposal to remain dormant, the branch decided instead to carry on in a limited way, meeting two to three times per year.

Edna Adams — Army Nurse

By the end of the war in 1945, over 70 local people had enlisted from the 70 homes at the Tub. No other area could beat this record of over one enlisted person per home. Tobermory residents had travelled all over the world and had seen many sights, that they would never forget. Two men, Gordon Belrose and Sidney Masterson, were killed in action and the community mourned their loss. Several men, including Reeve J. W. Ransbury, had served in the Royal Canadian Air Force while others showed more interest in areas such as the infantry, the rifle battalion, and the field ambulance brigade. Two young women, Gladys and Iona Davis, found a place for themselves in the Women's Royal Canadian Naval Service (W.R.E.N.S.), and Eva Wyonch became switchboard operator in the Canadian Women's Army Corp. (C.W.A.C.) in Kingston. Her sister Mrytle was also in the Army, and Edna Adams was an Army Nurse. Dr. Spenceley also put aside his local practice for several years to join the war effort.

Myrtle and Eva Wyonch — Army

During the Second World War, two Tobermory men received medals. Tom Hopkins received the "Military Medal" for bravery, and Cliff Woods received the "Order of the British Empire" for exceptional service.

There were many more notable enlisted residents who returned to their jobs after returning home. Most of these men had been fishermen. The reeve assumed his position again in 1948. Sheldon Ribbel returned to his Lion's Head Royal Mail Route, and others settled back with their new war brides, trying to reconstruct their lives as things had been before the war.

About a week after the war ended, the Canadian Legion met to discuss the construction of a new Legion Hall as a memorial to the community members who had given their lives or services in the Second World War. Members at the meeting contributed $230 to start a fund and the president, T. A. Golden, offered to donate a site for the building. By September, a lot had been chosen and a surprise gift of the former hunting clubhouse on Cove Island had been given to the Legion by Henry Bodman of Detroit.

Early in 1946, the following *Wiarton Echo* article was written regarding the formation of a Ladies' Auxiliary to the Legion:

"Nineteen wives of veterans gathered in the auditorium of the hall to hear Comrade Stewart Peacock, vice-president of the branch, explain the procedure required for formation of a Ladies' Auxiliary. The ladies agreed that Provincial Headquarters of the Legion should be asked to send an organizer to Tobermory for the purpose of starting an auxiliary."

Evelyn Young became the president of this new group consisting of 16 members.

In July of 1946, the Township received a grant of $500 from the County, to be used for a War Memorial. The Township granted an additional $1000 for this purpose, increasing the Legion Hall construction fund considerably. The Hall was under construction for 1947 and in February of 1948, the first Legion meeting was held in the new hall.

The Ladies' Auxiliary was very active during 1947 as they held a hunters dance in November and organized a Santa Claus Day celebration for the local children. Mr. and Mrs. Santa Claus arrived in the village in a one horse sleigh and distributed candies, nuts, and oranges. Carols were sung a little later and everyone had a good time.

In 1948, the Ladies' Auxiliary made up food parcels to be sent to families in Britain whose names had been submitted by members. Participation in the Blue Cross Hospital Plan was considered and it was announced that a piano had been bought for the hall. The next year, the ladies ordered dishes, glasses, and cutlery for use in the hall.

The ladies were of great help in 1951 when they prepared sandwiches and served tea for many hungry men who had spent hours searching for a lost boy. The boy was eventually found and no one returned home with an empty stomach.

WORLD WAR I
(1914-1918)
SERVED

C. Adair	C. Golden	E. Martin
W. Adams	T. Golden	J. Martin
H. Belrose	L. Graham	R. Martin
J. Belrose	A. Hopkins	J. McArtney
W. Belrose	J. Hopkins	J. McPhail
S. Craigie	M. Hopkins	H. Munn
J. Currie	R. Hopkins	L. Simpson
N. Currie	W. Hopkins	T. Spears
W. Currie	W. Hopkins	T. Spears
R. Dean	A. Martin	A. Young

KILLED IN ACTION

N. Campbell	J. McLeod	A. Smith
S. Campbell	F. Millwood	H. Willaughan

WORLD WAR II
(1939-1945)
SERVED

A. R. Adams	J. Barber Jr.	I. Connor
C. Adams	J. Barber	A. C. Coultis
E. H. Adams	B. Bartley	J. B. Craigie
J. H. S. Adams	B. Belrose	G. A. Craigie
J. J. Adams	K. C. Belrose	J. Cross
J. T. Adams	W. A. Belrose	A. Currie
T. J. Adams	V. Bravener	W. Currie
W. P. Adams	H. G. Chisholm	H. C. Davis
J. Davis	T. Knight	L. H. Smith
N. R. Davis	W. V. Leonard	R. V. Smith
W. W. Davis	N. Leslie	W. M. Smith
J. R. Desjardine	A. E. Martin	M. Spears
J. S. Desjardine	G. H. Martin	P. Spears
C. E. Eagles	L. J. Martin	W. A. Spears
E. W. Edmonstone	R. M. McArthur	E. C. Watson
D. Gibbons	W. McIvor	F. M. Watson
C. E. Golden	T. H. Munn	S. R. Watson
A. Hopkins	S. C. Peacock	J. White
B. H. A. Hopkins	J. Rae	F. Wipp
C. S. Hopkins	J. W. Ransbury	C. Woods O. BE.
G. Hopkins	W. E. Ransbury	F. Wright
G. B. Hopkins	E. Robinson	D. Wyonch
H. A. Hopkins	J. Rumley	J. S. Wyonch
J. Hopkins	A. T. M. Simpson	C. Young
R. Hopkins	G. B. Simpson	E. E. Young
T. A. Hopkins M. M.	H. C. Simpson	H. Young
W. S. Hopkins	E. M. Smith	M. E. Young
D. Hyde		

WOMEN WHO SERVED

E. Adams	I. Davis	M. Wyonch
G. Davis	E. Wyonch	

KILLED IN ACTION

J. E. Belrose	S. Masterson

SERVED IN KOREAN WAR (1949-1953)

G. Belrose	W. M. Ransbury

The Legion and the Auxiliary put a lot of effort into the community and contributed to many worthy causes in the late fifties. Donations were made to hospitals, the Children's Aid Society, the Institute for the Blind, the Byron Sanitorium, and the Tubercular Veteran's Summer Camp. Dances, banquets, bazaars, and teas were held and poppy canvasses were done to raise money.

A new building at the Legion Hall was officially opened in April of 1957. The addition was comprised of a kitchen, a store room, and toilets on the same floor level as the main hall. The Legion celebrated its 20th Anniversary in 1958 and a "past presidents" plaque was presented to the hall. That year membership was 47. During 1959, the Legion arranged for Tobermory donors to go to the Wiarton blood donor clinic. The Lion's Head Legion branch joined the local branch in bearing the cost for a plaque to be presented in connection with the Legion's Bruce Peninsula public speaking contest.

The sixties saw a continuation of the Legion's good works and in 1962, an honour roll plaque containing all the names of the local servicemen who had lost their lives in the war, and those that had died since, was dedicated by the Reverend Thomas Scott. In September of 1962, it was decided to write the District Department of Highways and the Deputy Minister asking that "the veterans' preference" be observed when men were hired for winter work in the district.

In 1963, a new electric stove was bought for the hall kitchen and a dinner was held to mark the Legion branch's 25th anniversary. At this dinner, Martin Hopkins, W. Earl McFarlane, Samuel Craigie, J. W. Hopkins, Charles Golden, and Weir Grieve received their 25 year membership badges.

Decoration Day was celebrated in the sixties. The Legion and Auxiliary members dressed in their formal uniforms, would attend a church service, and then go to the Dunk's Bay cemetery to place wreaths on the graves. In 1962, the Legion purchased a refrigerator for the hall and a committee was appointed to investigate the installing of a water supply in the hall. A cause that was considered worthy this year was the preservation of the shipwrecks of the area. To this end, the Legion sent a letter to the Department of Transport requesting their help and authority.

By 1981, many of the Legion men had passed away and the group was small and not very active. The Ladies' Auxiliary was still meeting regularly and holding penny sales, draws, dinners, bingo, and catering to wedding lunches. The big project for the year was to erect wings to the cenotaph and to update the list of servicemen on it to include all the servicemen from 1939 onward.

The biggest community event that the Legion now holds is the annual fish dinner which has been celebrated for years at the Community Hall. Today the Legion Hall is open most evenings and music can often be heard drifting out of it late in the evening. It is still a pleasant place to go for a drink and a chat.

Sidney Masterson — killed in action during World War II.

Gordon Belrose — killed in action World War II.

Alex (Andy) Young, Whit Hopkins, Alex McPhail, Barney Hopkins, World War I.

Howard Chisholm, Carl Hopkins, Bud Hopkins, Tom Hopkins, Harry Davis, Neil Leslie, World War II.

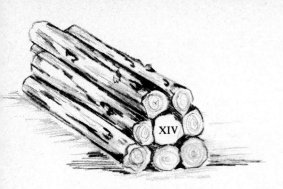

CHAPTER FOURTEEN

PLACES *in* ST. EDMUNDS

PLACE NAMES IN ST. EDMUNDS TOWNSHIP

The place names entered below are among those best remembered by the older residents of St. Edmunds Township. Some of these names originated in their own youth, and others were part of the folklore which they inherited from previous generations. Some names perpetuate particular incidents such as a shipwreck, the memory of an early settler, or a particular aspect of the natural environment. While the origin of some of these names has been lost, the inception of others at a later date means that they are well remembered. Although many of these names are well remembered, they have fallen out of everyday usage as the official names given on maps are more familiar to people who have not been living in the area for a long time. The large numbers of tourists have perhaps exerted a subtle influence on the disuse of place names and other local traditions. This reflects the fear that many area natives have of being considered a "country bumpkin". The disappearance of these colourful local names is unfortunate, for they relieve the urban cosmopolitan blandness that is found in many areas of this province.

Some of the following names were discovered by Patrick Folkes, and others came from the older residents of the area. The names in the quotation marks are the local names, and those bracketed are the official names. Wherever possible, the location and the origin of the place names have been given.

"Worts Shoal" (Southwest Bank) — after the wreck of the schooner 'James G. Worts', 1895.

"Plucky" (Middle Island) — origin unknown.

"Otter Nook" — a shallow bay one mile northeast of Cape Hurd.

"Pott's Crook" — a narrow inlet on the southeastern shore of Hay Bay.

"The Gap" — the termination point of Highway 6, overlooking the entrance of the Big Tub.

"Indian Bay" — a small indentation in the shore midway between Big Tub and Little Tub; formed on the west side by "Fish Gut Point"; a landing point until the 1920's of Indians arriving down from Manitoulin Island by sail boat.

"Burnt Point" (Dunk's Point) — in memory of a forest fire of unknown date.

"Wireless Point" (North Point) — after the nearby site of Marconi Wireless Station, now Trail's End Lodge.

"Dave's Bay" (Little Cove) — Dave Butchart was the early resident of this place.

"Whiskey Still Marsh" — a swamp two miles south, southeast of the head of Dorcas Bay.

"Old Coat Corner" — Highway 6 and Johnston Harbour Road. Someone hung an old coat on a tree at the corner to give directions and it remained there for many years.

"The Long Bridge" — on Highway 6, one half mile south of Willow; named after a bridge built across a swamp known as "Little Lake" in 1910.

"Wreck Point" — the outcrop of land north of China Cove.

"Ragged Bight" — the inlet of water south of China Cove at the base of Cape Hurd.

"Baptist Harbour" — the harbour on the south side of Cape Hurd.

"Newaygo Shoal" (Northwest Bank) — after the wreck of the steambarge 'Newaygo', 1903.

"Stag Island" — a small island lying off the west shore of Cove Island about midway between Channel Point and Gat Point.

"Ed's Harbour" — a narrow islet lying on the south side of Gat Point. Ed Young was the early resident.

"Cassels' Cove" (Boat Harbour) — a shallow inlet on the east side of Cove Island; so-called after Thomas Cassels' timbering camp, 1905-1909.

"George Lake" — the inland lake on Cove Island.

"Starlight Point" (Eagle Point) — after the stranding of the schooner 'Starlight', 1893.

"McRae's" — at the head of the Boat Passage, Cove Island; possibly commemorates the memory of a building or cabin.

"La Ronde's" — the large log cottage on the east shore of Cove Island Harbour; erected in the 1920's.

"Leslie's Shoal" — a reef running southwest of Turning Island.

"Rabbit Island" (Russel Island) — after the large number of rabbits said to inhabit the island; or in memory of the towbarges 'James C. King' and 'Brunette' (wrecked in 1901), a type of ship frequently referred to as "rabbits"; the island was also known as "Find Out Island".

"Gut Dock" — a small pier once situated on the southwest side of Doctor Island and used as a place to clean fish.

"Earl's Patches" — Patrick Earl is believed to have spotted a sunken chest in the water off one of the islands. He hired Archie Simpson, then about 10 years old, to row him out to the island where he could sit and try to hook the chest.

"Toenail Hill" — a steep hill on the highway where the horses and humans had to dig in their toenails in order to get up it.

"Orange Meadow" — a field covered in orange flowers in the summer, one mile north of Willow Creek on Highway 6.

"Mrs. Munn's Bathtub" — a curve in the road at which Mrs. Munn fell out of the buggy that her son was driving. It was during the wet spring weather and she fell into a deep puddle. When he turned around, she was sitting in water to her waist.

"Woods' Swamp" — Billy Woods lived on this lot and it is said that he lived downstairs in his home and kept his many hens upstairs.

"Nine Mile Stone" — marked the ninth mile along the road at Willow Creek on Highway 6.

"Willow Creek" — origin unknown.

"Hemlock Hill" — origin unknown.

"Smith's Gulley" — John Smith's timber shanty home, father of Mrs. Percy Adams.

"Dorcas Bay Swamp" — origin unknown.

"Old Bob Ransom's" — an abandoned cabin overlooking Shoal Bight, Tobermory Harbour, and said to be the only building between Little Tub and North Point until the 1920's.

"Little Lake" — origin unknown.

"Sandhills" — origin unknown. Dorcas Bay area.

"Singing Sands" — the head of Dorcas Bay so named because the sand blowing from the beach hums in the wind.

"Blueberry Marsh" — on Lot 47, Concession 1, WBR; traditionally the only spot where blueberries grew in the area and was in use until the 1950's.

"Black Alex's Corner" — named after Alex Campbell, a settler on Lot 51, Concession 3, WBR.

"Cooney's Hollow" — a small but well defined gulley that intersects Highway 6 about two hundred yards north of the Dunks Bay Road. Named after an early resident of that name.

"The Dead Horses" — a place where the carcasses of horses killed in a stable fire were dumped; located about two hundred yards west of Bee Haven Tourist Home on the original Hay Bay road.

"Dog Patch" — a small clearing in the old wagon road at the head of the Big Tub. In 1946, the Norisle docked at Big Tub. Two families, one named Edwards, built a booth on top of the hill on the north side at the head of Big Tub and called it Dog Patch. They sold pop, candies, cigarettes and other items.

"Greasy Meg's" — named after the site of Maggie Killbreath's home opposite Happy Heart's Campground.

"Munn's Corner" — intersection of Highway 6 and the 50th sideroad. Andrew Munn's farm is adjacent.

"School Corner" — the intersection of sideroad 45 and Highway 6 at the old Settlement School, which is now the Museum.

Bob Ransom's cabin

Lumbering Scenes

Big Tub Harbour approximately 1910

Left to Right: **Warren Adams' smoke house, dwelling of Ben and Mary Young, Buckeye Boat Shop of Alex (Candy) Young.**

Then — **Ferry leaving dock 1920's**

Now — **Ferry preparing to leave dock 1980's**

Then — **Tobermory Ferry Dock about 1948**

Now — **Tobermory Ferry Dock and Terminal 1983**

Then — **Kosy Kove Koffee Shoppe and Clayton Young
1930's.**

Now — **Vera Whit Hopkins house, driveway and
Peacocks Grocery 1983.**

Then — **Little Tub Harbour**

Then — **Little Tub Harbour**

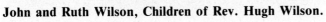

John and Ruth Wilson, Children of Rev. Hugh Wilson.

Then — **Little Tub Harbour**

Then — **Little Tub Harbour**

Then — **Golden's General Store between 1910-1920.**

Now — **The Peninsula Supply 1983**

Then — **Ritchie's Restaurant 1945**

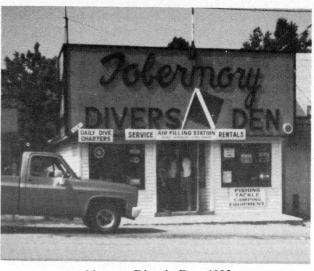

Now — **Diver's Den 1983**

Then — **William Gillies General Store before 1910**

Now — **Liquor Store 1983**

Then — **Overlooking village from Cenotaph area about 1936**

1983

COVE ISLAND LIGHTHOUSE

The sequence of events which led to the erection of the lighthouse on Cove Island are as yet unclear. The expansion of shipping and the hazards of navigating the entrance to Georgian Bay were doubtless the crucial factors. By 1852 the southwest extremity of the island had been proposed as a site. That same year, Captain A. Murray MacGregor of Goderich was appointed to select the positions of six lighthouses on Lake Huron and Georgian Bay — Clark Point, Chantry, Cove, Griffith, Nottawasaga, and Christian Islands.

In 1855, the contract for the chain of lights, along with harbour improvements at Kincardine, Inverhuron, and Southampton, was let to John Brown, a veteran Thorold contractor who had taken part in the enlargement of the Welland Canal during the eighteen forties. Each station, at a cost of $3,500, was to consist of a light tower and adjacent keeper's dwelling, both of ashlar or cut stone. The entire project was a massive undertaking and in the end cost in each case $1,500 above the original estimate. Supplies such as sand and cement had to be brought in great distances by steamboat or schooner, several of which were wrecked.

The construction on Gig Point of the Cove Island lighthouse began in the late summer or early autumn of 1855. By the end of navigation in November the keeper's cottage had been erected and the first storey of the 80-foot tower laid down. Work was resumed in May of 1856 and in July there were seven masons and stone cutters, ten labourers, one blacksmith, a foreman, and three horses engaged in the work. On August 23 when A. G. Robinson, chief engineer of the Board of Public Works, arrived at the island on board the schooner 'Indian Maid', the tower stood fifty-three feet above the base and carpenters were busily finishing the interior of the cottage. By October the tower had been raised to its full height, the first of the six structures to be so completed. There is no evidence to support the legend that the ashlar was brought from Scotland. Brown opened quaries at Inverhuron, the Fishing Islands, and Owen Sound, and Robinson noted in June of 1855 that the necessary stone could be procured at Gig Point.

Such were the demands of navigation that Brown's crew maintained a temporary light during their presence on the island. The arrival and installation of the permanent light, a device manufactured by L. Sautter of Paris, France, was attended by great delay. Through the season of 1857, no light of any sort was displayed, nor does any attempt appear to have been made to complete the lantern room. In the spring of 1858, George Collins was appointed keeper. He arrived at Cove Island on May 22 and kept a temporary beacon until the arrival of the permanent light in October.

The subsequent history of the lighthouse is as yet unexplored. A cursory examination of the known source material indicates that memorable and dramatic incidents were common to life at the station. Storms and shipwrecks, the physical evolution of the lighthouse, the background and life of each keeper, the relationship of the lighthouse to Tobermory, and the whole range of daily activities on the island — unique even within the context of the history of Georgian Bay — give to the maritime themes of Fathom Five Park an unbroken continuity spanning one hundred and twenty years.

Strategically located in a wilderness of uninhabited islands the lighthouse frequently provided shelter for mariners in distress, such as the crews of the schooners 'San Jacinto', lost at Yeo Island, and 'Sarah Jane', wrecked on Manitoulin Island (1881), and that of the 'Charles P. Minch' (1898). Technologically, the light passed through several stages, i.e., an Argand lamp utilizing sperm oil, then a flatwick coal oil lamp, and about 1900 an oil vapour light in which vapourized kerosene was burned in an incandescent mantle. Sometime during the nineteen fifties, electrification by means of an on-site generator was introduced, and in 1971 a submarine power cable was laid from the mainland. A steam powered fog-horn was erected in 1883 and a radio beacon prior to 1940. The lives of the keeper and his family revolved entirely around the maintenance of the light.

Until at least 1883 they wintered on the island, a duty of some peril, as is illustrated in the selection of documents appended to this report. From the meagre information presently at hand, it is evident that the keepers were individuals of singular experience. David McBeath, the second keeper, was formerly assistant keeper of a

Cove Island Lighthouse

Cove Island Light

Happy Reunions by Phone and in Person as Lightkeepers Rescued

Harold Banas assures his anxious mother in Toronto that he is alright and didn't catch cold after being adrift on Georgian Bay in an open twenty foot outboard motor boat for twenty hours and weathering a forty mile an hour westerly gale. Banas is lightkeeper at Cove Island at the extreme tip of the Bruce Peninsula, and shared his ordeal with Alva Stewart, his assistant at the Lighthouse. The two made a landing on Half Moon Island, eighteen miles northeast of Tobermory and were spotted by a seaplane. They were rescued by the Government Lighthouse Tender St. Heliers at six o'clock Monday evening. Picture on right shows Harold Banas as he stepped ashore from the St. Heliers to be greeted by his wife and a close friend, Barney Hopkins of Tobermory.—Sun-Times Staff Photos.

Marvin Graham, assistant lightkeeper at Cove Island, prepares to light the big lamp, which, flashing through giant lenses, can be seen as far as fifty miles away. The lamp revolves on a carriage cushioned in mercury, powered by weights strung to a clock-like drive.

lighthouse in Scotland and later an employee of the Hudson's Bay Company. George Collins transferred to the Nottawasaga light and in 1872 was awarded an inscribed gold watch by the Department of Marine and Fisheries in recognition of saving a life on Georgian Bay between 1860 and 1870.

Documents pertaining to David McBeath, keeper, Cove Island lighthouse, 1860

D. C. Smith, Superintendent of Light Houses, to T. Trudeau, Secretary, Department of Public Works, Quebec City:

Odessa 8th Novr 1860
Sir,

I beg leave to State for the information of the Hon. the Commissioner, that I have received a letter from Mr. David McBeath Light Keeper at the Isle of Coves, requesting me to write to the Department to have whatever monies may be due to him and his sons sent to the Bank of Upper Canada in Toronto.

I would recommend one quarter's salary advanced to him, as he is in indigent circumstances with a large family, and in winter season cannot lay in his stock of provisions.

Telegram: Captain Thomas Dick, Collingwood, to Commissioner of Public Works, Quebec City:

1 Decr 1860

The Collector & surveyor of Customs here informs me that the Light House Keeper at Isle of Coves Lake Huron is out of provisions & must starve unless supplied. The steamer 'Rescue' is about laying up but can be kept out long enough to take provisions if the Dept. will say she shall be paid.

Telegram: T. Trudeau, Secretary, Department of Public Works, to Captain Thomas Dick, Collingwood:

3 Decr 1860
Capt. Dick

Provisions must be sent immediately. Department has sent Instructions to Collector of Customs & Postmaster.

There have been a number of lighthouse keepers at the Cove Island Lighthouse, and each has many stories to tell about his experiences there. The *Wiarton Echo* has written a series of articles about the lighthouse over the years, and this is the main source of material for this section.

Life On Cove Island

In 1945, Lighthouse Keeper Harold Banas married Iris Hine in the first wedding ever performed at the lighthouse. The year following their wedding, the couple underwent a nerve-racking experience when Harold Banas was lost for twenty-seven hours.

Harold and his assistant light keeper had been testing out a new boat and outboard motor when the motor failed. The two men then tried to row back to the island, but the oarlocks broke, and the men were swept by the wind to Half Moon Island, almost eighteen miles away.

It was a few hours before Mrs. Banas realized that the two men had disappeared. As she had no means of communicating with the mainland, and as she did not know how to operate the lighthouse light, Mrs. Banas hoped that someone would notice that the light was not lit and would come to investigate. It was the next morning before help did arrive. Hugh Rumley, the Lighthouse

Keeper of the Flowerpot Island Light, had noticed that the light on Cove Island was not functioning but had not been able to investigate due to the poor weather. When he did arrive at Cove Island, he collected Mrs. Banas and boated to Tobermory to spread the alarm to search for the two missing men.

It was fortunate that there was a seaplane moored in the Big Tub, for this aided the search. Mr. Lentz, the owner of the plane, located the men on Half Moon Island after searching an area of two hundred square miles. As his plane was too small to pick up the two men, he informed the Department of Transport to pick up the two men in the "St. Heliers", a boat that had been dispatched from Midland to aid in the search. Both men were successfully rescued and returned to the safety of Tobermory.

The Lighthouse Equipment

Unlike the Big Tub Lighthouse and the Flowerpot Lighthouse, the Cove Island Lighthouse maintains a light, a foghorn, and a radio beam.

The light is actually a 500-watt bulb that is magnified by prisms to approximately ten times that power. This magnification causes the light or glow to be seen anywhere from seventeen to fifty miles away, depending on the atmospheric conditions. There are six of these prisms mounted on a frame that revolves around the light. The prisms are each separated by a section of the frame. This is what gives the impression that the light is being turned on and off when it is actually on all the time. All of the machinery of the light floats on a base of liquid mercury. The machinery that causes the light to revolve is the original material installed when the lighthouse was built. This machinery is powered by a set of weights that are wound and started by hand, much like the weights in a cuckoo clock.

In foggy weather, the light flashes at a rate of twelve flashes per minute.

The foghorn is a piece of equipment that has largely become outdated due to the use of radar. However, ships' captains are content that it still functions as they can verify the radar's operation by it. The foghorn is an air horn that is filled by an air compressor. It gives three blasts a minute on foggy days and can be heard up to twenty miles away.

The most recent addition to the lighthouse equipment is the radio beam. The radio beam sends out the signal for the letter "D" every hour. This signal helps ships to find their position in regards to the lighthouse. By taking a bearing on two lighthouses besides Cove, a ship is able to locate its exact position on the charts.

Bill Spears, keeper of the Cove Island light, relaxes with his daughter, Linda Kaye, 10 and Janet Graham, Daughter of his assistant, Marvin Graham. Mr. Spears, a native of Tobermory, has been on the job seven years.

FLOWERPOT ISLAND LIGHTHOUSE

In 1896, the Flowerpot Island Lighthouse was built to guide ships as they travelled from Georgian Bay to Lake Huron. Unlike the Cove Island Lighthouse, the Flowerpot Lighthouse was built of wood. Over the years, the elements took their toll and in 1968, it was decided that the old wooden lighthouse should be torn down. A new steel tower and a foghorn plant were installed in its place by the Ministry of Transport.

In constructing the new tower, the Ministry encountered a number of problems. They soon found that they had to unload building supplies directly off the boat by hoisting them up a seventy foot cliff to the building site. The difficulty in landing boats also prevented heavy machinery from being used.

A new dwelling has also been erected, but the original one still stands and is in good condition. The station has had thousands of visitors over the years as a point of interest for those visiting the island, which is a National Park.

Flowerpot

Flower Pot Light, the Old and the New.

167

CHAPTER FIFTEEN

THE PEOPLE *of* ST. EDMUNDS TOWNSHIP

TOBERMORY NICKNAMES

The first nicknames in Tobermory were probably an answer to the problem of having too many Williams, Johns, Roberts, Charles', James', and Marys.

The Hopkins were an especially troublesome family in this respect as there were two Roberts, several Johns and a couple of James'. To avoid confusion, some of these people had their second name or initial added to their first name when they were referred to. This led to a clearer distinction between just "Robert" and "Robert Allan" and between "John" and "John C." and between "James" and "James H.". To confuse matters further, James Whitmore Hopkins wife Vera is known today as Vera Whit. — and don't try to look that up in a phone book!

Many names originated in childhood and just seemed to stick over the years so that, even now, several oldtimers are known only by their nicknames. John Carlton Munn is one such as these. His friends named him "Bazoo" in fun when he was a child and over the years it was shortened to "Baise". This name sticks even today in his 83rd year.

Some names such as "Little Jimmy", "Husky" and "Blue-eyed Mary" describe discerning features or physical characteristics, while other names have no logical explanation.

The name in quotation marks is the nickname; the other is the proper or given name.

Local Residents' Nicknames

"Diddie"	Doreen Adams
"Nookie"	Norma Adams
"Bunny"	Yvonne Adams
"Dedee"	Marie Bartley
"Dot"	Mildred Bartley
"Biddle"	Vera Bartley
"Blue-eyed Mary"	Mary Belrose
"Tuck"	Russel Belrose
"Pid"	Howard Chisholm
"Sis"	Marie Chisholm
"Dick"	Bill Craigie
"Fritz"	Reg Craigie
"Ma Davey"	Mrs. Carroll Davey
"Ted"	Cecil Davis
"Pick"	Helen Edmonstone
"Tighe"	Gordon Gibbons
"Dimples"	Ailean Golden
"Little Jimmy"	James Hopkins
"Bud"	W. S. Hopkins
"Oee"	Zora Hopkins
"Buster"	Arnold Martin
"Bubbles"	Laura Martin
"Mezz"	Melvin Martin
"Jiggs"	R. M. McArthur
"Buff"	Ivor McLeod
"Oat"	Lawrence McLeod
"Toots"	Margaret McLeod
"Staring"	David Munn
"Hub"	Hiram Munn
"Baise"	John Carlton Munn
"Stub"	J. W. Ransbury
"Cy"	George Simpson
"Dode"	George Smith
"Tiny"	Gertrude Smith
"Bungee"	Oscar Smith
"Operator Billy"	W. J. Smith
"Indian Billy"	W. H. Smith
"Pop"	Ivan Watson
"Dot"	Loyais Wyonch
"Cap"	Clayton Young
"Buck"	Harold Young
"Nonie"	Kathleen Young
"Mattie"	Martha Young
"Husky"	Martin Young
"Candy"	William A. Young

BIOGRAPHIES
Tobermory Residents

Wiarton Echo, June, 1954

WEIR GRIEVE

Tobermory Scribe Wins Highest Ontario Honour

Weir Grieve, 72-year-old bachelor who has been Tobermory correspondent for the Wiarton Echo during the past thirteen years, brought honour to himself, this newspaper and his own community when he was named Champion Country Correspondent of Ontario at the convention of the Ontario Weekly Newspaper Association at London last week-end. (June 11th, 1954) The award, presented this year for the first time, by the Ontario Hydro Commission, was considered by daily newspapers to be one of the highest given at the convention.

Only Man Chosen

Of six country correspondents from Ontario weeklies picked out for prizes in the contest, Mr. Grieve was the only man. In awarding him the first prize, the chairman of the judges' committee, Clarence V. Charters, a former president of the Canadian weeklies, and a prominent publisher, paid tribute to Mr. Grieve's many years of service to his community in a multitude of roles.

Wins Bronze Plaque

Prize for winning the championship was a bronze plaque, engraved with his name and achievement. It was presented personally to Mr. Grieve at the weekly association's dinner in the Hotel London on Friday evening. Presentation was made by Jim Blay, director of information for the HEPC. Mr. Blay also presented the Wiarton Echo with an engraved scroll outlining the achievement of its correspondent. The latter was accepted by W. B. T. Smiley.

Mr. Grieve was a head-table celebrity at the dinner, along with Rixton Rafter, 70-year-old retired editor of the Arthur Enterprise, blind since childhood, who was honoured as "Newspaperman of the Year."

How He Does It

Other correspondents and Echo readers will be interested in the manner in which Weir Grieve picks up the news that won him the championship. To cover meetings in the village, he attends, or arranges to get the information from someone who is there. In most cases, he must be present himself, anyway, because he is on the executive.

For general news, in his own words, "I repair to the pool room and filling station run by Alex Holmes, where I learn a lot about who is visiting in town. I also frequent the village's two restaurants, where I quaff coffee and smoke and keep my ears open." Later in the day he might pay a visit to the docks, where he picks up all the latest items about guide boats, commercial fishing, ferry news and other marine activities.

If he has some late news that is important, he telephones it to the Echo. If it is not too important, he sends it along on Friday or Saturday, so that the Echo linotype operator gets an early start on next week's news. Again Monday morning, he sends down the week-end news, and a third lot often arrives Tuesday.

Mr. Grieve admits to being a nighthawk. He seldom goes to bed early and often writes his news at night, mailing it early in the morning before going to bed.

There are not many Ontario weeklies who have correspondents as far as fifty miles away, yet Mr. Grieve gets all the news of Tobermory and district in, and gets it in faithfully and on time.

He would be the first to admit that he has an exceptional chance to do a good job as a correspondent because he is a bachelor, and is retired. This gives him a lot more time to work at the job than the average correspondent, who is usually a busy housewife.

Army Service

A glimpse at Mr. Grieve's background shows that he has lived an interesting and useful life. Born in Scotland, he was educated in Glasgow. He graduated as a lawyer and spent seven years at his profession, until World War I broke out. A member of the famous Territorials, he went to war in August 1914 and served his country for five years as a soldier, rising to the rank of Captain. His army service included a spell in Ireland following the Easter Rebellion of 1916, and several months in Germany, in 1919, in the army of occupation.

Following the war, he decided to come to America and for seven years travelled through the U. S., working at all sorts of jobs. Then he read an advertisement about land for sale on the Bruce Peninsula. He arrived in Tobermory, bought some land, and built himself a log cabin. He has lived there ever since, and has become an integral part of the life of the village.

Busy Man

He has been an official or member of many community organizations, including the community hall, the township council, the United Church, the Orange Lodge, the school board, the library board and the badminton club. He was the first secretary of the Canadian Legion branch at Tobermory. He served the township as reeve for some years. He was active in a dramatic group in the village for several years.

The Echo is proud of all its correspondents, and especially so of Mr. Grieve for the honour he has won. We hope he has many years of happy and useful living ahead of him.

The following is a program of Weir Grieve night held by the Tobermory Legion before he left for Scotland. An appreciation night was also held at the community centre in his honour.

R O Y A L   C A N A D I A N   L E G I O N

Branch - 290 - TOBERMORY, Ontario, Canada.

OCTOBER, 23rd., 1965.

IN 1926, a former Captain of the 9th., Highland Light
Infantry, came to Tobermory and took up permanent Residence with us.

THIS PERSON, was Comrade, WEIR GRIEVE, but alas our High
ly Esteemed Comrade has decided to go back to
his Home in Bonny Scotland - His Native Land,
to spend the remainder of his days.

SINCE WEIR has been in our midst, he has been a valuable
Asset to our Community and a Friend to all. We
simply hate to see him take his departure.

TO GIVE a Brief Outline of some of his activities, below,
is a partial List of some of the various Duties
he undertook and performed Faithfully -

NINE YEARS on THE COUNCIL - SIX of them as REEVE

CHAIRMAN of THE LIBRARY BOARD

MEMBER of THE SCHOOL BOARD

CHAIRMAN of THE POPPY FUND - Branch 290.

CHAPLAIN of THE ORANGE LODGE

He Served the UNITED CHURCH as - CLERK of THE SESSION
CHAIRMAN of THE BOARD - TREASURER - SUNDAY SCHOOL
SUPERINTENDENT and at times CARETAKER.

He also Served as SECRETARY to Branch 290 - ROYAL
CANADIAN LEGION and incidently was one of the Original
Members who were Instrumental in the Formation of our
Branch.

In between times he managed to Serve us as NEWS REPORTER
for the OWEN SOUND SUN TIMES and THE WIARTON ECHO.

STAG DINNER and SOCIAL EVENING

in

HONOUR OF

Comrade, WEIR GRIEVE

LIFE MEMBER - CHARTER MEMBER - 25 YEAR PIN HOLDER

COMRADE, GRIEVE is leaving us to Return to his Native
Land.

BON VOYAGE and LANG MAY YOUR LUM REEK

COMRADES, this is truly a Record to be Proud of - and
we are all proud to have Comrade, GRIEVE as
one of our Members. It is too bad that we
have to lose him, but our Loss is anothers
gain.

IF EVER a man Deserves a Rest, Weir does although we are
all somewhat downcast at his leaving, we are
all Happy in the knowledge that, he still has
the Good Health to enjoy his Trip home ⊙ in
spite of the fact that he is only 83 Years
young. Needless to say it is our Sincere -
Wish that - Young Weir will have many - many
more years to sit back and Relax.

YES, COMRADES, the time comes when all Old War Horses
have to go out to Pasture - and it is our Hope
that Weir will take full advantage of the time
at his disposal. We will envy him as he Basks
under the Skies of his beloved Homeland may
his thoughts turn back to Tobermory - his
adopted Home and think of us, as we will never
forget him and the Services he has rendered
us. The thoughtful and kindly manner he used,
at all times when dealing with any Problems
that confronted him or his Colleagues, will
never be forgotten.

GOD SPEED and BON VOYAGE - Comrade GRIEVE - and may the
Good Lord Watch over you and Spare you for
a long time yet - this is our Fond Hope and
Finally - THANK YOU for a Job WELL DONE.

The MEMBERSHIP and LADIES

of Branch, 290, ROYAL CANADIAN LEGION

AFTER DINNER - Our Ladies have been Invited to join the
Men Folk for a SOCIAL EVENING - a SPECIAL
THANK YOU to our Ladies for the Wonderful
Dinner, they worked so hard to Prepare.
THANK YOU - Ladies.

Weir returned to his native Scotland and finally settled in Oban, and there he spent his remaining days.

It is at Oban that you catch the ferry to go to Tobermory, Scotland, on the Isle of Mull.

Weir touched everyone's life while living in Tobermory, Canada, and may he rest in peace in Oban, Scotland.

Weir Grieve Appreciation Night.
From left to right: **Eunice Wheildon, Cecil Davis, Weir Grieve, J. P. Johnstone** *(standing)*, **Rev. George Trigger, Ed Erb.**

MR. RAY HEPBURN

Owen Sound Sun Times, June, 1971
Retiring Principal, R. Hepburn
Always Happiest In Classroom
By Les Moyse

"I've had a rewarding career in teaching" said the principal pensively "and the classroom is where I am happiest" he added.

These are the sentiments of Raymond Hepburn who retires at the end of this month after over 40 years of school teaching and almost 16 years as principal of Strathcona public school.

Simultaneous with his retirement, a new era will emerge as the establishment becomes a senior school. Many of Mr. Hepburn's pupils will be moved elsewhere and the incoming principal will receive pupils from other schools on the east side who enter Grade 7.

Mr. Hepburn was born at Hope Bay, on the Bruce Peninsula and was educated in the one-room school prior to attending the OSCVI.

Upon graduation, he entered Stratford Teachers' College where he trained in 1927 and 1928. The two year stint was permitted due to the "depression".

Mr. Hepburn's first teaching assignment was at S. S. No. 1, St. Edmunds Township, Tobermory, where he remained for one year then moved to the three-room village school where he spent 12 years as principal and taught Grades 5 and 6, including industrial arts.

"There was a healthy type of rivalry in those days among families" Mr. Hepburn recalled "and the students were very capable."

During the summer holidays those days, Mr. Hepburn supplemented his income by taking a position as purser on the ferry and at other times as a commercial fisherman.

"We used to get up at 4 a.m. to lift the nets and in the evenings pitched ball in the Park Head-Hepworth area.

At the outbreak of the Second World War, Mr. Hepburn tried to enlist in the armed services. "I went to the army, navy and air force" he said "but although I was physically fit I never heard anything more." It was later thought the fact he was not called was due to his profession as a school teacher when teachers were in short supply.

But from 1943 until 1945 Mr. Hepburn took a position with Russell-Hipwell Ltd., in the engineering and sales department.

When hostilities ceased, Mr. Hepburn went to the Mount Forest elementary school as principal and commuted from Owen Sound each day because accommodation was not obtainable.

One year later he transferred to Strathcona school to become vice-principal where he remained for 7-1/2 years. Then for one year he taught at the OSCVI.

"Mr. Prudham then principal told me that because of my experience as an elementary school teacher, I was versatile and consequently I taught English, French, social studies and commercial mathematics, as well as doing guidance counselling and assisting with school sports" said Mr. Hepburn.

The final move came after the year spent at the OSCVI when he returned to Strathcona and was appointed principal.

Having received a bachelor of arts degree from the University of Western Ontario in 1953, Mr. Hepburn took post-graduate studies and obtained his bachelor of education degree. But he never went down to the convocation to receive it.

"I wrote many applications for supervisory positions but would sleep on them and tear them up next morning" said Mr. Hepburn. In all, he obtained 11 certificates from department of education courses.

Unlike many principals, Mr. Hepburn maintains a regular teaching schedule for himself and spends as much time in the classroom as he can. Many of his pupils are children of parents that he taught.

Former pupils often call upon him when visiting the city or coming to the school for special occasions.

Mr. Hepburn said it is very odd how a situation develops when some of these former pupils ask "do you remember this or that?"

"I clearly recall the pleasant experiences, but require a detailed account before remembering the unpleasant," he said. "But my concerns about the latter are usually erased when assured that my action, cruel as it may seem was appreciated and respected as a guiding influence in later life" he added.

Strathcona school has been cosmopolitan in its day and Mr. Hepburn still recalls some of the pupils of various national origins. One pupil came to the school only speaking French and was having difficulties in a lesson.

"When I wrote a sentence on the board in French, he became exhilarated" he said.

Another pupil could not speak any English and so Mr. Hepburn told a student to take him in the yard and show him the trees, tell him the words, and teach him to play ball. The pupil later progressed well and graduated from Oxford University and holds an important position.

Mr. Hepburn has been a member of the Owen Sound Kiwanis Club and the Y's Men and hopes to resume Kiwanis activities in the future. He has been associated with Knox United Church for 22 years and is presently an elder.

He has always been active in sports in the city and other parts of the district.

Asked what he plans to do in his retirement, he chuckled that his wife has "about eight years of work for him to do".

Mr. And Mrs. Hepburn plan to travel and will visit his brother in Vancouver, B. C., in the near future, as well as spend some time with their daughter, Carol and son-in-law and family in Oakville.

About 150 former students and staff members returned to honor Mr. Hepburn at Strathcona school Sunday afternoon. Cartoon sketches of his history were projected and many tributes from former and present staff members.

The sketches were prepared by Ron Prout, Strathcona art teacher, and two Grade 7 students, Terry McMillan and David Eldred.

Mr. Hepburn was presented with a chair.

MARGARET (BELROSE) PARKER

Wiarton Echo, May 9, 1946

First White Child Born In Tobermory
Sorry To Have Missed Film Premiere

One person who should have been present when Tobermory went "Hollywood" and opened its doors to the film premiere, "I Know Where I'm Going," was Mrs. John Parker of Wiarton. "I was the first white child born in the Village of Tobermory," Mrs. Parker proudly relates, "and I was sorry to have missed the show on Monday." It was a long time ago that Mrs. Parker first saw the light of day, in December, 1875, to be exact, but she can quite vividly remember things that happened after her fourth birthday.

At the age of six Mrs. Parker started to school as Margaret Belrose, and, as she says, the class at that time was not very large. Her parents, Mr. And Mrs. Jacob Belrose, settled one and one-half miles outside the village three months before their daughter was born. They arrived in Tobermory from Owen Sound, making the journey by boat, there being no road of any account through the Peninsula wilds. Mr. Belrose built their home, a log cabin, erected from logs hewn and carried by himself, and when the barn was later constructed every board had to be carried from Dyer's Bay, with the shingles for the roof being shaved by hand. To explain what it was like on the Peninsula in those early days, Mrs. Parker asked if we knew what an Indian trail was like, explaining that this would give us some inkling into pioneer times. Her father was the mailman for the village, and his duties included getting the mail in from Stokes Bay once a week — a feat he accomplished via horseback. "He left on Monday," Mrs. Parker recalled, "and was usually back on Tuesdays, if stormy weather didn't hold him up."

Mrs. Parker grew up in the Tobermory community, and in 1894 she was united in marriage to John Parker, by the Rev. Mr. Harnwell, now of Walkerton. Her husband was lighthouse-keeper on Flower Pot Island for nine years prior to the installing of electricity, and the fog lamp had to be operated by hand. In 1910 they took up residence in Wiarton where she has made her home since. Mr. Parker passed away in 1933. There were seven children born to the union, six of whom are still living, including John Parker of Port Dover, William of Wiarton, (Violet) Mrs. Roy King, Farmington, Mich., (Myrtle) Mrs. O. E. Langford, Wiarton, (Bertha) Mrs. Clarence Hardy, Toronto, and Clayton, a Great Lakes' sailor, who makes his winter home in town. (Lettie) Mrs. Wesley Allan, died in 1920.

Although the premiere film showing was successful in every detail, colour would have been added with the presence of the first white child born in the village, and Mrs. Parker would have enjoyed every minute of it.

MR. LLOYD SMITH

Wiarton Echo, October 1, 1980
Lloyd Smith Exhibit Opens In Tobermory

Lloyd Smith, long-time resident of Tobermory, lived between the years 1908 and 1978.

He saw many changes in his own area and in the world. He adapted to change in a way that explored the many facets of a talented and sensitive spirit.

Lloyd Smith grew and was many things: fisherman, musician, nature-lover, photographer, masterful wood carver, and furniture maker, guide, cook, boat builder, home builder, soldier.

He was always the same, too; and the image that remains in the mind is one of a young Lloyd Smith strumming his banjo to a boat full of friends under a moonlit sky.

A special exhibit of the life and works of Lloyd Smith prepared by the Grey-Bruce Arts Council opened in Tobermory last Friday, at Circle Arts.

The display is in a special room set aside on the second floor.

It includes examples of Lloyd's wood-carving art, some of his photographs, and a sketch of his life with other photographs.

Lloyd's father was a fisherman for forty years, and so was his older brother.

Lloyd himself got a commercial fishing license in 1928, and he was "in boats" for the rest of his life; in fact, he lived on a boat until he was married. That boat was the 'Albacore' a vessel that combined sail and motor power.

In 1942 Lloyd went into the Air Force.

After the war when he returned to the 'Tub' there were many changes.

The lake trout fell off drastically because of the increase in the smelt population and the appearance of the lamprey.

Tourism began to flourish, and Lloyd and others began to take tours by boat to the islands around Tobermory, especially Flowerpot.

The tours would include going ashore and cooking for the visitors, "Trout and potatoes, and tea as black as ink".

Lloyd took over caretaking at Flowerpot.

Then he became interested in plant life and "Everything that went with the park". He got a camera and started taking pictures, photographing the rich array of orchids and ferns.

He carved since he was a boy, but became more involved in wood-carving under the inspiration of a Mr. Lloyd Nixon, art director for the Detroit Free Press who used to spend his month's holidays with Lloyd on his boat, the 'Penguin', "And made wood shavings from one end of the boat to the other."

That boat Lloyd built himself in 1950.

He had used the 'Albacore' for a couple of years after the war, but burned it when someone offered to buy it because he consideres it unseaworthy.

In the winters Tobermory was often isolated by heavy storms.

There was always music around somewhere. Dances were called on the spur of the moment, and more often than not, there would be Lloyd fiddling with his special left handed technique, as described in the Arts Council exhibit.

The display will be circulated to different locations in the Grey-Bruce area on request.

MR. J. C. MUNN

Wiarton Echo, Jan. 25, 1973
Retires After 44 Years

More than 150 relatives and friends jammed the Tobermory Community Centre Friday night to honor J. C. Munn who retired in 1972 as an employee of St. Edmunds Township after 44 years.

Mr. And Mrs. Munn were presented with a reclining chair and a bouquet of roses by the township.

Presentations were also made by Dan Webb of the Owen Sound branch of the Ministry of Transportation and Communications and Laverne Culbert, Goderich on behalf of Dominion Road Machinery.

Reeve J. P. Johnstone presented Mr. Munn with a wall clock on behalf of the local Bruce Trail Club in recognition of his service to the area.

The presentation was attended by former reeves John Ransbury and Archie Simpson and Bill Weir, area road superintendent for many years.

Mr. Munn began his road-building career in 1928 as the road foreman. His starting pay was 15 cents an hour.

At that time, the township maintained 25 miles of road, including 13-1/4 miles of what is now Highway 6.

The township now maintains 63 miles of roads and four miles of paved road.

Mr. Munn, or, as he is better known, Baise, has seen many changes over the past 44 years.

The most notable changes he says, is in the type of machinery used for road construction.

In 1928, the road foreman was equipped with a team of horses, a sledgehammer, a crowbar and a couple of chains.

The first horse-drawn grader was purchased in the early 1930's at a cost of $150. It was not until 1965 that the first power grader was bought.

During the early years, stones were picked from nearby fields and from along the roadway and thrown by hand into the stone crusher powered by steam engine.

It produced about 40 yards a of gravel a day as compared to 1,200 yards a day produced by the modern crushers.

The gravel used for road building was hauled by a team and wagon in yard-load boxes. The first gravel trucks were hired by the township in the 1940's.

In 1937 the township road south of Tobermory was taken over by the Federal Department of Highways. The takeover required a special act of Parliament as the road had never been taken over by the Ontario government.

The road was widened and straightened and the first eight miles south of Tobermory were paved. This was the beginning of a program to improve the road to Wiarton.

Mr. Munn worked under eight reeves and four road superintendents.

J. C. Munn and wife Ada

MR. ALF CARVER

Wiarton Echo, 1949

Alf. Carver of Tobermory,
Wolf Trapper of Repute, Caught 400 in 40 years
(Special by Staff Writer)

TOBERMORY, May 4 — If you're troubled with wolves around your back yard call Alf. Carver at Tobermory and he'll eliminate them for you, just for the bounty, the price of the hide, and the fun he gets out of it. He's been in the trade for 40 years.

Carver had a poor season this past winter — he only caught six wolves. But his average per season, he says is 10 to 12. Around Tobermory, that is. When he was trapping in Northern Ontario, things were done on a bigger scale.

Trapper, hunter, fishing guide, mink rancher and sailer, the 60 year old Carver was born in England but has been in this country since his early youth. He has lived for the past 20 years here at the tip of Bruce Peninsula.

"I take a back seat to nobody in trapping wolves," he says, in justifiable pride. "I've done it all my life. The last one I caught had eight pups in her. But I hate catching a female wolf this time of year when they've got pups.

That's because they're my bread and butter for the next season, but I've got them pretty well cleaned out of here anyway." He gets "about twice as many wolves as all the rest of the trappers in Grey and Bruce Counties put together," he says.

This winter two Bruce County trappers got one each and a third got two, Carver says. His nearest competitor at present is a man at Red Bay. This fellow at Red Bay got some with hounds, but he'll find he can't get any more because they'll leave the area where the hounds are."

88lb-Wolf His Biggest

The weight of the average wolf Carver snares in the Tobermory area is 40 to 50 pounds, but the record size was 88 pounds, and that one was a female at that. These are brush wolves, of course. Timber wolves never come this far south.

"Anybody can catch muskrat and mink, but when you start on foxes you begin to learn trapping, and when you jump from foxes to wolves, you really know it. These wolves down here near settled country have a college education, but those up north of Port Arthur, where I was have only got a common schooling. There's that much difference between them. Down here they have to be smart to survive, but they are still on the increase in spite of it."

Foxes are no good any more, Carver says. "They're not worth bringing home." There is no township bounty for them and present day returns for their furs aren't worth the trouble. He sets his snares for wolves, never for foxes, but odd times a fox gets tangled up in a wolf snare, and then he lets it go free. "I don't suppose the farmers will thank me for that, but I've let five go so far this year."

He keeps hoping, Carver says, that fox pelt prices may increase and a bounty be paid for them. Then all the foxes he frees now will have multiplied and will pay him dividends.

Has caught 400
Four hundred wolves have fallen into Carver's snares since he first took up trapping, and 120 of them were caught in the Bruce Peninsula. "I wish they were all around now with pups — I'd be able to clean up next winter. That would be as good as the sweepstakes."

Born in England, Carver came to Canada at the age of 15. He first lived at Midland, and during his teens started sailing on the lakes. He received some of his education in Milwaukee, Wis., during the time he was sailing, and he also won his pilot's license, he says, while on the lakes.

Altogether he spent 14 years on the decks of lake vessels, and then for five years buried himself in the bush 200 miles north of Port Arthur, where he operated a narrow-gauge copper mine locomotive. On the side he carried on with his trapping, having learned the trade at Midland.

"I went up there figuring I knew it all, but I found I knew practically nothing," he remarks: "The scent is the whole thing when you're trapping wolves.

Miles of Traplines
Carver has about 50 miles of traplines in St. Edmunds Township around Tobermory, but he no longer extends his lines down into Lindsay Township as he once did. Trapping isn't as good now as it was ten or 20 years ago.

During the winter he goes out along his traps practically every day, although it takes him quite a few days to cover all his lines. He travels through the bush on snowshoes and finds it much easier to get around that way than it is to walk on the bare ground in the summer.

By this time of year he has taken up most, if not all of his traps and snares, for the season.

Gets $45 Per Wolf
Carver collects a $35-bounty per wolf from the province and ten dollars from Bruce County. He first sends his pelts to be examined by county officials, and when they are returned he ships them away to Toronto for the provincial bounty. "It takes three weeks or more for them to get through with them and send me the bounty."

One time he sent in a pelt which government men swore belonged to a dog. "But I knew it wasn't a dog. It probably was a cross between a dog and a wolf away back somewhere," he says.

"I still have hopes I may catch one or two more this season," he says optimistically. The most he ever snared in St. Edmunds in one season was 14. But during the war

years lumber became so valuable that many little saw mills were started up in the Peninsula bush, and they scared off a lot of the wolves.

Carver tells of a letter he got not long ago from north of Vancouver, B. C., with a clipping taken from a Vancouver paper "about me catching wolves." His fame has spread a long way from home.

He recently received a letter from officials at Algonquin Park, Ontario, asking him to go up there to let the game wardens study his methods. "But I don't want to go up there unless I get a pretty good offer, although I wouldn't mind trying it for awhile, just for the fun of it, to see how many I could get."

Occupational Hazards
The occupation is not without its hazards, though. The snares he uses are loops of wire hung like a noose at the height of a wolf's head. They are equipped with a very sturdy lock so that when the unfortunate wolf unwarily gets his head into the noose the more he struggles the tighter it becomes until he finally suffocates. Up to that point he's inclined to be vicious, particularly with trappers.

Carver locates the wolves' trails and there sets his snare among low bushes. It is almost invisible. The wolf walks right into it. And he can't back out. Sometimes they try to chew to pieces the stout wire holding the noose which is slowly strangling them.

He's seen wolves dead with their lips and gums and teeth all torn and blood-covered from their violent, panicky struggle as the noose grew tighter and tighter. "There are 19 strands of 22-gauge wire of the very finest steel in those snares, but the wolves some times destroy them before they die," he explains.

Lots of Deer
Last winter he found a dead deer, shot and left by hunters only a few feet from the Peninsula highway. The wolves had been at it, so Carver set a few snares in the area, and caught a wolf. Now, with the snow gone he himself had difficulty locating these snares. And all that's left of the deer is the hair, hoofs and bones.

"There are lots of deer around here, but I never bother with them. There's no money in them. Lots of times when I go out I don't even carry a gun except in the spring.

"I carry a gun now, because the bears are coming out and if one of the cubs happened to get caught in a snare I wouldn't want to come upon it without a gun. The old bear is always close by."

Carver looks with disdain upon hunters who lie in wait for their prey, or who organize drives to force the prey into the open. In fact he doesn't even call them hunters. "What I call hunting is the way I do it, I go out and stalk my game through the bush. Sometimes I follow it for a whole day. That is hunting!"

Fishing Guide, Mink Rancher

For several years when he first came to Tobermory Carver was a summer fishing guide, taking tourists out trolling in his launch. But he gave that up. Now for seven years he has been raising mink, and this spring he has 41 females in a yard-full of pens at the rear of his house. He breeds several kinds of mink, but these days he's talking about Royal Pastelles. "Two years ago I paid $750 for three of them, and this year I'll sell three of the same kind for only $100. That's the way prices are."

Before prices dropped he laid a cement floor in his yard for a refrigeration unit he hoped to build. Now he's postponed that project.

Carver lives in a neat little frame house near the highway entrance to Tobermory, at the corner of the road leading west to Hay Bay. With him live his wife and daughter.

He looks like a story-book trapper and woodsman, with his heavy breeches, knee-high boots, mackinaw and ski cap. He's tall and lean and weatherbeaten and his hair is turning grey. But, keen-eyed and lithe as an Indian, at 60 he's as active and capable in the bush he knows so well as he ever was.

MRS. MARTHA WATSON

The Owen Sound Sun Times, Sat. Jan. 18, 1964
Old Age Pensioner Spends Hours Preparing Bundles Of Clothing To Help Needy

You probably have never heard of Mrs. Martha Watson. There aren't many of her kind left. She is a woman who lives on her old age pension — and believes in helping the needy.

Just the other day 90 pounds of good, clean used clothing was delivered to the Unitarian Service Committee in Toronto. It was all prepared by Mrs. Watson. Up around Tobermory she is almost a legend — and with good reason.

This cheery, forthright woman is a widow of 78 and still lives on the farm where she and her husband raised 15 children. Every child was born at home and none of them had any help from a doctor. What is more surprising every one survived the occasion. There are now nearly 60 grandchildren and 27 great grandchildren.

In spite of this — or perhaps because of it — this energetic woman retains a delightful sense of humor and is as resourceful as ever. She sold strawberries from her garden to pay express charges on the 90 pounds of clothing that went to the Unitarian Service Committee. Recently she completed a dozen pairs of cosy slippers made from parts of an old rug and old blankets.

A few years ago she read about the U.S.C. in the paper. They were appealing for good used clothing, cleaned and mended, to send to people all over the world who were in need. Mrs. Watson spoke to her neighbours and asked them to bring her their old clothes. Soon her

attic began to look as she puts it "like a junk man's heaven". And she has been getting clothes, not only for U.S.C. but for other organizations ever since.

From around the world, Africa, India, British Buiana, Barbados have come letters of appreciation and thanks. These letters, and the knowledge that her efforts have helped someone in need give her a deep sense of satisfaction and purpose.

Tell of Happiness

Some letters recount more than the usual measure of happiness, such as the time three African brides wrote to Mrs. Watson telling her of their triple wedding, wearing veils which she had made. Others tell of tragedy. At Mont Frere in Africa, Rev. Mr. Gray struggled to establish a small mission church. In a letter to Mrs. Watson, he told of the disappearance of his two small children, aged five and seven. One day they wandered off into the swampy, crocodile infested jungle and were never seen again. Their fate has never been established.

Born in Shelburne in January, 1886, Mrs. Watson was one year old when her parents moved to Tobermory. Her father, Charles William Hodge, was a mason and plasterer by trade. Tobermory before the turn of the century was a very small, isolated collection of fishing shacks and a few houses. There was no brick construction. The best houses were plastered on the outside or were made of stone.

During the winter season, any building construction came to a halt. A mason was obliged to take any work he could find to make ends meet during the off season. As a child, Mrs. Watson remembers sitting in the window of their home watching her father cut ice in the bay.

Charles Hodge must have been an extraordinary person. He instilled a love and affection that even now, as Mrs. Watson talked of him, caused a catch in her throat. For a moment she was deeply serious and said simply, "He was a man I worshipped."

It is possible she inherited her resourcefulness from her father. She recalls a Sunday trip across the ice of the bay to visit Abraham Davis, the lighthouse keeper. Her parents, with two small daughters, spent the day visiting their friend who lived at the lighthouse the year round.

Became Lost

Returning in the late afternoon, the early darkness fell around them and the little family became lost. In the dark they finally stumbled on the shore with no idea where they were. There was no light to guide them. Since he had no idea of direction, her father decided the best course was to stay where they were.

She has a lasting recollection of the shelter he made for her sister and herself. Against a rock, in the shelter of a few small pine trees, her father drove sticks into the snow and over them arranged his large, heavy cape which provided protection from the wind. Then, lighting a fire in front, father and mother sat beside it all through the night, talking to keep themselves awake. Meanwhile, the two little girls slept safe and warm in the shelter of their father's cape. With the morning light, Charles Hodge discovered their whereabouts and the parents set out for home, each carrying a small, sleepy child.

As a girl of 17 she married Arthur Watson and moved into a frame farmhouse, three miles southwest of Tobermory. For awhile the young couple were without transportation of any kind. In any case, there was no road, only a couple of cart tracks through the rough area.

Groceries were carried on foot from Tobermory. Many times Arthur Watson toted a 100-pound sack of flour on his shoulders from the village to the farm. Their weekly trips were made through all kinds of weather.

Good Country

Though the first years were hard, Mrs. Watson says it was good farm country. Farm machinery is not suited to the land found at the top of the Bruce. She is of the opinion that small farms can still provide a good living if people are willing to work the land without elaborate equipment.

In the original frame house she gave birth to all of her 15 children except one. Louis, the eldest, first saw the world in a woodsman's log shanty on a cold winter night. Like others who went into the woods to take out timber, Arthur Watson took his family with him. Warm and snug in the log shelter, Mrs. Watson and her mother and the late Mrs. Robert Hopkins held and kept her company during the short winter days while her husband worked to bring out the logs.

None of her children were attended by a doctor when they were born. The closest doctors were at Lion's Head and Wiarton. It must be said that self reliance early became an integral part of Mrs. Watson's character.

Many are the tales she can tell of problems encountered and overcome. It took planning to patch pants, wash and sew, darn socks and do many daily tasks and feed 17 people on a small, isolated farm. She still has memories of nights when she went to bed "dog tired" in the late hours.

During those years she baked 12 to 15 loaves of bread each day. Three to four loaves disappeared from her larder at every meal. She had baked as many as 30 loaves in one day. And many nights, as she crawled into bed, she would suddenly find herself asking the question "Oh dear, did I forget to set the bread?" Bread for 15 people required approximately 100 pounds of flour each week.

Light Moments

But if life had its dark side, it also had a few lighter moments. A well known Indian chief named Chitooa (the spelling may not be correct) had a big wigwam on an area known as The Bight, near the village. The chief, a familiar arrow-straight figure, travelled about the countryside on missions known only to himself. Many times he visited the Watson farm and any hospitality he received was always returned in the form of a giant lake trout or other gift.

One winter's night, from her bed where she lay ill, Mrs. Watson arose and went into the kitchen. A moment later she came flying back to her husband, startled and saying excitedly, "There is a dead man lying on the kitchen floor!"

Her husband laughed sleepily, "It's all right Martha, it's only the chief sleeping by the fire."

He went on to explain that Chitooa had appeared out of the cold asking for shelter, a warm spot by the fire for the night.

Mrs. Watson had gone into the kitchen to find the Indian with his hands folded on his chest, wrapped in deerskin, sleeping peacefully on the kitchen floor in front of the fire.

About 20 years ago the original house burned to the ground, taking practically everything with it. On the same spot Arthur Watson built a seven-room stone house, without plans, but according to Mrs. Watson's wishes.

Of her large family, 13 children are still living. One girl Joy, died of pneumonia as a child. The oldest girl married a Wesleyan Methodist minister and was herself ordained in the same church. She died six years ago, a year after Arthur Watson. The surviving children are scattered all over Ontario.

Home For Summer

Mrs. Watson insists on returning to the farm each summer. She lives alone but her son Archie lives only a short distance away. During the winter she leaves the farm to stay with various members of her family in more populous places. At present she is staying with her eldest son Louis at 1795 6th Avenue East.

She finds great satisfaction and pleasure in bringing help and happiness to people of all kinds all over the world. During the past year she gathered, mended, and washed seven bales of clothing, each weighing 70 to 90 pounds which went out to people in many lands. Sometimes she buys articles at rummage sales, paid for from her small resources. On one occasion she heard of a needy missionary in India and promptly sent him clothes from her late husband's wardrobe. From her many friends and neighbours and from the large source of supply represented by her own large family, Mrs. Watson has high hopes of carrying on her work for a long time to come.

Come spring, she will return to the farm at the tip of the Bruce Peninsula where she has lived for so many years. Here she will carry on her work of kindness and goodwill towards all.

Mrs. Watson lived to celebrate her 90th birthday.

**Martha Watson, son A.J. and great grandson
Brent Adams 1973**

MR. ORRIE VAIL

Owen Sound Sun Times, 1970
**Early Fisherman, Orrie Vail, Tobermory wins wide fame
White House has one of his knives, has drill tool secret**
(By Ann Kelly)

"If you want something go ahead and make it," is the philosophy of Orrie Vail of Tobermory. Further he states, "If man made it, man can fix it," and leads the way to proving his theory sound.

Orford Cleveland Vail has probably amassed more Bruce Peninsula history, general knowledge, and realized more ambitions in his 78-year history than most in the district with more extensive formal training. He was unable to complete his senior years in elementary school, but his constant thirst for knowledge has never left him wanting. It is ironic that a man of such diversity and talent has lived most of his life within calling distance of his childhood home.

As a boy he well remembers fetching water for his mother and meeting a rattlesnake curled in the path. His mother was unnerved and killed the snake with an oar. In error he once mistook a rattler on the bedroom floor, for his brother's tie. Apparently the reptile had come up through a knot in the floor.

Although Orrie Vail proudly calls himself a Canadian, and has a birth certificate to prove it, he was actually born in the U.S. where his parents were visiting. This probably explains why his luggage is never examined when crossing the border. He made his American debut on January 25, 1893.

Perfect Record

Like his father before him, Orrie Vail was a commercial fisherman until the spring of 1955. In his 44 years of commercial fishing he was never towed by any other craft.

Only twice did he stay out overnight because of engine problems. These he repaired in daylight and came home under his own power. In this period of time he never banged up a shaft or propellor which says much for his abilities as a navigator.

It was Orrie Vail who started shipping fish independently while his father was still living, even though he was denied the right to put his fish on a company dock. At that time companies were paying fishermen by cents per pound with Orrie earning 10 cents per pound as a dependent shipper. Many in the community followed his example and each built an independent ice-house. It was common practice for each to help the other put up ice in the winter. His last shipment of fish left Tobermory at 4 o'clock and was in Cleveland at 10 the same day with shipment cheaper than rail.

In 1953, he wrote an article entitled "Depletion of the Great Lakes. When and How" and mailed it to district biologist Dr. John Budd, now deceased. Mr. Vail quit fishing in the spring of 1955 and by the summer of that year commercial fishing of trout had virtually ended. His interest in fishing didn't end with his career, however, Orrie Vail still makes all his own fishing lures, and sealers, popular items with sportsmen.

Knives Popular

It may take a woman to know her knives, but it takes a man to make them. Such a man is Orrie Vail whose hobby began when his fishing career ended. He wanted to make something usable by everybody all year and decided knives were the answer. He didn't want a seasonal hobby because he wanted to keep a loaf of bread on his table in the winter. To date, Mr. Vail has shipped knives to every country in the world except Russia and Sweden. In fact he declined a Swedish order for 10,000 knives contending that it was better that the representative be disappointed than Orrie be overworked. The Swede left the weathered shingled shed with only one knife in his possesion.

Swedish steel and Sandvik steel, also from Sweden, are purchased by Mr. Vail for the blades of his knives. The one is razor steel and the other forged steel which he uses for hunting knives because it is durable, takes a good edge and won't break easily. The Sandvik steel is hand-hammered and, consequently, expensive to buy. With moose-horn handles atop such a blade, however, his hunting knives are almost indestructible. He rivets and laces the natural-coloured sheaths for such knives. When one woman asked, "Don't you have different colors for your sheaths?" His reply was, "they're all the same color on the cow."

Another tourist's question "do you sell moose antlers?" brought the reply, "Even the moose themselves won't sell them." Such is the spontaneous wit of Orrie Vail, his remarks always made with a twinkle in his blue eyes.

For kitchen use he makes any type of knife from paring knife to carving knife, even sets in wooden cases to complement any home. Although he personally prefers applewood handles, he uses ironwood from the Bruce, walnut from Lake Erie, hickory from many parts of the province, black walnut from a U.S. gun stock factory cuttings, and moose horns from as far away as Sudbury, Nipigon, Quebec, and Tacoma, Washington. In fact he has even used elk horns, but these are difficult to acquire and not as durable as moose. His knives have been purchased for Benson and Edith Ford, the White House in Washington, and by Deputy Minister Hail to name but a few. The greatest tribute to their quality, according to Mr. Vail, is the fact that there are few homes in the village without one.

Mr. Vail enjoys the quiet tranquility of Tobermory in the winter. He is happy pursuing his hobbies in his little shop. When asked by an American tourist if Tobermory has much snow in winter he replied, "When I look out and see the squirrels digging down in the snow to try to find a tree to climb I know the snow is deep."

Tool, Boat Designer

Orrie Vail's talents don't end with making knives, fishing lures, lamps, scalers and other such sought-after items. He has designed and built a tool that will put a hole through any piece of steel, no matter how hard it is. Although men have come to his shop dressed as casual fishermen trying to learn for big companies, his secret, only his grandson has been told. The grandson works as a machinist in an atomic energy plant. In this way Mr. Vail will keep his secret from being lost. He has been working on this discovery since 1918 but it took him this long to make the application useable.

While fishing he designed and built his first two boats. The model of one is in a boat works in Michigan. It was because of the shape of the bottom and design of the hull (there were no dead spots and she just made one sea) that the craft could do nine miles per hour on a 15 horsepower motor. Although he didn't build his third vessel, still in operation around Kilarney, he did implement many changes, including an ice breaking bow that was built into her.

Orrie Vail had the first metal turning lathe in his part of the country. It is still in operation, run by an International Harvester 1917 gasoline engine with all its original parts. Early in his building career he made his own electricity. The instructions on the lathe state: Do not put axle grease in grease cup of this engine. "It's still a pretty quiet engine," operator Vail admits.

The grinder he uses was built by Mr. Vail from an old cream separator. Because of his philosophy about making something when you want it, very little equipment is ever purchased new.

He also owned the first tour cycle gas engine in Tobermory. His gas was purchased in wooden barrels from Northern Paint and Varnish in Owen Sound for 11 cents per gallon.

As a boy Orrie Vail used to fish near the remains of an ancient boat. The remains of this ship provoked great controversy among the experts as to its origin, controversy that some aren't willing even yet to terminate. As Mr. Vail explains it: "I knew the fastenings were old, but I had no way of knowing what it was. I let the experts figure it out."

Established to be the remains of the "Griffon", the first vessel to sail the Upper Lakes the information brought Mr. Vail a barrage of criticism. As a guest on "Front Page Challenge" he skillfully answered all the caustic questions that panelist Gordon Sinclair could muster. Despite the fact that "Griffon" wreckage continues to be found most recently on Manitoulin Island, experts remain adamant in their stand that it is easier to believe than to doubt that Mr. Vail has in his possession the remains of La Salle's ship, built in 1679.

C. H. J. Snider, government authority on ships and Rowley Murphy, artist for the Royal Canadian Navy and British Navy, contend that the material recovered in 1955 by Mr. Vail corresponds in every respect to the known dimension of the Griffon. They are united in their original conclusion that what Mr. Vail recovered cannot be other than the original vessel.

Mr. Vail's little workshop houses the valuable treasure including bones of Griffon crew members. In addition his little museum boasts such valuable objects as an 1819 gear clock, the bell from a CNR locomotive, a wicker basket that was among the first wind instruments when sailing vessels were at Tobermory, arrowheads, ox shoes, corral, a wood carving from the Congo, a Japanese sword and other priceless relics.

Orrie Vail's six-foot four-inch frame with broad shoulders that demand a size 20 shirt, becomes his years. He is very fond of young people but has reservations about hippies. Of long-haired hitch-hikers he says: "if you want to look like old people do, then walk like them."

In a three-year period 5,000 people signed the guest book in his little work shop. He has gifts from all over the world, including a mounted piece of wood from the Florencia, a ship of the Spanish armada in 1588.

He believes that if you build a better mousetrap than your neighbour the world will build a highway to your door and Orrie Vail, in his 78-year-history has never lacked company.

Left to Right: **Orrie Vail, Marmaduke Vail, Woodland Vail**

MR. GEORGE BELROSE

Owen Sound Sun-Times, 1947
**Long Lived, Enjoying Life, Tobermory
Pioneers' Sons Look Back at "Tub's" Past
Names Like Belrose, Simpson and Hopkins made
Tobermory History — Sons of Original Settlers
are still prominent in Village and Settlement Life**

Although the original pioneer settlers of the Tobermory district have all passed on, many sons and daughters of these pioneers, who came with their parents are still here to recall the old days. Among these is George Belrose, who came to Tobermory from Owen Sound with his father, the late Micheal Belrose, in the year 1876. The family settled on Lot 50, Concession 3, W. B. R. At that time there were only two other families in the area, Abraham Davis on Lot 48 of Concession 1, E. B. R., and Charles Earl, who spent the summer at the Big Tub and the winter in the farming section, now known as the Settlement.

There were, Mr. Belrose says, no permanent residents then at the harbor around which the village of Tobermory has since grown. There was one little fish shanty just about where Ransbury's net shed stands today and a small log cabin behind the house now occupied by Whitmore Hopkins. Tom Boyter lived in it while fishing from the harbor in the summer season.

The next family to arrive in the district was that of James Seaman, who settled on a lot on Concession 2, right across the road from the Belrose Homestead. Everything in these early days Mr. Belrose states, had to be brought in by boat as there were no roads in the district.

Returns After Absence

Mr. Belrose farmed in the Settlement until 1908, in which year he built a house in the village and moved in to take up fishing. The house is now owned and occupied by Donald McIver. Mr. Belrose lived in it until 1916, when he sold out his interest in a fishing business and moved to Southampton. During part of his sojourn there, he also engaged in fishing. In 1931 he returned to Tobermory, having purchased the house in which he has been residing ever since.

Although he reached 81 years of age last January, Mr. Belrose is as spry as many a man twenty years younger. He is now living in retirement, but to relieve the monotony he still does the odd bit of net mending, or takes a trip as pilot on a visiting boat unacquainted with the dangerous channels, familiar to Mr. Belrose through his early fishing career.

Wife Came In 1883

But George Belrose is not the only old-timer in his household of two, for his wife, the former Sarah Jane Spears, now 80 years of age, arrived in Tobermory in 1883. She came with her parents, the late Mr. and Mrs. Solomon Spears from near Holland Centre. George and Sarah recently celebrated the 61st anniversary of their wedding. They were married by the Rev. Philip Sparling at the old homestead on Lot 50 on May 5, 1886.

Mr. Sparling was the second resident minister stationed in Tobermory by the Methodist Church and it was during his term here that the Harbor Church was built, the first church building.

Mrs. Belrose recalls the many inconveniences of housekeeping in her early days. She baked all the bread and made most of the sugar used in her household out of sap obtained from maple trees on the farm.

Brother Follows Him

The year after Jacob Belrose had arrived in Tobermory his brother, Michael Belrose came, settling on Lot 47, Concession 1, E. B. R. That was in 1877 and with him came his son, Andrew, now 73 years of age and another of Tobermory's highly respected sons of pioneers Mr. Belrose, who was born in Annan, nine miles from Owen Sound, says he cannot remember what his first impressions of Tobermory were, as he was only three years old at the time of his arrival. Later in young manhood he shared with his father all the hardships that were the lot of the early pioneers.

In 1898 he married the former Mamie Spears and took up farming on Lot 51, Concession 1, W. B. R. In 1912 he moved into the village of Tobermory on being appointed postmaster, a position he still holds and has held continuously for 35 years. About 1920 he opened a general store and hotel. Under Mr. Belrose's management these businesses developed greatly in the succeeding years and now rank among the best in the district.

In his younger days, Mr. Belrose took an active part in community affairs. He acted as treasurer for 25 years for the trustee board of the village school and also served from 1916 to 1926 as township treasurer. Prior to his appointment as township treasurer, he had served as a member of council, being first elected in 1904. He was chaplain of L.O.L. 382 for several terms, and also gave many years of faithful service on the Methodist and United Church Boards.

MR. W. J. SMITH

Wiarton Echo, 1943-1944
**William J. Smith Has Been Resident
Of Tobermory for More Than Half A Century**
Went to Picturesque Fishing Village at Head of Bruce Peninsula as Telegraph Operator — Mail Was Received Once a Week at Log Cabin — Recalls Days of Sailing Vessels — Family of Seven Children Are All Married and All Reside at Tobermory

In 1889, when he was barely sixteen years old, William John Smith arrived in Tobermory to act as agent and operator for the Great North Western Telegraph Company of Canada. At that time, Mr. Smith says, there were only four houses and the present United Church building on the south eastern bank of the harbor and only four or five shanties on the other side. William Hill then was running Tobermory's first store in the house afterwards occupied by the late Wm. J. Spears, lightkeeper at Flower Pot Island. It was the only store in the district and, besides being patronized by the few families at the harbor, served the settlers in what is now known as the Settlement. This is the small area close to the village suitable for farming which in the early days, when Mr. Smith first came to Tobermory, had a more numerous population than existed around the harbor. The roads leading into Tobermory in those days, Mr. Smith recalls, were just timber roads, and he remembers how in spring and fall it was not practicable to drive a wagon over them, due to floods, the residents having to walk to and from Wiarton, if they had any occasion to go to town at these periods.

When Mr. Smith first arrived in 1889 and for some years afterwards, mail was only received once a week. The post office then was in a log cabin, situated at a point on the main road two and a half miles out from the present village, almost opposite the farm-house now owned by Gordon Hopkins. This old building was demolished only a few years ago.

Was Telegraph Operator

For three years, from 1889 to 1892, Mr. Smith satisfactorily conducted the Great North Western Telegraph Company's office at Tobermory, which had been established mainly for navigation purposes. As a result, in 1892 his employers placed him in charge of the whole of their land telegraph line from Wiarton north to Tobermory. This line ran to Lion's Head, then across to Stokes Bay and up to the Tub. Traversing the roads in the district, as he does now, with ease, Mr. Smith looks back grimly to the many difficulties he had to contend with in the nineties while supervising his line. This job kept Mr. Smith fully employed until 1913. In that year the Wireless Station having been built, the land telegraph line on the peninsula was abandoned. Mr. Smith acted as an operator at the Wireless Station for about eight months, then he went into the commercial fishing business, in which he has been engaged ever since, a period of thirty years. His son Oscar, has been associated with him in the business in recent years, and this past summer Mr. Smith, although still taking an active part in the fishing business, did not spend as much time on the lake as had been his custom in former years.

Recalls Sailing Vessels

Mr. Smith says, when he first arrived at Tobermory, most of the boats in use were sailing vessels. Gradually, however, a change came over the scene, until the days came when a sail became a rare sight in the harbor. In early times the village was practically dependent on the water for receiving its supplies, and Mr. Smith remembers how eagerly the inhabitants awaited the arrival of the first boat in Spring. One of the early boats, with which Mr. Smith was familiar, was the steamer "J. H. Jones", shown as she enters the harbour in a picture taken about the turn of the century by Edgar Macdonald, a Wiarton photographer of the period. Later, in 1906, the J. H. Jones foundered with all on board while on her way from Owen Sound to Tobermory, Mr. Smith recalls that two of Tobermory's pioneers, George and Frank Fellon, went down with her.

Storm Signal Agent

In May of the year 1889, shortly after Mr. Smith's first arrival in Tobermory, he was appointed storm signal agent, a post which he has faithfully filled down through the years and which he still fills. In recognition of his long and valuable services he received King George's coronation medal and in 1940 on the completing fifty one years at the post, he was the recipient of a letter from the Assistant Controller of the Air Services, Meteorological Division, Department of Transport, complimenting him on the manner in which he had carried out his duties and stating that there was no other storm signal agent on the records with a length of service comparable to his.

Served On Council

That is not the only record breaking episode in Mr. Smith's career, for he has all records in St. Edmunds Township eclipsed for service as a councillor. In 1908 he first entered the Township Council. He has been a member without intermission from that year on and is still going strong.

Mr. Smith is of mixed Scottish and English origin. He was born at London, Ontario, in April 1873. His father, William Smith, was a native of Scotland, who had come to Canada, at about the age of sixteen. His mother was born in England. Her maiden name was Marie Coulson.

Mr. Smith first attended public school at London and then continued as far as the third form in the Collegiate there. After that he took a course at Forest City Business College in London, an institution which, Mr. Smith says, is still carrying on in that city. While at business college Mr. Smith specialized in telegraphy which led to his early appointments on the peninsula in that line.

Married in 1897

On March 8th, 1897, Mr. Smith took his bride, Helena May Belrose, a daughter of Michael Belrose, one of the earliest pioneers in the Tobermory settlement, who had settled there in 1877. The young couple had to journey to Hepworth to be married. The Rev. H. J. Harnwell was the Methodist minister there at the time and he officiated at the ceremony in the Hepworth parsonage. Journeying back by horse and cutter, it took the young couple three days to reach home. Mr. and Mrs. Smith both recall that the snow in the valleys was up to the top of the telephone poles. They made Wiarton the first day, Lion's Head by the end of the second day, and finally reached Tobermory on the third night. They still occupy the house they entered as newly-weds over forty-six years ago. Of this union were born one son and six daughters, all of whom are married and are residents of Tobermory. The son is Oscar and the daughters are Dorothy, Mrs. J. W. Ransbury; Kathleen, Mrs. Carleton Young; Lizzie, Mrs. Gordon Gibbons; Marjory, Mrs. Donald McIver; Madelene, Mrs. Lawrence MacLeod; and Norah, Mrs. R. J. Hopkins. There are sixteen grandchildren and one great grandchild. In these days of shifting populations, it is quite remarkable that Mr. and Mrs. Smith's family have remained so loyally rooted to the old home town. Mr. and Mrs. Smith, indeed, feel it a great joy to be able to pass their older years surrounded by the unbroken circle of their children and their children's children, even unto — in one case at least — the fourth generation.

CAPT. WILLIAM J. SIMPSON

Wiarton Echo, 1942
CAPT. WILLIAM J. SIMPSON
Veteran Tobermory Man
Oldest Living Ratepayer
Resided 62 years in Bruce Village at the "Tip of the Top"
Fisherman, Lumberman, Mill Owner
Community Leader, Municipal Official
Member of Pioneer Family
HISTORY OF FISHING INDUSTRY
Capt. Simpson Served as Police Magistrate
and Postmaster, School Trustee, Lighthouse Keeper,
and Took Active and Progressive Part in Progress
of the Village
(By Weir Grieve)

Not many of those who visit Tobermory are un-aquainted with Captain William James Simpson, veteran fisherman, and lumberman of Tobermory. Retired now, after sixty-two years residence in the village, his six-foot-two figure is a familiar sight around the harbor, where the genial "Irishman" is a noted raconteur.

Captain Simpson was born on December 21, 1869, at Lennoxville, Quebec. He was the son of James Simpson, whose father, also named James Simpson, was a native of Tipperary, Ireland, and came to Canada, with the 100th Regiment, which was disbanded in Quebec. On disbandment the soldiers were given grants of land, James Simpson getting a grant at Richmond in the Township of Goulburn, twenty miles from Ottawa. As he had served twenty one years in the British Army he received a pension, and small though it was, the receipt of this pension every three months made him the envy of many of the other settlers in the bush.

Early Education
Captain Simpson attended school for a short period at Lennoxville, to which place his father had moved from Richmond on his marriage. The teacher's name was Miss La Rush and he recalls that she was very kind to him, then a mischievous little boy of six. The people settled there at that time were mostly of British origin, but quite a number of French families were there also. All went to the same school, played together and were best of friends. English was the only language taught.

Moved to Bentinck
In 1871, when Captain Simpson was barely two years old, his mother, Matilda Wood, died. Six years later, in 1877, his father like the old frontiersman he was, moved to Bentinck Township in Grey County, where his sister, Mrs. Thomas Blaney already lived. He took with him his three daughters, Marie, Matilda and Emily, and his only son William James. On arrival he found the good land had all been filled in Bentinck Township and the call to go farther afield came to him. Along with Dick, John C. and James H. Hopkins, he moved to St. Edmunds Township, Bruce County, and took up land in 1879. The journey was made via Owen Sound from which place the tug "Prince Albert",[1] bore them to Tobermory. When they arrived at Tobermory they found already settled there, Abraham Davis and his wife and son, Henry, also

Michael and Jacob Belrose, George Peffer,[2] James Fellon, Alexander Parker, and William, Benjamin, Edward and George Young. Most of these had moved their families into the bush.

First Land Owners
The first to take land in St. Edmunds had been Abraham Davis, who filed on Lot 48, Concession 1 W B R in 1868 (sic) and Henry Davis, who filed on Lot 48, Con. 1 E B R. At that time the whole township was heavily timbered with maple, birch, beech, pine, cedar, hemlock, spruce and balsam. The year following his father's arrival in St. Edmunds, Captain Simpson joined him. There were no roads then and he made the journey by water on the ill-fated "Jane Miller", a boat that went down with all hands in Colpoy's Bay a year later. Captain Porte (sic) was her master and owner.

Store Established
The first store established in Tobermory, Captain Simpson remembers, was in 1881, by Maitland, Rixon and Company. They bought ties, posts and cord wood, for which there was a brisk demand. A line of steamboats running from Collingwood to Chicago called at the harbor regularly for wood. There were four boats on the run, the "Northern Queen", the "Lake Erie", the "Canada" and the "Columbia". All used wood entirely and each took forty cords of hard wood on each call. The company's store was a large log building on the property now owned by Albert Leslie, Jr. It was a lumber camp van and besides being used as a store, served as a boarding house and as sleeping quarters. In the fall enough supplies had to be brought in by boat to last until a fresh supply could be brought in the spring. Captain Simpson recalls that sometimes food became very scarce. In March 1882 the supply of flour was used up, but nearly every settler had a supply of Indian corn to fall back on. John Shearer, an old Scotsman, was the local miller. He had a large coffee mill and for grinding the meal took part as toll. The result was he had meal and some to spare. One year for six weeks, Captain Simpson says, he and his father and sister lived on Johnny cake, cornmeal mush, and maple syrup. The last mentioned was plentiful in those days.

During his first winter in the bush, Captain Simpson helped his father cut cord wood out of big maples, two and three feet across. As he only had leather boots, and the winter was cold with snow three feet deep, he says it was a stiff job for a boy of eleven years.

Started Fishing Industry
Captain Simpson recollects clearly the commencement of the Tobermory fishing industry. The first fishermen to come to the district came to Big Tub in 1881. They were Bill Vail and his son, Marmaduke, Sam Parsley, Sid Doran, John Savalley and his two sons, Denney and Michael, Alexander, John, Hector and Archie Kennedy, and Dick and Young (sic) Chapman. Prior to coming to Tobermory the Vails had fished at Flower Pot Island and at Half Moon Island, salting their fish in one hundred pound kegs. In 1881 the late Gilbert MacIntosh of Meaford commenced buying fish at Big Tub. He shipped them to Meaford on a little steam tug owned by Dick Chapman. Lige Rumley was the engineer. Later Mr.

MacIntosh built a larger tug for the run, to which he gave his own name "The MacIntosh".[3] Captain Chapman, who is still hale and hearty (and) lives in Wiarton, was her skipper. In 1883 Mr. MacIntosh transferred his fish business to the Little Tub, where the village of Tobermory had become established. Later he sold out to McKay and Clark, who joined up with the old Buffalo Fish Company. They in time sold out to the J. R. Boothe Fish Company of Chicago.

Fished in Sail Boats

Up until 1882, Captain Simpson states, all fishing was carried on by sail boats. A number of the fishermen, who came to the Tub from Southampton, used square stern boats with a large wooden centre board. Others who came from Meaford, Cape Rich and Vail's Point, favored sharp sterned boats with an iron centre board. The rivalry between these two groups of owners as to which type of boat was the speedier was great. Among the Southampton fishermen at Tobermory in those days were Dougal MacAulay, George McAulay, Dan McAulay, Murdock Matheson, and Malcolm McKenzie. The rival group consisted of John and Duncan McInnis of Meaford, John, Alexander and Archie Kennedy, and Bob Webber, of Cape Rich, William and Marmaduke Vail, James and William McReynolds, Bob Edmonstone, and Charles Vail, of Vail's Point.

Many Fishing Tugs

Captain Simpson, who has a wonderful memory, can recount all the tugs that have operated from Tobermory and can name their skippers. In 1882 the "Clucas", owned by McKay and Clark of Goderich, came to the harbour. Captain John McKay was in charge at first, but on his appointment as lightkeeper at Loyal Island,[4] he was succeeded in turn by Captains Young, Chapman, Angus McKenzie, Malcolm McDonald, Alexander Craigie and George McAulay.

Another early comer was the tug "Juno",[5] owned first by Malcolm McKenzie of Southampton and later by the Boothe Company. She was commanded by Captain Neil Matheson, a fine type of Highland Scotsman, from the time she was built until she became unfit for further service. Captain Matheson also was Master of the tug "Evelyn" for a number of years. His widow, Mrs. Neil Matheson, still lives in Tobermory, operating the Matheson House tourist home.[6] The Boothe Company also had the tug "Seabold" fishing from the Tub, with Captain Duncan McInnis of Meaford in charge.

Built Ice House

In 1903, Captain Simpson recalls, Robert Gillies built an icehouse and dock where the present ferry dock is. Mr. Gillies carried on as a fish dealer there, later selling out to the F. T. James' Company of Toronto, who after a number of years sold out to the G. W. Golden and Sons, who still carry on the business. In 1905 William Leslie, Albert Leslie and George Belrose built and launched the tug "David Marwick". They also built an ice-house, and besides operating their fishing boats, bought and shipped fish. W. W. Ransbury later sold out his interest to Captain Simpson and Mr. Smith, purchasing the Boothe Company's ice-house, dock, and net sheds. Mr. Ransbury

still carries on the business along with his sons. Of the first very early group of fishermen, Captain Simpson says O. C. Vail is the only direct descendant still carrying on a fish business in Tobermory, with his own boat, icehouse and dock.

Was Lumberman Too

In the early days Captain Simpson was a fisherman in the summer and a lumberman in the winter. For twenty-two winters he went lumbering in the bush around Tobermory, only leaving the district for the winter of 1909-10, when he was in charge of a lumber camp on the Circle River for the Grand Trunk Pacific, taking out ties for the railroad and cofferdam timber for bridge work. He has vivid recollections of the time when the Tobermory district hummed with the sound of saw-mills. The first to be built was in 1878 at Crane River. It was a small water powered mill. A. E. Pedwell now has a steam saw mill there. In 1881 Maitland, Rixon and Company built a large sawmill at the Little Tub. It was burned down in March 1882, but was rebuilt the same year. They operated until 1888, when they moved to Owen Sound. In 1893 Richard Badstone built a small mill at the head of the harbor, which he sold to Hector Currie in 1902.

Owned a Mill

Captain Simpson himself went into the mill owning business, when Simpson and Culbert bought a mill from J. P. Newman of Wiarton, which they moved to Tobermory. After running if for some time, Captain Simpson and his partner disposed of the mill to John Neil and Hector Currie, who later sold it to William Gillies. Mr. Gillies ran it until it was destroyed by fire. About the same time E. M. Miers built and operated a large sawmill and box factory, which he later moved to Wiarton. In 1907 Murphy and Willischroft erected a large mill at the harbor. After running it for a while they sold out to Deible and Eldridge. Later that firm sold the building to G. W. Golden and Sons, who still have it, using it as an ice-house and net shed. About twenty years ago Thomas Spears built a saw and planing mill on the shore of the Wireless Bay. He operated it until 1939 when he sold out to E. O. Erb, who rebuilt it and now has an up-to-date saw and planing mill run by a large motor.

Active in Community Life

Notwithstanding his activities in the fish and timber business, Captain Simpson has found time to take an active part in many phases of community life. When Lindsay and St. Edmunds became separate townships in 1903, he served on the first St. Edmunds Council with Reeve Solomon Spears and Councillors John Smith, Henry Davis, H. Hopkins. In the following year, 1904, he became reeve and held the office again in the next year. After that he rested from municipal honors until 1919, when he returned to the council. He served then as a councillor for three years and was again elected to the reeveship in 1922, remaining reeve till the end of 1925. After three years out of office, Captain Simpson again filled the post in 1929 and 1930. He has thus been reeve of St. Edmunds for eight terms, beating his nearest rival, Andrew Munn, by one year. He was police magistrate for the township for twenty-seven years, retiring in 1932. For a number of years he was President of the local Conservative Association.

School Trustee

Captain Simpson also served several terms on the Trustee Board of school section No. 2, the harbor section. The first log schoolhouse in St. Edmunds was built in 1881 in school section No. 1 in the Settlement. Miss Ella Coughlin was the first teacher. The harbor had no school until 1901, when the main part of the present school was erected. C. J. Hamilton was appointed teacher at the princely salary of $300 a year.

Was Postmaster

Capt. Simpson acted as postmaster. His father had been the second postmaster in St. Edmunds, succeeding Donald McDonald who was appointed in 1884 until 1889, the year of his death. When Captain Simpson gave up the postmastershop, his sister, Mrs. Archie Currie, carried on until 1913, when the present postmaster, Andrew Belrose, took office. The first post office was on the site of Gordon Hopkin's present farm-house. Benjamin Butchard was the first mail carrier and Captain Simpson recalls how he used to carry the mail on his back, walking to and from Stokes Bay once weekly.

Lighthouse Keeper

From 1912 to 1915, Captain Simpson was in charge of the lighthouse at Cove Island. He well remembers the terrible storm of November 9, 1913, during which two hundred and sixty-two sailors were lost on the Great Lakes. Most of those who have motored to Tobermory know the long bridge at Little Lake. In 1910 Captain Simpson took the contract for building the bridge and says he put three hundred and sixty-five cords of stone into the job. In 1911 he contracted for clearing the ground for the Wireless Station. It was established in that year with Sam Currie head operator and John MaCartney and Fiddes Rennie as his assistants.

When a library association was formed in Tobermory in 1921, largely through the efforts of David Robertson, K. C., Captain Simpson acted as first chairman of the board. Mrs. Simpson was the first librarian and held the position until the library became a public library in the fall of 1929. Captain Simpson is at present a member of the library board.

Church Affairs

In the building of both the Harbor and Settlement Churches, Captain Simpson and his father, James Simpson, had a hand. The foundation of the village church was laid in 1884, when the Rev. Philip Sparling was minister. There had been a Methodist minister placed in the township the year before, the Rev. James Walker, but there was no church for his congregation to worship in. The Maitland, Rixon Company helped much in the building of this first Methodist Church in the village. The Settlement Church was built in 1889, while the Rev. W. B. Danard was pastor. Along with Captain Simpson and his father, others who helped at the building were James H. Hopkins, William Spears, Michael Belrose, Jacob Belrose and John C. Hopkins.

Enthusiastic Orangeman

Captain Simpson was one of the first trustees of the Methodist Church. He served for many years as a member of the church board, first when it was Methodist and also later when it became United. Captain Simpson is a member of the United Church. His father belonged to the Methodist persuasion, while his mother was Anglican. He is an enthusiastic Orangeman and has held every office in the Tobermory Lodge except Deputy Master and Treasurer. He has been Master for three separate terms and three of his sons, George, Bill, and Archie, have been Masters. He is a member of the Royal Black Knights of Ireland.

Oldest Living Ratepayer

Although not the oldest person in the community, Captain Simpson claims that he is the oldest living ratepayer in the Township of St. Edmunds, having owned property and paid taxes since he was seventeen years of age. The captain was united in marriage to Christena Martin at Glamis in 1893. The Rev. Richard MacDonald, Presbyterian minister there, performed the ceremony. Mrs. Simpson's father, Murdock L. Martin, came to Canada direct from the Island of Lewis. Her parents settled on Lot 35, Concession 4, Bruce Township, which they cleared. Their whole married life was spent on that lot and both died there. Captain and Mrs. Simpson have three sons serving the Canadian Armed Forces, George, in the Army, Archie in the Air Force, and Hugh in the Navy, Lindsay, the oldest son, now deceased, served overseas in the last war.

Last April, Captain Simpson had the misfortune to have his house burned down, but he has converted his former garage into a very comfortable cabin, and he and Mrs. Simpson are living cosily there now.

The Captain has always been much in demand as a chairman for social gatherings, his specialty being a pie social. He can give a fine rendering of the many of Henry Drummond. His supply of humorous stories is inexaustible and his geniality contagious. His many friends in Tobermory, and all over Bruce County, hope that he may long continue to enjoy his present good health.

---

[1] No such vessel existed. The reference is to the 'Prince Alfred' built at Sarnia in 1859, and in service as a passenger and freight boat out of Wiarton and Owen Sound in 1879.
[2] Probably George Pepper who settled on Lot 44, Con. 2, EBR.
[3] The 'G. P. McIntosh', 40.6 tons, built at Meaford in 1888.
[4] Lyal Island, Stokes Bay.
[5] The 'Juno', 19.3 tons, was built at Goderich in 1887.
[6] Now the George'n

MR. W. A. SPEARS

Owen Sound Sun Times, 1970

Travellers taking the ferry from Tobermory to South Bay Mouth, or a yacht through the McGregor Channel, dividing Georgian Bay and Lake Huron, need have no fear.

Standing guard over what is believed to be the most dangerous stretch of water in the Lakes, are a light and a keeper with combined experience of more than 160 years in guiding ships through treacherous waters.

Bill Spears and the Cove Island light will play a part in seeing to it that you arrive safely at your destination.

Situated six miles north-west of Tobermory, on the north-east corner of Cove Island, the light is a landmark which has stood watch over the channel since 1856.

Bill Spears has been keeper of the light since 1950. He previously kept lights at Flower Pot Island, and Angus Island in Lake Superior.

Mr. Spears was only six months old when his father and mother moved to Flower Pot Island to keep the light there. At 17, Bill became an assistant. Upon his father's death, Bill maintained the light, while waiting for the department of transport to send out a full time replacement.

Upon leaving Flower Pot, in 1936, Mr. Spears returned to Tobermory where he worked on the fishing tugs for three years. With the outbreak of war in 1939, he enlisted and became a member of the Perth regiment, which went overseas in 1941.

Boat Builder

Upon returning to the 'Tub' in '45, the lightkeeper took up an old hobby of building boats, in order to make a living. To supplement the small income from the boat construction, he worked as a guide for tourists.

When the Angus Island Light came open in 1948, Mr. Spears' application for the position was accepted. While serving on Angus Island, Mr. Spears travelled to Toronto during the winter to earn his second class commercial ticket in morse code. With this ticket, he was able to get the position he holds now, on Cove Island.

When Mr. and Mrs. Spears and their three small children landed on Cove for the first time in 1950, it was like stepping into the past. Water had to be dipped out of the bay, toilet facilities were outside, and the keeper had to cut his own firewood.

In his 22 seasons on the island, Mr. Spears has seen many changes. In 1950, there was only one helper on the island. In 1960, the department of transport hired a second assistant, making the keeper's job a little easier. The work of the three men on Cove Island is varied and difficult but never boring. They may be cutting the grass, winding the big light, or keeping the floor of the generator room painted amidst the noise of two diesel generator engines and a fog horn.

When one first arrives on the island, after a 45-minute ride by water taxi it is difficult to believe that just three men keep the buildings in as good a shape as they are. There are three dwellings, a boat house, a generator house, and the light house, all to maintain.

Since coming to the island, Mr. Spears and his assistants, Harry Horton and Ken Armstrong, have found time to put in 200 yards of cement sidewalks, and to build a landing pad for the department of transport helicopter.

As well as the routine of maintenance the keeper and his assistants are responsible for giving regular weather reports to the department of transport offices in Wiarton, and for making sure that the fog horn is turned on if there is even a small amount of fog on the water.

The big light, the fog horn and the radio signal 'D' are all part of the ability of ships to recognize their position in regard to the lighthouse. The light flashes 12 times a minute; the fog horn sounds three blasts in a row, every minute; and the radio signal is beamed out every hour to allow ships to home-in on Cove Island.

By taking a bearing on two other lights besides Cove Island, the particular ship can locate its exact position on a chart.

"Fog horns are pretty well outdated now," Mr. Spears said, "with the ships equipped with radar. However, when I have spoken to skippers about it, they have expressed the feeling that it is nice to hear the horn, just to be sure that the radar is O.K."

One of the most unforgettable experiences of the keeper took place in 1954, when he contracted mumps late in the season. Since his help was inexperienced, Mr. Spears had a man sent out from town to cook for him; and he spent 14 days in the radio transmitting room of the generator house.

Stayed on the Job

In the room, he carried on the duties of regular radio reports to Midland, while attempting to recover from the mumps. The radio room is located beside the fog horn and the two generator engines, which ran continually during the time that he was sick.

One thing which really makes the keeper see red, is "city people who think they are A-1 navigators because they have a captain's cap on." Mr. Spears relates stories of people who have come to his dock without life jackets, oars or charts. He has seen some come up with 12 people in one 12-foot boat.

"Just this month," the keeper said, "I had a lad come to the dock, with a road map for a chart. When I attempted to assist him, he was so sarcastic I couldn't believe it."

Mrs. Spears fills her hours with the regular household tasks, and gardening; using any free hours to read or write. At present, she is corresponding with a lightkeeper's wife from Tasmania.

The Spears have three children, two girls and a boy. Their oldest daughter, Ila, is now Mrs. Tom Klienknecht and lives in Kitchener. Linda is married to Grant Watson, a businessman in Tobermory. Bill junior, his father's pride and joy, is the light keeper on Angus Island, his father's previous position. Bill is now in his second year there.

The second half of the light keeping partnership is the light. Built between 1856 and 1859, the lighthouse towers 85 feet above the rocky beach. Virtually all stone that went into the construction of the light was brought in from Edinborough, Scotland. Many of the slabs of granite are so large that they could not possibly be lifted by manpower. As Mr. Spears puts it: "You couldn't get enough people around it to lift the weight."

Capstan Used

Spears believes that the stones were lifted into place with the aid of a capstan and pulleys. The capstan was operated by eight men.

The light itself operates on a system of weights, much the same as a grandfather clock. It is wound and started by hand. The equipment that turns the light is all original.

In September 1960, the light was converted from oil to electricity. Other than that, it remains the same as the day it was built in 1858.

During the winter, a battery operated light, much the same as a buoy light, flashes automatically. It is also important as an emergency light in case of a power failure.

The big light is powered by a 500-watt bulb, magnified through a 1-1/2 inch thick glass. The machinery of the light is floating on a base of liquid mercury.

The story of Bill Spears and the Cove Island light would not be complete without the mention of the ghost of Cove Island.

According to the light keeper's log of 1881; "the body of Captain Tripp, skipper of the Schooner Regina that was wrecked off the west shore of the island in 1881, was swept ashore Sept. 25 of that year." The log states that the skipper was buried where he was found.

Spears, the soft spoken keeper of 1970, says "whenever a door bangs, or the wind whistles around the eaves of the house, in the evening, we say, "It's Captain Tripp.""

W. A. Spears

MR. ROY HATT

Four decades at the centre of life in Tobermory, and St. Edmunds in all its spheres; educational, social, cultural, municipal and spiritual.

By Lloyd Adams

When Roy Hatt arrived here in 1931 as a young twenty-one year old fresh out of normal school, few if any would realize the benefit accruing to the area for the next forty-one years flowing from his talents as a country school teacher and his outstanding personality.

He was born in Eastnor Township in 1911, the son of Mr. and Mrs. Frank Hatt and raised on the family farm along with two sisters and two brothers. His education was received at Lion's Head, Wiarton and Stratford in normal school.

Installed as the new school teacher of S. S. No. 1 with its 40 pupils and the magnificent salary of $808.50 per year, his youthful good looks and engaging personality soon caught the attention of the local young misses. However, Mildred Dean, daughter of Mr. and Mrs. John Dean soon had the upper hand. Shortly after that Roy and his violin were banished to the granary for his practice sessions. Her motive might be questioned but anyone with first hand experience of hearing a violin taking punishment from a beginner could sympathize. Fortunately for the livestock the granary was a detached building.

Roy and Mildred were married in 1933 and moved into a house on her father's farm formerly occupied by Jerry Parker. They lived there for awhile and then moved to the George Bartman farm just south of the school where their first child, Elizabeth, was born in 1935. The following year he purchased a building lot just behind the school from his brother-in-law Gordon Hopkins and began building a home doing most of the work himself. There were very few homes being built at this time in the very heart of the depression years but with the relative security of his teaching job and proximity of the building to the school seemed like a good idea. These were economically tough times but in many ways simpler, happier times.

About this time a life long active involvement with the Tobermory United Church began in the Settlement United Church just a stones throw away from the school.

Softball was a very important area sport at this time involving teams from Tobermory to Clavering to Shallow Lake and Roy became a key player with the local team. A very agile fielder, he had an uncanny ability to place his hits where opposing fielders were not. Roy and Mildred's new home soon became a mecca for friends and relatives with Saturday night being particularly lively with card games, Foster Hewitt and Hockey Night in Canada and of course lunch with much discussion of the merits of the game.

Roy was now also an enthusiastic and active member of the Tobermory Ladies Orange Lodge eventually holding all the offices and becoming County Master of North Bruce Orange Lodge with forty years of membership.

In 1941 a son, Frances Maurice, was born and in 1942 Roy moved as principal to the larger S. S. No. 2 school in the village completing his first decade of teaching. At this time he purchased a farm and dairy business from Cecil Davis situated a mile south of town and moved there from his home by the settlement school. To see Roy now was to see a person in constant motion with a full time teaching position, operating a dairy and farm and many community activities and in spite of the demands on his time his home remained a gathering place for many and he always seemed to find time for a smile, some fun and conversation.

In 1943 Roy and Mildred suffered a personal tragedy in the death of their son Frances Maurice. Work and responsibilities had to be carried on, however, and these were there in abundance. Two years later in 1945 an event occurred which gave a new meaning to the term "Hatt trick" for area residents. Triplet sons, Barry, Raymond, and Billie were born to Mildred and Roy at the Wiarton Spears Nursing Home February 15th, the fathers birthday! Needless to say this created much interest and a newspaper account at the time said that the mother and the babies although premature were doing quite well but that Roy was being treated for severe shock. They eventually matured into healthy young adults and were a source of joy and of course considerable help to their parents in operating the farm and dairy. Their lone sister, Elizabeth, maintains that to her they were sometimes an exasperation also.

In 1951 Roy added the job of Township Treasurer to his growing portfolio of jobs and duties. About the time he sold the Davis farm to Aaron Dean and moved to dairy to the Cosgrove farm on lot 47 W. B. R. the same farm on which he had boarded as a new arrival twenty some years earlier. The Cosgroves assumed possession of the house at the settlement School which Roy had built years earlier and still owned. A new home was now built on the Cosgrove farm and the farm across the road lot 47 E. B. R. was purchased from Cliff Woods. Throughout all this activity Roy was still the prinicipal of the three room village school. In 1964, deep personal tragedy again struck the Roy Hatt family with the accidental death of one of the triplet boys, Raymond, at the age of nineteen years.

Within the next three years the dairy business was sold to Wiarton dairy interests and the Hatt family moved to the village in 1966 having sold the farms to William Willoughan and Archie Watson. One would think Roy Hatt would be ready to slow down but instead he added the job of Clerk to that of Treasurer for the Township and began selling real estate.

As well, he became a member of the Tobermory Rotary Club and was soon its secretary. A square dance club was formed and proved successful due largely to Roy's enthusiasm. He never became proficient on the violin which probably was not due to lack of musical talent but more likely lack of time for concentration.

There was little time for personal leisure but when a golf course was built south of town for two or three brief summers Roy could be seen enthusiastically swinging away on the occasional weekend with his sons or relatives and friends.

In robust good health up to this time he now began showing symptoms of fatigue and illness and decided to retire as principal of S. S. No. 2 St. Edmunds at the end of December 1971. A "Tribute to Mr. Hatt" night was held in the Community Hall to honour his four decades of teaching service to St. Edmunds residents. The esteem in which he was held was evident by the large number in attendance.

On April 15, 1972, the community was shocked and saddened to learn of the sudden death of Roy Hatt in the Wiarton Hospital. His passing was a tremendous blow to his family and to this community but fond memories will remain for all who were fortunate enough to have known such an unassuming and generous person who gave so much of his time and talents to others.

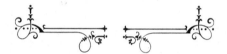

Roy Hatt

Mr. and Mrs. Roy Hatt at school retirement party December, 1972.

FAMILY TREES

In this section, a number of family trees are presented. The families thus represented were chosen because their ancestors arrived in the early years of settlement, and there are still family members living in the area today.

There are a number of reasons for including these family trees. They are useful in identifying the characters mentioned in other sections of this book. They help to show how the community developed into the closely knit, inter-related one that it is today. Trends in marriages can be observed as the years pass, showing how people married others within the area until after the isolation between St. Edmunds and the rest of the world was broken, when names from outside the area appear. Statistical information such as the changes in family size and the age at death can be found in these trees as well.

Each family tree begins with the first member of the family who arrived in the area, and continues only with those who continue the family name, mainly the sons. The family trees are as complete as possible up to the period of 1945-50. After this period, the number of people leaving the area rose dramatically as did the number of divorces, both of which made it difficult to carry the trees on.

There are a number of mistakes in these trees in spite of all the sources we used to make sure that the information presented was correct. These mistakes are due to incorrect information on tombstones and in obituaries and records; hidden information; and simply the fact that some branches of different families have moved out of the area and are no longer in contact with people in St. Edmunds.

ADAMS 1

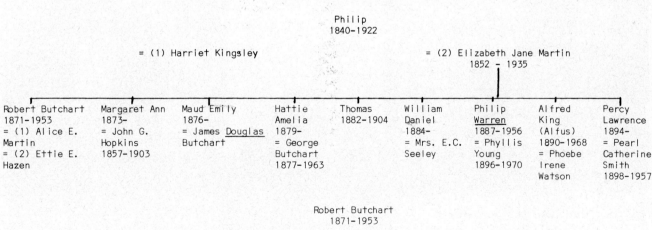

Philip
1840-1922

= (1) Harriet Kingsley   = (2) Elizabeth Jane Martin
                                      1852 - 1935

| Robert Butchart 1871-1953 = (1) Alice E. Martin = (2) Ettie E. Hazen | Margaret Ann 1873- = John G. Hopkins 1857-1903 | Maud Emily 1876- = James Douglas Butchart | Hattie Amelia 1879- = George Butchart 1877-1963 | Thomas 1882-1904 | William Daniel 1884- = Mrs. E.C. Seeley | Philip Warren 1887-1956 = Phyllis Young 1896-1970 | Alfred King (Alfus) 1890-1968 = Phoebe Irene Watson | Percy Lawrence 1894- = Pearl Catherine Smith 1898-1957 |

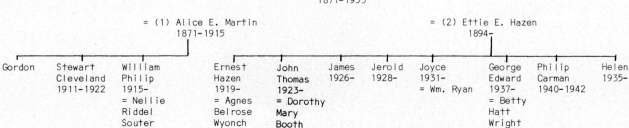

Robert Butchart
1871-1953

= (1) Alice E. Martin   = (2) Ettie E. Hazen
        1871-1915   1894-

| Gordon | Stewart Cleveland 1911-1922 | William Philip 1915- = Nellie Riddel Souter | Ernest Hazen 1919- = Agnes Belrose Wyonch | John Thomas 1923- = Dorothy Mary Booth | James 1926- | Jerold 1928- | Joyce 1931- = Wm. Ryan | George Edward 1937- = Betty Hatt Wright | Philip Carman 1940-1942 | Helen 1935- |

Philip Adams family home

Alf Adams and sons Jack,
Glen and Stan

Thomas Adams

Alfred King (Alfus) Adams 1906

Bob Adams and wife Ettie

Percy Adams and wife Pearl (Smith) Adams

Percy Adams and Vida Jordan

Percy and Pearl Adams with son Lloyd
and grandson Brooke

ADAMS 2

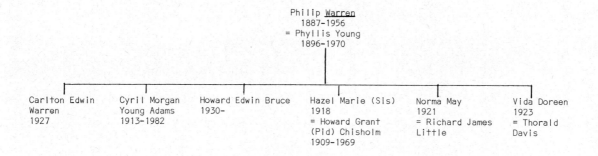

```
                            Philip Warren
                             1887-1956
                           = Phyllis Young
                             1896-1970
                                 |
  ┌───────────┬──────────┬───────────┬──────────┬──────────┬──────────┐
Carlton Edwin  Cyril Morgan  Howard Edwin Bruce  Hazel Marie (Sis)  Norma May   Vida Doreen
Warren         Young Adams   1930-               1918               1921        1923
1927           1913-1982                         = Howard Grant     = Richard James  = Thorald
                                                 (Pid) Chisholm     Little       Davis
                                                 1909-1969
```

```
                       Alfred King (Alfus)
                            1890-1968
                      = Phoebe Irene Watson
                                 |
          ┌──────────────────────┼──────────────────────┐
       Stanley                  Glen                    Jack
       = Mary              = Joyce Adams            = Dorothy
```

ADAMS 3

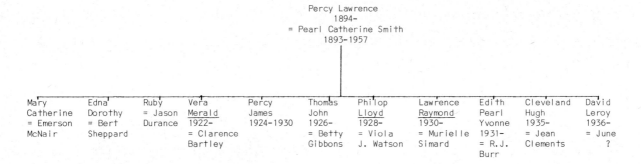

```
                       Percy Lawrence
                           1894-
                    = Pearl Catherine Smith
                           1893-1957
                                 |
```

| Mary Catherine = Emerson McNair | Edna Dorothy = Bert Sheppard | Ruby = Jason Durance | Vera Merald 1922- = Clarence Bartley | Percy James 1924-1930 | Thomas John 1926- = Betty Gibbons | Philop Lloyd 1928- = Viola J. Watson | Lawrence Raymond 1930- = Murielle Simard | Edith Pearl Yvonne 1931- = R.J. Burr | Cleveland Hugh 1935- = Jean Clements | David Leroy 1936- = June ? |

BARTMAN 1

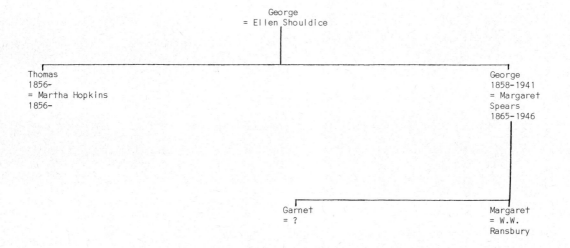

```
                          George
                     = Ellen Shouldice
                                 |
          ┌──────────────────────────────────────────────────┐
       Thomas                                              George
       1856-                                               1858-1941
       = Martha Hopkins                                    = Margaret
       1856-                                               Spears
                                                           1865-1946
                                                               |
                                    ┌──────────────────────────┴──────┐
                                 Garnet                            Margaret
                                 = ?                               = W.W.
                                                                   Ransbury
```

BARTMAN 2

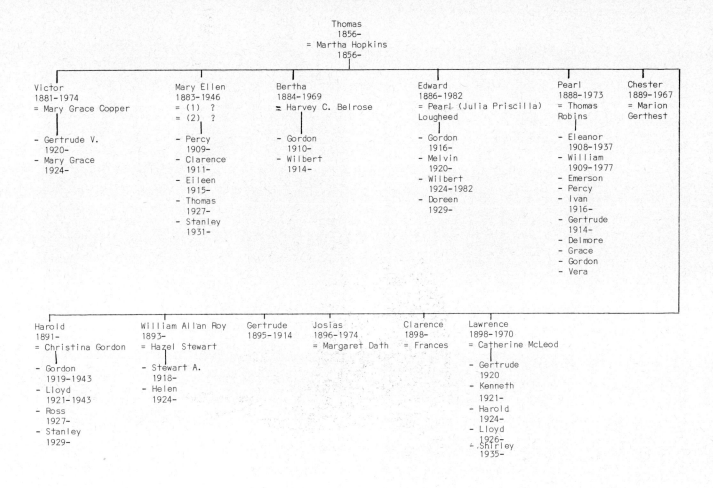

```
                                    Thomas
                                    1856-
                                  = Martha Hopkins
                                    1856-
 ┌──────────────┬───────────────┬──────────────────────┬──────────────────┬──────────────┐
Victor          Mary Ellen      Bertha                 Edward             Pearl          Chester
1881-1974       1883-1946       1884-1969              1886-1982          1888-1973      1889-1967
= Mary Grace    = (1)  ?        = Harvey C. Belrose    = Pearl (Julia     = Thomas       = Marion
  Cooper        = (2)  ?                                 Priscilla)         Robins         Gerthest
                                                         Lougheed
- Gertrude V.   - Percy         - Gordon               - Gordon           - Eleanor
  1920            1909-           1910-                  1916-              1908-1937
- Mary Grace    - Clarence      - Wilbert              - Melvin           - William
  1924            1911-           1914-                  1920-              1909-1977
                - Eileen                               - Wilbert          - Emerson
                  1915-                                  1924-1982        - Percy
                - Thomas                                - Doreen          - Ivan
                  1927-                                   1929-             1916-
                - Stanley                                                 - Gertrude
                  1931-                                                     1914-
                                                                          - Delmore
                                                                          - Grace
                                                                          - Gordon
                                                                          - Vera

 ┌──────────────┬───────────────┬──────────────────────┬──────────────────┬──────────────┐
Harold          William Allan   Gertrude               Josias             Clarence       Lawrence
1891-            Roy            1895-1914               1896-1974          1898-          1898-1970
= Christina      1893-                                 = Margaret Dath    = Frances      = Catherine McLeod
  Gordon        = Hazel Stewart
                                                                                         - Gertrude
- Gordon        - Stewart A.                                                               1920
  1919-1943       1918-                                                                  - Kenneth
- Lloyd         - Helen                                                                     1921-
  1921-1943       1924-                                                                  - Harold
- Ross                                                                                     1924-
  1927-                                                                                  - Lloyd
- Stanley                                                                                  1926-
  1929-                                                                                  - Shirley
                                                                                           1935-
```

BELROSE 1

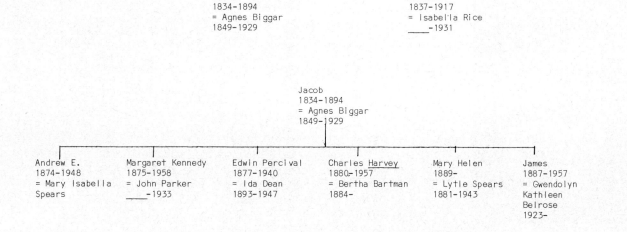

```
          Jacob                              Michael
          1834-1894                          1837-1917
          = Agnes Biggar                     = Isabella Rice
            1849-1929                           ____-1931


                          Jacob
                          1834-1894
                          = Agnes Biggar
                            1849-1929
 ┌──────────────┬───────────────┬──────────────────┬──────────────┬──────────────┐
Andrew E.       Margaret        Edwin Percival     Charles Harvey  Mary Helen     James
1874-1948       Kennedy         1877-1940          1880-1957       1889-          1887-1957
= Mary Isabella 1875-1958       = Ida Dean         = Bertha Bartman = Lytle Spears = Gwendolyn
  Spears        = John Parker     1893-1947          1884-           1881-1943       Kathleen
                  ____-1933                                                          Belrose
                                                                                     1923-
```

Howard Belrose 1916

Wesley, Debbie and son Kingsley Belrose 1912

**Mary Ellen Bartman
(Mrs. T. Spears
before 1920)**

Michael Belrose's family 1910

BELROSE 2

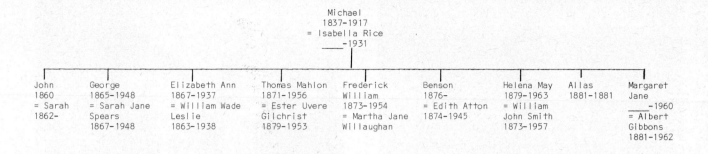

Michael
1837-1917
= Isabella Rice
____ -1931

| John 1860 = Sarah 1862- | George 1865-1948 = Sarah Jane Spears 1867-1948 | Elizabeth Ann 1867-1937 = William Wade Leslie 1863-1938 | Thomas Mahlon 1871-1956 = Ester Uvere Gilchrist 1879-1953 | Frederick William 1873-1954 = Martha Jane Willaughan | Benson 1876- = Edith Atton 1874-1945 | Helena May 1879-1963 = William John Smith 1873-1957 | Allas 1881-1881 | Margaret Jane ____ -1960 = Albert Gibbons 1881-1962 |

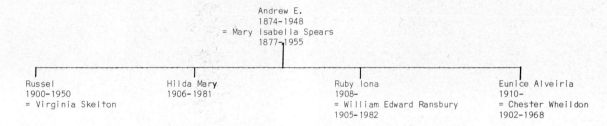

Andrew E.
1874-1948
= Mary Isabella Spears
1877-1955

| Russel 1900-1950 = Virginia Skelton | Hilda Mary 1906-1981 | Ruby Iona 1908- = William Edward Ransbury 1905-1982 | Eunice Alveiria 1910- = Chester Wheildon 1902-1968 |

BELROSE 3

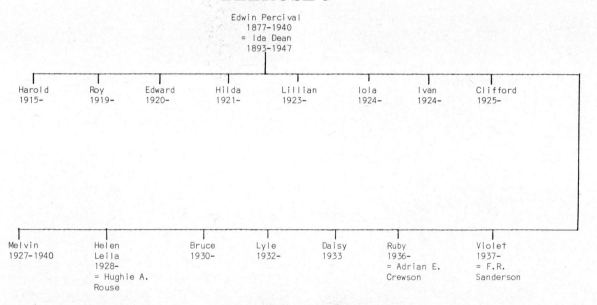

Edwin Percival
1877-1940
= Ida Dean
1893-1947

| Harold 1915- | Roy 1919- | Edward 1920- | Hilda 1921- | Lillian 1923- | Iola 1924- | Ivan 1924- | Clifford 1925- |

| Melvin 1927-1940 | Helen Leila 1928- = Hughie A. Rouse | Bruce 1930- | Lyle 1932- | Daisy 1933 | Ruby 1936- = Adrian E. Crewson | Violet 1937- = F.R. Sanderson |

BELROSE 4

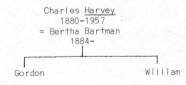

Charles Harvey
1880-1957
= Bertha Bartman
1884-

| Gordon | William |

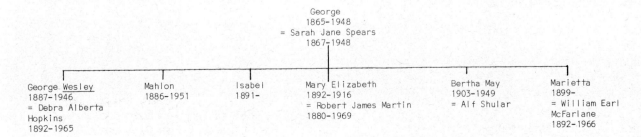

George
1865-1948
= Sarah Jane Spears
1867-1948

| George Wesley 1887-1946 = Debra Alberta Hopkins 1892-1965 | Mahlon 1886-1951 | Isabel 1891- | Mary Elizabeth 1892-1916 = Robert James Martin 1880-1969 | Bertha May 1903-1949 = Alf Shular | Marietta 1899- = William Earl McFarlane 1892-1966 |

Andrew Belrose

Mamie Belrose

Hilda Belrose 1927

**Hilda Belrose and Harriet Hopkins
with Charlie Longstaff in mid-1920's.**

BELROSE 5

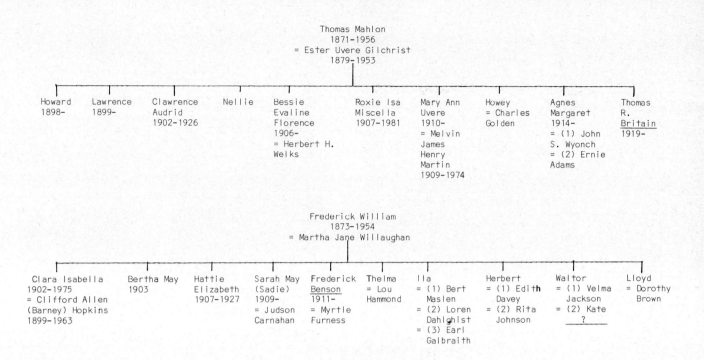

Thomas Mahlon
1871-1956
= Ester Uvere Gilchrist
1879-1953

| Howard 1898- | Lawrence 1899- | Clawrence Audrid 1902-1926 | Nellie | Bessie Evaline Florence 1906- = Herbert H. Welks | Roxie Isa Miscella 1907-1981 | Mary Ann Uvere 1910- = Melvin James Henry Martin 1909-1974 | Howey = Charles Golden | Agnes Margaret 1914- = (1) John S. Wyonch = (2) Ernie Adams | Thomas R. Britain 1919- |

Frederick William
1873-1954
= Martha Jane Willaughan

| Clara Isabella 1902-1975 = Clifford Allen (Barney) Hopkins 1899-1963 | Bertha May 1903 | Hattie Elizabeth 1907-1927 | Sarah May (Sadie) 1909- = Judson Carnahan | Frederick Benson 1911- = Myrtle Furness | Thelma = Lou Hammond | Ila = (1) Bert Maslen = (2) Loren Dahlghist = (3) Earl Galbraith | Herbert = (1) Edith Davey = (2) Rita Johnson | Waltor = (1) Velma Jackson = (2) Kate ? | Lloyd = Dorothy Brown |

BELROSE 6

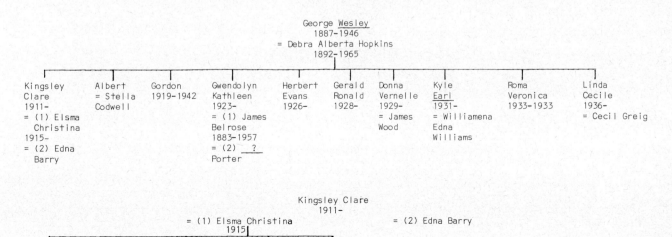

George Wesley
1887-1946
= Debra Alberta Hopkins
1892-1965

| Kingsley Clare 1911- = (1) Elsma Christina 1915- = (2) Edna Barry | Albert = Stella Codwell | Gordon 1919-1942 | Gwendolyn Kathleen 1923- = (1) James Belrose 1883-1957 = (2) ? Porter | Herbert Evans 1926- | Gerald Ronald 1928- | Donna Vernelle 1929- = James Wood | Kyle Earl 1931- = Williamena Edna Williams | Roma Veronica 1933-1933 | Linda Cecile 1936- = Cecil Greig |

Kingsley Clare
1911-

= (1) Elsma Christina   = (2) Edna Barry
        1915-

| James Wesley Morris 1940 - 19? | Sheldon = Erma Berry | Robert | George Maitland 1932-1939 |

BUTCHART 1

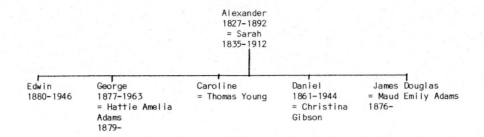

```
                              Alexander
                              1827-1892
                              = Sarah
                              1835-1912

  Edwin          George              Caroline        Daniel          James Douglas
  1880-1946      1877-1963           = Thomas Young  1861-1944       = Maud Emily Adams
                 = Hattie Amelia                     = Christina     1876-
                   Adams                               Gibson
                   1879-
```

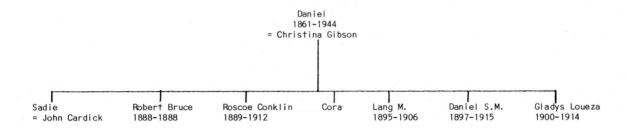

```
                              Daniel
                              1861-1944
                              = Christina Gibson

Sadie          Robert Bruce    Roscoe Conklin   Cora    Lang M.      Daniel S.M.    Gladys Loueza
= John Cardick 1888-1888       1889-1912                1895-1906    1897-1915      1900-1914
```

BUTCHART 2

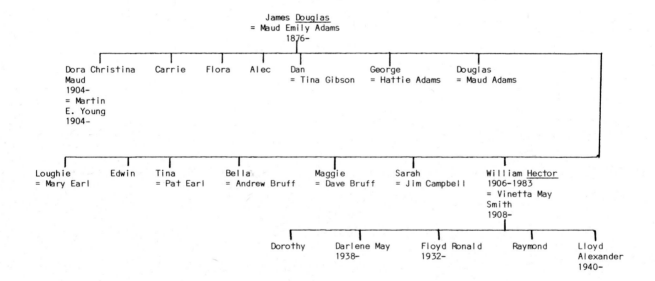

```
                              James Douglas
                              = Maud Emily Adams
                              1876-

  Dora Christina  Carrie  Flora  Alec  Dan            George         Douglas
  Maud                                 = Tina Gibson  = Hattie Adams  = Maud Adams
  1904-
  = Martin
    E. Young
    1904-

Loughie      Edwin   Tina        Bella             Maggie          Sarah           William Hector
= Mary Earl          = Pat Earl  = Andrew Bruff    = Dave Bruff    = Jim Campbell  1906-1983
                                                                                   = Vinetta May
                                                                                     Smith
                                                                                     1908-

        Dorothy       Darlene May     Floyd Ronald      Raymond       Lloyd
                      1938-           1932-                           Alexander
                                                                      1940-
```

BUTCHART 3

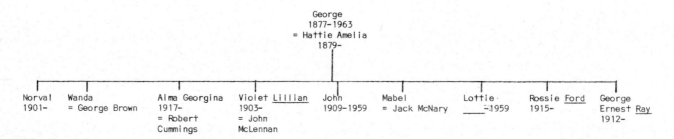

```
                              George
                              1877-1963
                              = Hattie Amelia
                              1879-

Norval   Wanda          Alma Georgina  Violet Lillian   John         Mabel         Lottie      Rossie Ford   George
1901-    = George Brown  1917-          1903-            1909-1959    = Jack McNary  -1959      1915-         Ernest Ray
                         = Robert       = John                                                               1912-
                           Cummings       McLennan
```

198

CHISHOLM

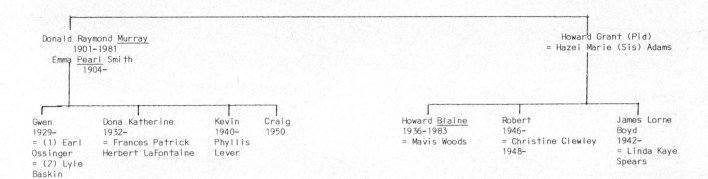

Donald Raymond Murray
1901-1981
Emma Pearl Smith
1904-

Howard Grant (Pid)
= Hazel Marie (Sis) Adams

Gwen
1929-
= (1) Earl
Ossinger
= (2) Lyle
Baskin

Dona Katherine
1932-
= Frances Patrick
Herbert LaFontaine

Kevin
1940-
Phyllis
Lever

Craig
1950

Howard Blaine
1936-1983
= Mavis Woods

Robert
1946-
= Christine Clewley
1948-

James Lorne
Boyd
1942-
= Linda Kaye
Spears

CRAIGIE

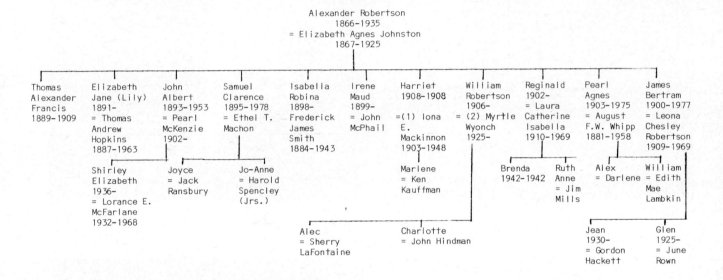

Alexander Robertson
1866-1935
= Elizabeth Agnes Johnston
1867-1925

Thomas
Alexander
Francis
1889-1909

Elizabeth
Jane (Lily)
1891-
= Thomas
Andrew
Hopkins
1887-1963

John
Albert
1893-1953
= Pearl
McKenzie
1902-

Samuel
Clarence
1895-1978
= Ethel T.
Machon

Isabella
Robina
1898-
Frederick
James
Smith
1884-1943

Irene
Maud
1899-
= John
McPhail

Harriet
1908-1908

=(1) Iona
E.
Mackinnon
1903-1948

William
Robertson
1906-
= (2) Myrtle
Wyonch
1925-

Reginald
1902-
= Laura
Catherine
Isabella
1910-1969

Pearl
Agnes
1903-1975
= August
F.W. Whipp
1881-1958

James
Bertram
1900-1977
= Leona
Chesley
Robertson
1909-1969

Shirley
Elizabeth
1936-
= Lorance E.
McFarlane
1932-1968

Joyce
= Jack
Ransbury

Jo-Anne
= Harold
Spencley
(Jrs.)

Marlene
= Ken
Kauffman

Brenda
1942-1942

Ruth
Anne
= Jim
Mills

Alex
= Darlene

William
= Edith
Mae
Lambkin

Alec
= Sherry
LaFontaine

Charlotte
= John Hindman

Jean
1930-
= Gordon
Hackett

Glen
1925-
= June
Rown

DAVIS

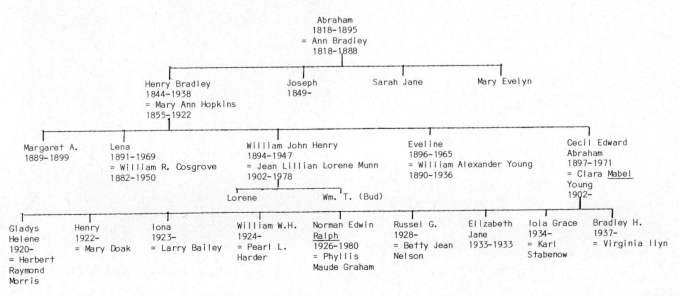

Abraham
1818-1895
= Ann Bradley
1818-1888

Henry Bradley
1844-1938
= Mary Ann Hopkins
1855-1922

Joseph
1849-

Sarah Jane

Mary Evelyn

Margaret A.
1889-1899

Lena
1891-1969
= William R. Cosgrove
1882-1950

William John Henry
1894-1947
= Jean Lillian Lorene Munn
1902-1978

Eveline
1896-1965
= William Alexander Young
1890-1936

Cecil Edward
Abraham
1897-1971
= Clara Mabel
Young
1902-

Lorene

Wm. T. (Bud)

Gladys
Helene
1920-
= Herbert
Raymond
Morris

Henry
1922-
= Mary Doak

Iona
1923-
= Larry Bailey

William W.H.
1924-
= Pearl L.
Harder

Norman Edwin
Ralph
1926-1980
= Phyllis
Maude Graham

Russel G.
1928-
= Betty Jean
Nelson

Elizabeth
Jane
1933-1933

Iola Grace
1934-
= Karl
Stabenow

Bradley H.
1937-
= Virginia Ilyn

199

Craigie family

Craigie home 1904

Murray Chisholm and wife Pearl (Smith)

Henry Bradley Davis family:
Evelyn, Lena, Mary Ann Hopkins, Henry Bradley, Bill and Cecil 1900.

Henry Bradley Davis and wife Mary Ann Hopkins 1900 or before.

Left to Right: Mary Ann Hopkins, Isaac Hopkins, Ilene Rae Hopkins, Henry Bradley Davis about 1910.

Cecil "Teddy" Davis, Henry Bradley Davis, Bill Cosgrove and Bill Davis.

Cecil Davis and wife Mabel (Young).

William Cosgrove and wife Lena Davis about 1910.

Granny Young and Ralph Davis 1940's

Back Row: **Harry and Bill Davis.**
Middle Row: **Ralph and Russel Davis.**
Front Row: **Bradley Davis 1940**

Dorine Adams and Iona Davis 1920

Left to Right: **Norma Adams, Diddie Adams, "Sis" Adams, Iona Davis, Gladys Davis and Harry Davis 1920.**

DEAN 1

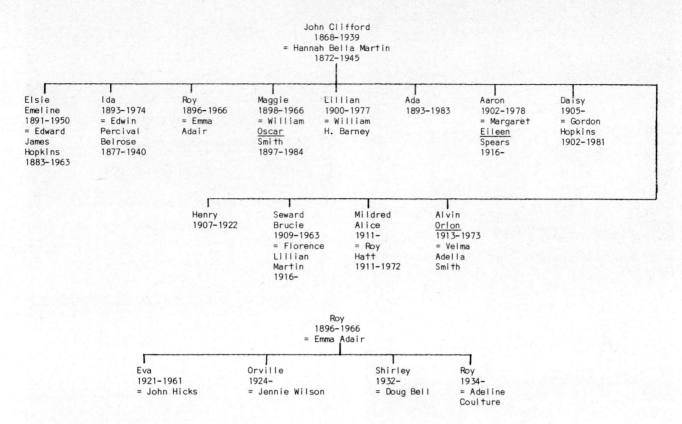

John Clifford
1868-1939
= Hannah Bella Martin
1872-1945

| Elsie Emeline 1891-1950 = Edward James Hopkins 1883-1963 | Ida 1893-1974 = Edwin Percival Belrose 1877-1940 | Roy 1896-1966 = Emma Adair | Maggie 1898-1966 = William Oscar Smith 1897-1984 | Lillian 1900-1977 = William H. Barney | Ada 1893-1983 | Aaron 1902-1978 = Margaret Eileen Spears 1916- | Daisy 1905- = Gordon Hopkins 1902-1981 |

| Henry 1907-1922 | Seward Brucie 1909-1963 = Florence Lillian Martin 1916- | Mildred Alice 1911- = Roy Hatt 1911-1972 | Alvin Orlon 1913-1973 = Velma Adella Smith |

Roy
1896-1966
= Emma Adair

| Eva 1921-1961 = John Hicks | Orville 1924- = Jennie Wilson | Shirley 1932- = Doug Bell | Roy 1934- = Adeline Coulture |

DEAN 2

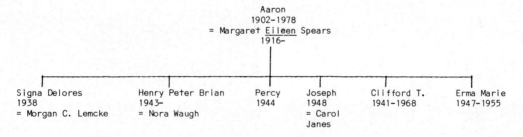

Aaron
1902-1978
= Margaret Eileen Spears
1916-

| Signa Delores 1938 = Morgan C. Lemcke | Henry Peter Brian 1943- = Nora Waugh | Percy 1944 | Joseph 1948 = Carol Janes | Clifford T. 1941-1968 | Erma Marie 1947-1955 |

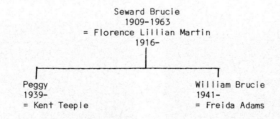

Seward Brucie
1909-1963
= Florence Lillian Martin
1916-

| Peggy 1939- = Kent Teeple | William Brucie 1941- = Freida Adams |

DEAN 3

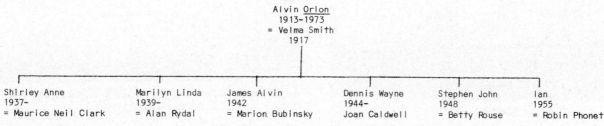

Alvin Orlon
1913-1973
= Velma Smith
1917

| Shirley Anne 1937- = Maurice Neil Clark | Marilyn Linda 1939- = Alan Rydal | James Alvin 1942 = Marion Bubinsky | Dennis Wayne 1944- Joan Caldwell | Stephen John 1948 = Betty Rouse | Ian 1955 = Robin Phonet |

Left to Right: **Orlon Dean, Mildred Dean, Viney Martin and George Martin 1916.**

The Hatt triplets

Orville Dean, Ray Hopkins, Eva Dean, Bert Hopkins mid-1920's

Orlon Dean and wife Velma (Smith)

Maggie Dean

Aaron Dean and wife Eileen (Spears) Signa, Clifford and Peter

GOLDEN

William
= Annie

George Wellington
1860-1948

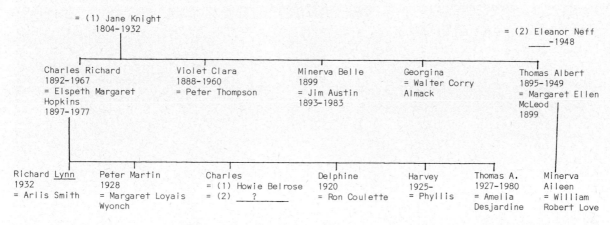

= (1) Jane Knight
1804-1932

= (2) Eleanor Neff
____-1948

Charles Richard	Violet Clara	Minerva Belle	Georgina	Thomas Albert
1892-1967	1888-1960	1899	= Walter Corry	1895-1949
= Elspeth Margaret	= Peter Thompson	= Jim Austin	Almack	= Margaret Ellen
Hopkins		1893-1983		McLeod
1897-1977				1899

Richard Lynn	Peter Martin	Charles	Delphine	Harvey	Thomas A.	Minerva
1932	1928	= (1) Howie Belrose	1920	1925-	1927-1980	Aileen
= Arlis Smith	= Margaret Loyais	= (2) ___?___	= Ron Coulette	= Phyllis	= Amelia	= William
	Wyonch				Desjardine	Robert Love

HOPKINS 1

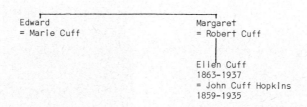

Edward
= Marie Cuff

Margaret
= Robert Cuff

Ellen Cuff
1863-1937
= John Cuff Hopkins
1859-1935

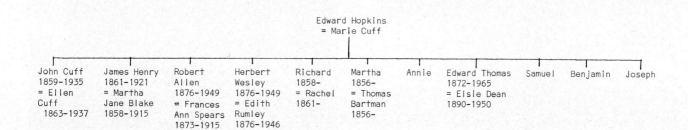

Edward Hopkins
= Marie Cuff

John Cuff	James Henry	Robert	Herbert	Richard	Martha	Annie	Edward Thomas	Samuel	Benjamin	Joseph
1859-1935	1861-1921	Allen	Wesley	1858-	1856-		1872-1965			
= Ellen	= Martha	1876-1949	1876-1949	= Rachel	= Thomas		= Elsie Dean			
Cuff	Jane Blake	= Frances	= Edith	1861-	Bartman		1890-1950			
1863-1937	1858-1915	Ann Spears	Rumley		1856-					
		1873-1915	1876-1946							

205

G. W. Golden family about 1912.
Left to Right: **Georgina, Bert, Minerva, Charlie, son-in-law Peter Thompson, Violet, Jane (Knight), G. W.**

Left to Right: **Willard Currie, George Simpson, T. A. Golden, Ross Butchart, John McLeod and Gordon McLeod 1910.**

G. W. Golden and wife Eleanor Neff 1930's.

Bert Golden   Margaret (McLeod) Golden

Mr. and Mrs. Edward Hopkins and their twin sons
Robert Allen and Herbert Wesley 1877.

Charlie Golden and wife Elsie (Hopkins)

William Henry Hopkins before 1910

PEARL SOAP
A WHITE NAPTHA
ALWAYS SAVE THE WRAPPERS

Delphine Golden

Mary Jane Hopkins, daughter of James Henry Hopkins
about 1905.

HOPKINS 2

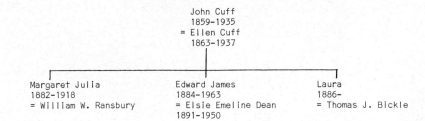

John Cuff
1859-1935
= Ellen Cuff
1863-1937

Margaret Julia	Edward James	Laura
1882-1918	1884-1963	1886-
= William W. Ransbury	= Elsie Emeline Dean	= Thomas J. Bickle
	1891-1950	

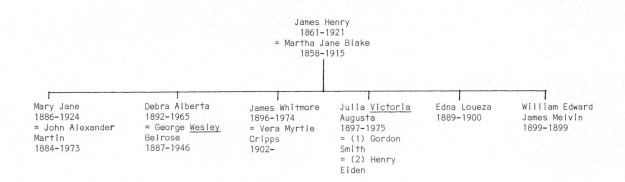

James Henry
1861-1921
= Martha Jane Blake
1858-1915

Mary Jane	Debra Alberta	James Whitmore	Julia Victoria	Edna Loueza	William Edward
1886-1924	1892-1965	1896-1974	Augusta	1889-1900	James Melvin
= John Alexander	= George Wesley	= Vera Myrtle	1897-1975		1899-1899
Martin	Belrose	Cripps	= (1) Gordon		
1884-1973	1887-1946	1902-	Smith		
			= (2) Henry		
			Eiden		

HOPKINS 3

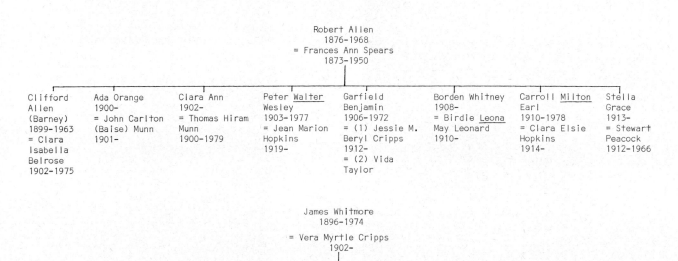

Robert Allen
1876-1968
= Frances Ann Spears
1873-1950

Clifford Allen (Barney)	Ada Orange	Clara Ann	Peter Walter Wesley	Garfield Benjamin	Borden Whitney	Carroll Milton Earl	Stella Grace
1899-1963	1900-	1902-	1903-1977	1906-1972	1908-	1910-1978	1913-
= Clara Isabella Belrose	= John Carlton (Baise) Munn	= Thomas Hiram Munn	= Jean Marion Hopkins	= (1) Jessie M. Beryl Cripps	= Birdie Leona May Leonard	= Clara Elsie Hopkins	= Stewart Peacock
1902-1975	1901-	1900-1979	1919-	1912-	1910-	1914-	1912-1966
				= (2) Vida Taylor			

James Whitmore
1896-1974
= Vera Myrtle Cripps
1902-

Arras Blake	Emery Rae	John James	Hilda Augusta Jane	Loyais Vera Ruth	Elizabeth Annie
1920-1922	1922-1924	1926-	1929-	1931-	1938-1941
		= Tillie Margaret (Marjory) Knowles	= Stan Jorgenson	= J.R. Lambert	

Davis' and Hopkins':
Noriene, Ruby and Zora Hopkins, Iona and Gladys Davis and Marion Hopkins early 1930's.

Edward James Hopkins and wife Elsie Dean 1905

Victor Bartman and Isaac Hopkins 1896

Mr. and Mrs. J. C. Hopkins, Julia, Edward James and Laura about 1905.

Left to Right: Milton, Borden, Walter, Garfield, Clara, Ada and Clifford (Barney) 1911 or 1912.

Sitting, Left to Right: **Martha Jane Blake, Victoria, James Henry Hopkins.**
Standing, Left to Right: **Mary Jane, Whit and Debbie Hopkins.**

**William Robert Hopkins
between 1914 - 1918.**

**Laura Bickle
(nee Hopkins)
about 1905.**

**Tom Hopkins, Hattie Martin and Elsie Hopkins
about 1923**

HOPKINS 4

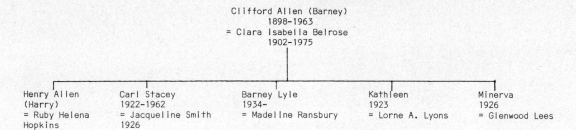

Clifford Allen (Barney)
1898-1963
= Clara Isabella Belrose
1902-1975

| Henry Allen (Harry) = Ruby Helena Hopkins | Carl Stacey 1922-1962 = Jacqueline Smith 1926 | Barney Lyle 1934- = Madeline Ransbury | Kathleen 1923 = Lorne A. Lyons | Minerva 1926 = Glenwood Lees |

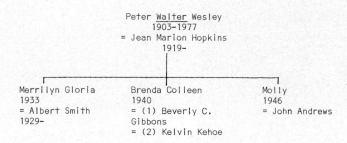

Peter <u>Walter</u> Wesley
1903-1977
= Jean Marion Hopkins
1919-

| Merrilyn Gloria 1933 = Albert Smith 1929- | Brenda Colleen 1940 = (1) Beverly C. Gibbons = (2) Kelvin Kehoe | Molly 1946 = John Andrews |

HOPKINS 5

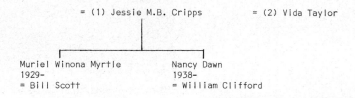

Garfield Benjamin
1906-1972

= (1) Jessie M.B. Cripps   = (2) Vida Taylor

| Muriel Winona Myrtle 1929- = Bill Scott | Nancy Dawn 1938- = William Clifford |

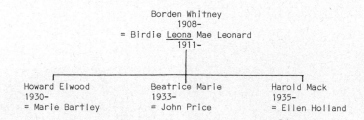

Borden Whitney
1908-
= Birdie <u>Leona</u> Mae Leonard
1911-

| Howard Elwood 1930- = Marie Bartley | Beatrice Marie 1933- = John Price | Harold Mack 1935- = Ellen Holland |

HOPKINS 6

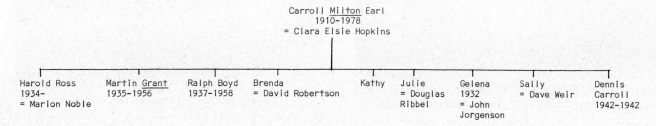

Carroll <u>Milton</u> Earl
1910-1978
= Clara Elsie Hopkins

| Harold Ross 1934- = Marion Noble | Martin <u>Grant</u> 1935-1956 | Ralph Boyd 1937-1958 | Brenda = David Robertson | Kathy | Julie = Douglas Ribbel | Gelena 1932 = John Jorgenson | Sally = Dave Weir | Dennis Carroll 1942-1942 |

Sitting: **Harriet Martin, Elsie Hopkins, Edward Hopkins.**
Standing: **Andrew Hopkins and Martin Hopkins 1906.**

J. C. Hopkins house in Tobermory

Barn on same farm built by Edward James Hopkins

James Henry Hopkins, wife Martha Jane Blake and daughters Mary Jane and Debra Alberta mid-1890's.

House on J. C. Hopkins farm 1910

Robert Allen Hopkins and wife Annie Spears 1948.

Martin Hopkins

Elsie (Hopkins) Golden

Clifford (Barney) Hopkins, and wife Clara (Belrose) early 1920's.

Ollie Hopkins

HOPKINS 7

Robert
1824-1920

= (1) Irene Rae Hopkins   = (2) Julia Ann
                                                                                                        1836-1927

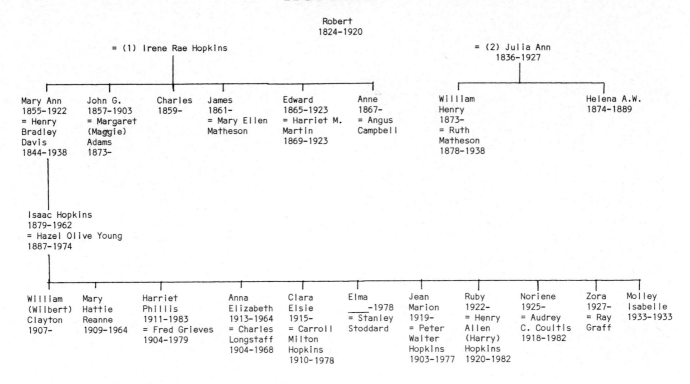

Mary Ann	John G.	Charles	James	Edward	Anne	William	Helena A.W.
1855-1922	1857-1903	1859-	1861-	1865-1923	1867-	Henry	1874-1889
= Henry	= Margaret		= Mary Ellen	= Harriet M.	= Angus	1873-	
Bradley	(Maggie)		Matheson	Martin	Campbell	= Ruth	
Davis	Adams			1869-1923		Matheson	
1844-1938	1873-					1878-1938	

Isaac Hopkins
1879-1962
= Hazel Olive Young
1887-1974

| William (Wilbert) Clayton 1907- | Mary Hattie Reanne 1909-1964 | Harriet Phillis 1911-1983 = Fred Grieves 1904-1979 | Anna Elizabeth 1913-1964 = Charles Longstaff 1904-1968 | Clara Elsie 1915- = Carroll Milton Hopkins 1910-1978 | Elma ___-1978 = Stanley Stoddard | Jean Marion 1919- = Peter Walter Hopkins 1903-1977 | Ruby 1922- = Henry Allen (Harry) Hopkins 1920-1982 | Noriene 1925- = Audrey C. Coultis 1918-1982 | Zora 1927- = Ray Graff | Molley Isabelle 1933-1933 |

HOPKINS 8

John G.
1857-1903
= Margaret Adams
1873-

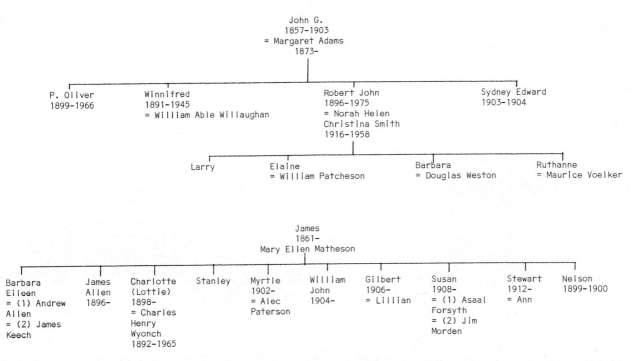

P. Oliver	Winnifred	Robert John	Sydney Edward
1899-1966	1891-1945	1896-1975	1903-1904
	= William Able Willaughan	= Norah Helen Christina Smith 1916-1958	

Larry	Elaine = William Patcheson	Barbara = Douglas Weston	Ruthanne = Maurice Voelker

James
1861-
Mary Ellen Matheson

| Barbara Eileen = (1) Andrew Allen = (2) James Keech | James Allen 1896- | Charlotte (Lottie) 1898- = Charles Henry Wyonch 1892-1965 | Stanley | Myrtle 1902- = Alec Paterson | William John 1904- | Gilbert 1906- = Lillian | Susan 1908- = (1) Asaal Forsyth = (2) Jim Morden | Stewart 1912- = Ann | Nelson 1899-1900 |

HOPKINS 9

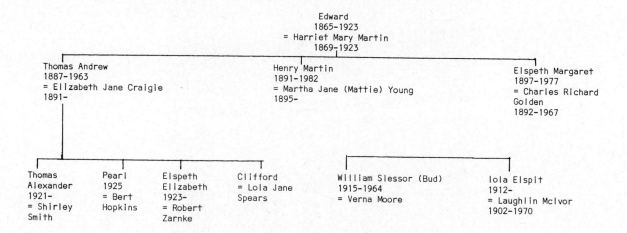

Edward
1865-1923
= Harriet Mary Martin
1869-1923

Thomas Andrew
1887-1963
= Elizabeth Jane Craigie
1891-

Henry Martin
1891-1982
= Martha Jane (Mattie) Young
1895-

Elspeth Margaret
1897-1977
= Charles Richard
Golden
1892-1967

Thomas
Alexander
1921-
= Shirley
Smith

Pearl
1925
= Bert
Hopkins

Elspeth
Elizabeth
1923-
= Robert
Zarnke

Clifford
= Lola Jane
Spears

William Slessor (Bud)
1915-1964
= Verna Moore

Iola Elspit
1912-
= Laughlin McIvor
1902-1970

HOPKINS 10

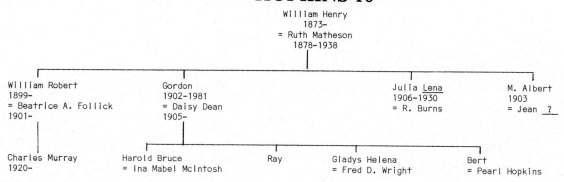

William Henry
1873-
= Ruth Matheson
1878-1938

William Robert
1899-
= Beatrice A. Follick
1901-

Gordon
1902-1981
= Daisy Dean
1905-

Julia Lena
1906-1930
= R. Burns

M. Albert
1903
= Jean ?

Charles Murray
1920-

Harold Bruce
= Ina Mabel McIntosh

Ray

Gladys Helena
= Fred D. Wright

Bert
= Pearl Hopkins

MARTIN 1

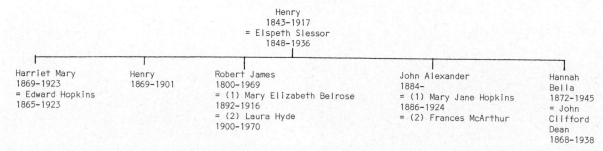

Henry
1843-1917
= Elspeth Slessor
1848-1936

Harriet Mary
1869-1923
= Edward Hopkins
1865-1923

Henry
1869-1901

Robert James
1800-1969
= (1) Mary Elizabeth Belrose
1892-1916
= (2) Laura Hyde
1900-1970

John Alexander
1884-
= (1) Mary Jane Hopkins
1886-1924
= (2) Frances McArthur

Hannah
Bella
1872-1945
= John
Clifford
Dean
1868-1938

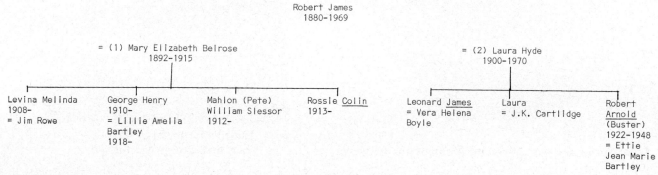

Robert James
1880-1969

= (1) Mary Elizabeth Belrose
1892-1915

= (2) Laura Hyde
1900-1970

Levina Melinda
1908-
= Jim Rowe

George Henry
1910-
= Lillie Amelia
Bartley
1918-

Mahlon (Pete)
William Slessor
1912-

Rossie Colin
1913-

Leonard James
= Vera Helena
Boyle

Laura
= J.K. Cartlidge

Robert
Arnold
(Buster)
1922-1948
= Ettie
Jean Marie
Bartley

Henry Martin and wife Elspeth Slessor before 1910.

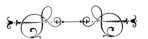

John Martin and wife May Jane Hopkins about 1905.

**Robert Martin, Mary Belrose,
Viney and George Martin, 1909**

MARTINS 2

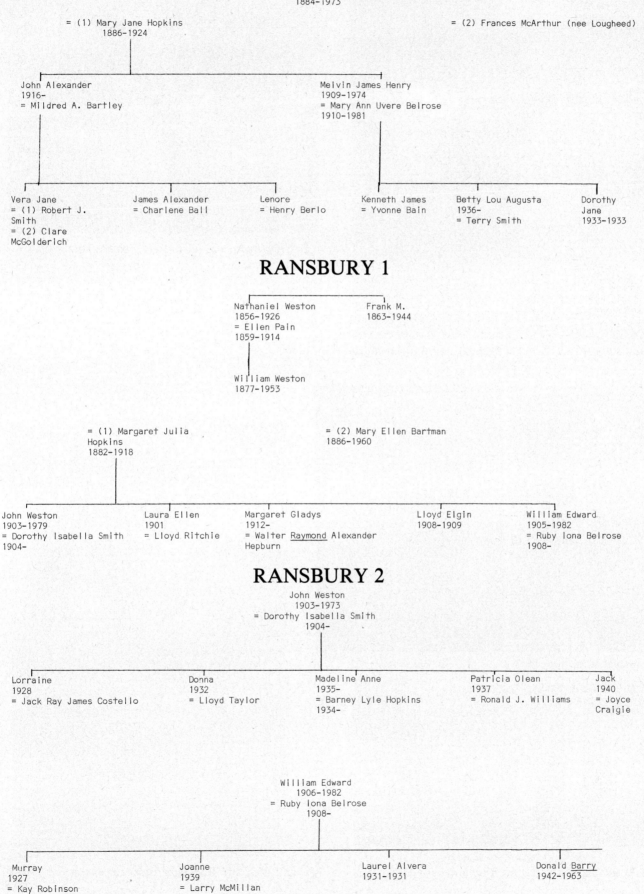

John Alexander
1884-1973

= (1) Mary Jane Hopkins
1886-1924

= (2) Frances McArthur (nee Lougheed)

John Alexander
1916-
= Mildred A. Bartley

Melvin James Henry
1909-1974
= Mary Ann Uvere Belrose
1910-1981

Vera Jane
= (1) Robert J.
Smith
= (2) Clare
McGolderich

James Alexander
= Charlene Ball

Lenore
= Henry Berlo

Kenneth James
= Yvonne Bain

Betty Lou Augusta
1936-
= Terry Smith

Dorothy
Jane
1933-1933

RANSBURY 1

Nathaniel Weston
1856-1926
= Ellen Pain
1859-1914

Frank M.
1863-1944

William Weston
1877-1953

= (1) Margaret Julia
Hopkins
1882-1918

= (2) Mary Ellen Bartman
1886-1960

John Weston
1903-1979
= Dorothy Isabella Smith
1904-

Laura Ellen
1901
= Lloyd Ritchie

Margaret Gladys
1912-
= Walter Raymond Alexander
Hepburn

Lloyd Elgin
1908-1909

William Edward
1905-1982
= Ruby Iona Belrose
1908-

RANSBURY 2

John Weston
1903-1973
= Dorothy Isabella Smith
1904-

Lorraine
1928
= Jack Ray James Costello

Donna
1932
= Lloyd Taylor

Madeline Anne
1935-
= Barney Lyle Hopkins
1934-

Patricia Olean
1937
= Ronald J. Williams

Jack
1940
= Joyce
Craigie

William Edward
1906-1982
= Ruby Iona Belrose
1908-

Murray
1927
= Kay Robinson

Joanne
1939
= Larry McMillan

Laurel Alvera
1931-1931

Donald Barry
1942-1963

Frank Ransbury with nephews John and Bill Ransbury
1906

Bill Ransbury and wife Ruby Belrose about 1980.

Nathaniel Ransbury 1905

Laura Ransbury 1903

Mr. and Mrs. Nat Ransbury
(grandparents of Laura Ritchie) about 1900.

Mr. and Mrs. Bill Ransbury and daughter about 1900.

SIMPSON

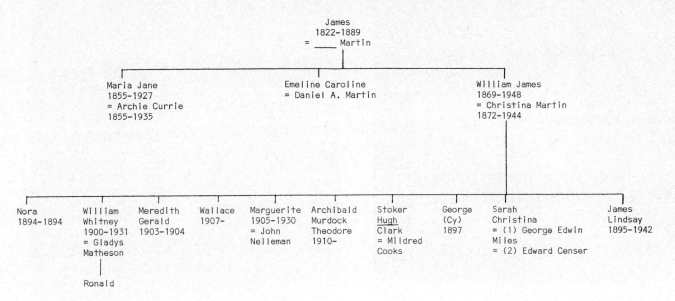

```
                                    James
                                  1822-1889
                               = _____ Martin


         Maria Jane              Emeline Caroline          William James
         1855-1927               = Daniel A. Martin        1869-1948
         = Archie Currie                                   = Christina Martin
         1855-1935                                         1872-1944


Nora      William     Meredith   Wallace   Marguerite   Archibald   Stoker    George   Sarah                        James
1894-1894 Whitney     Gerald     1907-     1905-1930    Murdock     Hugh      (Cy)     Christina                    Lindsay
          1900-1931   1903-1904            = John       Theodore    Clark     1897     = (1) George Edwin           1895-1942
          = Gladys                         Nelleman     1910-       = Mildred          Miles
          Matheson                                                 Cooks              = (2) Edward Censer

          Ronald
```

SMITH 1

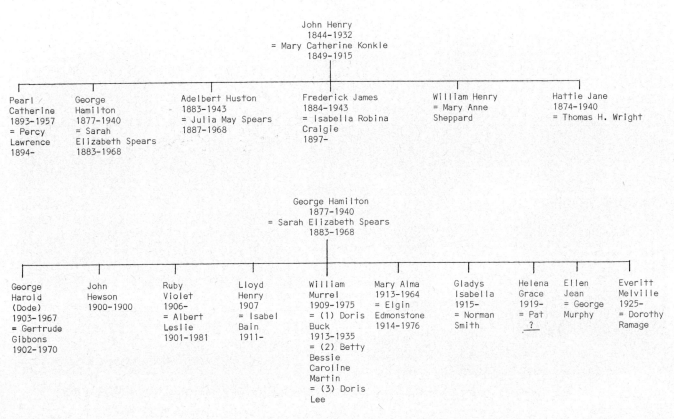

```
                                    John Henry
                                   1844-1932
                            = Mary Catherine Konkle
                                   1849-1915


Pearl            George          Adelbert Huston        Frederick James      William Henry      Hattie Jane
Catherine        Hamilton        1883-1943              1884-1943            = Mary Anne         1874-1940
1893-1957        1877-1940       = Julia May Spears     = Isabella Robina    Sheppard            = Thomas H. Wright
= Percy          = Sarah         1887-1968              Craigie
Lawrence         Elizabeth Spears                       1897-
1894-            1883-1968
```

```
                                 George Hamilton
                                   1877-1940
                            = Sarah Elizabeth Spears
                                   1883-1968


George      John       Ruby       Lloyd      William      Mary Alma    Gladys      Helena    Ellen      Everitt
Harold      Hewson     Violet     Henry      Murrel       1913-1964    Isabella    Grace     Jean       Melville
(Dode)      1900-1900  1906-      1907       1909-1975    = Elgin      1915-       1919-     = George   1925-
1903-1967              = Albert    = Isabel   = (1) Doris  Edmonstone   = Norman    = Pat     Murphy     = Dorothy
= Gertrude            Leslie      Bain       Buck         1914-1976    Smith        ?                   Ramage
Gibbons               1901-1981   1911-      1913-1935
1902-1970                                    = (2) Betty
                                             Bessie
                                             Caroline
                                             Martin
                                             = (3) Doris
                                             Lee
```

George (Cy) Simpson

Mr. and Mrs. William Henry Smith

Left to Right: **Mrs. Dell Smith, Vinetta Smith, Dell Smith, Laura Smith, George Fitzhenry, Mrs. George Fitzhenry about 1906.**

George Harold (Dode) Smith and wife Gertrude Gibbons.

George Hamilton Smith and wife Sara Elizabeth Spears.

Marjorie and Madeline Smith

William John Smith and wife Helena May Belrose.

Pearl (Smith) Chisholm

SMITH 2

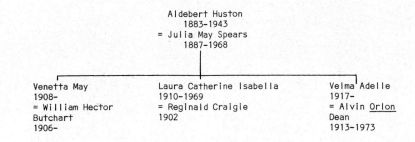

Aldebert Huston
1883-1943
= Julia May Spears
1887-1968

Venetta May 1908- = William Hector Butchart 1906-	Laura Catherine Isabella 1910-1969 = Reginald Craigie 1902	Velma Adelle 1917- = Alvin Orlon Dean 1913-1973

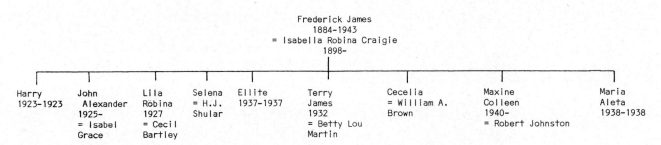

Frederick James
1884-1943
= Isabella Robina Craigie
1898-

Harry 1923-1923

John Alexander 1925- = Isabel Grace

Lila Robina 1927 = Cecil Bartley

Selena = H.J. Shular

Ellite 1937-1937

Terry James 1932 = Betty Lou Martin

Cecelia = William A. Brown

Maxine Colleen 1940- = Robert Johnston

Maria Aleta 1938-1938

SMITH 3

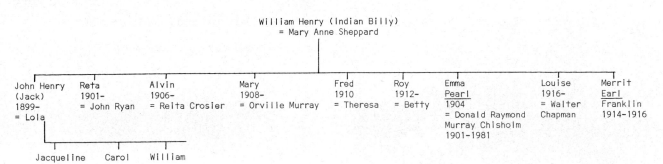

William Henry (Indian Billy)
= Mary Anne Sheppard

John Henry (Jack) 1899- = Lola

Reta 1901- = John Ryan

Alvin 1906- = Reita Crosier

Mary 1908- = Orville Murray

Fred 1910 = Theresa

Roy 1912- = Betty

Emma Pearl 1904 = Donald Raymond Murray Chisholm 1901-1981

Louise 1916- = Walter Chapman

Merrit Earl Franklin 1914-1916

Jacqueline   Carol   William

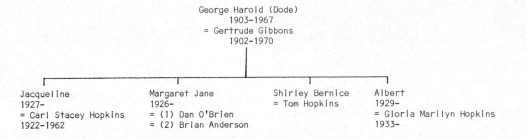

George Harold (Dode)
1903-1967
= Gertrude Gibbons
1902-1970

Jacqueline 1927- = Carl Stacey Hopkins 1922-1962

Margaret Jane 1926- = (1) Dan O'Brien = (2) Brian Anderson

Shirley Bernice = Tom Hopkins

Albert 1929- = Gloria Marilyn Hopkins 1933-

SMITH 4

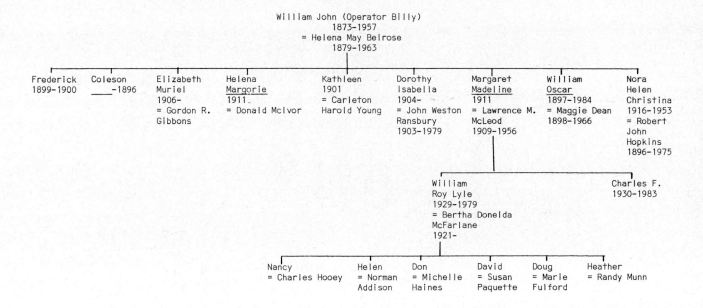

William John (Operator Billy)
1873-1957
= Helena May Belrose
1879-1963

Frederick 1899-1900	Coleson ____-1896	Elizabeth Muriel 1906- = Gordon R. Gibbons	Helena Margorie 1911 = Donald McIvor	Kathleen 1901 = Carleton Harold Young	Dorothy Isabella 1904- = John Weston Ransbury 1903-1979	Margaret Madeline 1911 = Lawrence M. McLeod 1909-1956	William Oscar 1897-1984 = Maggie Dean 1898-1966	Nora Helen Christina 1916-1953 = Robert John Hopkins 1896-1975

William
Roy Lyle
1929-1979
= Bertha Donelda
McFarlane
1921-

Charles F.
1930-1983

Nancy = Charles Hooey	Helen = Norman Addison	Don = Michelle Haines	David = Susan Paquette	Doug = Marie Fulford	Heather = Randy Munn

<u>NOTE</u>: This is a separate family of Smiths. Only William Oscar carried on this family.

SPEARS 1

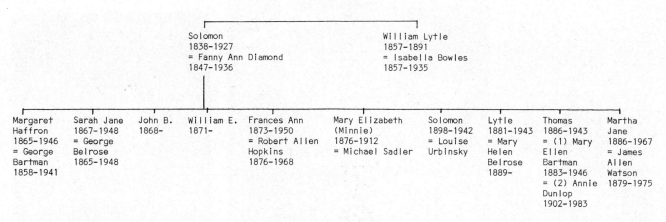

Solomon
1838-1927
= Fanny Ann Diamond
1847-1936

William Lytle
1857-1891
= Isabella Bowles
1857-1935

Margaret Haffron 1865-1946 = George Bartman 1858-1941	Sarah Jane 1867-1948 = George Belrose 1865-1948	John B. 1868-	William E. 1871-	Frances Ann 1873-1950 = Robert Allen Hopkins 1876-1968	Mary Elizabeth (Minnie) 1876-1912 = Michael Sadler	Solomon 1898-1942 = Louise Urbinsky	Lytle 1881-1943 = Mary Helen Belrose 1889-	Thomas 1886-1943 = (1) Mary Ellen Bartman 1883-1946 = (2) Annie Dunlop 1902-1983	Martha Jane 1886-1967 = James Allen Watson 1879-1975

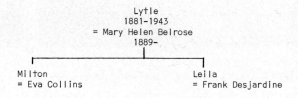

Lytle
1881-1943
= Mary Helen Belrose
1889-

Milton = Eva Collins	Leila = Frank Desjardine

Left to Right: **Reg Craigie, Bill Smith, Wilbert Hopkins, Bill Ransbury, Lawrence McLeod, Wally McIver.**

**John Spears
1890's**

Hazel Young holding Vera Vail about 1900

Lytle Spears 1900

SPEARS 2

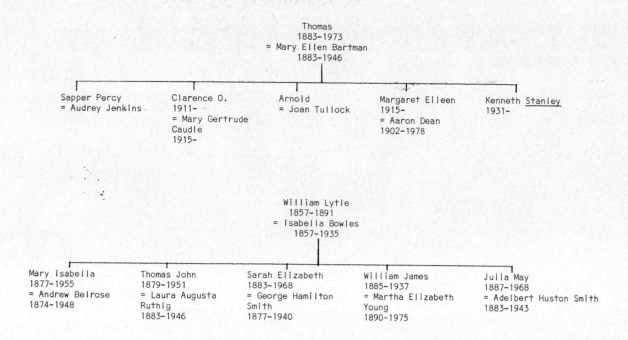

```
                              Thomas
                            1883-1973
                      = Mary Ellen Bartman
                            1883-1946
```

| Sapper Percy = Audrey Jenkins | Clarence O. 1911- = Mary Gertrude Caudle 1915- | Arnold = Joan Tullock | Margaret Eileen 1915- = Aaron Dean 1902-1978 | Kenneth <u>Stanley</u> 1931- |

```
                           William Lytle
                            1857-1891
                        = Isabella Bowles
                            1857-1935
```

| Mary Isabella 1877-1955 = Andrew Belrose 1874-1948 | Thomas John 1879-1951 = Laura Augusta Ruthig 1883-1946 | Sarah Elizabeth 1883-1968 = George Hamilton Smith 1877-1940 | William James 1885-1937 = Martha Elizabeth Young 1890-1975 | Julia May 1887-1968 = Adelbert Huston Smith 1883-1943 |

SPEARS 3

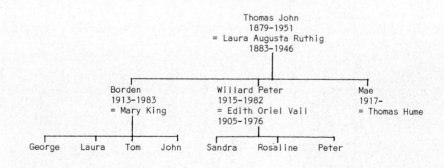

```
                           Thomas John
                            1879-1951
                      = Laura Augusta Ruthig
                            1883-1946
```

| Borden 1913-1983 = Mary King | Willard Peter 1915-1982 = Edith Oriel Vail 1905-1976 | Mae 1917- = Thomas Hume |

| George | Laura | Tom | John | Sandra | Rosaline | Peter |

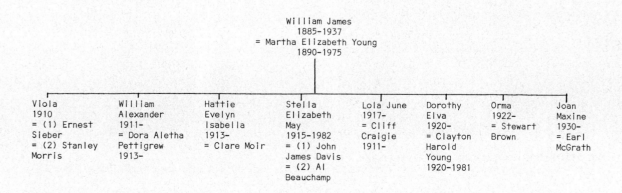

```
                           William James
                            1885-1937
                   = Martha Elizabeth Young
                            1890-1975
```

| Viola 1910 = (1) Ernest Sieber = (2) Stanley Morris | William Alexander 1911- = Dora Aletha Pettigrew 1913- | Hattie Evelyn Isabella 1913- = Clare Moir | Stella Elizabeth May 1915-1982 = (1) John James Davis = (2) Al Beauchamp | Lola June 1917- = Cliff Craigie 1911- | Dorothy Elva 1920- = Clayton Harold Young 1920-1981 | Orma 1922- = Stewart Brown | Joan Maxine 1930- = Earl McGrath |

Vail clan about 1910

Orrie, Marmaduke, Grandma and Edith Vail
early 1930's.

David and Jane Vail 1934-1935

VAIL

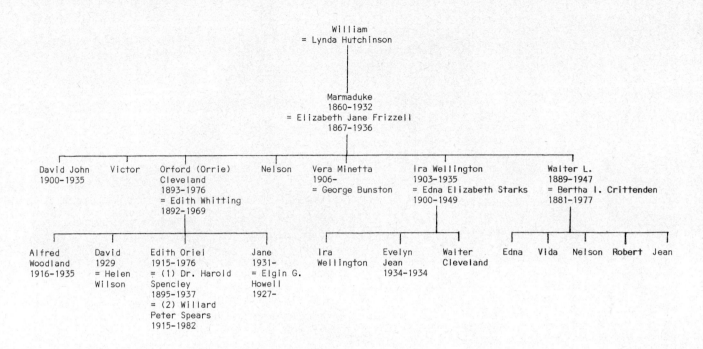

William
= Lynda Hutchinson

Marmaduke
1860-1932
= Elizabeth Jane Frizzell
1867-1936

David John 1900-1935 | Victor | Orford (Orrie) Cleveland 1893-1976 = Edith Whitting 1892-1969 | Nelson | Vera Minetta 1906- = George Bunston | Ira Wellington 1903-1935 = Edna Elizabeth Starks 1900-1949 | Walter L. 1889-1947 = Bertha I. Crittenden 1881-1977

Alfred Woodland 1916-1935 | David 1929 = Helen Wilson | Edith Oriel 1915-1976 = (1) Dr. Harold Spencley 1895-1937 = (2) Willard Peter Spears 1915-1982 | Jane 1931- = Elgin G. Howell 1927-

Ira Wellington | Evelyn Jean 1934-1934 | Walter Cleveland

Edna | Vida | Nelson | Robert | Jean

WATSON 1

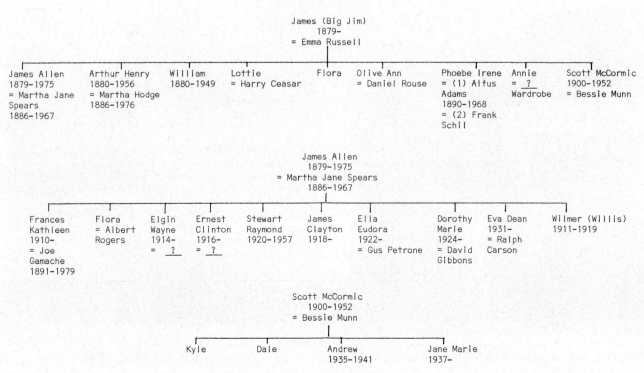

James (Big Jim)
1879-
= Emma Russell

James Allen 1879-1975 = Martha Jane Spears 1886-1967 | Arthur Henry 1880-1956 = Martha Hodge 1886-1976 | William 1880-1949 | Lottie = Harry Ceasar | Flora | Olive Ann = Daniel Rouse | Phoebe Irene = (1) Alfus Adams 1890-1968 = (2) Frank Schil | Annie = ? Wardrobe | Scott McCormic 1900-1952 = Bessie Munn

James Allen
1879-1975
= Martha Jane Spears
1886-1967

Frances Kathleen 1910- = Joe Gamache 1891-1979 | Flora = Albert Rogers | Elgin Wayne 1914- = ? | Ernest Clinton 1916- = ? | Stewart Raymond 1920-1957 | James Clayton 1918- | Ella Eudora 1922- = Gus Petrone | Dorothy Marie 1924- = David Gibbons | Eva Dean 1931- = Ralph Carson | Wilmer (Willis) 1911-1919

Scott McCormic
1900-1952
= Bessie Munn

Kyle | Dale | Andrew 1935-1941 | Jane Marie 1937-

227

Vail House in the 1930's

James (Big Jim) Watson and wife Emma Russel 1870's.

James (Big Jim) Watson's family, Jim, Arthur, William, Annie, Olive and Flora 1890's.

WATSON 2

Arthur Henry
1880-1956
= Martha E. Hodge
1886-1976

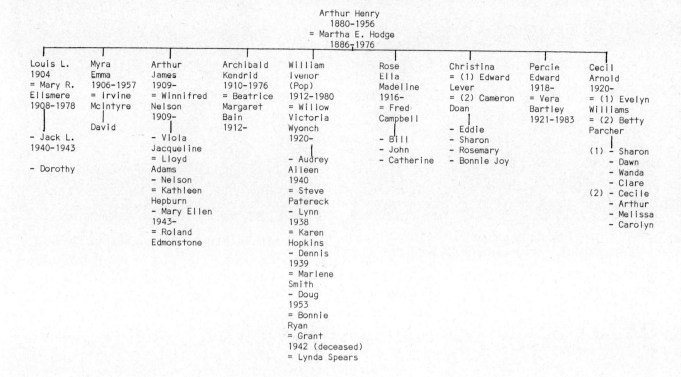

Louis L.	Myra	Arthur	Archibald	William	Rose	Christina	Percie	Cecil
1904	Emma	James	Kendrid	Ivenor	Ella	= (1) Edward	Edward	Arnold
= Mary R.	1906-1957	1909-	1910-1976	(Pop)	Madeline	Lever	1918-	1920-
Ellsmere	= Irvine	= Winnifred	= Beatrice	1912-1980	1916-	= (2) Cameron	= Vera	= (1) Evelyn
1908-1978	McIntyre	Nelson	Margaret	= Willow	= Fred	Doan	Bartley	Williams
		1909-	Bain	Victoria	Campbell		1921-1983	= (2) Betty
- Jack L.	- David		1912-	Wyonch		- Eddie		Parcher
1940-1943		- Viola		1920-	- Bill	- Sharon		
		Jacqueline			- John	- Rosemary		(1) - Sharon
- Dorothy		= Lloyd		- Audrey	- Catherine	- Bonnie Joy		- Dawn
		Adams		Aileen				- Wanda
		- Nelson		1940				- Clare
		= Kathleen		= Steve				(2) - Cecile
		Hepburn		Patereck				- Arthur
		- Mary Ellen		- Lynn				- Melissa
		1943-		1938				- Carolyn
		= Roland		= Karen				
		Edmonstone		Hopkins				
				- Dennis				
				1939				
				= Marlene				
				Smith				
				- Doug				
				1953				
				= Bonnie				
				Ryan				
				= Grant				
				1942 (deceased)				
				= Lynda Spears				

WATSON 2

(continued)

Arthur Henry
1880-1956
= Martha E. Hodge
1886-1976

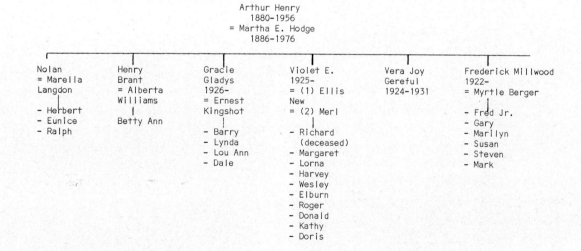

Nolan	Henry	Gracie	Violet E.	Vera Joy	Frederick Millwood
= Marella	Brant	Gladys	1925-	Gereful	1922-
Langdon	= Alberta	1926-	= (1) Ellis	1924-1931	= Myrtle Berger
	Williams	= Ernest	New		
- Herbert		Kingshot	= (2) Merl		- Fred Jr.
- Eunice	Betty Ann				- Gary
- Ralph		- Barry	- Richard		- Marilyn
		- Lynda	(deceased)		- Susan
		- Lou Ann	- Margaret		- Steven
		- Dale	- Lorna		- Mark
			- Harvey		
			- Wesley		
			- Elburn		
			- Roger		
			- Donald		
			- Kathy		
			- Doris		

**Wedding picture of
Arthur Henry Watson and Martha E. Hodge.**

Archie Watson and wife Beatrice (Bain)

Arthur Henry Watson family

WATSON 3

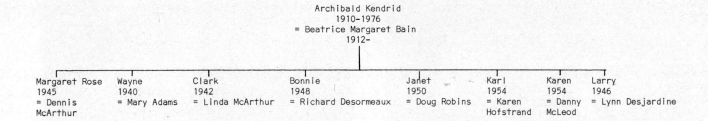

Archibald Kendrid
1910-1976
= Beatrice Margaret Bain
1912-

| Margaret Rose
1945
= Dennis
McArthur | Wayne
1940
= Mary Adams | Clark
1942
= Linda McArthur | Bonnie
1948
= Richard Desormeaux | Janet
1950
= Doug Robins | Karl
1954
= Karen
Hofstrand | Karen
1954
= Danny
McLeod | Larry
1946
= Lynn Desjardine |

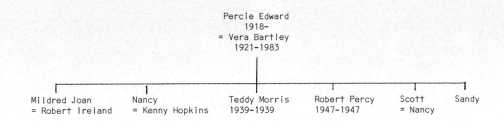

Percie Edward
1918-
= Vera Bartley
1921-1983

| Mildred Joan
= Robert Ireland | Nancy
= Kenny Hopkins | Teddy Morris
1939-1939 | Robert Percy
1947-1947 | Scott
= Nancy | Sandy |

WYONCH 1

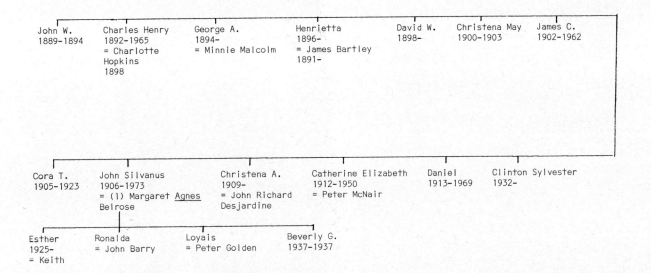

George
1864-1937
= Christina McArthur
1870-1942

| John W.
1889-1894 | Charles Henry
1892-1965
= Charlotte
Hopkins
1898 | George A.
1894-
= Minnie Malcolm | Henrietta
1896-
= James Bartley
1891- | David W.
1898- | Christena May
1900-1903 | James C.
1902-1962 |

| Cora T.
1905-1923 | John Silvanus
1906-1973
= (1) Margaret Agnes
Belrose | Christena A.
1909-
= John Richard
Desjardine | Catherine Elizabeth
1912-1950
= Peter McNair | Daniel
1913-1969 | Clinton Sylvester
1932- |

| Esther
1925-
= Keith | Ronalda
= John Barry | Loyais
= Peter Golden | Beverly G.
1937-1937 |

WYONCH 2

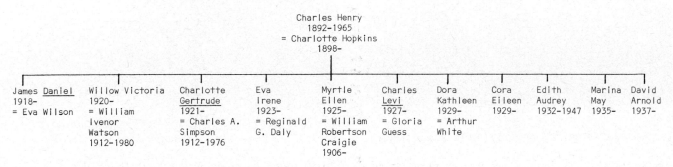

Charles Henry
1892-1965
= Charlotte Hopkins
1898-

| James Daniel
1918-
= Eva Wilson | Willow Victoria
1920-
= William
Ivenor
Watson
1912-1980 | Charlotte
Gertrude
1921-
= Charles A.
Simpson
1912-1976 | Eva
Irene
1923-
= Reginald
G. Daly | Myrtle
Ellen
1925-
= William
Robertson
Craigie
1906- | Charles
Levi
1927-
= Gloria
Guess | Dora
Kathleen
1929-
= Arthur
White | Cora
Eileen
1929- | Edith
Audrey
1932-1947 | Marina
May
1935- | David
Arnold
1937- |

Charles Henry Wyonch and wife Charlotte "Lottie" Hopkins on their 45th wedding anniversary.

Granny Young, "Sis" Adams, Phylis Young and Blaine Chisholm? 1930's.

Martha (Mattie) Young and Harold Young 1900

Hazel (Young) Hopkins and granddaughter Mary Ellen Grieves

Flora Webb and husband William Young about 1900

Martha Jane
(Young) Hopkins

Martin E. Young
1917

Phylis (Dudie) Young, Mabel (Mumm) Young
late 1920's.

Granny (Mrs. Alex) Young 1930's

Left to Right: Gladys Davis, Mabel Davis (nee Young) and Verna Young
1900

233

YOUNG 1

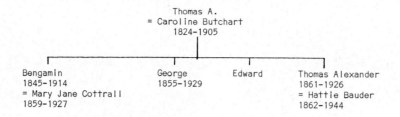

Thomas A.
= Caroline Butchart
1824-1905

Bengamin 1845-1914 = Mary Jane Cottrall 1859-1927	George 1855-1929	Edward	Thomas Alexander 1861-1926 = Hattie Bauder 1862-1944

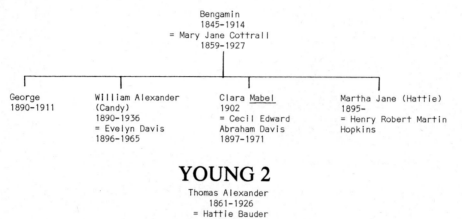

Bengamin
1845-1914
= Mary Jane Cottrall
1859-1927

George 1890-1911	William Alexander (Candy) 1890-1936 = Evelyn Davis 1896-1965	Clara Mabel 1902 = Cecil Edward Abraham Davis 1897-1971	Martha Jane (Hattie) 1895- = Henry Robert Martin Hopkins

YOUNG 2

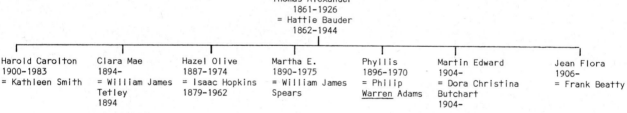

Thomas Alexander
1861-1926
= Hattie Bauder
1862-1944

Harold Carolton 1900-1983 = Kathleen Smith	Clara Mae 1894- = William James Tetley 1894	Hazel Olive 1887-1974 = Isaac Hopkins 1879-1962	Martha E. 1890-1975 = William James Spears	Phyllis 1896-1970 = Philip Warren Adams	Martin Edward 1904- = Dora Christina Butchart 1904-	Jean Flora 1906- = Frank Beatty

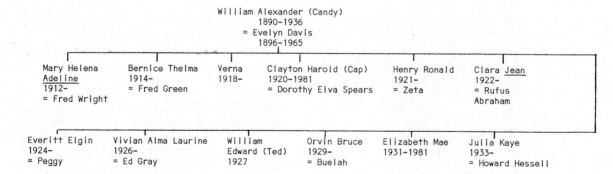

William Alexander (Candy)
1890-1936
= Evelyn Davis
1896-1965

Mary Helena Adeline 1912- = Fred Wright	Bernice Thelma 1914- = Fred Green	Verna 1918-	Clayton Harold (Cap) 1920-1981 = Dorothy Elva Spears	Henry Ronald 1921- = Zeta	Clara Jean 1922- = Rufus Abraham

Everitt Elgin 1924- = Peggy	Vivian Alma Laurine 1926- = Ed Gray	William Edward (Ted) 1927	Orvin Bruce 1929- = Buelah	Elizabeth Mae 1931-1981	Julia Kaye 1933- = Howard Hessell

YOUNG 3

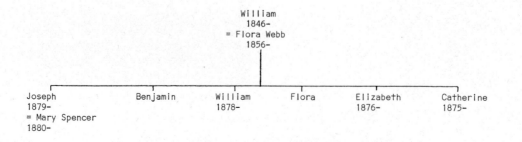

William
1846-
= Flora Webb
1856-

Joseph 1879- = Mary Spencer 1880-	Benjamin	William 1878-	Flora	Elizabeth 1876-	Catherine 1875-

CHAPTER SIXTEEN

MISCELLANEOUS PIECES

This chapter consists of pieces that do not fit into any of the subjects mentioned in prior chapters, and therefore a chapter of their own has been invented to accommodate them.

TOBERMORY

At the north of the rocky headland,
Where the great two waters meet,
And the winds are madly howling
In a grey November sleet,
Any ship upon those waters,
Hardly pressed and puzzled sore,
Will find instant hope by glimpsing
Of the lights of Tobermore.

It was fashioned to perfection
In the days when earth was new,
And the Mason dropped his plummet
That the walls be straight and true;
It has gained world wide approval,
For without e'er plank or dock
You can walk from deck of vessel
To the flat and solid rock.

And while standing on foundations
That have stood the ages long,
You'd best button up your ulster,
For the wind is blowing strong.
Then with air so clear and bracing
You can view the landscape for
Tho, the land is but a fancy
Where the rocks and waves wage war.

They say in Bonnie Scotland,
With its banks and braes so dear,
And its firths and forths all scattered
On its broken bold frontier
They have such another harbour
For the storm-tossed ones to win,
And if you can talk the Gaelic,
You're at home with kith and kin.

Unknown

A FALSE ALARM

Now if you chaps will listen.
For it will do you no harm.
I'll tell you of what might have been a tragedy
But turned out to be a false alarm.
Last fall, five strong and healthy youths
From home they chose to stray
To work upon an island.
Out in the Georgian Bay.
They made arrangements with their folks
Before they did depart.
That if trouble came upon them
A bonfire signal they would start.
Then through a freak of nature
Hid by a mighty screen.
The signal showed up plainly
By many it was seen.
The news it did spread quickly
And soon we all did know
That help at once was wanted.
On an Island called the Yoe.
Four chaps at once got started.
With grub enough for ten.
A pirate and a bootlegger.
The other two honest men.
We landed out at Flower Pot.
The situation we looked over.
And we cursed the Georgian Bay.
For such a bleak and ice bound shore
But after a good stiff dinner
With plenty of tea to cheer.
We set out to work with right good will
And the way we soon had to clear.
Then we quickly shoved in the gas boat.
The weather was not so nice.
But by 3 o'clock in the afternoon.
We had pulled her clear of ice.
We headed for Yoe Island.

We were clear of all ice cakes
Our engine gave us trouble
By stopping off the Snakes.
As we rolled and turned about
The trouble was soon found.
As we proceeded on our way
For Yoe Island we were bound.
We landed on the Island,
Then to the camp we went.
To find five strong and healthy youths
No Message they had sent.
The Cook gave us a good supper
Tho' his name I ne'er will tell
His bread it tasted mighty good.
But his doughnuts were tough as you know what.
They wished us a pleasant voyage.
And soon we were homeward bound.
But our steering gear it broke
And we went round and round.
If a gas boat gives you trouble
It is sure to be at night.
And we thought ourselves quite lucky
when a fish tug came in sight.
It was the "John and Alex"
And the skipper's name was "Stub"
Our troubles soon were over.
And we landed in the "Tub"
On the dock was a mighty gathering
For reporters they had come.
But the bootleggers beat us to it
And the sucker he got the rum
That signal is still a mystery.
But this to you I'll say.
An Irishman holds the answer
For it was on St. Patrick's Day.

Warren Adams, 1937

TOBERMORY HARBOUR

Within the harbour motor launches laze
Reflected in the placid water's depth,
While overhead the white gulls wheel and dip
Describing neat parabolas and whorls,
Their mewing supplications echoing
Along the harbour's rocky limestone ledges
Where purple vetch embraces juniper
And white birch paternize with cedar hedge.

Out on the rocks a swarthy fisherman.
Intently winds his net upon a reel
His patient toil throughout the night, his zeal
Has furnished plenitude for present need
For greedy gulls as well as man — and he
Now rest content, knowing security.
Out in the Georgian Bay wild winds are sweeping
Within the harbour little boats are sleeping.

Alice Ann Dorey

MY FARM

My farm to me is not just land
where bare unpainted buildings stand.
My farm to me is nothing less
than all created loveliness.

My farm is not a place
where I must soil
My hands in endless dreary toil
But where through seed and swelling pod
I've learned to walk and talk with God.

My farm to me is not a place
outmoded by a modern race.
I like to think I just see less
of evil, greed and selfishness.

My farms not lonely for all day
I hear my children shout and play
and when age comes free from fears
I'll live again long joyous years.

My farms a heaven, here dwells rest,
security and happiness.
What ere befall the world outside
Here faith and hope and love abide.

No, my farm to me is not just land,
where bare unpainted buildings stand
My farm to me is nothing less
than all God's hoarded loveliness.

Percy Adams, Tobermory

LITTLE DUNKS BAY AT NIGHT

Little Dunks talks to itself in the night,
The stars are so many, the stars are so bright!
The birches so that with their plumes and white bars —
And Little Dunks talks to itself and the stars.

Moonlight in the clearing makes magic untold
Where the Scotch pines are young and the red pines are old;
In the birch grove white beauty — unearthly — supreme
Little Dunks smiles — and disturbs not the dream.

Comes rolling the fog with its gray banners flown,
Hiding heaven and earth, leaving each soul alone.
Little Dunks, lying silver, is silent, serene;
It knows, beyond veils, that the bush is still green.

The wind is northeast. The pines swing with a roar.
Heavy surf pounds on the far, outer shore.
Boats tighten and strain on their lines at the dock.
Little Dunks laughs, smashes high on the rock.

O Son, can you hear it? You've gone on so far —
Where you paint with a meteor and chop with a star!
In that land of all loveliness, laughter and light,
Can you hear Little Dunks chuckle softly at night?

Miriam Russel Alburn

SINKING OF THE STEAMER JONES

The Steamer Jones of Wiarton lay in Owen Sound's
sheltered "swatch"
Whilst Captain Crawford paced the deck a-fumbling with
his watch,
Foreboding skies revealed so well a "blow" from north
and west
Which meant the little cargo ships would face a gruel-
ling test —
The wind blew strong and reached a gale 'way out on
Georgian Bay,
But Captain Jim, so tall and prim, just itched to get away!

Dominion Fish's Caribou, the flagship of her fleet,
Came sailing in with decks awash through angry winds
and sleet,
She docked astern the Steamer Jones as Captain Batten
cried, —
"Don't try it, Jim, stay right in here, — it's mighty rough
outside!
The Captain quipped, "My faithful ship has never failed
me yet,
Though we've been through a blow or two that we shall
ne'er forget"

Her whistle screamed to call the crew — each man to take
his post —
Twelve boys whom Jim could ever trust and drink a
captain's toast,
His passengers were also paged to board the vessel too —
What odds a storm when Captain Jim would see them
safely though!
Ah! faith and trust rode high that day for gallant men
and ship
As from her berth she steamed away to leave the sheltered
slip.

Protected well from howling wind by Owen Sound's
western shore
She pointed north to breast the gale around Cape
Commodore,
Then, on she pushed toward Griffiths Isle where
lighthouse keeper
Boyd could view the graceful little ship that soon would
be destroyed
And as he watched, his heart would tune to say a fervent
prayer
For Captain Jim and those with him so rudely battered
there.

Beyond them stood Cape Croker light, (Dick Chapman's
Summer-Post),
He spied her reaching through the spray, intent on
pushing through
The rampant storm to claim her goal like all good
steamers do —
He saw her cut the angry waves — the bay looked mighty
grim,
But Richard knew that all was well in charge of Captain
Jim.

Thus, on she sailed for Lion's Head through billows
rolling high
With little sign the hour had come when all on board
would die —

Dick proved to be the last to see the Steamer Jones afloat
Still pressing toward the "Head" and "Tub" — a faithful
little boat!
He saw her skirt the Cove-o'-Cork, then pass from out
his view
With firm resolved she'd best the gale that she was passing
through.

What happened next is purely guess, but men who ought
to know,
Believe the windward shutters sprung before the pounding
blow,
In seconds flat great pressure forced the vessel to capsize
Amidst the roar of violent seas and muffled, anguished
cries, —
One lonely body washed ashore seems proof that we
assume
Death swiftly came to those on board and locked them
in a tomb.

Hope turned to fear at Lion's Head, and likewise, at the
"Tub",
They knew so well that violent storms are born of
Beelzebulb,
Days came and went, nights lingered on, fears grew that
all were lost,
Then comes the word from Christian Isle, "On shore,
Jones' wreckage tossed" —
Life boat with name, the wheelhouse, too, but told a
bitter tale
About a valiant little ship that never would sail.

"But what', you ask, means this to us, — we knew no-
one on board!"
Alas, how true! but they loved life, and someone, each
adored,
The days of little cargo ships on Georgian Bay have gone,
Let's not forget the sailor lads with risks they thrived
upon,
They helped to build, along with us, a Nation strong and
brave —
Whilst we enjoy their labour's fruit, they fill a wat'ry
grave!

LIZZIE GIBBONS' CAKE

As I sat by my window last evening
Our postman brought unto me
A little gift edged invitation
Saying Mrs. Eagles come over for tea.

Sure I knew it was the Gibbons who sent it
So I went for old friendship sake
And the first thing they gave me to tackle
Was a piece of Lizzie's cake

Mildred Hatt wanted to taste it
But really, there wasn't much use
For they worked at it over an hour
And couldn't get none of it loose.

Till Gordon went out for the hatchet
And Soup went out for a saw
That cake was enough by the powers
To paralyze anyone's jaw.

In it were cloves, nutmeg and berries
Raisins, citrons and cinnamon too.
There was sugar, pepper and cherries
And the crust was nailed on with glue.

Lizzie, as proud as a peacock
Kept winking and blinking away
Till she fell over Gordon's shoes
And spilt a whole brew of tea.

"Ada" she cried, "you're not eating"
"Just take another piece for my sake"
"No thanks Lizzie" says I
But I'd like the recipe for that cake.

Winnie was took with the colic
Debbie complained of her head
Maretta fell down on the sofa
And swore that she wished she were dead.

Leona fell down in hysterics
And there she did wiggle and shake
While everyone swore they were poisoned
By eating Lizzie Gibbons' cake.

Pearl Eagles

WHEN DAD WAS YOUNG

Kids were so queer when Dad was young,
They always liked to work they never seemed to want
to play and never tried to shirk.
They never made a racket in the house or on the street,
And never came inside the door with dirt upon their feet,
They never had to be waked up
but when the rooster crew,
They sprang right up — put on their clothes
and down the stairs they flew!
When school time came away they went
As happy as a King.
And studied — my how they did work
and mastered everything.
Sometimes at noon they would forget
their dinner and their skates,
And stayed right at their desk to work
with pencil and with slates.
I wish I'd lived when Dad was young
things were so different then,
For all the boys were studious
and acted just like men.
My Uncle Paul he sometimes comes
to visit us awhile,
And when I tell him how it was
you ought to see him smile,
He never says a word you know
but acts just like he thought,
There were some things which boys did then
Which my Dad has forgot!

Lily Martin, 1974

THE LEGEND *of the* FLOWERPOTS *of* FLOWERPOT ISLAND

Of all the legends that come from the Ottawa concerning that area of St. Edmunds, the one that tells about the formation of the flowerpots is probably the most famous. Time and the elements have gradually weathered these rocks to their present shapes and dimensions, but long ago, they closely resembled two human figures *The Owen Sound Sun Times* printed this story in 1944.

"She was Shining Rainbow, daughter of Waubesee, a chief of the Ottawa. He was Bounding Deer, a son of an enemy tribe of Chippewa. While the tribes were on peace terms for a season, the two met at a camp at the mouth of the beautiful Saugeen River at Southampton. There Bounding Deer brought Shining Rainbow dainty birch bark baskets filled with glossy blackberries and later, with her eyes upon him he far outshone his brother braves in the games which entertained the visitors. Soon she promised him that she would leave her people and go with him to the Saugeen. Their elopement was hastened because her mother, Spotted Turtle, had whispered to her that Waubesee had promised her to Swift Arrow, great warrior of their own band. Further, she said that the Chippewa would soon make war on Bounding Deer's People.

So one night in the Moon of Strawberries (June), Bounding Deer pushed his canoe away for the last time from the flat rock that had been their trysting place for a long time. The fact that it was the last time did not worry him for in the centre of his graceful canoe sat Shining Rainbow and she was leaving her people forever.

Out on the lake they moved as the canoe slipped like a slim, swift bird through the waters, for pursuit was expected. For hours Bounding Deer's paddle rose and turned in the moonlight, and when the moon had made the shadows short, they were within sight of Manitoueses. This was a sacred island off the mainland of the long-point-that-juts-out-into-Lake Huron, as the Indians called the Bruce Peninsula. This was the home of the lesser devils and of Little Spirit, and of a thunder bird egg. No Indian who had set foot on this island ever returned. It was shunned by all, and Bounding Deer, though glad to see the island for it told him that he was nearing home, instinctively drew his course away from it. Scarcely had he done so when a thrill of horror ran through him, for Shining Rainbow was calling "Look! Look!" and looking, he saw, far behind, three large canoes — and the moonlight gleaming on twenty paddles!

What chance had the frightened fugitives? Bounding Deer knew only too well that they had none. Shining Rainbow knew it too. She offered to throw herself over the side of the canoe and swim back to meet her fate, allowing her lover to escape, but he would not listen to her.

"It might be that the Little Spirit would have more pity on us than your brothers" he suggested. Shining Rainbow agreed, so when they saw that their pursuers would not fail to take them, they turned straight to the shore.

Shining Rainbow's brothers, who really loved her, saw with horror what was planned. They tried to call to the desperate pair and the big canoes flashed through the water in a last minute effort, but the solitary canoe was now in the shadow of the headland of the island, and they were too late. No sooner had the bow of Bounding Deer's canoe touched the shore that the watchers in the other canoes felt the waves rise in billows as the result of a mighty upheaval, and their ears were deafened by a loud crash. When the canoes were steadied again, it could be seen that the island had split in two! There on the shore were the petrified figures of the two they had followed. The Little Spirit had once again spoken to his people!

BITS ABOUT BOATS

In more recent times, the popularity of privately owned watercraft increased dramatically. The first yacht to visit Tobermory was probably the "Alice Smith", owned by Dr. Francis Smith. The "Alice Smith" travelled around the shores of Lake Huron through the summers of 1869-71. (1) The "Wanda", the "Explorer" and the "Star" were several other yachts that visited Tobermory and Cove Island in the late 1800's. (2) Dodges' yacht "Dauphine", which was the largest freshwater yacht on the Great Lakes at that time, was a regular visitor in the 1920-30's.

In the post World War II period, yachters took an increased interest in the Tobermory Harbour. Now, over two hundred yachts visit the harbour each year.

There have been a number of unusual vessels to visit the waters around St. Edmunds. One such vessel was the royal yacht, "Britannia". The "Britannia" cruised nearby Tobermory in 1959. Many small boats were out and about hoping to catch a glimpse of this ship as it sailed gracefully by. A less graceful ship but equally well known was Jacques Costeau's ship, the "Calypso", which docked briefly in Tobermory in 1980. Those who were able to see the "Calypso" were captivated by the amount of equipment aboard the ship as well as the ship's reputation and fame.

Some unusual watercraft have been tested in these waters. In 1971, the "Pisces III", a three man submarine belonging to the army, was tested near Tobermory. Another interesting experimental craft was "Sublimnos", which was tested off Dunks Bay from 1969-71. This submerged sphere allowed people to scuba down to the sphere and then remove their breathing apparatus inside the sphere. This sphere was used to make observations on geology and limnology.

THE "GRIFFON"

The subject of the "Griffon" was introduced in the first chapter of this book. It was stated that in 1679, Rene Robert Cavalier, Sieur de la Salle, built a small ship at Niagara, which he christened the "Griffon". The "Griffon" sailed to Green Bay, Wisconsin, where she picked up a load of furs. After leaving Green Bay, the "Griffon" and her crew of six disappeared. There are many different theories about the fate of the "Griffon". Some say that she was simply lost at sea during a storm. Others say that the crew stole the furs and burned the ship. The true answer to the riddle of the "Griffon's" disappearance has not yet been discovered, even though there are more than ten shipwrecks around the Great Lakes that different people claim to be the "Griffon".

One of these shipwrecks was brought to the public's attention by Orrie Vail of Tobermory. In 1955, Orrie Vail announced that for one hundred and twenty-three years, the location of the "Griffon" had been a family secret. The location of this wreck was in an inner cove on Russel Island.

In 1956, the remains of this mystery ship were raised. A keel and the ribs and planking from the port side of the ship remained. These were brought to Tobermory where Orrie Vail installed them in an old fishing shed that stood where the Ferry Dock is located.

A lively debate carried on through the years as experts attempted to prove or disprove Vail's claim that his wreck was the "Griffon". Vail appeared in newspapers, on interviews and even on televison in such shows as Front Page Challenge! The remains of the "Griffon" were subjected to every test that people could think of. Nails from the ship underwent spectro-chemical analysis, and wood underwent Carbon-14 dating. Unfortunately none of these tests helped in dating the wreck.

Photographs were sent to marine museums in France in order that they could compare the remains of the ship at Tobermory to the ships and drawings of ships that were built in the same period as La Salle's "Griffon". The French experts found that there were a number of differences apparent. The spacing of the ribs, the junction of the keel to the stern post, and the way that the floor timbers were notched into the keel were some of the construction methods in Vail's wreck that lead the French to believe that Vail's boat was actually built in the eighteenth century or later, not the seventeenth century in which La Salle had lived.

In spite of the opinion that the French experts offered, a large number of historians and others believed that Vail's wreck was the "Griffon". When Vail later produced some human bones, this group was even more convinced. Vail stated that he found the bones on Russel Island within six miles of the wreck. Some of these bones belonged to a child and others belonged to a very tall man. These bones seemed to confirm that this was the "Griffon" for La Salle's crew had included a young cabin boy and a very large man who was the pilot of the ship!

The controversy continued for years and the remains of this wreck continued to attract large numbers of people to Tobermory to view them in Vail's small shed until Orrie Vail's death in 1976.

In 1977, the Ministry of Natural Resources bought the wreck and the other remains connected with it. They studied these until 1981, when they announced that they believed that Vail's wreck was not the "Griffon". They reached this conclusion after studying the shipwreck material, timbers, fastenings, and the pieces of pottery and utensils found with the wreck. They believed that these items indicated that the shipwreck was actually from a mid-nineteeth century, "mackinaw boat" — like vessel. (1).

Today the Ministry still possesses the remains of Vail's wreck but many people in the area still secretly believe that Russel Island was indeed the final resting place of La Salle's ship, the "Griffon".

MONSTERS!

It seems that every isolated area of the globe has stories about rarely seen creatures whose presence cannot be explained. St. Edmunds Township is no exception to this rule. As St. Edmunds is surrounded by huge bodies of water, it is rather appropriate that the water is the home of one such beast.

This story took place one warm July afternoon in 1948, in the waters off Flowerpot Island. All of the people who saw this monster were aboard the cruise ship, the "City of Detroit"! The ship was touring the islands, and many merry makers lined the rails of the decks in order to catch a glimpse of the famous rock formations of Flowerpot Island. Suddenly, cries of surprise filled the air as a sixty foot long creature with a snake-like body and a horned head broke the surface and swam along for a few hundred yards. Just as suddenly as it appeared, the creature dived and no further sign was seen of the beast.

As soon as the ship arrived in Tobermory, the passengers began to tell their tale. When the local fishermen heard the tale, they laughed and said that like so many other "spirits", the sea serpent had been bottled in the United States and was a result of too much sun and too much liquor! (2).

The other mysterious creature that has also been seen only once, lives on the land. This animal was about two feet long and emitted a strange cry that sounded like a child wailing according to one witness. One resident, whose dog had been attacked, stated that the animal would be shot if it harmed any more animals, even if it was a monster! (3).

As Ripley says, "Believe it or not", but all of these stories are part of the spoken heritage of St. Edmunds.

THE KENDALL MURDER CASE

The history of St. Edmunds Township has not been without incidents that have been sensationalized throughout the country by newspapers' headlines. In the 1800's, it was the Davis Indian murders and in the 1900's, it was the Kendall murder case that focussed national attention on this small community.

In 1952, Arthur Kendall came to the Bruce Peninsula on an early springtime fishing trip. In an impulsive gesture, he accepted employment with Ashford Pedwell's sawmill at Johnston Harbour, even though he had a family and farm waiting for him in Monkton. Kendall stayed at Johnston Harbour until the summer when he suddenly summoned his wife and five children to join him. However, in the period that Kendall had been by himself, he had developed an intimate relationship with Beatrice Hogue, a worker in a Wiarton restaurant.

It seems that nothing out of the usual happened to this family until August 2, 1952. On this day, Mrs. Helen Kendall disappeared. Also that day, Kendall quickly gathered his five children and all of their possessions together and left their small cabin at Johnston Harbour, after leaving a note for his employer saying that he would not be back to work due to family problems. Kendall and his children drove to Wiarton where Kendall stopped to pick up Beatrice and her six children and their possessions. From Wiarton they drove to Kendall's farm in Monkton.

In Monkton, a neighbour of Kendall's soon noticed his arrival with Beatrice and the six new children. When he asked about Helen's absence, Kendall told him that Helen had deserted him. A week later, the neighbour again visited Kendall. This time Kendall told him that Helen was with her mother. On returning to his home, the neighbour phoned Helen's mother only to learn that Helen had not been there or called in a long time. The neighbour was alarmed so he then called and reported Helen's absence to the O.P.P. After his phone call to Helen's mother, Helen's brother had also become alarmed and had immediately driven to Kendall's farm in order to ask Kendall about Helen's disappearance. As he too was unconvinced by Kendall's anwsers, he reported Helen's disappearance to the O.P.P.

The next day, August 12, 1952, the police investigation began. Kendall's statement, although it matched that of his children perfectly, did not match what other witnesses told the police. As a result, the area around Johnston Harbour was searched extensively and many people were questioned. However, Helen's body was never found and no other incriminating evidence was found, therefore, Kendall was not charged then.

In 1960, Helen was declared legally dead and Kendall and Beatrice married.

In 1961, the case was opened again when one of Kendall's daughters went to the police after leaving home. Her sister also came forward and made a statement. Together they told the same story about the shocking events of August 2, 1952. Both stated that on August 2,

1952, they had been sleeping in the bunk above that of their parents, when they were wakened by their mother screaming "Don't Art! Oh, please don't". Their father had then thrown a bloody butcher knife on the table and dragged his wife's body out of the cabin. After being gone for about half an hour he returned, cleaned up the blood with the bedsheets, collected the knife and his wife's clothing, and then disappeared again. After his second return, he scrubbed the cabin and told the children the story that they were to tell anyone who asked about their mother's disappearance.

The Kendall trial began on October 22, 1961, and was soon completed. Kendall was found guilty of murder and was sentenced to be hanged. This sentence was later changed to life imprisonment, but Kendall was released on parole in 1975.

This case is still talked about in law schools, for it was the first case in Canada where a man was found guilty of murder without the body being found, and Kendall's death sentence was the first to be changed to life imprisonment (4).

LIQUOR STILLS *and* BOOTLEGGING

Long before the days of the Liquor Control Board of Ontario, and long before St. Edmunds had a police force, some of the men in St. Edmunds used to make their own liquor. As the region was settled largely by Methodists of Scottish descent, liquor was frowned upon especially by the women and preachers of the community. Even in the days of Prohibition, the whisky traffic somehow continued.

Liquor was made in stills that were often cleverly hidden in areas where few people travelled. Wheat and corn were used as raw products with sugar to help along the fermentation. In the past, when a ship ran aground with a load of wheat aboard, the wet wheat that had begun to sprout was also used.

Sometimes the stills were accidently discovered. One was discovered on the west side of the Big Tub by the road crews who were extending the roads around. This still was thought to have belonged to Charles Earl. Another still was discovered by a herd of cattle who drank its contents after pushing it over. Their owner, who had found them lying all over the field, was somewhat relieved to find that they were only drunk, not dead as he had first thought upon seeing them. One wife, whose suspicions were aroused by her husband's sudden desire for a walk every evening, secretly followed him one evening. After finding the still she returned the next day and destroyed it with her husband's axe. Other stills were only detected after they exploded because of the fermentation process.

One band of bootleggers had a boat to help them transport their product. One side of the boat was painted red, and the other side was painted green. People who saw the boat from shore would think that there were two boats out rather than just one going back and forth repeatedly.

Bootlegger's Cave and Whisky Harbour are two places that owe their names to the practice of making home-brewed liquor.

CONCLUSIONS

Patrick Folkes' conclusions still hold regarding the evolution of the settlement.

The evolution of Tobermory and St. Edmunds township is the story of a very small number of people, about whom almost nothing is known, who settled in the most isolated region of Ontario, south of the Precambrian Shield. Unlike the rest of the Bruce Peninsula, the Tobermory settlement was effectively isolated, for at least the first twenty years of its existence, by a barrier of forest and swamp. It was this wasteland that reduced the intended cultivation of the upper Peninsula to that of a small enclave on the edge of the Bury townplot and molded the individualism and exclusivism of the present community. The sale of lots for farming purposes spread out from the homesteads of Charles Earl and Abraham Davis, and then trickled along the route of the Bury Road. Elsewhere in the township land sales were limited, due for the most part to the inhospitable nature of the terrain. Not until the eighteen 'eighties, following the collapse of the Cook Brothers timbering monopoly, are large numbers of lots purchased, and only then by a multitude of other timber and lumber operators.

The patterns of development were firmly set during the 'seventies and early 'eighties. They differed substantially from that which occurred elsewhere on the Peninsula where the other townships had better and more soil and better access, either by road or steamboat, to centers of population. While the St. Edmunds settlers were limited to one relatively small tract, the townships of Lindsay and Eastnor enjoyed a wide proliferation of farms, particularly along the Bury Road.

The prosperity of the farms in the western part of the township continued to be a marginal affair, at least until after the turn of the century. A generation consumed itself in an attempt to consolidate its grip on a very harsh landscape, and experience which shaped the quality and character of their lives. Fortunately, the setting itself provided alternatives in the struggle for survival. The forest lay close at hand and from the beginning provided extra means of income, first as an individual undertaking and then in the form of collective employment. The latter arose among the shanties of "foreign" entrepreneurs and then at Green's sawmill on the Little Tub. In that event lies the real beginnings of Tobermory as a village. Simultaneously, the harbour established itself as a permanent base for commercial fishing. The manpower for both endeavours came in part from the neighbouring farms and after 1886, when the townplot was opened for sale, most of the original settlers were among the purchasers. Not only did a village evolve on the shores of the Little Tub, but also a mixture of farm, timber, and fishery interests. This amalgamate lasted with little change until after World War II, when the collapse of the timber industry, the decline of the fishery and the abandonment of some of the farms occurred.

Also, Tobermory seemed to thrive on three separate industries, each one succeeding the other. First came timbering that carried Tobermory into the twentieth century and extended the township's population to a great height. Eventually the timbering died out as the primeval forest was completely taken off. Fishing served as an alternative industry, rising to strong heights until the lake trout disaster. As fishing began to die out in the forties, a new industry filled the gap. Tourism had been developing at a slow pace previously, but with the need for a new source of income it became, as it is today, the major industry that supports most citizens in the township. The population rose to new heights that rivaled earlier timbering industry populations.

These three waves of prosperity left their mark on the settlement and their families. It is only the families with strong roots in the community who remain since the late 1800's. With each end of an industry, some families commonly left to other parts of Canada never to return. Thus, St. Edmunds' history is veiled by an exodus of its inhabitants. Those who stayed behind in these lull periods were victims of the isolation and poor services that accompanied it.

**Kenneth McLeod's children in 1906:
Ivor, Margaret and John.**

**Michael Belrose, Hector Currie, John MacLeod.
All over 90 years of age.**

Left to Right: **Margaret Currie, Annie McLeod, Vina Schauntz, Pearl Smith, Tena Smith, Annie Matheson, Margaret Matheson, Georgina Golden 1912.**

APPENDIX

APPENDIX A

This is the 1836 Manito treaty that frees the Manitoulin Islands as reserves for all Indian and surrenders generally the Bruce Peninsula to the Governments from the Sauking Indians.

"My Children:

"Seventy snow seasons have now passed away since we met in Council at the crooked place (Niagara), at which time and place your Great Father, the King and the Indians of North America tied their hands together by the wampum of friendship.

"Since that period various circumstances have occurred to separate from your Great Father many of his red children, and as an unavoidable increase of white population, as well as the progress of cultivation, have had the natural effect of impoverishing your hunting grounds it has become necessary that new arrangements should be entered into for the purpose of protecting you from the encroachments of the whites.

"In all parts of the world farmers seek for uncultivated land as eagerly as you, my red children, hunt in your forest for game. If you would cultivate your land it would then be considered your own property, in the same way as your dogs are considered among your-selves to belong to those who have reared them; but uncultivated land is like wild animals, and your Great Father, who has hitherto protected you, has now great difficulty in securing it for you from the whites, who are hunting to cultivate it.

"Under these circumstances, I have been obliged to consider what is best to be done for the red children of the forest, and I now tell you my thoughts.

"It appears that these islands on which we are now assembled in Council are, as well as all those on the north shore of Lake Huron, alike claimed by the English, the Ottawas and the Chippewas.

"I consider that from their facilities and from their being surrounded by innumerable fishing islands, they might be made a most desirable place of residence for many Indians who wish to be civilized, as well as to be totally separated from the whites; and I now tell you that your Great Father will withdraw his claim to these islands and allow them to be applied for that purpose.

"Are you, therefore, the Ottawas and Chippewas, willing to relinquish your respective claims to these Islands and make them the property (under your Great Father's control) for all Indians whom he shall allow to reside on them: if so, affix your marks to this my proposal.

"F. B. HEAD.
"J. B. ASSEKINACK.
"MOKOMMUNISH (totem).

"TAWACKUCK.
"KIMEWEN (totem).
"KITCHEMOKOMON (totem).
"PESIATAWICK (totem).
"PAIMAUSEGAI (totem).
"NAINAWMUTTEBE (totem).
"MOSUNEKO (totem).
"KEWUCKANCE (totem).
"SHAWENAUSEWAY (totem).
"ESPANIOLE (totem).
"SNAKE (totem).
"PAUTUNSEWAY (totem).
"PAIMAUGUMESTCAM (totem).
"WAGEMAUQUIN (totem).

"MANITOWANING, 9th August, 1836."

"TO THE SAUKINGS:
"My Children,

"You have heard the proposal I have just made to the Chippewas and Ottawas, by which it has been agreed between them and your Great Father that these Islands (Manitoulin), on which we are now assembled, should be made, in Council, the property (under your Great Father's control) of all Indians whom he shall allow to reside on them.

"I now propose to you that you should surrender to your Great Father the Sauking (Saugeen) Territory you at present occupy and that you shall repair either to this Island or to that part of your territory which lies on the North of Owen Sound, upon which proper houses shall be built for you, and proper assistance to enable you to become civilized and to cultivate land, which your Great Father engages forever to protect for you from the encroachments of the whites.

"Are you, therefore, the Sauking Indians, willing to accede to this arrangement; if so, affix your marks to this my proposal.

"MANITOWANING, 9th August, 1836.

"Witness:

"T. G. ANDERSON, S.I.A.
"JOSEPH STINSON, Genl. Supt. Of
  Wesleyan Missions.
"ADAM ELLIOT.
"JAMES EVANS.
"F. L. INGALL, Lieut. 15th Regt.,
  Commanding Detacht.
"TALFOURD W. FIELD, Distrt. Agent.

"F. B. HEAL.
"METTIEWABE (totem).
"ALEXANDER (totem)
"KAQUTA BUNEVAIREAR.
"KOWGISAWIS (totem).
"METTAWANAHS (totem).

APPENDIX B

This is the 1854 treaty that specifically surrenders certain areas of the peninsula.

INDIAN TREATY RELATING TO THE SURRENDER OF THE SAUGEEN PENINSULA

"We, the Chiefs, Sachems and Principal Men of the Indian Tribes resident at Saugeen, Owen Sound, confiding in the wisdom and protecting care of our Great Mother across the Big Lake, and believing that our Good Father, His Excellency the Earl of Elgin and Kincardine, Governor-General of Canada, is anxiously desirous to promote those interests which will most largely conduce to the Welfare of His red children, have now, being in full Council assembled, in presence of the Superintendent General of Indian Affairs, and of the young men of both tribes, agreed that it will be highly desirable for us to make a full and complete surrender unto the Crown of that Peninsula known as the Saugeen and Owen Sound Indian Reserve, subject to certain restrictions and reservations to be hereinafter set forth. We have therefore set our marks to this document, after having heard the same read to us, and do hereby surrender the whole of the above named tract of country, bounded on the south by a straight line drawn from the Indian village of Saugeen to the Indian village of Nawash, in continuation of the northern limits of the narrow strip recently surrendered by us to the Crown; and bounded on the north-east and west by Georgian Bay and Lake Huron, with the following reservations, to wit: 1st. For the benefit of the Saugeen Indians we reserve all that block of land bounded on the west by a straight line running due north from the River Saugeen, at the spot where it is entered by a ravine, immediately to the west of the village, and over which a bridge has recently been constructed, to the shore of Lake Huron; on the south by the aforesaid northern limit of the lately surrendered strip; on the east by a line drawn from a spot upon the coast at a distance of about (9-1/2) nine miles and a half from the western boundary aforesaid, and running parallel thereto until it touches the aforementioned northern limits of the recently surrendered strip; and we wish it to be clearly understood that we wish the Peninsula at the mouth of the Saugeen River to the west of the western boundary aforesaid to be laid out in townpark lots and sold for our benefit without delay; and we also wish to be understood that our surrender includes that parcel of land which is in continuation of the strip recently surrendered to the Saugeen River.

We do also reserve to ourselves that tract of land called Chief's Point, bounded on the east by a line drawn from a spot half a mile up the Sable River, and continued in a northerly direction to the bay, and upon all other sides by the lakes.

2nd. We reserve for the benefit of the Owen Sound Indians all that tract bounded on the south by the northern limit of the continuation of the strip recently surrendered; on the north-west by a line drawn from the north-easterly angle of the aforesaid strip (as it was surrendered in 1851, in a north-easterly direction); on the south-east by the sound extending to the southern limit of the Caughnawaga Settlement; on the north by a line two miles in length and forming the said southern limit. And we also reserve to Ourselves all tract of land called Cape Crocker, bounded on three sides by Georgian Bay, on the south-west side by a line drawn from the bottom of Nochemowenaing Bay to the mouth of Sucker River, and we include in the aforesaid surrender the parcel of land contained in the continuation to Owen's Sound of the recently surrendered strip aforesaid.

3rd. We do reserve for the benefit of the Colpoy's Bay Indians, in the presence and with the concurrence of John Beattie, who represents the tribe at this Council, a block of land containing 6,000 acres, and including their village, and bounded on the north by Colpoy's Bay.

All which reserves we hereby retain to ourselves and our children in perpetuity, and it is agreed that the interest of the principal sum arising out of the sale of our lands be regularly paid to them so long as there are Indians left to represent our tribe without diminution at half-yearly periods.

And we hereby request the sanction of our Great Father the Governor-General to this surrender, which we consider highly conducive to our general interests.

Done in Council, at Saugeen, this thirteenth day of October, 1854. It is understood that no islands are included in this surrender.

Signed and sealed:
L. Oliphant,
Supt. Genl. Indian Affairs
Peter Jacobs,
Missionary.

JOHN (totem) KADUHGEKWUN, (L.S.)
ALEX (totem) MADWAYOSH, (L.S.)
JOHN (totem) MANEDSWAB, (L.S.)
JNO. THOS. (totem) WAHBUHDICK, (L.S.)
PETER (totem) JONES, (L.S.)
DAVID SAWYER, (L.S.)
JOHN (totem) JOHNSTON, (L.S.)
JOHN H. BEATY, (L.S.)
THOMAS (totem) PABAHMOSH, (L.S.)
JOHN (totem) MADWASHEMIND, (L.S.)
JOHN AUNJEGAHBOWH, (L.S.)

Witnesses:
JAS. ROSS, M.P.P.,
C. RANKIN, P.L.S.,
A. McNABB,
    Crown Land Agent.

JAMES NEWASH, (L.S.)
THOMAS (totem) WAHBUHDICK, (L.S.)
CHARLES KEESHICK. (L.S.)

APPENDIX C

LAND SALES, ST. EDMUNDS TOWNSHIP
c/o Patrick Folkes
July, 1870 — Sept., 1883

Sale No.	Date of Sale	Purchaser	Lot & Concession
2464	July 11, 1870	John Wesley Colwell	Lot 47, Con. 1, W.B.R.
2465	July 11, 1870	Abraham Davis	Lot 48, Con. 1, W.B.R.
2466	July 11, 1870	Abraham Davis	Lot 48, Con. 1, E.B.R.
2471	Sept. 6, 1870	David Reed	Lot 49, Con. 1, W.B.R.
2482	Oct. 15, 1870	Darius Doty	Lot 14, Con. 6, W.B.R.
2483	Oct. 15, 1870	Darius Doty	Lot 15, Con. 6, W.B.R.
2484	Oct. 15, 1870	Darius Doty	Lot 14 & 15, Con. 7, W.B.R.
2541	May 19, 1871	A. A. Thompson	Lot 24, Con. 5, W.B.R.
2542	May 19, 1871	A. A. Thompson	Lot 25, Con. 5, W.B.R.
2548	July 13, 1871	A. A. Thompson	Lot 54, Con. 5, W.B.R.
2549	July 13, 1871	A. A. Thompson	Lot 55, Con. 5, W.B.R.
2610	June 25, 1872	John Leathorn	Lot 7, Con. 1, E.B.R.
2612	July 2, 1872	James Cockwill	Lot 6, Con. 2, E.B.R.
2613	July 2, 1872	James Cockwill	Lot 7, Con. 2, E.B.R.
2614	July 2, 1872	James Cockwill	Lot 6, Con. 3, E.B.R.
2645	Oct. 4, 1872	George Campbell	Lot 32, Con. 1, E.B.R.
2646	Oct. 4, 1872	George Campbell	Lot 33, Con. 1, E.B.R.
2647	Oct. 4, 1872	George Campbell	Lot 33, Con. 2, E.B.R.
2648	Oct. 4, 1872	Donald McIntosh	Lot 31, Con. 4, E.B.R.
2649	Oct. 4, 1872	Donald McIntosh	Lot 32, Con. 4, E.B.R.
2650	Oct. 4, 1872	Donald McIntosh	Lot 33, Con. 3, E.B.R.
2711	Apr. 23, 1873	Mark Mathews	Lot 5, Con. 2, E.B.R.
2712	Apr. 23, 1873	Mark Mathews	Lot 5, Con. 3, E.B.R.
2713	Apr. 29, 1873	George Sidwell	Lot 1, Con. 8, E.B.R.
2714	Apr. 29, 1873	Donald McDonald	Lot 4, Con. 4, E.B.R.
2715	Apr. 29, 1873	Donald McDonald	Lot 5, Con. 4, E.B.R.
2716	Apr. 29, 1873	Adam McTavish	Lot 30, Con. 4, E.B.R.
2717	May 9, 1873	William Grant	Lot 8, Con. 2, W.B.R.
2718	May 9, 1873	William Grant	Lot 8, Con. 3, W.B.R.
2719	May 9, 1873	Thomas Cockwill	Lot 1, Con. 8, E.B.R.
2720	May 9, 1873	Thomas Cockwill	Lot 2, Con. 8, E.B.R.
2741	June 21, 1873	John Ellicot	Lot 1, Con. 4, E.B.R.
2591	June 18, 1875	Jacob Belrose	Lot 47, Con. 1, e.B.R.
2973	Sept. 9, 1875	John Shearer	Lot 49, Con. 1, E.B.R.
2976	Sept 20, 1875	Alexander Hay	Lot 47, Con. 3, W.B.R.
2977	Sept 20, 1875	Alexander Hay	Lot 48, Con. 3, W.B.R.
3005	Nov. 25, 1875	Thomas H. Lee	Lot 1, Con. 7, E.B.R.
3046	June 20, 1876	Patrick Earl	Lot 49, Con. 2, W.B.R.
3047	June 20, 1876	Alexander Marks	Lot 49, Con. 3, W.B.R.
3059	July 26, 1876	Isabella Belrose	Lot 50, Con. 3, W.B.R.
3060	July 26, 1876	Mary E. Geareau (Sp?)	Lot 50, Con. 2, W.B.R.
4018	July 11, 1877	William Soper	Lot 45, Con. 1, W.B.R.
4140	Aug. 7, 1877	George Pepper	Lot 44, Con. 1, W.B.R.
4141	Aug. 7, 1877	George Pepper	Lot 46, Con. 1, W.B.R.
4151	Sept. 22, 1877	Hugh Henderson	Lot 48, Con. 2, W.B.R.
4268	Apr. 30, 1878	Adeline McDonald	Lot 46, Con. 1, E.B.R.
4318	July 5, 1878	Edwin F. Pond	Lot 31, Con. 1, W.B.R.
4322	July 11, 1878	James Fallon	Lot 43, Con. 1, W.B.R.
4343	Aug. 21, 1878	William John Warren	Lot 33, Con. 5, E.B.R.
4344	Aug. 21, 1878	William John Warren	Lot 34, Con. 5, E.B.R.
4345	Aug. 21, 1878	Thomas McDermott	Lot 31, Con. 5, E.B.R.
4346	Aug. 21, 1878	Thomas McDermott	Lot 31, Con. 6, E.B.R.
4348	Aug. 22, 1878	Volney William Foster	Lot 33, Con. 2, W.B.R.
4394	Oct. 21, 1878	Louisa Amelia Nelson	Lot 35, Con. 1, W.B.R.
4399	Oct. 24, 1878	Neil Currie	Lot 42, Con. 1, W.B.R.
4403	Oct. 30, 1878	Volney William Foster	Lot 30, Con. 1, E.B.R.
4414	Nov. 11, 1878	William Burny (sp?)	Lot 36, Con. 1, W.B.R.
4415	Nov. 11, 1878	Charles Grey	Lot 36, Con. 1, E.B.R.
4416	Nov. 11, 1878	George Dunkley	Lot 44, Con. 2, W.B.R.
4417	Nov. 11, 1878	George Dunkley	Lot 45, Con. 2, W.B.R.
4418	Nov. 11, 1878	George Dunkley	Lot 44, Con. 1, E.B.R.
4455	Dec. 16, 1878	Volney William Foster	Lot 29, Con. 1, W.B.R.
4482	March 1, 1879	George Dunkley	Lot 46, Con. 2, W.B.R.
4486	March 8, 1879	Volney William Foster	Lot 29, Con. 2, W.B.R.
4529	July 30, 1879	Thomas Earl	Lot 39, Con. 1, E.B.R.
4550	Aug. 22, 1879	Edwrd Hopkins	Lot 46, Con. 3, W.B.R.
4551	Aug. 22, 1879	Edward Hopkins	Lot 46, Con. 4, W.B.R.
4552	Aug. 22, 1879	John C. Hopkins	Lot 44, Con. 4, W.B.R.
4553	Aug. 22, 1879	James Hopkins	Lot 45, Con. 3, W.B.R.
4554	Aug. 22, 1879	Richard Hopkins	Lot 47, Con. 4, W.B.R.
4557	Aug. 27, 1879	William Grant	Lot 10, Con. 5, W.B.R.
4574	Oct. 15, 1879	James Simpson	Lot 43, Con. 2, W.B.R.
4575	Oct. 16, 1879	James McDermott	Lot 46, Con. 2, E.B.R.
4628	Dec. 6, 1879	Walter Millar	Lot 38, Con. 1, E.B.R.
4624	Dec. 27, 1879	George Bartman	Lot 48, Con. 2, E.B.R.
4630	Jan. 2, 1880	Robert Hopkins	Lot 45, Con. 4, W.B.R.
4633	Jan. 12, 1880	Elizabeth Dunkley	Lot 43, Con. 1, E.B.R.
4635	Feb. 10, 1880	Thomas Cockwell	Lot 4, E.B.R.
4650	Apr. 12, 1880	Alexander Green	Lot 51, Con. 3, W.B.R.
4651	Apr. 12, 1880	James Maitland	Lot 54, Con. 4, W.B.R.
4652	Apr. 12, 1880	James Maitland	Lot 55, Con. 4, W.B.R.
4660	May 7, 1880	William Hicks	Lot 37, Con. 2, W.B.R.
4661	May 7, 1880	William Blake	Lot 41, Con. 4, W.B.R.
4662	May 7, 1880	John Sanders	Lot 45, Con. 2, W.B.R.
4688	Sept. 10, 1880	Angus McRae	Lot 47, Con. 2, E.B.R.
4697	Oct. 6, 1880	Hector McDonald	Lot 50, Con. 1, W.B.R.
4715	Oct. 12, 1880	Donald McDonald	Lot 45, Con. 1, E.B.R.
4731	Nov. 3, 1880	James Blair	Lot 4, Con. 6, E.B.R.
4753	Nov. 11, 1880	James Coleman	Lot 36, Con. 4, E.B.R.
4754	Nov. 11, 1880	James Coleman	Lot 37, Con. 4, E.B.R.
4778	Dec. 13, 1880	John Blair	Lot 4, Con. 1, E.B.R.
4782	Jan. 10, 1881	Charles Fox (sp?)	Lot 36, Con. 2, E.B.R.
4783	Jan. 10, 1881	Charles Fox	Lot 37, Con. 2, E.B.R.
4784	Jan. 10, 1881	Robert Crawford	Lot 33, Con. 3, E.B.R.
4785	Jan. 10, 1881	Robert Crawford	Lot 32, Con. 4, E.B.R.
4786	Jan. 10, 1881	Robert Crawford	Lot 31, Con. 4, E.B.R.
4807	Feb. 4, 1881	George Bartman	Lot 47, Con. 2, W.B.R.
4812	Feb. 22, 1881	Benjamin Young	Lot 37, Con. 1, W.B.R.
4825	Mar. 15, 1881	William Young	Lot 42, Con. 1, E.B.R.
4826	Mar. 15, 1881	John Webb	Lot 39, Con. 3, W.B.R.
4840	Apr. 6, 1881	Henry Rixon	Lot 32, Con. 1, W.B.R.
4841	Apr. 6, 1881	Henry Rixon	Lot 28, Con. 1, E.B.R.
4846	Apr. 12, 1881	Henry Rixon	Lot 23, Con. 3, W.B.R.
4847	Apr. 12, 1881	Alexander Green	Lot 26, Con. 2, W.B.R.
4865	May 21, 1881	Thomas McDowell	Lot 49, Con. 1, W.B.R.
4871	June 3, 1881	Edward Hopkins	Lot 34, Con. 1, W.B.R.
4872	June 3, 1881	James Hopkins	Lot 37, Con. 1, E.B.R.
4886	June 25, 1881	James Maitland	Lot 38, Con. 1, W.B.R.
4909	Aug. 19, 1881	Hugh J. McMillan	Lot 17, Con. 7, E.B.R.
4910	Aug. 19, 1881	Hugh J. McMillan	Lot 18, Con. 7, E.B.R.
4936	Oct. 1, 1881	Alexander Campbell	Lot 9, Con. 6, W.B.R.
5057	Jan. 18, 1882	Ann Pepper	Lot 44, Con. 2, E.B.R.
5063	Jan. 25, 1882	John Trout Jr.	Lot 26, Con. 1, W.B.R.
5064	Jan. 25, 1882	John Trout Jr.	Lot 27, Con. 1, W.B.R.
5065	Jan. 25, 1882	John Trout Jr.	Lot 28, Con. 1, W.B.R.
5071	Feb. 8, 1882	Martin P. Hayes	Lot 51, Con. 1, W.B.R.
5072	Feb. 8, 1882	Martin P. Hayes	Lot 51, Con. 2, W.B.R.
5073	Feb. 8, 1882	Martin P. Hayes	Lot 50, Con. 1, W.B.R.
5074	Feb. 8, 1882	Martin P. Hayes	Lot 50, Con. 2, W.B.R.
5078	Feb. 11, 1882	Andrew Quinlan	Lot 1, Con. 11, E.B.R.
5080	Feb. 11, 1882	Andrew Quinlan	Lot 1, Con. 10, E.B.R.
5095	Feb. 21, 1882	Robert Hayes	Lot 1, Con. 13, E.B.R.
5096	Feb. 21, 1882	John Ceasor	Lot 2, Con. 13, E.B.R.
5103	Mar. 1, 1882	William Young	Lot 36, Con. 2, W.B.R.
5104	Mar. 1, 1882	John Ainslie	Lot 41, Con. 2, W.B.R.
5105	Mar. 1, 1882	John Ainslie	Lot 42, Con. 2, W.B.R.
5106	Mar. 1, 1882	James W. Maitland	Lot 41, Con. 3, W.B.R.
5107	Mar. 1, 1882	James W. Maitland	Lot 42, Con. 3, W.B.R.
5112	Mar. 11, 1882	Jacob Moshier	Lot 11, Con. 10, E.B.R.
5113	Mar. 11, 1882	Jacob Moshier	Lot 9, Con. 11, E.B.R.
5115	Mar. 13, 1882	Geo. E. Smith	Lot 24, Con. 3, W.B.R.
5116	Mar. 13, 1882	Geo. E. Smith	Lot 23, Con. 4, W.B.R.
5121	Mar. 21, 1882	Jacob Moshier	Lot 12, Con. 10, E.B.R.
5122	Mar. 21, 1882	Jacob Moshier	Lot 10, Con. 11, E.B.R.
5123	Mar. 21, 1882	Jacob Moshier	Lot 11, Con. 11, E.B.R.
5125	Mar. 21, 1882	Albert C. Bridge	Lot 3, Con. 13, E.B.R.
5137	Mar. 25, 1882	Alexander Butchart	Lot 44, Con. 3, E.B.R.
5142	Mar. 31, 1882	Thomas Maitland	Lot 18, Con. 4, W.B.R.
5143	Mar. 31, 1882	Thomas Maitland	Lot 19, Con. 4, W.B.R.
5166	May 12, 1882	Thomas Penton	Lot 5, Con. 4, W.B.R.
5167	May 12, 1882	Anna Penton	Lot 6, Con. 4, W.B.R.
5168	May 12, 1882	Anna Penton	Lot 6, Con. 5, W.B.R.
5188	June 3, 1882	Hugh J. McMillan	Lot 23, Con. 4, E.B.R.
5195	June 26, 1882	Robert Conolly	Lot 1, Con. 12, E.B.R.
5196	June 26, 1882	Robert Conolly	Lot 2, Con. 12, E.B.R.
5228	Aug. 19, 1882	John Kilbourne	Lot 8, Con. 10, E.B.R.
5229	Aug. 19, 1882	John Kilbourne	Lot 9, Con. 10, E.B.R.
5230	Aug. 19, 1882	John Kilbourne	Lot 10, Con. 10, E.B.R.
5231	Aug. 19, 1882	Maria A. Kibourn (sic)	Lot 1, Con. 14, E.B.R.
5232	Aug. 19, 1882	Maria A. Kibourn	Lot 3, Con. 14, E.B.R.
5233	Aug. 19, 1882	Maria A. Kibourn	Lot 3, Con. 14, E.B.R.
5234	Aug. 19, 1882	William H. Bishop	Lot 3, Con. 12, E.B.R.
5235	Aug. 19, 1882	William H. Bishop	Lot 41, Con. 12, E.B.R.
5240	Sept. 11, 1882	Absolem S. Allen	Lot 6, Con. 11, E.B.R.
5241	Sept. 11, 1882	Absolem S. Allen	Lot 6, Con. 10, E.B.R.
5242	Sept. 11, 1882	Absolem S. Allen	Lot 7, Con. 10, E.B.R.
5243	Sept. 11, 1882	Absolem S. Allen	Lot 12, Con. 9, E.B.R.
5244	Sept. 11, 1882	Kate Allan	Lot 6, Con. 9, E.B.R.
5245	Sept. 11, 1882	Kate Allan	Lot 7, Con. 9, E.B.R.
5246	Sept. 11, 1882	Kate Allan	Lot 11, Con. 9, E.B.R.
5247	Sept. 11, 1882	Jane Webster	Lot 5, Con. 9, E.B.R.
5248	Sept. 11, 1882	Jane Webster	Lot 5, Con. 10, E.B.R.
5249	Sept. 11, 1882	Jane Webster	Lot 5, Con. 11, E.B.R.
5251	Sept. 15, 1882	George Webster	Lot 12, Con. 9, E.B.R.
5252	Sept. 15, 1882	George Webster	Lot 12, Con. 8, E.B.R.
5257	Sept. 21, 1882	Jessie Webster	Lot 2, Con. 10, E.B.R.

5258	Sept. 21, 1882	Jessie Webster	Lot 3, Con. 10, E.B.R.
5259	Sept. 21, 1882	Jessie Webster	Lot 4, Con. 10, E.B.R.
5270	Oct. 3, 1882	Alexander Campbell	Lot 24, Con. 4, W.B.R.
5272	Oct. 13, 1882	Hiram Quinlan	Lot 2, Con. 9, E.B.R.
5273	Oct. 13, 1882	Hiram Quinlan	Lot 1, Con. 9, E.B.R.
5274	Oct. 13, 1882	Hiram Quinlan	Lot 3, Con. 9, E.B.R.
5275	Oct. 13, 1882	James Quinlan	Lot 4, Con. 9, E.B.R.
5276	Oct. 13, 1882	James Quinlan	Lot 2, Con. 11, E.B.R.
5283	Oct. 14, 1882	John Cranston	Lot 1, Con. 4, W.B.R.
5284	Oct. 16, 1882	Francis Noble	Lot 22, Con. 7, E.B.R.
5285	Oct. 16, 1882	Francis Noble	Lot 23, Con. 7, E.B.R.
5355	Mar. 5, 1883	Thomas Penton	Lot 5, Con. 7, W.B.R.
5356	Mar. 6, 1883	James W. Maitland	Lot 29, Con. 1, E.B.R.
5357	Mar. 6, 1883	James W. Maitland	Lot 40, Con. 4, E.B.R.
5358	Mar. 6, 1883	Henry Rixon	Lot 39, Con. 3, E.B.R.
5359	Mar. 6, 1883	Henry Rixon	Lot 37, Con. 3, E.B.R.
5368	Mar. 30, 1883	George McLandress	Lot 34, Con. 3, E.B.R.
5369	Mar. 30, 1883	George McLandress	Lot 35, Con. 3, E.B.R.
5370	Mar. 30, 1883	George McLandress	Lot 36, Con. 3, E.B.R.
5371	Mar. 30, 1883	Alex McLandress	Lot 33, Con. 4, E.B.R.
5372	Mar. 30, 1883	Alex McLandress	Lot 34, Con. 4, E.B.R.
5373	Mar. 30, 1883	Alex McLandress	Lot 35, Con. 4, E.B.R.
5374	Mar. 30, 1883	Herman Spence	Lot 32, Con. 5, E.B.R.
5375	Mar. 30, 1883	Herman Spence	Lot 35, Con. 5, E.B.R.
5376	Mar. 30, 1883	James Paterson	Lot 32, Con. 6, E.B.R.
5377	Mar. 30, 1883	James Paterson	Lot 33, Con. 6, E.B.R.
5405	May 16, 1883	Beaville Bredgmen	Lot 5, Con. 6, E.B.R.
5406	May 16, 1883	William Channon	Lot 3, Con. 10, E.B.R.
5408	May 17, 1883	James Lynch	Lot 21, Con. 1, E.B.R.
5429	July 11, 1883	Robert Hopkins	Lot 44, Con. 4, W.B.R.
5445	Aug. 1, 1883	John Tyndall	Lot 11, Con. 7, E.B.R.
5446	Aug. 1, 1883	John Tyndall	Lot 12, Con. 7, E.B.R.
5447	Aug. 1, 1883	John Tyndall	Lot 12, Con. 7, E.B.R.
5448	Aug. 1, 1883	Amelia Tyndall	Lot 14, Con. 7, E.B.R.
5449	Aug. 1, 1883	Amelia Tyndall	Lot 15, Con. 7, E.B.R.
5450	Aug. 1, 1883	Amelia Tyndall	Lot 16, Con. 7, E.B.R.
5451	Aug. 1, 1883	William Duke	Lot 18, Con. 7, E.B.R.
5452	Aug. 1, 1883	William Duke	Lot 20, Con. 7, E.B.R.
5453	Aug. 1, 1883	Ann Duke	Lot 14, Con. 8, E.B.R.
5454	Aug. 1, 1883	Ann Duke	Lot 15, Con. 8, E.B.R.
5455	Aug. 1, 1883	George Ames	Lot 16, Con. 8, E.B.R.
5456	Aug. 1, 1883	George Ames	Lot 17, Con. 8, E.B.R.
5457	Aug. 1, 1883	Mary Ames	Lot 8, Con. 9, E.B.R.
5458	Aug. 1, 1883	Mary Ames	Lot 9, Con. 9, E.B.R.
5459	Aug. 1, 1883	Mary Ames	Lot 10, Con. 9, E.B.R.
5460	Aug. 1, 1883	Albert Ames	Lot 13, Con. 9, E.B.R.
5461	Aug. 1, 1883	Albert Ames	Lot 7, Con. 11, E.B.R.
5462	Aug. 1, 1883	Robert Tyndall	Lot 3, Con. 11, E.B.R.
5463	Aug. 1, 1883	Robert Tyndall	Lot 4, Con. 11, E.B.R.
5465	Aug. 15, 1883	Peter McVicar	Lot 30, Con. 6, E.B.R.
5472	Aug. 30, 1883	Hiram Charleton	Lot 1, Con. 6, W.B.R.
5474	Sept. 1, 1883	William McVicar	Lot 6, Con. 4, E.B.R.
5475	Sept. 1, 1883	Thomas Bearman	Lot 7, Con. 4, E.B.R.
5476	Sept. 1, 1883	Thomas Bearman	Lot 6, Con. 5, E.B.R.
5477	Sept. 1, 1883	Fred W. Bearman	Lot 3, Con. 2, E.B.R.
5478	Sept. 1, 1883	Fred W. Bearman	Lot 4, Con. 2, E.B.R.
5479	Sept. 1, 1883	John Bearman	Lot 24, Con. 3, E.B.R.
5480	Sept. 1, 1883	John Bearman	Lot 4, Con. 3, E.B.R.
5481	Sept. 1, 1883	Alexander Walker	Lot 22, Con. 4, E.B.R.
5482	Sept. 1, 1883	Alexander Walker	Lot 23, Con. 4, E.B.R.
5483	Sept. 1, 1883	Solomon Spears	Lot 40, Con. 1, E.B.R.
5486	Sept. 8, 1883	James A. McKay	Lot 3, Con. 7, E.B.R.
5487	Sept. 8, 1883	James A. McKay	Lot 4, Con. 7, E.B.R.
5488	Sept. 8, 1883	J. S. Allan (sp?)	Lot 5, Con. 7, E.B.R.
5489	Sept. 8, 1883	J. S. Allan (sp?)	Lot 6, Con. 7, E.B.R.
5490	Sept. 8 1883	James Clark	Lot 7, Con. 7, E.B.R.
5491	Sept. 8 1883	James Clark	Lot 8, Con. 7, E.B.R.
5493	Sept. 15, 1883	Charles Clifford	Lot 2, Con. 7, E.B.R.
5494	Sept. 15, 1883	Charles Clifford	Lot 9, Con. 7, E.B.R.
5495	Sept. 15, 1883	Charles Clifford	Lot 10, Con. 7, E.B.R.
5496	Sept. 15, 1883	Henry Duncan	Lot 2, Con. 6, E.B.R.
5497	Sept. 15, 1883	Henry Duncan	Lot 6, Con. 6, E.B.R.
5498	Sept. 15, 1883	Henry Duncan	Lot 7, Con. 6, E.B.R.
5499	Sept. 15, 1883	Frank Fowler	Lot 10, Con. 6, E.B.R.
5500	Sept. 15, 1883	Frank Fowler	Lot 11, Con. 6, E.B.R.
5501	Sept. 15, 1883	Frank Fowler	Lot 12, Con. 6, E.B.R.
5502	Sept. 15, 1883	Charles Plewes	Lot 13, Con. 6, E.B.R.
5503	Sept. 15, 1883	Charles Plewes	Lot 14, Con. 6, E.B.R.
5504	Sept. 15, 1883	Charles Plewes	Lot 15, Con. 6, E.B.R.
5505	Sept. 15, 1883	G. T. Ames	Lot 16, Con. 6, E.B.R.
5506	Sept. 15, 1883	G. T. Ames	Lot 17, Con. 6, E.B.R.
5507	Sept. 15, 1883	G. T. Ames	Lot 10, Con. 5, E.B.R.
5508	Sept. 15, 1883	M. Builder	Lot 11, Con. 5, E.B.R.
5509	Sept. 15, 1883	M. Builder	Lot 12, Con. 5, E.B.R.
5510	Sept. 15, 1883	Charles Builder	Lot 13, Con. 5, E.B.R.
5511	Sept. 15, 1883	Chalres Builder	Lot 14, Con. 5, E.B.R.
5512	Sept. 15, 1883	Emma Whitehouse	Lot 15, Con. 5, E.B.R.
5513	Sept. 15, 1883	Emma Whitehouse	Lot 16, Con. 5, E.B.R.
5514	Sept. 15, 1883	Emma Whitehouse	Lot 20, Con. 5, E.B.R.
5515	Sept. 15, 1883	G. W. Ames	Lot 21, Con. 5, E.B.R.

Sources:

Public Archives of Canada, Record Group, *Land Returns, Saugeen Peninsula, 1855-74* (Vol. 772), *Journal of Land Sales, Toronto Office, 1869-78* (Vol. 686), *Day Book of Land and Timber Transactions, 1878-81* (Vol. 1030), *Day Book of Land and Timber Transactions, 1881-83* (Vol. 1031).

APPENDIX D

PETITION OF THE RATEPAYERS OF LINDSAY & ST. EDMUNDS TOWNSHIPS 1888

To the Honourable
The Superintendent of Indian Affairs
Ottawa

The Petition of the Ratepayers of the
Townships of Lindsay & St. Edmunds

Humbly petition

that you may consider the following statement and act as herein suggested.

The Summer season of 1888 has indeed been so very severe one to settlers on the Indian Peninsula the great drought lasting as it did from May to August prevented early crops from producing much more than the seed sown and in many instances not even so much. Grain sown late remained unsprouted until the wet season came on in August. It then shot up rapidly but a severe frost towards the end of September destroyed the chances of much of this late grain maturing. Many settlers have been deprived of any means to pay even their taxes from the produce of their farms and are endeavouring to cut and sell sufficient timber to enable them to pay their taxes and support their families. To do this it is necessary to pay a certain fee for licenses and to have a certain percentage of the price of the timber retained to meet the demands of your Department for dues.

The price of timber is exceedingly low this year and when License fees and dues are deducted there remains little if any to the settler over the cost of getting the timber to market.

In the face of all this trouble and distress a great number of the Settlers have received notice from the Indian lands Agent at Wiarton (acting presumably under your instruction) to pay up all arrears immediately or the sale of their land would be cancelled.

In many cases a poor Settler who has recently taken up land requires all his means to clear a little patch of ground and build himself a house hiring out in intervals to earn a living for his family it is quite evident that such a resident could have nothing left to meet the demands of your Department for a second payment on his farm and if your Department insist on such a procedure as outlined in your Agent's Notices it will be financial ruin to many already burdened to the extreme limit of endurance. Your petitioners therefore pray that for this Winter Season of 1889 your Department will not insist on arrears due to be paid up but will extend the time for another year trusting that Providence next Summer may bless this Peninsula with better crops to enable them to meet all arrears.

Further your Petitioners pray that you will grant **free licenses** to **actual resident** Settlers for this winter to cut timber and dispose of it and still further that such timber may be **free of dues** hoping that another year may see the Settlers above want and confidence and prosperity may be restored your petitioners as in duty bound will ever pray.

(Wiarton Land Office Correspondence, 1864-1906, Vol. 991, No. 27)

APPENDIX E

SETTLERS' PETITION FOR A SAWMILL AT TOBERMORY, 1883

To the Right Hon Sir John A. McDonald (sic)

Minister of the Interior ec.

Sir: We the undersigned settlers of the Township of St. Edmunds Co of Bruce Respectfully request that you will grant a saw mill site and piling grounds at Tobermory Harbour to the firm of H. Rixon & Co. who purpose rebuilding their mill lately destroyed by fire.

We ask this favor on the following ground

That rebuilding the mill site will enhance the value of property in this neighbourhood

It will be the means of bringing in settlers and giving them steady employment

They have expended a good deal of money on roads here which is a great benefit to us

(Signed)Donald McDonald   Neil Currie
    Jas Simpson   Alex Marks
    Charles Earl   Michael Belrose
    Thomas Earl   William Leslie
    Thomas Bartman
    Charles Hopkins
    John C. Hopkins
    Ed Hopkins
    James Hopkins
    George Bartman
    Thomas Anderson
    Will Moshier
    William Hall

(Indian Affairs, Red Series, Vo. 2207, File 41811)

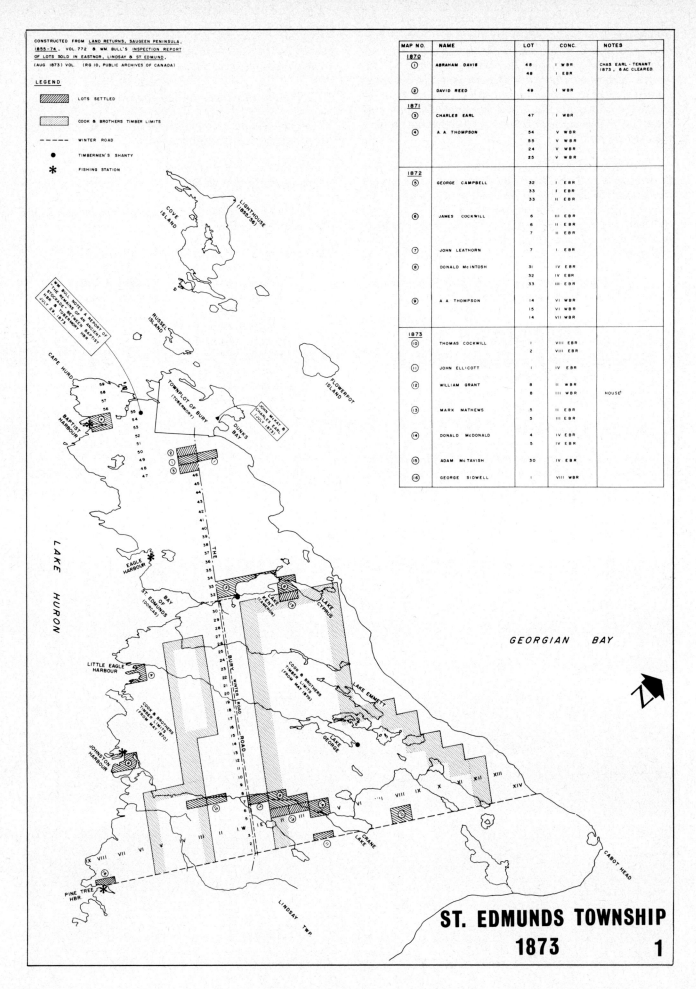

CONSTRUCTED FROM LAND RETURNS, SAUGEEN PENINSULA, 1855-74, VOL. 772 & WM. BULL'S INSPECTION REPORT OF LOTS SOLD IN EASTNOR, LINDSAY & ST EDMUND, (AUG 1873) VOL. (RG 10, PUBLIC ARCHIVES OF CANADA)

LEGEND

	LOTS SETTLED
	COOK & BROTHERS TIMBER LIMITS
---	WINTER ROAD
●	TIMBERMEN'S SHANTY
*	FISHING STATION

MAP NO.	NAME	LOT	CONC.	NOTES
1870				
①	ABRAHAM DAVIS	48	I WBR	CHAS EARL - TENANT 1873 , 8 AC CLEARED.
		48	I EBR	
②	DAVID REED	49	I WBR	
1871				
③	CHARLES EARL	47	I WBR	
④	A A THOMPSON	54	V WBR	
		55	V WBR	
		24	V WBR	
		25	V WBR	
1872				
⑤	GEORGE CAMPBELL	32	I EBR	
		33	I EBR	
		33	II EBR	
⑥	JAMES COCKWILL	6	III EBR	
		6	II EBR	
		7	II EBR	
⑦	JOHN LEATHORN	7	I EBR	
⑧	DONALD McINTOSH	31	IV EBR	
		32	IV EBR	
		33	III EBR	
⑨	A A THOMPSON	14	VI WBR	
		15	VI WBR	
		14	VII WBR	
1873				
⑩	THOMAS COCKWILL	1	VIII EBR	
		2	VIII EBR	
⑪	JOHN ELLICOTT	1	IV EBR	
⑫	WILLIAM GRANT	8	II WBR	
		8	III WBR	HOUSE¹
⑬	MARK MATHEWS	5	II EBR	
		5	III EBR	
⑭	DONALD McDONALD	4	IV EBR	
		5	IV EBR	
⑮	ADAM McTAVISH	30	IV EBR	
⑯	GEORGE SIDWELL	1	VIII WBR	

WM. BULL NOTES A REPORT OF THE REMAINS OF AN ANCIENT STOCKADE BETWEEN BAPTIST HBR & TOBERMORY HBR. JULY 29 1873

COVE ISLAND

LIGHTHOUSE (1855/56)

RUSSEL ISLAND

FLOWERPOT ISLAND

CAPE HURD

TOWNPLOT OF BURY (TOBERMORY)

JOHN McKAY & CHARLES EARL JULY 1873

DUNKS BAY

BAPTIST HARBOUR

LAKE HURON

EAGLE HARBOUR

BAY OF ST EDMUNDS (DORCAS)

LAKE KENT (HERRON)

LAKE CYPRUS

GEORGIAN BAY

LITTLE EAGLE HARBOUR

COOK & BROTHERS TIMBER LIMITS (FROM MAY 1870)

LAKE EMMETT

BURY WINTER ROAD

THE

COOK & BROTHERS TIMBER LIMITS (FROM MAY 1870)

LAKE GEORGE

JOHNSON HARBOUR

N

PINE TREE HBR.

CRANE LAKE

CABOT HEAD

LINDSAY TWP.

ST. EDMUNDS TOWNSHIP
1873

1

248

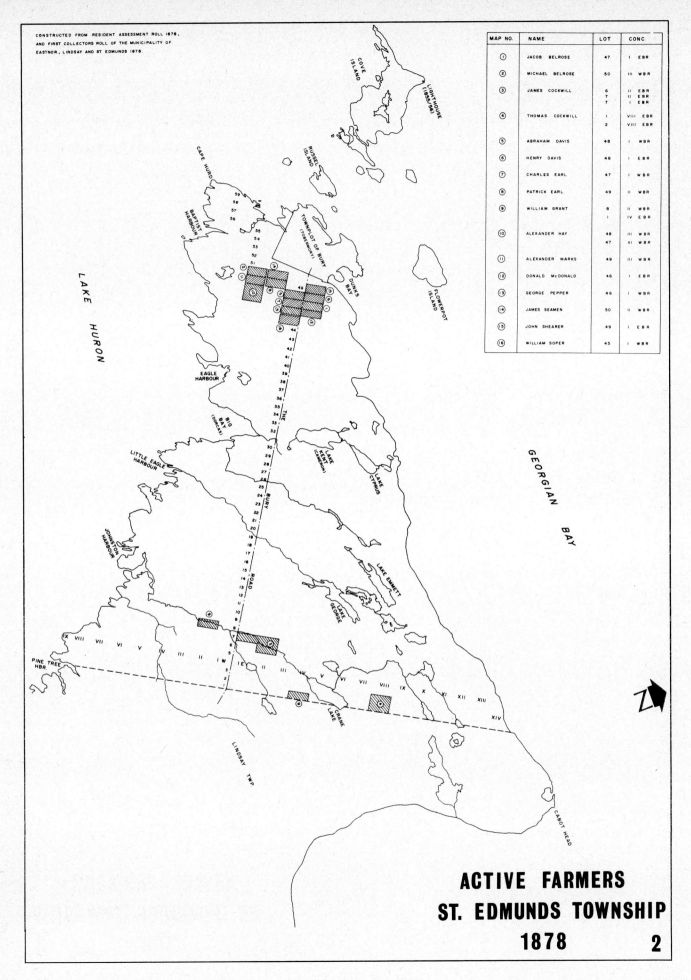

CONSTRUCTED FROM RESIDENT ASSESSMENT ROLL 1878,
AND FIRST COLLECTORS ROLL OF THE MUNICIPALITY OF
EASTNOR, LINDSAY AND ST. EDMUNDS 1878.

MAP NO.	NAME	LOT	CONC.
①	JACOB BELROSE	47	I EBR
②	MICHAEL BELROSE	50	III WBR
③	JAMES COCKWILL	6	II EBR
		7	II EBR
		7	I EBR
④	THOMAS COCKWILL	1	VIII EBR
		2	VIII EBR
⑤	ABRAHAM DAVIS	48	I WBR
⑥	HENRY DAVIS	48	I EBR
⑦	CHARLES EARL	47	I WBR
⑧	PATRICK EARL	49	II WBR
⑨	WILLIAM GRANT	8	II EBR
		1	IV EBR
⑩	ALEXANDER HAY	48	III WBR
		47	III WBR
⑪	ALEXANDER MARKS	49	III WBR
⑫	DONALD McDONALD	46	I EBR
⑬	GEORGE PEPPER	46	I WBR
⑭	JAMES SEAMEN	50	II WBR
⑮	JOHN SHEARER	49	I EBR
⑯	WILLIAM SOPER	45	I WBR

ACTIVE FARMERS
ST. EDMUNDS TOWNSHIP
1878

2

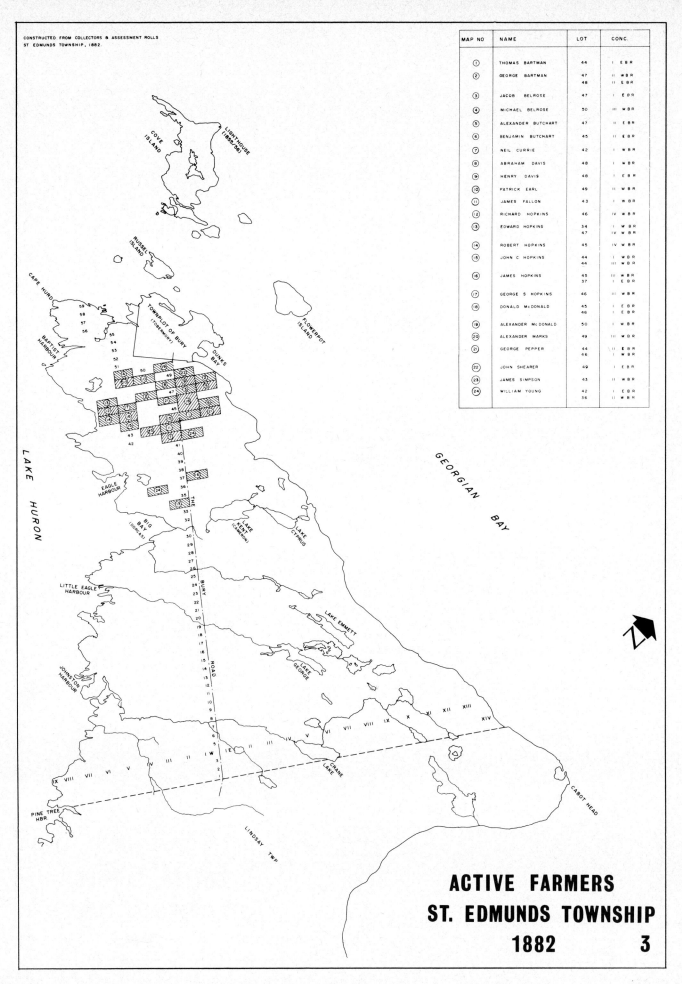

CONSTRUCTED FROM COLLECTORS & ASSESSMENT ROLLS
ST EDMUNDS TOWNSHIP, 1882.

MAP NO	NAME	LOT	CONC.
1	THOMAS BARTMAN	44	I E B R
2	GEORGE BARTMAN	47	II W B R
		48	II E B R
3	JACOB BELROSE	47	I E B R
4	MICHAEL BELROSE	50	III W B R
5	ALEXANDER BUTCHART	47	II E B R
6	BENJAMIN BUTCHART	45	II E B R
7	NEIL CURRIE	42	I W B R
8	ABRAHAM DAVIS	48	I W B R
9	HENRY DAVIS	48	I E B R
10	PATRICK EARL	49	II W B R
11	JAMES FALLON	43	I W B R
12	RICHARD HOPKINS	46	IV W B R
13	EDWARD HOPKINS	34	I W B R
		47	IV W B R
14	ROBERT HOPKINS	45	IV W B R
15	JOHN C HOPKINS	44	I W B R
		44	III W B R
16	JAMES HOPKINS	45	III W B R
		37	I E B R
17	GEORGE S HOPKINS	46	III W B R
18	DONALD McDONALD	45	I E B R
		46	I E B R
19	ALEXANDER McDONALD	50	I W B R
20	ALEXANDER MARKS	49	III W B R
21	GEORGE PEPPER	44	II E B R
		46	II W B R
22	JOHN SHEARER	49	I E B R
23	JAMES SIMPSON	43	II W B R
24	WILLIAM YOUNG	42	I E B R
		36	I W B R

ACTIVE FARMERS
ST. EDMUNDS TOWNSHIP
1882   3

APPENDIX G

July 27: Sunday, spent in Tobermory

28: Examined the north west part of the Township of St. Edmund's. The Town plot of Bury is all rock as well as the Cape Hurd Point. The timber has been nearly all burnt off, leaving the white rocky ridges quite bare — There is a block of land of about 4000 acres adjoining the Town Plot fit for settlement. The good land extends from the Town Plot of Bury to Lot 42 on the Bury line; from Lots 40 to 47 on the 2nd and 3rd Cons E.B.R., from 43 to 50 on Con 2 W.B.R. and on parts of 45 to 50 Con 3 W.B.R. From Lots 40 to 34 (sic) on Cons 1, 2 & 3 E.B.R. the land is rocky with Cedar and Hemlock timber. This block of land like all the land in the Peninsula is more or less broken with rock and stone, but is equal to the average of the lands that are already settled. As there is good fishing around this part of the Coast and on the adjacent Islands, it is very probable that all the land fit for settlement would soon be taken up and settled if a winter road was opened.

There are two families residing at Dunk's Bay — John McKay a fisherman, and Charles Earl, who owns lot 47 Con 1 W.B.R. These men informed me that a number of Fishermen and others would purchase land and settle if there were a road opened for winter use.

Tobermory Harbour is one of the best in the Country and as it lies at a Point where a good Harbour of Refuge is needed, vessels frequently enter it in Stormy weather. Several Propellers and sailing vessels, ran into it for shelter whilst we were around this part of the Coast. There is a possibility that it may become a railway terminus and be used for commercial purposes. This would be a convenient point for communication with the Manitoulin Island in Winter.

There is not much merchantable timber near Tobermory except Cordwood, which would doubtless sell well, if the Captains of Steamers knew that a supply could always be obtained. At Dunk's Bay there is about a mile square of Pine timber on rocky ground which has been burnt over and the timber killed, — most of the Pines are still standing and appear to be sound. They are not of first quality, many of them being small and scrubby, but still a good many would do for Saw logs and Shingle timber.

29: Left Tobermory and sailed round to Baptist Harbour - Lots 54 and 55 Con 5 W.B.R. (These two lots are sold and are reported on separately)

This is a fishing station and a fine Harbour for small vessels, but the land around is all rock and the timber small.

I was informed by a person who occasionally hunts and traps along this Coast, that in going through the Bush from Baptist Harbour to Tobermory he came upon the remains of an ancient Stockade, that the stumps of the Cedar Posts of which it was composed, though quite rotten above the ground were quite plainly to be seen, and that they were sound beneath the surface, and had been set in the earth to a depth of about 3 feet; and that large trees were growing over the place now.

(William Bull, *Inspection Report of Lots Sold In Eastnor, Lindsay & St. Edmund*, Vol. 736, RG 10, P.A.C.)

FOOTNOTES

These footnotes merely tell the author. Look to Reference List for more information about the book concerned.

Chapter One
1. written by Andrew Hodgkinson
2. Jenness, page 277
3. Jenness, page 277
4. Geographic Board of Canada
5. Geographic Board of Canada
6. Trigger
7. Wiarton Echo, 1967
8. Geographic Board of Canada
9. Wiarton Echo
10. Wiarton Echo
11. Wiarton Echo
12. Wiarton Echo, 1958
13. Trigger
14. Geographic Board of Canada
15. Geographic Board of Canada

Chapter Two
1. Owen Sound Sun Times, 1946
2. Owen Sound Sun Times, 1946
3. Folkes
4. Folkes
5. Folkes
6. Robertson
7. Folkes
8. Folkes
9. Folkes
10. Folkes
11. Atlas, 1880
12. Folkes
13. Folkes
14. Folkes and Atlas, 1880
15. Atlas, 1880
16. Atlas, 1880
17. Folkes

18. Folkes
19. Atlas, 1880
20. Atlas, 1880
21. Folkes
22. Folkes
23. Folkes
24. Folkes
25. Folkes
26. Folkes
27. Wiarton Echo, 1901

Chapter Three
1. Folkes
2. Folkes
3. Folkes

Chapter Four
1. Folkes, 1973
2. Folkes, 1973
3. Folkes, 1973

Chapter Five
1. Folkes, 1970, 1975
2. Folkes, 1970, 1975

Chapter Six
1. Wiarton Echo, 1894
2. Wiarton Echo, 1894
3. Wiarton Echo, 1894

Chapter Eleven
1. Folkes, 1973

Chapter Sixteen
1. Wiarton Echo, 1981
2. Owen Sound Sun Times, 1948
3. Wiarton Echo, 1952
4. Murdoch & Wiarton Echo

REFERENCE LIST

Folkes, Patrick
1970
Shipwrecks of the Saugeen: 1828-1938 A History of Marine Disasters of Bruce County: Clark Point-Tobermory-Owen Sound.

1973
The Early History of Tobermory and St. Edmunds Township. Fathom Five Provincial Park

Fox, William S.
1952
The Bruce Beckons: The Story of Lake Huron's Great Peninsula University of Toronto Press, Toronto.

Gardiner, H.
1899
Nothing But Names. George Morany and Co. Ltd. Toronto.

Jenness, D.
1932
The Indians of Canada: 4th Edition Bulletin 65, Anthropological Series No. 15, National Museum of Canada, Ottawa.

McKay, H. H.
1963
Fishes of Ontario. The Ontario Department of Lands and Forests.

Murdoch, D.
1983
Disappearances: Truce Accounts of Canadians who Have Disappeared. Doubleday Canada Ltd., Toronto.

Robertson, N.
1969
The History of the County of Bruce. Richardson, Bond and Wright, Owen Sound.

Salen, R.
Salen, J.
The Tobermory Shipwrecks: A History and Description. The Mariner Chart Shop, Tobermory.

Trigger, B.
1976
The Children of Aataentsic, A History of the Huron People to 1660. McGill-Queen's University Press, Montreal.

Warder, W.
1977
Between You, Me, and the Gatepost: A Historic View of the Lion's Head Area.

1880
Illustrated Atlas of the County of Bruce: 1880. H. Belden and Co., Toronto. Offset Edition, Port Elgin, 1970.

1913
Handbook of the Indians of Canada. Appendix to the Tenth Report of the Geographic Board of Canada C. H. Parmell, Toronto Reprinted by Coles, Toronto, 1974, Coles Canadiana Collection.

ERRATA

Page 50   J. W. Ransbury photo caption should read:
           "Shown here with son Jack," — Not Paul.

Page 67   Bottom Left photo caption should read:
           "Tobermory Garage late 1960's" not 1940's

Page 209   Upper Right, Davis' and Hopkins' photo
           caption should read: "1920's" - not 1930's

Page 232   Bottom Left photo caption should read:
           "Martha (Young) Spears and Harold
           Young, 1900" — not (Mattie) Young.